THE MAKING OF THE
CROFTING COMMUNITY

By the same author

Skye: The Island

For the People's Cause: From the Writings of John Murdoch

The Claim of Crofting: The Scottish Highlands, 1930–1990

Scottish Highlanders: A People and their Place

A Dance Called America: The Scottish Highlands, the United States and Canada

On the Other Side of Sorrow: Nature and People in the Scottish Highlands

Glencoe and the Indians

Last of the Free: A Millennial History of the Highlands and Islands of Scotland

THE MAKING OF THE CROFTING COMMUNITY

James Hunter

New Edition

JOHN DONALD
EDINBURGH

This new edition published in 2000 by John Donald, an imprint of
Birlinn Ltd
8 Canongate Venture
5 New Street
Edinburgh
EH8 8BH

First published 1976 by John Donald Publishers Ltd

ISBN 0 85976 537 7

British Library Cataloguing in Publication Data
A catalogue record for this book is available from the British Library

Typeset in Sabon by Brinnoven, Livingston
Printed and bound by Redwood Books, Trowbridge

CONTENTS

'I cannot bear evidence to the distress of my people without bearing evidence to the oppression and high-handedness of the landlord and his factor.'

— Angus Stewart, crofter at Peinchorran, Braes, 8 May 1883.

For Evelyn

PREFACE TO THE NEW EDITION

The histories of our land have mostly been written to serve the political purposes, and flatter the conceits, of our aristocracy. When the historian knew of happenings calculated to cast odium on our landed gentry, he carefully excised the records, and where he did not know, he was careful to assume, and lead others to assume, that the periods of which he was ignorant were periods of intense social happiness, wherein a glad and thankful populace spent their days and nights in devising Hallelujahs in honour of the neighbouring nobleman.
— Tom Johnston, *Our Scots Noble Families.*

When, in 1996, the *Scottish Historical Review* got round, 20 years after its appearance, to reviewing the original version of this book, *SHR*'s reviewer, Ewen A. Cameron, despite his disagreements with its methodology and conclusions, was kind enough to call *The Making of the Crofting Community* 'one of the most significant Scottish books of its generation'. Cameron, among the more productive of Scotland's younger historians, went on to comment that, if *The Making of the Crofting Community* is properly to be understood, 'it is vital to consider the historiographical and political context in which it was originally published'. It is a moot point, I admit, as to whether I am the person best equipped to embark on an exercise of the sort Cameron advises. But by way of preface to this new edition of *The Making of the Crofting Community*, its publishers have asked me to reflect both on the book's approach to Highland history and on how that approach has been received by other historians of the Highlands. In so reflecting, of course, I run the risk of appearing hopelessly self-indulgent. But given that 'much of the material' published on the modern history of the Highlands during the last quarter century — and I quote again from Ewen Cameron's review — 'has been produced . . . in direct response' to *The Making of the Crofting Community*, it is, perhaps, legitimate for me to make my own contribution to a continuing debate which, it appears, I helped initiate.

In the acknowledgements section of this book's 1976 edition, I attributed my perspective on the Highland past 'to my . . . family and to my Highland

1

upbringing'. That upbringing took place in Duror, North Argyll, where, as a small boy, I absorbed, principally from my maternal grandfather, John Cameron, who stayed with my parents, my sister and I until his death in 1963, something of what it meant to be caught up in events, not least the Highland Clearances, which *The Making of the Crofting Community* was afterwards to describe. My grandfather, who lived into his nineties, had himself been raised on a Strontian croft tenanted by his father and my great-grandfather, Alan Cameron, who, having been born in 1815, lived through, and was personally affected by, the clearances. What I learned of such happenings from John Cameron, then, I learned from a man whose knowledge of them had been gained from folk – such as his father – who had either fallen victim to clearance or who had witnessed its impact on their relatives, friends and neighbours. It was from John Cameron, to give a specific instance, that I first heard of the evictions carried out on the Morvern estate of Ardtornish – where my grandfather worked, towards the nineteenth century's close, as a ghillie – on the orders of the most notorious of all the Highland Clearances' many perpetrators, Patrick Sellar. And it was from John Cameron, a teenager when the legislation in question was passed, that I first gained some inkling of the extent to which the Crofters Act of 1886 was regarded by its beneficiaries – who were provided by that Act with security of tenure – as a hard-won charter of liberation from landlord-directed tyranny and oppression.

Since I was only fourteen when John Cameron died, I do not claim that what he had to say about the nineteenth-century Highlands made an immediate and deep impression on me. It did not. But something of my grandfather's outlook – an outlook shared by my parents and by others of my close relatives – nevertheless remained with me when, as an undergraduate student of history in the University of Aberdeen in the late 1960s, I started to encounter academic interpretations of nineteenth-century occurrences in the Highlands. As Ewen Cameron remarked in the review with which I began, there existed then no 'coherent account' of the background to the Crofters Act of 1886 – a deficiency which *The Making of the Crofting Community* would seek to remedy. But there were in circulation a number of academic analyses of the causes and consequences of the Highland Clearances. Most of those I found to be wholly at odds with what I had absorbed – more or less unconciously – in the course of my childhood. To John Cameron, as to most folk of his background, the clearances were an overwhelming tragedy resulting from the brutally self-interested conduct of the individuals owning the land from which thousands of nineteenth-century Highlanders were forcibly removed. By academic historians, I now discovered, the clearances were approached from a quite different standpoint.

Serious academic study of the clearance epoch in the north of Scotland began with the publication, in 1956, of *The Highland Economy, 1750–1850,* by Malcolm Gray. Gray's work has many merits. But what struck me as surprising when I first came upon his book was how little space – perhaps ten pages out of 280 – this book devotes to the numerous mass-evictions which took place during the 100-year period Gray scrutinised. What I thought still more surprising was the tone of Gray's few remarks about processes which, however one regards them, involved so many families being summarily ejected from their homes that hundreds of communities ceased absolutely to exist. There is little in Gray's book about the victims of eviction; there is nothing about how such victims reacted to what was done to them. Instead there is a pervasive implication that no professional historian should be seen to give credence to – let alone identify with – anti-landlord attitudes of the sort to which the clearances gave rise. The policies pursued by the owners of the Highland properties on which evictions occurred, Gray admitted, 'were mistaken and short-sighted, even greedy'. But to attribute any 'special malignity' to the originators of those policies, he insisted, is simply to exhibit 'social prejudice'.

During the two decades separating *The Highland Economy* from *The Making of the Crofting Community*, Malcolm Gray's reading of the clearance period became standard among his fellow academics. Alternative interpretations – especially those which hinted that nineteenth-century landlords might have been so committed to boosting the revenue-generating capacities of their estates as to be willing, in certain circumstances, to maltreat their tenantries – were rubbished, ignored, set aside. By the mid-1960s, in fact, it had become something of a test of one's credibility as a university-based historian of Scotland to be able to deal with the Highland Clearances in a manner that (a) exculpated nineteenth-century landlords from any personal responsibility for what happened on their properties and (b) displayed absolutely no vestige of sympathy for the men, women and children whose lives were wrecked and devastated as a result of their eviction. Thus A. J. Youngson, noting that 'it is easy to declaim against the inhumanity of turning families out of their customary possessions', went on (in *After the Forty-Five*) to take the more praiseworthy course – as he saw it – of attributing the clearances to forces so 'irresistible' as to be beyond human jurisdiction. George H. Pryde (in *Scotland from 1603 to the Present Day*) thought the clearances a consequence of 'the silent operation of economic laws'. Rosalind Mitchison (in *A History of Scotland*) wrote – incredibly – of evictions conducted 'with consideration and skill'. And Eric Richards, surveying the outcome of clearance in Sutherland, found it 'difficult to avoid the conclusion' (in *The Leviathan of Wealth*) that 'employment and even subsistence opportunities would have been even smaller' had policies which depopulated some of the most productive straths in northern Scotland 'not been implemented'.

Others went further. Clearing landlords may have driven their tenantries overseas, Roy H. Campbell acknowledged (in *Scotland Since 1707*). But 'by forcing him to emigrate a landlord was . . . frequently only forcing a tenant to act as he would have had to do eventually'. To be evicted, then, was practically to be done a favour. It was definitely not to be turned out of house and home, as generations of Highlanders had assumed, in order that a profit-hungry laird might expand his sheep farming interests. Campbell, it appears, looked hard for evidence of such conduct, but found none. 'It is not easy', he reported, 'to substantiate the accusation that the landlords were forwarding their own ends selfishly at the expense of the welfare of their tenants.' 'Like tenants,' Campbell added, 'landlords . . . were the victims of economic forces over which they had little control'.

Re-reading Roy Campbell and his colleagues today, after a quarter-century that has taken me to every corner of the Highlands and Islands, one thought constantly intrudes. Why do Scotland's historians, living and working in a country where nowhere is more than a few hours from anywhere else, so neglect what Simon Schama – an outstandingly successful explorer of the world's past – calls 'the archive of the feet'? Nowhere is that archive more easily accessed than in Sutherland. Go to Strathnaver and spend an hour or two among the wide, sheltered fields whose cultivators Patrick Sellar evicted in 1815. Travel next to the desperately exposed coastal locations – Strathy Point and Bettyhill, for example – where Sellar's men installed Strathnaver's former residents on five-acre plots of windswept rock and bog. Nothing is more implausible, in the light of such a journey, than the notion that Strathnaver's occupants were evicted solely to enhance their wellbeing. And so grimly inhospitable – when compared with the places they had formerly inhabited – are the spots where refugees from Strathnaver were expected to set up home that it is hard to understand, having glimpsed the spots in question, how anyone could imagine, as Roy Campbell seems to have imagined, that those folk were somehow on a par with landed proprietors of the type inhabiting, in the early nineteenth century, Dunrobin Castle, Armadale Castle, Inverary Castle and all the other grand residences where the Highland Clearances were conceived. Victims come in many guises, of course. But it is stretching the language more than slightly to apply the term both to evicted Highlanders and to the men – men whose wealth and position enabled them to exercise a truly dazzling range of choices – who ordered those Highlanders' eviction.

Their eccentricity notwithstanding, Roy Campbell's views of the Highland Clearances were of a piece with opinions expressed, throughout the 1960s and into the 1970s, by virtually all of Scotland's professional historians. The books which such historians wrote may not have been written – like the histories to which Tom Johnston took exception in that most splendid of socialist polemics, *Our Scots Noble Families* – with a view to burnishing the posthumous reputations of the landowners on whose careers they touched. But that was indubitably their effect. By implying, first, that the effects of the clearances had been greatly exaggerated, and by suggesting, second, that the clearances were inherently unavoidable, Campbell and his colleagues bestowed – whether intentionally or not – a retrospective legitimacy on mass evictions of the Strathnaver variety. For if such happenings are regarded as the product of 'economic forces' pure and simple, then it makes no more sense to be concerned about their consequences than it would to be angered by the effects of gravity. Hence, perhaps, the impatience with which T. C. Smout – a more than usually influential academic – dismissed (in *A History of the Scottish People*) the 'emotion' the Highland Clearances had engendered in minds other than those of historians like himself. When the clearances were viewed in 'a deeper perspective' of the sort he brought to them, Smout wrote, it became evident that 'nothing could have been done that would have provided the Highlands with an alternative' to what took place there in the nineteenth century. The Highland Clearances, in other words, were nobody's fault. Most decidedly, they were not the fault of the region's landlords.

By the late 1960s and early 1970s, then, the typical academic historian's approach to the Highland Clearances was that of counsel for landlordism's defence – a role adopted with particular relish by Philip Gaskell in *Morvern Transformed: A Highland Parish in the Nineteenth Century*. This book, published in 1968, deals mainly with the various Victorian proprietors of the Ardtornish estate. And I can still recall the sense of excitement with which, on picking it up in an Aberdeen bookshop, I found Gaskell's pages replete with references to places and incidents which had featured in my grandfather's stories. I can still recall, too, the disappointment I felt as Gaskell proceeded to scorn, as well as to reject, beliefs of the kind John Cameron's tales had been intended, I suppose, to inculcate in their hearers – the belief, for example, that the Highland Clearances were unalterably and inescapably wrong.

Philip Gaskell's extraordinarily amoral treatment of the clearances is all the more striking in view of the fact that he acknowledges both the scale of Morvern's evictions and the intensity of the suffering they caused. From the mid-1820s onwards, Gaskell comments, 'the number of evictions increased rapidly . . . and, until the last clearance of 1868, hundreds of Morvern people suffered unhappiness and distress as a result'. 'Nevertheless,' Gaskell stresses, 'we must reject an emotional approach if the clearances are to be understood.'

I have never grasped why some historians – though not, in my experience, the greatest historians – see virtue in thus declining to empathise with the people whose lives they survey. But what makes Philip Gaskell's stance peculiarly off-putting is that feeling of the sort he refuses to extend to evicted crofters is readily extended to the Ardtornish landlords whose doings his book so approvingly, even fawningly, chronicles.

In 1979, Ian Carter, a sociologist rather than a historian, had occasion to comment (in *Farm Life in Northeast Scotland*) on the contrast – a contrast to which *The Making of the Crofting Community* had drawn Carter's attention – between the crofting population's collective view of the crofting past and the quite different view of this past to be found in books of the sort turned out by Gray, Youngson, Mitchison, Pryde, Richards, Campbell, Smout and Gaskell. Commenting that crofters had 'kept alive an account of Highland history that differs markedly from the account usually provided by sleek academic commentators', Carter cited *Morvern Transformed* as 'the epitome' of the 'sleekness' he had in mind. I agree with Ian Carter. And I mention *Morvern Transformed* here principally because it was responsible for first raising in my mind the possibility that I might one day take issue in print with its author and with all those other historians who, I felt, were doing violence to the deeply-held convictions of the many people, myself included, to whom the Highland Clearances were no more and no less than a crime – by no means the worst or biggest such crime, but a crime all the same – against humanity.

Even in the 1960s, to be sure, it was possible to read alternatives to the Gray-Youngson-Mitchison-Pryde-Richards-Campbell-Smout-Gaskell line on the clearances. Ian Grimble's *The Trial of Patrick Sellar* and John Prebble's *The Highland Clearances* were products of that decade, and both, particularly the latter, were written from a standpoint with which I warmly identified. On his opening page, Prebble summarises that standpoint thus:

> This book . . . is the story of how the Highlanders were deserted and then betrayed. It concerns itself with people, how sheep were preferred to them, and how bayonet, truncheon and fire were used to drive them from their homes. It has been said that the clearances are now far enough away from us to be decently forgotten. But the hills are still empty. In all of Britain only among them can one find real solitude, and if their history is known there is no satisfaction to be got from the experience.

Long afterwards, I would undertake my own elaboration of that last point in a book entitled *On the Other Side of Sorrow* – a book which attempts to show, among other things, that Highland 'wilderness', as celebrated by today's conservationists, is not so much natural as the wholly artificial result of nineteenth-century landlords having excluded humanity from ecosystems of which people had been part for ten millennia. In the years around 1970, however, my interests lay more in the short-run than in the long-run impact of the clearances. Like Prebble, I wanted to demonstrate that evictions of the Morvern or Strathnaver type were inextricably bound up with landlord-organised 'exploitation' – Prebble's term – of those evictions' victims. But unlike Prebble, I was – in the late 1960s and early 1970s anyway – anxious to challenge academic historians on their own ground. I was duly conscious of the 'absence of footnotes' – the phrase is Malcolm Gray's – both from John Prebble's book and from *The Trial of Patrick Sellar*, Ian Grimble's raging denunciation of Sellar's actions in Sutherland. By not burdening their work with detailed references to their sources, I believed, Grimble and Prebble made it all too easy for that work to be treated with the disdain which academics reserve for those they call 'popularisers'. Hence the one passage I wish I had excised from *The Making of the Crofting Community*: a passage, towards the end of the book's Introduction, which damns with faint praise two men whom I later came to know, and greatly to admire, as meticulous researchers and superb stylists.

That passage can be explained, though I do not think now it can be justified, by my younger self's strong sense that it was essential, if the academic take on the Highland Clearances was to be countered effectively, to construct an account of the nineteenth-century Highlands which, while remaining true to John Cameron (standing here for the wider crofting population from which my grandfather stemmed), was also sustainable and defensible academically. *The Making of the Crofting Community*, in essence the PhD thesis I researched and compiled while a postgraduate student in Edinburgh University's Department of Scottish History from 1971 to 1974, was intended to be such an account. But if this thesis owed its original inspiration to what I heard of the nineteenth-century Highlands when a boy in Duror, it owed much of its shape and thrust to two quite different influences. One was Edward P. Thompson's wonderful book, *The Making of the English Working Class*, which was published in 1963 and which, for reasons shortly to be examined, helped underpin my instinctive conviction that there could be advanced a historiographically worthwhile alternative to histories of the Campbell, Mitchison and Gaskell sort. The other huge influence on *The Making of the Crofting Communtiy* – its title, of course, a tribute to Thompson – is maybe less explicitly acknowledged in the book than it ought to have been. Be that as it may, it has long been clear to me that such confidence as I displayed in handling the subject matter of *The Making of the Crofting Community* derived, in large measure, from my having had the good fortune, before getting to Edinburgh, to be exposed to the history of sub-Saharan Africa.

In *The Making of the English Working Class*, E. P. Thompson set out, as he memorably expressed it, 'to rescue . . . from the enormous condescension of posterity' the southern and urban equivalents of the Highland folk who, in much the same period as the one with which Thompson's book deals, were being removed *en masse* from their townships. The people Thompson wrote about were people whom historians, especially the economic historians who were Thompson's particular *bêtes noires*, had mostly thought of no account. In the writings of such historians, Thompson conceded, working people might put in an appearance 'as a labour force, as migrants, or as the data for statistical series'. But few economic historians, Thompson continued, had been prepared to embrace the possibility that working men and women might have had anything other than the most passive of historical roles. And no economic historian had imagined that working folk might, 'by conscious efforts', have themselves 'contributed . . . to the making of history'. It was this 'enormous condescension' – to repeat its author's magnificent phrase – that *The Making of the English Working Class* so triumphantly challenged by demonstrating that working people were worthy and important objects of historical enquiry in their own right.

Of 'the poor stockinger', 'the Luddite cropper', 'the "obsolete" hand-loom weaver' and all the other formerly ignored individuals who bulk large in his book, E. P. Thompson observed:

> Their crafts and traditions may have been dying. Their hostility to the new industrialism may have been backward-looking. Their communitarian ideals may have been fantasies. Their insurrectionary conspiracies may have been foolhardy. But they lived through these times of acute social disturbance, and we did not. Their aspirations were valid in terms of their own experience.

From such sentences I derived a substantial part of my belief – a belief expressed at the start of *The Making of the Crofting Community* – that it is possible 'to write the modern history of the Gaelic Highlands from the crofting community's point of view'. Just as Thompson had spectacularly exposed the inadequacies of the economic historians who had dealt dismissively with England's working people, so *The Making of the Crofting Community* was meant to point up the similar inadequacies, as they appeared to me, in the work of that other set of economic historians – Gray, Youngson, Mitchison, Pryde, Richards, Campbell, Smout, Gaskell – who had been permitted, in my opinion, to make far too much of the running with regard to northern Scotland's past. And just as Thompson had put working folk at the centre of his book, so crofters were placed firmly at the centre of mine.

But if E. P. Thompson helped confirm my suspicion that the modern history of the Highlands did not have to be written the way that Gray and his successors had written it, Thompson was, as I have already attested, by no means the only source of such confirmation. At Aberdeen, I was taught by two historians of Africa, John Hargreaves and Roy Bridges. During the years following the Second World War, Hargreaves and Bridges were among a number of Europeans who – on becoming staff members of the universities then being established in black Africa – became convinced that, if African history was to be rendered meaningful to peoples engaged in anti-colonial struggle, it would have to be conceived in novel ways. No longer could the history of Africa consist – as it had consisted in every textbook produced under the British Empire's aegis – of the doings of white explorers, white missionaries, white administrators. Henceforth, or so African-based historians like Bridges and Hargreaves began to argue, Africa's history would have to be approached from the perspective of the continent's black inhabitants – a perspective, it goes almost without saying, the historians of empire had ignored. Of this historiographical upheaval,

I guess, I would have remained largely ignorant had it not chanced that, shortly before my arrival there in 1967, both John Hargreaves and Roy Bridges had been recruited by the University of Aberdeen. There they gave Aberdeen a leading role – which, sadly, it has since lost – in African studies. And there Bridges and Hargreaves made it their business to introduce students to the frequently heated debate surrounding a historiographical revolution in which they had themselves participated.

Among the more reactionary contributors to this debate was Hugh Trevor-Roper (afterwards Lord Dacre), then regius professor of history at the University of Oxford and a man who, in 1965, dismissed African history as nothing more than 'the unrewarding gyrations of barbarous tribes in picturesque but irrelevant corners of the globe'. By way of substantiating that remark, Trevor-Roper commented:

> Perhaps, in the future, there will be some African history to teach. But at present there is none, or very little: there is only the history of the Europeans in Africa. The rest is largely darkness, like the history of pre-European, pre-Columbian America. And darkness is not a subject for history.

This was, and is, claptrap – highly offensive claptrap at that. But Trevor-Roper's outburst (in *The Rise of Christian Europe*) was nevertheless of great assistance in clarifying my thinking about the Highlands. With regard to the latter area, I concluded, Gray, Campbell, Mitchison, Smout and all the rest stood in much the same relation as Hugh Trevor-Roper stood in regard to Africa. Believing the Africans on whom Africa's colonisers imposed their policies to have had none of the qualities – cultural, intellectual or otherwise – which give people a history, Trevor-Roper, as he openly averred, saw no point in taking seriously anything that had been said or done in Africa by people who were not Europeans. The academic historians of the Highlands, to be sure, were a little less explicitly dismissive of the generality of Highlanders than Trevor-Roper was of black Africa's population. But their outlook and methodologies were such, I felt, as to produce a strictly analogous outcome. The Gray-Youngson-Mitchison-Pryde-Richards-Campbell-Smout-Gaskell interpretation of Highland history was one which gave no credence to – in fact, virtually never cited – the many Gaelic and other sources from which one can form some impression of how the Highland Clearances and associated developments were perceived by the folk on their receiving end. Instead the Gray-Youngson-Mitchison-Pryde-Richards-Campbell-Smout-Gaskell school relied on the records of estate managements, on travelogues produced by visitors from the south, on the correspondence and reports of public officials. In its setting aside of the Highland perspective on the Highland past, this school's output, I duly felt, was the precise counterpart of Trevor-Roper's 'history of the Europeans in Africa'. And it seemed to me imperative, when I commenced work on *The Making of the Crofting Community*, that this anti-Highland travesty of Highland history be overthrown in the same spirit – and with the same liberating purpose – as imperialist and Eurocentric interpretations of Africa's past had already been overthrown.

With the overweening self-confidence – not to say arrogance – of youth, I wanted *The Making of the Crofting Community*, then, to have as innovative an impact in a Highland context as Afrocentric analyses of that continent's past had had in an African one. My aim, to make the point another way, was to write ordinary Highlanders – my own forebears among them – into nineteenth-century Highland history with much the same effect as Africans, during the 1950s and 1960s, had begun to be written into the history of Africa.

In January 1977, just five or six months after *The Making of the Crofting Community* was published, there erupted one of those rows which, from time to time, make the Highland Clearances a topic of renewed public controversy. This particular furore was occasioned by dispute as to whether the organising committee of that year's National Mod, Scotland's premier Gaelic festival, had been wise to invite the Countess of Sutherland – a descendant of the family responsible for clearances such as the Strathnaver one and owner of what remained of the estate on which the Strathnaver clearance had occurred – to play a prominent part in the Mod's proceedings. Although the countess had defenders as well as attackers, the position which she had been asked to occupy became eventually so untenable that she stood down from it. By so doing, she provided *The Scotsman* – a newspaper which had followed an unswervingly pro-landlord course throughout the nineteenth century – with an opportunity to revert, as it were, to type.

What particularly aggravated *The Scotsman* was the fact that, among the more prominent critics of the Countess of Sutherland's proposed association with the National Mod, were people committed, as the paper remarked, to 'agrarian reforms' intended to 'sweep away the landlord system'. In targeting the 'innocent and vulnerable' countess, the paper continued, those land reformers had engineered 'one of the meanest and pettiest episodes to have disfigured Highland politics in recent years'. This episode's entire character, *The Scotsman* declared, was such as to demonstrate why advocates of land reform were no friends of the Highlands:

> For them, the matter seems above all to be one of class hatred. This they have pursued with a vindictiveness and spite which makes one tremble at the thought of the social order they wish to substitute in the Highlands for the present one.

This was legitimate, if slanted, comment. And had *The Scotsman* stopped at that point, the story of the countess and the Mod committee might have ended there. But not content with rushing to the aid of the Countess of Sutherland, the paper also tried to rehabilitate her ancestors by mounting a late twentieth-century version of the many defences it had mounted – 100 or more years earlier – of the Highland Clearances:

> For the record, let it be stated that the main motive of the Sutherlands, and of the many other landlords who followed the same course, was to improve the wretched condition of the people on their estates. A way of life was thereby destroyed, but it could probably not have survived in any case. All enlightened opinion agreed at the time that the numbers living on the congested lands in the north had to fall if any economic progress was to be achieved . . . The clearances, in fact, probably saved the Highlands from the dreadful famines which, in the nineteenth century, afflicted rural Ireland, a region of much the same character.

In the days that followed this pronouncement, *The Scotsman* received – predictably – a shoal of letters. Most of them opposed the paper's stance. Some, however, were supportive. In the latter category was a brief missive from Gordon Donaldson, then professor of Scottish history at Edinburgh University and someone who ought to have known, even if leader-writers at *The Scotsman* did not, that the Highlands had, in fact, suffered a famine of the sort the clearances were – preposterously – being credited with preventing:

> It is most refreshing, in a country where so much that passes for history is the plaything of propagandists, to read your wholly admirable leader on the Countess of Sutherland and 'The Clearances'.

Although he was no historian of the Highlands, interventions of this sort in Highland affairs were something of a Gordon Donaldson trademark. A decade after his involvement in the affair of the Countess of Sutherland and the Mod, for instance, Donaldson, acting this time in his capacity as Scotland's historiographer royal, responded to a Crofters Commission suggestion that a commemorative stamp be issued to mark the centenary of the Crofters Act of 1886 by informing the postal authorities – who consequently turned down the commission's request – that such a stamp would be contentious. The projected stamp's fate is neither here nor there. Nor have I ever met any crofters who were greatly troubled by Gordon Donaldson's conviction – stated more than once – that the measure which guaranteed their security of tenure had been a serious error. But it does say something, I feel, about his profession's overall attitude to the Highlands that a historian as eminent and well-respected as Gordon Donaldson, while unprepared to countenance condemnation of the Highland Clearances, was perfectly happy to denounce the legislation which brought the clearances to an end.

Judged by the standards set by some other historians, to be fair, Gordon Donaldson's opinions of the Crofters Act of 1886 seem wildly enthusiastic. When, in the mid-1990s, Allan I. Macinnes, then professor of history at Aberdeen University, chaired a Scottish National Party enquiry into landownership in Scotland, he helped produce a report which 'looked favourably on crofting as a system of landholding', which advocated 'expansion of . . . crofting land' and which favoured 'the introduction of new crofting tenancies'. Ten years previously, however, Macinnes had celebrated the 1886 Act's centenary with an article (in *Radical Scotland*) in which crofters are described – by way of an extended metaphor – as 'pampered' and 'privileged' jailbirds. The Crofters Act, Allan Macinnes wrote, had created 'a legislative prison to benefit a peasant class of quasi-proprietors at the expense of the Gaelic community as a whole'. This prison's crofting occupants, Macinnes thought, had been turned into 'institutionalised . . . old lags'. And that was why the Scottish Crofters Union, launched a year or so prior to the appearance of his article, was best understood, Allan Macinnes asserted, as 'a prisoners' rights society'.

Although I have long since concluded that it is usually counter-productive to respond to diatribes of the Donaldson or Macinnes type, I made my own contribution – a 'provocative' contribution, Eric Richards subsequently labelled it – to the debate initiated by that *Scotsman* leader of January 1977. What I wrote then, I would not write in quite the same manner today. But given that my 1977 opinions were much more directly the opinions of the author of *The Making of the Crofting Community* than the opinions I hold now, they are, I think, of some relevance in the present context. Here, at all events, is an extract from my reply to Gordon Donaldson's endorsement of the notion that the clearance of Sutherland had been a good thing:

> In the context of the more grandiose brutalities of our time, or even in the context of the war which was then being waged against Napoleon, the removal of a peasant people [in 1815 or thereabouts] from the interior of a remote Highland county might seem an event of no great importance. But while Waterloo is now no more than a name in history books, the simultaneous occurrences in Sutherland retain a virtually undiminished capacity for the generation of controversy and dispute . . . The result, since history consists as much of interpretation as of fact, is that – as far as the Highland Clearances are concerned – no generally agreed history is possible. If this were universally admitted, all would be well. The trouble is that the version of modern Highland history which has won general acceptance among professional historians – and which consequently tends to be paraded as the 'correct', 'objective' and otherwise irreproachable account of events – is little more than an apology for Highland landlordism, past and present.

Given the 'significance' of *The Making of the Crofting Community*, Ewen Cameron remarked in the course of his 1996 assessment of the book in the pages of the *Scottish Historical Review*, it was 'surprising that *SHR* did not accord it a review when it was originally published'. Mischievously, Cameron added:

> Conspiracy theorists will note that the joint editor of the *SHR* at the time was that scourge of Gaels, excoriator of crofters and reputed opponent of

a philatelic commemoration of the Crofter Holdings Act, Professor Gordon Donaldson.

The idea that Gordon Donaldson may have been so piqued by my writings as to withhold publicity for them is not one, I should make clear, I take seriously. *SHR*'s ignoring of *The Making of the Crofting Community*, I suspect, was more a product of its editors' incompetence than of their malevolence. And since I expected most academic historians to be hostile to a publication which constituted, after all, something of an attack on them, I was, in any case, a lot less anxious about academic reactions to *The Making of the Crofting Community*, when it first appeared, than I was about the book's reception in the area with which it deals.

By commentators living and working in the Highlands, *The Making of the Crofting Community*, was, as luck would have it, positively reviewed. Sorley MacLean – then head teacher at Plockton High School and a poet whose output was earning him a deserved reputation as the leading Gaelic literary figure of recent times – thought the book 'marvellously comprehensive, just and profound'. Roddy MacFarquhar – secretary of the Highland Fund and a man who, in that capacity, worked closely with the crofters the fund had been established to assist – was equally complimentary. For 'the first time', MacFarquhar wrote, there had 'been assembled' a 'cogent . . . and accurate history of the social, economic, cultural and religious events . . . which have sculptured the modern Gaelic Highlands and Islands'. From Charles MacLeod, a leading crofting activist, there came similar praise. *The Making of the Crofting Community*, MacLeod wrote, deserved the widest possible readership: 'Every Highland administrator, every councillor, every school, should have a copy . . . And so, ideally, should every crofter.'

As far as I am aware, only one professional historian, John Simpson, reviewed *The Making of the Crofting Community* in the months immediately following its publication. Simpson commented:

> Dr Hunter's commitment, his desire to discover the history of his own people, is similar to that of historians like Edward Thompson, from whom he has learned a lot. The version of history offered by either man could be countered by an alternative version written from somewhere politically further to the right. Dr Hunter, for instance, might be told that Highland landlords were the victims of the onset of capitalism just as the Highland peasantry were. Dr Hunter might well reply – so let me do it for him – that while some landlords suffered a fall from high social position . . . others lost merely all their scruples in dealing with their dependants and behaved with a kind of brutality unthinkable to their ancestors.

John Simpson's description of *The Making of the Crofting Community* as 'admirable' was echoed, a little later, by Bruce Lenman, who deemed the book 'excellent', and by Christopher Harvie, who thought it 'rightly acclaimed'. But Simpson, Lenman and Harvie were political historians, not economic historians of the sort who then, and subsequently, occupied so dominating a position in university-based study of Highland history. By virtually all such economic historians, inevitably, *The Making of the Crofting Community* was regarded with the darkest of suspicion. While finding the book 'highly readable', T. C. Smout, for example, believed it 'one-sided'. And others were much more explicitly hostile. Thus Rosalind Mitchison, although considering *The Making of the Crofting Community* 'a remarkable achievement', declared herself unconvinced by its arguments. Mitchison was especially unconvinced, as she made obvious in a 1981 article in *Scottish Economic and Social History*, by my sympathetic treatment of material such as that collected in Victorian times by the pioneer folklorist, Alexander Carmichael, from Peggy MacCormack, then an elderly resident of South Uist.

Talking, first, about the South Uist of her pre-clearance childhood and, next, about the clearances themselves, Peggy MacCormack said:

> How we enjoyed ourselves in those faraway days – the old as much as the young. I often saw three, and sometimes four, generations dancing together on the green grass in the golden summer sunset: men and boys of fourscore or more, for they lived long in those days, dancing with the boys and girls of five on the green grass . . . The thought of those young days makes my old heart both glad and sad, even at this distance of time. But the clearances came upon us, destroying all, turning our small crofts into big farms for the stranger, and turning our joy into misery, our gladness into bitterness, our blessing into blasphemy and our Christianity into mockery. *O a dhuine ghaolaich, thig na deoir air mo shuilean le linn smaoininn air na dh'fhuilig sinn agus na duirb thainig sinn 'roimhe.* O dear man, the tears come on my eyes when I think of all we suffered and of the sorrows, hardships, oppressions we came through.

While recognising that Peggy MacCormack's account of developments in South Uist contains 'a great deal that is obviously unhistorical', *The Making of the Crofting Community* interprets her few surviving sentiments as an attempt to make a key distinction between the world into which she had been born and the quite different world she inhabited in her old age. The South Uist of Peggy MacCormack's youth was hardly the paradise she evoked in her description of that youth. But the society of which the young Peggy MacCormack had been a member was a cohesive and culturally vibrant society in a way that the society to which she later belonged was not. By thus setting 'the grim realities of the nineteenth-century present against a vision of an older order in which material plenty was combined with security and social justice', *The Making of the Crofting Community* contends of comments like Peggy MacCormack's, 'crofters . . . were provided with an effective, if unsophisticated, critique of the social and economic system which was necessarily associated with commercial landlordism'.

By Rosalind Mitchison, however, this judgement was reckoned worthy only of derision. Quoting Peggy MacCormack's comments as a preliminary to ridiculing them, Mitchison observed of those comments that they were 'clearly rubbish, and it is the prime duty of the historian to label rubbish as such when he meets it'.

In Rosalind Mitchison's dismissal of Peggy MacCormack, I feel, there is to be found a classic example of what E. P. Thompson had in mind when he wrote about 'the enormous condescension of posterity'. But if Mitchison's complaints about *The Making of the Crofting Community* – or, rather, of Peggy MacCormack's brief appearance in it – are best ignored, the more thoughtful criticisms made of the book by Eric Richards in the course of his two-volume study, *A History of the Highland Clearances*, require an answer.

Nearly a decade separates the first volume of *A History of the Highland Clearances*, which appeared in 1982, from *Leviathan of Wealth*, Eric Richards' earlier account of the Sutherland family's business and land management practices. Since *The Making of the Crofting Community* was published some three years into this period, it may be that my efforts helped ensure that Richards' previous – and generally emollient – portrayal of the Highland Clearances had given way, by 1982, to a harder-edged verdict:

> The iron fist of landlord power in the Highlands was employed without restraint in many cases; there was almost certainly a number of deaths among the victims of eviction; the poverty of the people was often desperate; fire was used as a method of finalising a clearance in many instances; people were forced on to emigrant ships; the forces of the law were recruited to implement cruel evictions; the government refused to intercede on behalf of the common people. It is an ugly story . . . When all the qualifications have been made, it is beyond dispute that large but unknown numbers of Highlanders were cleared from their ancestral homes: a peasant society and an independent culture were, in many places, razed from the face of the land, and the benefits which accrued from the great upheaval never flowed in the direction of the people who inhabited the region.

Of my treatment of the clearances and of what came after them, Eric Richards has this to say:

> The work of James Hunter . . . is erected on elaborate and scholarly analytical foundations and [is] informed by a detailed study of archival sources . . . His book on *The Making of the Crofting Community*, written with great flair, has clearly advanced the study of the Highlands during the clearance period. He opens up entirely original lines of research on religion in the Highlands, on the impact of famine and sheep farming, and on the origins and form of crofting protest. It is impressive and path-breaking writing in the best tradition of Scottish social history.

Eric Richards is sceptical, however, of the possibility of anyone ever effectively accomplishing what *The Making of the Crofting Community* tried to do. The materials needed for a worthwhile history of the kind the book is meant to be, Richards states baldly, do not exist:

> Any writer attempting a history-from-below, for the people of the Highlands or elsewhere, is invariably impeded by the dearth of direct primary sources. The inescapable fact is that the poor, the powerless and the illiterate leave very little residue of their lives amongst which a historian may seek material for their reconstruction. This presents a great challenge and there is a danger that, in the full flood of sympathy for the underdog, the historian will interpolate thoughts and emotions for people of whom there is no direct knowledge. Dr Hunter has by no means solved this problem.

Despite the 'penetration and subtlety' of its analysis, therefore, *The Making of the Crofting Community*, Eric Richards concludes, is marred by my importing into my reading of Highland history, as Richards sees it, 'judgements about political equity, economic justice and the rights of property'. Because of this lapse on my part, Richards reckons, *The Making of the Crofting Community* 'fails to address . . . objective conditions of economic change', takes 'a somewhat romanticised view of pre-clearance circumstances in the Highlands' and, more reprehensibly still, 'entertains the . . . dream of Highland reform by which the land and its allied resources would be returned to the common people'.

For reasons explored later, I accept the validity of one of Eric Richards' contentions. *The Making of the Crofting Community*, though it did not set out deliberately to romanticise the epoch in question, certainly falls far short of satisfactorily elucidating the nature of social change in the Highlands during the seventeenth and eighteenth centuries.

But this is by no means to concede Richards' wider point. Writing the history of the powerless, as opposed to the powerful, is difficult, of course. But it is by no means impossible – as has been shown by historian after historian, right across the world, in recent decades. Of relevance, in this connection, is work I have already cited – such as E. P. Thompson's *Making of the English Working Class* and the many successful attempts which have been made to reinterpret Africa's history in ways that give due weight to the experiences and viewpoints of Africans. Of relevance, too, is Emmanuel Le Roy Ladurie's masterly book, *Montaillou*, in which Ladurie, a French historian, painstakingly reconstructs the lives of fourteenth-century Pyrenean villagers. Of relevance, finally, are the numerous accounts which now exist of social groups and social classes – African-American slaves, for instance – once thought so lacking in control over their own lives as to have had almost no autonomous existence, let alone recoverable histories, of any kind.

As compared with historians of slavery, to stick with my last example, the historian of crofting – Eric Richards' strictures notwithstanding – is faced by no 'dearth of direct primary sources'. In Gaelic song and poetry, in the testimony given by crofters to royal commissions and tribunals, in newspaper accounts of speeches made at crofters' meetings, in police reports dealing with the same meetings and in the letters with which crofters eventually began to bombard politicians and civil servants, there is, in fact, a wealth of evidence as to what crofters thought, said and did at various points in the nineteenth century. While it is certainly legitimate to question the use made of this material in *The Making of the Crofting Community*, it makes no sense to deny, as Eric Richards does, such material's existence.

What Richards calls history-from-below, then, is certainly feasible in a Highland context, and I make no apology for having attempted it. Nor do I regret the way in which *The Making of the Crofting Community* 'entertains' the 'dream' of land reform, advocates 'political equity' and is on the side of 'economic justice'. For better or worse, *The Making of the Crofting Community* – as Brian Smith, a Shetland historian, has remarked of Eric Richards' criticisms of my writings – is openly, and intentionally, *about* the crofting population's long, and still to be concluded, struggle for equity, justice and, indeed, land reform. While it would undoubtedly have been possible for me to write an account of crofting history which treated this struggle in a more off-hand and uninvolved manner than the one adopted in *The Making of the Crofting Community*, that would have been to produce simply yet another in the long line of books – some of Eric Richards' own productions among them – which focus primarily on what Richards calls 'the objective conditions of economic change' in the Highlands. It would have been, in other words, to identify with, and to embrace, an approach to Highland history which, as already explained, I reject totally.

But for all that *The Making of the Crofting Community* commences with a clearly enunciated proclamation to the effect that its interpretation of the Highland past is radically at variance with the interpretations advanced by academic historians of the region, there clearly continues to be feeling among such historians that it would have been better for my standing and reputation had I been prepared to sink my differences with them. Something of this is discernible in Eric Richards' reaction to *The Making of the Crofting Community*. And it is a point of view expressed more forcefully still by Tom Devine – whose work on the modern history of the Highlands, contained in books like *The Great Highland Famine* and *Clanship to Crofters' War* – is essential reading for anyone with an interest in the subject.

While recognising the manner in which 'the popular mind' continues to connect 'the depopulation of northern Scotland' with the 'forced removal' of the area's people, Devine explicitly aligns himself with the numerous other academic commentators who, as he remarks, consider such linkage 'simplistic'. He continues:

> Perhaps only James Hunter, among recent writers, in his *The Making of the Crofting Community*, has tried to provide some scholarly support for the more popular interpretation of Highland history. In Hunter's book the landlords are once again cast in their traditional role as villains, dominating and exploiting their people and systematically pursuing policies of clearance

and forced emigration. But Hunter's analysis has not been generally accepted within the mainstream of historical scholarship despite its foundations in wide-ranging archival research. This is partly because of the author's unwillingness to set landlord activity in its social and cultural context and his failure to combine demographic and economic analysis with an evalutation of élite behaviour.

The 'mainstream' to which Devine refers is, of course, the historiographical tradition represented by Malcolm Gray, Rosalind Mitchison and all those other historians I have already listed more than once. Tom Devine – a man, I should make clear at this point, I both like and admire – is very much in that tradition. But as is obvious from *The Great Highland Famine*, easily his most substantial piece of work on the Highlands, Devine brings to bear on the modern history of the area a range of skills which make him, in key respects, a far more impressive operator than his predecessors. Not least among the skills in question is Devine's ability to engage in statistical analysis of a sort never before undertaken in a Highland context. Dealing with topics as varied as death rates, wool prices, evictions and emigration patterns, the 80 or so statistical tables which appear in *The Great Highland Famine* are prominent among the methodological tools which enable Tom Devine to subject the famine period to scrutiny of a far more detailed kind than it receives in *The Making of the Crofting Community*. And while some of Devine's conclusions reinforce mine, notably with regard to the sheer extent and scope of clearance, others of his findings place the two of us at odds. Devine, for instance, disagrees with my assertion that, on the Highland potato crop failing in 1846 and people beginning to go hungry, most landowners did little to assist their tenantries.

The way Devine tackles this issue is indicative of his wider approach. He comments:

> It proved possible to assemble documentation on the activities of 59 (or 67 per cent) of the total of 86 landlords in the distressed districts. This is a much bigger sample than that considered by Dr Hunter who refers to only 11 individual proprietors in the course of his discussion. Furthermore, this evidence comes from a variety of sources and allows for some cross-checking. In most cases, commentators were often government officials independent of landlord influence . . . Their exhaustive and sometimes highly critical reports are a major source for the evaluation of landlord strategies in the first year of the famine. To these can be added information derived from local and national destitution committees which also undertook regular investigations of the stricken areas, statements from law officers, such as sheriffs and procurators-fiscal, and from the Free Church and Established Church of Scotland. The estate papers of eight of the 12 landlords on whose properties 86 per cent of the famine-stricken population lived are extant and have also been consulted in this survey. What follows are the general conclusions derived from evaluation of these varied sources of information.

Those conclusions are such as to enable Tom Devine to be 'more positive . . . about the role of Highland landowners during the early years of the famine' than I was in *The Making of the Crofting Community*. On such points of detail, I duly stand – if only because, in the face of so much assiduous effort, I can do no other – corrected. While recognising its strengths, however, I do not accept that Devine's overall approach to Highland history is – as he implies in the course of his comments on 'popular interpretations' of that history – automatically to be considered superior to, or in advance of, my own. I take comfort, in this connection, from the fact that thinking of the kind which underpins *The Making of the Crofting Community* has been reinforced recently, at the international level if not yet at the Scottish one, by innovative developments in history writing. Those developments have begun to impact, with fascinating results, on Ireland – a country which, as *The Making of the Crofting Community* recognises, has long been of particular interest from a Highland standpoint. And despite the parochialism in which academic historians of Scotland – a singularly isolationist breed – have always wallowed, the new ideas which historians elsewhere have started to embrace will eventually impact on historical studies here also. When they do, I suspect, the 'mainstream' in which Tom Devine so confidently locates himself will be shown to be – both intellectually and methodologically – something of a backwater.

The Irish equivalent of what Devine calls 'the popular interpretation' of Highland history is to be found in Irish people's longstanding and ineradicable tendency to blame Ireland's landlords – aided and abetted, most Irish folk would add, by the British politicians then in charge of their country – for the many miseries endured by Ireland's rural population in the nineteenth century. Against this 'popular interpretation' of the Irish past, many of Ireland's academic historians – the Irish counterparts of Malcolm Gray, Rosalind Mitchison, Tom Devine and their collaborators – have waged a long war. This war's ultimate aim – one, of course, with all sorts of political, social and cultural ramifications – was to replace anti-landlord and anti-British analyses of Irish history with a perspective on Ireland's past that would ideally be so drained of emotion and ideology as to be completely 'objective' and 'value-free'. For a time, it has to be admitted, Ireland's revisionist academics – rather like Tom Devine's 'mainstream' in the Scottish case – looked to be carrying all before them. Today, however, their project has begun to falter – principally because revisionism's numerous inadequacies have been cruelly exposed by a younger, and excitingly original, generation of Irish historians.*

To historians of this generation, revisionist treatments of the Irish famine – as contained in books which, both in style and purpose, mirror Tom Devine's work on the famine's Highland equivalent – seem especially

---

*Anyone interested in pursuing those Irish issues further is referred to C. Brady (ed), *Interpreting Irish History: The Debate on Historical Revisionism*, Dublin, 1994. Also important is C. Kinealy, 'Beyond Revisionism: Reassessing the Great Irish Famine', *History Ireland*, Vol. 3, No. 4, 1995.

unsatisfactory. Such treatments, it has been claimed, avoid 'the issue of culpability' by portraying landlords 'as hapless victims' of allegedly uncontrollable events; they adopt 'an austerely clinical tone' as a means of 'cerebralising and thereby desensitising trauma'; in their anxiety to be free of anything approximating to moral judgement, they make the mistake, as Christine Kinealy has forcefully put it, of throwing 'the starving baby out with the purified bath-water':

> Suffering, emotion and the sense of catastrophe have been removed from revisionist interpretations of the famine . . . The obscenity and degradation of starvation . . . have been marginalised. Popular books . . . which place suffering at the heart of the famine have been derided or dismissed.

What troubles critics of revisionism in Ireland, then, is identical to what troubled me, back in the 1960s, about the Gray-Youngson-Mitchison-Pryde-Richards-Campbell-Smout-Gaskell school's treatment of the Highland Clearances. And although this school – in the guise nowadays of Tom Devine's 'mainstream' – easily rode the punch I tried to land on it in the shape of *The Making of the Crofting Community*, I find it pleasing, I confess, to see its Irish *alter ego* take so many punishing blows. Among the more effective deliverers of such blows is Brendan Bradshaw:

> Confronted by the catastrophic dimension of Irish history, the discomfiture of the modern [or revisionist] school of value-free historians is apparent. So is the source of their discomfiture: a conception of professionalism which denies the historian recourse to value-judgements and, therefore, access to the kind of moral and emotional register necessary to respond to human tragedy.

Revisionism's most unforgivable error, Bradshaw continues, lies in its deliberate abandonment of historical scholarship's central and essential function of 'mediating between the actuality of the historical experience and contemporary perceptions of it':

> That function acquires a particular urgency, it may be claimed, when, as in the case of Ireland, the communal memory retains a keen sense of the tragic dimension of the national history. In such circumstances, the mediating function of the historian is manifestly *not* fulfilled by stoking the memory of ancient wrongs and the bitterness of bygone times. But neither is it constructive to conspire 'to remove the pain from Irish history' as a recent critic of the modern school has protested . . . As sorry experience has shown, such stratagems serve only to establish a credibility gap between the professional historian's account of the past and the public perception of it: the bitter reality, recalled in song and story, continues to haunt the popular memory.

It was exactly this type of credibility gap – between 'the crofter's conception of his own past' and 'the typical historian's portrayal of it' – that *The Making of the Crofting Community* was intended, as its Introduction states, to bridge. Hence the gratification I get from the spectacle of views akin to my own beginning to gather heavyweight support in Ireland.

Nor are historiographical advances in Ireland the only ones presently helping to sustain my conviction that, notwithstanding the evident unacceptability of my opinions in 'mainstream' circles, *The Making of the Crofting Community* might not, after all, have been so outlandish an exercise as Tom Devine has made it out to be. Internationally, in fact, it is Devine's own preferred methodology, the statistically and mathematically based brand of history known as econometrics or cliometrics, which is starting to look more than slightly *passé*. Having first noted the recent relegation of cliometrics to the status of a 'sub-specialism', Richard J. Evans, professor of modern history at the University of Cambridge and author (in 1997) of *In Defence of History*, a brilliant survey of current historiographical thinking, goes on to comment more generally about historical writing of the kind which has long loomed so large in relation to the Highlands:

> One of the very great drawbacks of generalizing social-science history, with its reliance on averages and statistics, was its virtual elimination of the individual human being in favour of anonymous groups and trends. To reduce every human being to a statistic, a social type, or the mouthpiece of a collective discourse is to do violence to the complexity of human nature, social circumstance and cultural life.

Increasingly taking the place of what Evans calls 'social-science history' is the variant of history which has become known as 'postmodern'. Of such postmodern history, Evans has this to say:

> Postmodernism in its more constructive modes . . . has shifted the emphasis in historical writing . . . back from social-scientific to literary models . . . It has restored individual human beings to history, where social science approaches had more or less written them out. And it has inspired, or at least informed, many outstanding historical works.

Among the works which Evans mentions in this context is Orlando Figes's *A People's Tragedy: The Russian Revolution, 1891–1921*. At the start of that extraordinarily fine book, Figes has this to say about its structure:

> The narrative of *A People's Tragedy* weaves between the private and the public spheres. Wherever possible, I have tried to emphasise the human aspect of great events by listening to the voices of individual people whose lives became caught up in the storm . . . In following the fortunes of these figures, my aim has been to convey the chaos of these years, as it must have been felt by ordinary men and women.

Were I looking – metaphorically speaking – for expert testimony of a sort that might help to counter Tom Devine's dismissal of *The Making of the Crofting Community*, I should definitely ask Orlando Figes to speak on my behalf. This I would do on the grounds that Figes understands, as Devine apparently does not, that the past can be comprehended by means other than those involving what Tom calls 'demographic and economic analysis'. Such analysis has its place. So, no doubt, has the 'evaluation of élite behaviour' and the setting of 'landlord activity in its social and cultural context'. But unlike Tom, I prefer to concentrate, as Orlando Figes does, on people. And among the people on whom it is essential to focus in a Highland context are those whose shattered lives, I believe, books like Tom Devine's tend to conceal below their endless layers of data.

In relation to the clearances, two such shattered lives can readily be made emblematic of all the others. The lives in question were those of Ellen and Anne MacRae, little girls whose names I came across in 1993 when researches I was then conducting into emigration from the Highlands took me to Grosse Île, the Quebec quarantine station which, in the 1840s, became the last resting place, in all too many instances, of folk from Ireland and from Scotland's crofting districts.

Ellen and Anne belonged to Lochalsh. They arrived at Grosse Île in the fall of 1847. Their father's name is given in the Grosse Île records as *Farre*. This was as near as a French-speaking nurse or orderly could get, I guess, to the Gaelic *Fearchar* or Farquhar – still a common first name among Lochalsh's MacRaes. What happened exactly to Farquhar MacRae, his wife (whose name was Margaret) and any other children they may have had, I do not know. Perhaps they died at sea. Perhaps they died, as lots of others did at that time, on Grosse Île itself. If so, they doubtless lie in one of the mass graves – their shapes reminiscent of the abandoned rigs surrounding the ruins of cleared Highland townships – to be seen on the shores of the Grosse Île inlet which, at about the point that Anne and Ellen reached this colonial quarantine station, became known as Cholera Bay.

Anne and Ellen, at all events, were left parentless. On 18 October 1847, they were accordingly admitted to an orphanage operated by nuns of the *Société Charitable des Dames Catholiques de Québec*. Ellen, aged 12, was eventually adopted by a Quebec family. Anne, aged ten, was found a home in the United States.

Did they ever meet again? Probably not. And even if they had done, other than by means of what little they might have recalled of their childhood Gaelic, they could scarcely have communicated – for Ellen would have grown up speaking *Québecois* French, and the adult Anne would have spoken American English.

Try to imagine what it would have been like, in the famine year of 1847, to be a little girl leaving the home and the community where you had spent your childhood; what it would have been like to make an ocean crossing in the dark, stinking and disease-ridden hold of one of the run-down cargo ships then dominating the emigrant trade; what it would have been like, in the course of this journey or at its end, to watch your mother and your father die; what it would have been like thus to have been left to cope unaided on a strange continent where – knowing no French and, at best, a word or two of English – you would not even have understood, to start with, what was being said to you; what it would have been like, following all of this, to be separated from your surviving sister by many hundreds of miles.

When set in its 'social and cultural context', Tom Devine contends, the conduct of the landlords responsible for what was done, in the nineteenth century, to Highlanders was a good deal less reprehensible than those of us 'outside the mainstream of historical scholarship' have alleged. Maybe Tom is right. That is certainly what his careful tabulations suggest to him. But the experiences of Anne and Ellen MacRae, I submit, suggest something else entirely.

Assessing the impact of postmodernism's assault on what he calls 'the rebarbative social science jargon' with which university-based historians began to fill their books during the 1960s and 1970s, Richard Evans comments: 'One thing which the postmodernist treatment of history as a form of literature has done is to reinstate good writing as legitimate historical practice.' I welcome this. In part, I suspect, my quarrel with academic historians of the Highlands – though it had other causes – was intensified by the way such historians have so frequently managed to turn hugely eventful raw material into tomes of awesome turgidity. When embarking on *The Making of the Crofting Community*, therefore, I was determined, as John Simpson recognised in his 1976 review of the book, to do justice to what is, whatever else it may be, a quite tremendous story:

> History books written on an ambitious scale (as this one is) are expected to convey a good deal of detailed information (as this one does). But many historians seem to construct their books for quarrying in and not for reading through. Dr Hunter displays the comparatively rare knack of subordinating a wealth of telling detail to the needs of a readable, indeed an exciting, narrative.

The Making of the Crofting Community, I hope, remains a reasonably good read. But being of its time, it is not the book I would write if I were commencing it today. While continuing to adhere – as I have emphasised – to the overall direction of *The Making of the Crofting Community*, I am less happy than once I was with the book's treatment of a number of subsidiary topics.

Two of those I have already mentioned. *The Making of the Crofting Community* ought, first, to have aligned itself unreservedly with Ian Grimble and, still more, with John Prebble. The book should have displayed more awareness, second, of the processes responsible for the emergence of the profit-driven landlordism which did so much to shape the pattern of events in the Highlands during the decades following the Battle of Culloden.

In the opening chapter of *The Making of the Crofting Community*, I argue that the transformation of clan chiefs from essentially tribal leaders into cash-obsessed owners of commercially organised estates was 'the great fact' of modern Highland history. From this fact, I add a trifle portentously, 'all else follows'. That remains, I feel, correct. The researches I conducted in the early 1970s, however, focused on the nineteenth century rather than on the period during which this key change actually took place. The book resulting from those researches has comparatively little to say, therefore, about the eighteenth century – and nothing at all to say about the century before. That is partly because those 200 years seemed, in the 1970s, dauntingly inaccessible. A good deal had been written about them. But very little of this material was at all illuminating about social changes of the sort in which I was interested.

Today that situation has altered enormously, not least as a result of the publication of three books which either touch on, or deal directly with, landlordism's emergence. The books in question, in order of appearance, are: *Alasdair MacColla and the Highland Problem in the Seventeenth Century*, by David Stevenson; *Clanship, Commerce and the House of Stuart, 1603–1788*, by Allan I. Macinnes; *From Chiefs to Landlords: Social and Economic Change in the Western Highlands and Islands, 1493–1820*, by Robert A. Dodgshon. Of those three publications, the most important, in the present context, is Allan Macinnes's. His opinions of the Crofters Act may be – and, I think, are – erroneous. But Macinnes is right to observe, in the course of *Clanship, Commerce and the House of Stuart*, that his highly persuasive account of Highland landlordism's origins cannot be reconciled with the way in which I present pre-1745 clanship, at the start of *The Making of the Crofting Community*, as – in Allan Macinnes's words – 'monolithic, static and undeveloped'. As Macinnes has demonstrated, I believe irrefutably, the beginnings of commercially orientated land management, in a Highland context, are to be found, not in the eighteenth century as I assumed in 1976, but in the seventeenth century. That new perspective is one I have incorporated into my own most recent book, *Last of the Free: A Millennial History of the Highlands and Islands*. It is a perspective which, if I were rewriting *The Making of the Crofting Community* as opposed to merely providing it with this preface, I should incorporate into this book also.

What other changes might I make to a wholly revised version of *The Making of the Crofting Community*? I would not, to begin with, make the mistake of implying – as I tended to do in 1976 – that the crofting population is almost exclusively male. I would extend my field of enquiry into the Northern Isles – more especially into Shetland where, as I stress in *Last of the Free*, both crofting and the landlord-directed exploitation with which crofting was so closely bound up, got underway earlier than anywhere else. I would also attach greater importance – and again I have attempted to remedy the deficiency in *Last of the Free* – to the remote origins of the beliefs underpinning the crofting community's eventual assault, in 1882

and subsequently, on landlordism. The antiquity of such beliefs is acknowledged in *The Making of the Crofting Community*. But despite one of my
research supervisors, John Bannerman, having drawn my attention to the
way in which some of the ideas expressed by crofters in the 1880s can be
traced to sources as distant as Gaelic law tracts of a thousand or more years
before, I did not make as much of this, in 1976, as I should have done.

Neither did I draw as heavily as I might have on more modern Gaelic
material of the sort Donald E. Meek has recently brought together in his
outstanding anthology, *Tuath is Tighearna: Tenants and Landlords*. Had
Tuath is Tighearna been available when I was researching *The Making of
the Crofting Community*, the book would have been better than it is.

It would have been better, too, had I had access, in the 1970s, to the
subsequently published researches of the only historian of the modern Highlands – and this may say more about me, I recognise, than it says about
my critics – who has changed my mind about the manner in which the
Highland Clearances ought to be interpreted. The historian in question,
Marianne McLean, is a Canadian whose family roots reach deep into Glengarry County, Ontario. This is one of several North American districts
settled, in the years around 1800, by emigrants from the Highlands. And
in McLean's magnificent book, *The People of Glengarry: Highlanders in
Transition*, it has generated much the best and most thought-provoking
account of the transoceanic population movements to which the Highland
Clearances gave rise.

In *The People of Glengarry*, Marianne McLean has this to say of the
views expressed in *The Making of the Crofting Community*:

> James Hunter has argued that the clearances psychologically devastated
> the clansmen. Their world was turned upside down when their erstwhile
> leaders suddenly jettisoned ancient social values and substituted individual
> self-interest for the common good. The Highlanders who experienced the
> transformation of their society and, in particular, the betrayal of the clear-
> ances were, according to Hunter, demoralized and unable to mount an effec-
> tive resistance to their landlords until they rebuilt their confidence through
> the religious revivals of the first half of the nineteenth century. But if Hunter
> and others who take this line are correct, how are we to explain the quite
> different attitude of the Glengarry settlers? The community of Glengarry
> County was extraordinarily self-confident, a fact that argues that at least
> some of the clansmen had quite a different experience.

The Making of the Crofting Community, Marianne McLean contends, is
too prone to present emigration in terms of a defeat imposed on people
who, in a better ordered world, would have been permitted to remain in
the places where they had been born. From a North American standpoint,
she maintains, it makes more sense to interpret the outflow of Highlanders
which commenced in the later eighteenth century as 'a radical protest
against the impact of economic transformation'. By removing themselves
from the Highlands to places like Glengarry County, McLean points out,

significant numbers of people – all of whom would otherwise have been totally at the mercy of their landlords – were able both to retain a degree of control over their lives and to recreate, in North America, communities of the sort destroyed, on this side of the Atlantic, by clearance and eviction. Something of this viewpoint, I think, is present in *The Making of the Crofting Community* – where quite a lot is made of the fact that Highland landlords, prior to 1815 or thereby, regarded emigration as a threat to the supplies of cheap labour they needed to make a success of the seaweed-harvesting operations which, at that time, were a major source of revenue on many west coast and Hebridean estates. But what I did not appreciate when working on *The Making of the Crofting Community* – and what I came fully to appreciate only by making several visits, some of them in Marianne McLean's company, to localities such as Glengarry County, Cape Breton Island and the Cape Fear River country of North Carolina – was the extent to which North America was, from a Highland perspective, a land of liberation. This perspective is the dominant one in my later book, *A Dance Called America: The Scottish Highlands, the United States and Canada*. But it would be good if it had been incorporated into *The Making of the Crofting Community* as well.

While being willing to contemplate modifications of this sort to the positions I stake out in the first three or four chapters of *The Making of the Crofting Community*, I see no reason to give ground on the line taken in those later chapters which deal with the half-century commencing in 1880. Since I first wrote about it, two academic historians have separately examined various aspects of this period. *Fit for Heroes?: Land Settlement in Scotland after World War I*, by Leah Leneman, concentrates, as its title suggests, on the years following 1918. *Land for the People?: The British Government and the Scottish Highlands, 1880–1925*, by Ewen Cameron, is wider ranging. Both Leneman and Cameron, more especially the latter, are critical of *The Making of the Crofting Community*. Cameron, having described the book as 'important but controversial', lambasts it thus:

> *The Making of the Crofting Community* is important because it was the first survey of the modern history of the Highlands; further, it reacted against a historiographical tradition which, during the preceding decades, had been attacking the 1886 [Crofters] Act . . . The controversy surrounding Hunter's book stems from its specific aim, which was to write a history with the crofter at its centre. This technique conveys the impression of the crofter as a figure of unique virtue, universally oppressed by a group of monolithic landowners; thus there are elements of the work which resemble ahistorical propaganda more than vigorous historical exposition.

Like Leah Leneman, whose approach is similar, Ewen Cameron – very much in the manner of those earlier historians whose work *The Making of the Crofting Community* sought to challenge – adopts a perspective on Highland history in which the mass of Highlanders drop largely from view.

Cameron mainly concerns himself, in other words, with politicians, with civil servants and with landed proprietors. Having thus taken up a historiographical stance which is the opposite of mine, Cameron concludes – and it would have been astonishing if his chosen methodology had resulted in any other finding – that the people on whom he concentrates, especially the landlords among them, exercised more influence over events both in the 1880s and subsequently than is suggested by *The Making of the Crofting Community*. That is fair enough. Had the region's proprietorial class not retained a good deal of political weight – maybe rather more weight than I indicated – in the later nineteenth century, we would not be stuck with this class in the Highlands still. But it is wholly unconvincing to suggest, as Ewen Cameron seems occasionally to do, that the landowning influence on Highland policy remained, after the 1880s as before, the decisive one. Had crofters not fought – often literally – for security of tenure, and had they not effectively pressed the case for a proportion of their lost lands to be restored to them, neither the Crofters Act of 1886 nor the land settlement legislation which followed it would have seen the light of day. It is in this very basic sense that the events of the 1880s constitute a shifting of the initiative from landlords to those crofters who, by organising themselves politically under the banner of the Highland Land League, ensured crofting's survival into the twentieth and twenty-first centuries.

In part at least, the analytical framework employed in *The Making of the Crofting Community* is Marxist in origin. Today, of course, Marxism is everywhere out of favour. But irrespective of the failings of the political ideology he inspired, and irrespective of the many horrors perpetrated in his name, Karl Marx, it seems to me, continues to offer all sorts of indispensable insights into the nature of social conflict. Without recourse to terminology which derives ultimately from Marx's writings, I should find it as impossible now as I did nearly 30 years ago to analyse, in any half meaningful manner, the hostilities in which ninteenth-century crofters and their landlords became embroiled. And if I were presently setting out to tackle the subject matter of *The Making of the Crofting Community* for the first time, I would still do so, I trust, in the spirit which the young Karl Marx displayed when commenting: 'The philosophers have *interpreted* the world in various ways; the point, however, is to *change* it.'

In addition to grappling with the area's history, then, *The Making of the Crofting Community* was meant to make some small contribution to Highland betterment. This, in itself, immediately distinguished the book from those produced by historians of the sort *The Making of the Crofting Community* was intended to counter. By such historians, the predicament in which Highlanders of the 1960s found themselves – a predicament arising from the closely linked phenomena of depopulation and economic contraction – was thought to be every bit as unavoidable and inevitable as the Highland Clearances were alleged, by the same historians, to have been. Thus Roy Campbell, writing in 1965, saw no prospect of repopulating or regenerating the Highlands – while T. C. Smout, writing in 1969, was firmly of the belief that 'the grim facts of economic geography' would always defeat 'the good intentions of planners'. As far back as the eighteenth century, Smout noted, people had aspired to improve conditions in the Highlands:

> There have been men ever since with one version or other of this dream. But perhaps it is all to the good that they do not allow themselves to be diverted from their vision by so dismaying a subject as history.

Because of their implication that it was pointless to embrace the possibility of achieving worthwhile progress in the Highlands, views of this sort were as reactionary as they were pessimistic. It is pleasant to record, therefore, that they were also wrong. In the period since T. C. Smout and Roy Cambell ruled out all prospect of economic and demographic advance in the Highlands, the region has seen its total workforce expand by some 40 per cent and its total population rise – during decades when the population of Scotland as a whole was virtually static – by around 20 per cent. Much remains to be done. But to go today to a crofting locality like Skye – its population massively up on that of the 1960s, its economy significantly diversified, its townships filling with new houses – is to see all around you the most striking evidence of a transformation which, if historians like Campbell and Smout had been right, could never have occurred.

The Making of the Crofting Community, whatever its weaknesses, did not make that sort of error. When studying African history at Aberdeen University, I had been directed to Frantz Fanon's classic of anti-colonial struggle, *The Wretched of the Earth*. There Fanon writes movingly of the importance – when trying to convince folk that the solution to their problems might lie in their own hands – of drawing attention to, and inspiration from, the accomplishments of such folk's forebears. Hence the stress laid in *The Making of the Crofting Community* on the tremendous gains made in the Highlands during the 1880s. In the course of that decade, the book argues, Highlanders imposed their agenda, for the first time in ages, on the Highlands. And what had been done once, *The Making of the Crofting Community* was intended subliminally – or maybe not so subliminally – to suggest could surely be done again.

As I have already made clear, then, Eric Richards was right to discern in *The Making of the Crofting Community* a plea for 'land and its allied resources' to be 'returned to the common people'. But in labelling my land reform aspirations a 'dream', Richards, I feel, made much the same mistake as T. C. Smout and Roy Campbell. He assumed that the Highland circumstances prevailing when he wrote were necessarily fixed and unalterable.

I have never made that assumption. I have always been convinced that radical change, not excluding a further round of 1880s-style land reform, can be brought about in the Highlands. That is why *The Making of the Crofting Community* – written when no such administration existed and when the cause of Highland land reform was embraced by only a tiny number of individuals – ended by looking forward to a time when a Scottish government, building on foundations laid in 1886, would enable Highlanders to take control of the land on which they lived. Today, primarily as a result of actions taken by the communities in question, such control has become a reality in Assynt, Eigg, Valtos, Borve, Knoydart and elsewhere. And today we have a Scottish government which is giving a high priority to enabling other rural residents, both in the Highlands and beyond, to opt for similar arrangements.

The Making of the Crofting Community was by no means the only, and certainly not the principal, originator of the land reform campaign which began in the Highlands in the 1970s and which is now, at last, yielding real and measurable results. Much more important in this connection were: the founding, by Brian Wilson and others, of the *West Highland Free Press*; the publication of John McEwen's remarkable book, *Who Owns Scotland?*; the success of John McGrath's great play, *The Cheviot, the Stag and the Black, Black Oil*; the acceptance by the Highlands and Islands Development Board, when under the chairmanship of Kenneth Alexander, that land reform might legitimately be undertaken by a major public agency. And if I have contributed personally to making land reform happen, then my contribution is maybe more to be discovered in my subsequent involvement with organisations like the Scottish Crofters Union and Highlands and Islands Enterprise than it is to be found in a book I put together in my twenties. But when, in September 1998, I went to Aviemore to hear Donald Dewar – then Secretary of State for Scotland, now First Minister in Scotland's devolved government – deliver that year's John McEwen Memorial Lecture, it was with some gratification, all the same, that I heard this leading politician say that *The Making of the Crofting Community* had helped persuade him of the need for a land reform package of the kind to which he proceeded, in his lecture, to commit himself. That package is now before the Scottish parliament. I would be happier, to be honest, if it went further than it does. But if *The Making of the Crofting Community* played any part, however small, in effecting land reform, however modest, then this book was well worth writing.

In 1976, Cuthbert Graham – whose retirement that summer from the features department of the *Press and Journal* created the vacancy which took me, for some years, into journalism – made this comment in the course of one of his numerous review articles:

> It cannot be often that an academic thesis is a potential best-seller, and the price of James Hunter's *The Making of the Crofting Community*, which is published with its full apparatus of detailed source references and an exhaustive biliography, may in the meantime stand between it and the wide general public which it undoubtedly ought to reach . . . It is greatly to be desired that this splendid narrative should soon be reissued in a popular version, shortened perhaps by the omission of the source list which occupies fully a third of the volume, and docked of the reference numbers which, while establishing its authority, impede the flow of an engrossing saga.

It has taken me a long time to act on Bert Graham's advice. But this version of *The Making of the Crofting Community* is as he suggested it should be. Those in search of references or bibliography will have to consult one of the five printings of the original edition which appeared between 1976 and 1997. Other changes, however, are minimal. The book has been tidied stylistically. But except where I have incorporated information relegated originally to an endnote, its contents are unaltered.

It remains only to thank some of the people who made *The Making of the Crofting Community* possible. Hugh Andrew of the new John Donald requested this preface. John Tuckwell of the original John Donald ensured the book got into print in the first place. Bill Ferguson as well as John Bannerman supervised my researches at Edinburgh University. At Aberdeen University, Don Withrington and Terry Brotherstone, as well as John Hargreaves and Roy Bridges, encouraged me to start on those researches. In Edinburgh, Aberdeenshire, Skye and Kiltarlity, Evelyn, my wife, has had to live with crofting, with Highland history, and sometimes with both simultaneously, since 1972. *The Making of the Crofting Community* was dedicated to her in 1976. It's dedicated to her still. But in its new shape it also owes something to our daughter, Anna, a fourth-year student at Edinburgh University when the foregoing pages were written and the source of a good deal of my information as to the progress of anti-revisionism in Ireland. Having begun this preface with a tribute to John Cameron, I'm glad to be able to end it with a mention of his great-granddaughter. Anna's opinions are her own. But she holds them, as I have cause to know, with all her great-grandfather's force of character.

INTRODUCTION

There are today in the north-west Highlands and Islands of Scotland some 10,000 crofters. A few hundred live on the west coast of the mainland and in Mull. The remainder live in Skye, Tiree and the Outer Hebrides where crofters and their families constitute the greater part of the population and where crofting townships – typically consisting of straggling groups of variously designed houses surrounded by long narrow fields – are the predominant form of human settlement on the land.

As in other parts of Europe's fragmented north-western fringe, the land itself is poor and could not, one might think, be more unsuited to its task of maintaining a smallholding population. From the bare and rocky hills of Skye and Harris to the undulating peat bogs of Lewis or the loch-bespattered surface of North Uist, the dominating impression is one of infertility. Only in a few areas – in the Sleat peninsula in Skye and in some unusually sheltered parts of the mainland, for example – are there any trees worthy of the name. Elsewhere in the region, especially in the islands, there are almost none – the uniformly brown, heathy landscape being broken only by a few relatively fertile straths, by the raised beaches that occasionally provide small, low plateaus of gravelly soil between the hills and the sea, and by the swathes of green machair land that delineate the Hebrides' outermost rim.

All these sites and particularly the machairs – natural grasslands which rest on the shellsands thrown up by the Atlantic and which occur spasmodically in Lewis, more widely in Harris and more extensively still in the Uists and Tiree – are the natural foci of crofting settlement, and the crofts that occupy them are conspicuously more productive than those consisting of a few acres of sour, shallow soil reclaimed, over many generations, from peat. But nowhere in the region is the crofter's lot an easy one. Even the most fertile croft cannot escape the frequent rain and gales that are a consequence of the proximity of the Highlands to the Atlantic depressions that track incessantly north-eastwards between Scotland and Iceland. Of all the numerous uncertainties of the crofter's condition, therefore, none is more permanent than the weather. In this book the natural hazards of geography and climate figure only occasionally: when a harvest does not ripen because

31

of an unusually wet summer or is destroyed by an exceptionally severe autumnal gale; when crofters are confronted with the task of winning hold-ings from previously uncultivated moorland. But the difficulties inherent in the Highlands' geographical position and circumstances are a constant backdrop to crofting history, and they should never be overlooked. That they are relatively unemphasised in this account is not because they are judged unimportant but because crofters have always considered the hard-ships that are the unavoidable consequences of their natural environment to be more bearable than those that have resulted from human action. The excessive and ostentatious comfort of a privileged few; their oppressive and unjust conduct: these have always seemed less tolerable than the vagaries of the climate and the general scarcity of resources. It is for that reason that this book deals more with the exploitation of man by man than with the unalterable conditions which have long defied humanity's efforts to create a prosperous agriculture in the Highlands.

Numerically insignificant and geographically distant from the centres of British industry, trade and political power, crofters exercise no great influence on the country as a whole. Nor have they done so in the past. Crofters and their families are, however, a distinctive social group. They possess their own culture, sometimes speak their own language and gener-ally live their lives in a way long since abandoned in the rest of Britain. The uniqueness of the crofting way of life – itself a reason for studying the crofting past – has long been apparent. At one time, it tended to provoke in outsiders a desire to sweep crofters and crofting into the dustbin of history and to remake the Highlands in the image of the southern British coun-tryside. Today, principally because of the steady erosion of the nineteenth-century belief in the self-evident virtue of 'progress', a quite opposite reac-tion is more common. In 1954, for example, a royal commission concluded that the crofting system deserved to be maintained if only for the reason that it supported 'a free and independent way of life which, in a civilisa-tion predominantly urban and industrial in character, is worth preserving for its own intrinsic quality'. In the last 20 years that opinion has gained a growing number of adherents – a development accompanied by a radical revision of the crofter's popular image. To the nineteenth century advocate of industry and empire, the crofter was an idle, feckless fellow whose diffi-culties were largely of his own making – 'the natural fruits' of his own 'indolence and ignorance', as one writer put it. In the increasingly congested and polluted environment of urban Britain in the 1970s, on the other hand, the crofter is frequently idealised, his way of life romanticised, and the region in which he lives depicted as a placid, pastoral haven in an ever more frantic world.

The Highlands of the tourist brochure and the holiday cottage are not, however, the Highlands of the crofter. The crofter has never been immune from the pressures generated by capitalist civilisation. Indeed, he has suffered from them more than most. And today, as the effects of a rapidly expanding tourist trade are supplemented by the consequences of oil-related industrialisation, such pressures are stronger than ever. The crofting tenant is no longer threatened with starvation when his crops fail or when the herring shoals do not materialise. And when his land is expropriated the process is more subtle and less violent than it once was. But the uncertainties of the crofter's day-to-day existence are nonetheless real and worrying. He has still to work hard for a meagre return. His holding is almost invariably small; his land often poor; his financial resources far from ample. His life, the crofter would agree, has its compensations. That is why he does not abandon it. But his independence is often more apparent than real, while such freedom as he does enjoy is purchased at a price which few of his urban admirers would be willing to pay. The crofter is consequently entitled to respect, not as a quaint anachronism who lives closer to nature's bosom than the rest of us, but as one of that majority of mankind which, in the face of immense difficulties, still wins a part of its living by its own efforts from the land.

Like that of peasant cultivators the world over, the crofter's way of life is more easily described than defined. The Napier Commission, the small body of men charged in 1883 with the task of conducting the first official enquiry into crofting conditions, tackled the problem by stating that the term crofter referred to 'a small tenant of land, with or without a lease, who finds in the cultivation of his holding a material portion of his occupation, earnings, and sustenance, and who pays rent directly to the proprietor'. Legislation passed since 1883 has modified the crofter's tenurial status, but as a delimitation of his social and economic position the Napier Commission's definition has yet to be bettered. The crofter, it makes clear, is the tenant of an individual holding. The returns from that holding usually meet only a part of his needs and consequently have to be supplemented in some way if he and his family are to attain an adequate standard of living. And the crofter rents his land from a landlord, not from a superior tenant.

The second of these points – that the crofter is not a subsistence agriculturalist but a man who, while retaining his stake in the land, has always had to have an occupation ancillary to that of farming his holding – will be returned to again and again in this book. For present purposes, however, the first and last of the Napier Commission's three statements about the crofter's essential characteristics are of most significance – showing, as they do, that the crofter is a relatively modern phenomenon. Until the end of the eighteenth century, smallholdings occupied by single tenants paying rent to a landowner had little or no place in the Highland scheme of things. The origins of the crofting system are consequently to be found, not in the middle ages, as is often loosely supposed, but in the period which also witnessed the appearance of the cotton mill and the steam engine.

Apart from a brief glance at eighteenth-century occurrences, this book is concerned, therefore, with the development of crofting and of crofting life from its beginnings around 1800 until 1930 when, with the virtual completion of the Board of Agriculture's land settlement programme, the modern pattern of crofting settlement was delineated. What follows is not, however, a history of the crofting counties as that expression has been understood since the passing of the first Crofters Act in 1886. Within the larger region, the Gaelic areas are separated from the Northern Isles and much of Caithness by important historical and geographical differences. These have led not only to obvious cultural divergences but also to the physical structure of crofting in the Gaelic west being quite dissimilar to that prevailing in the three northern counties or, for that matter, in the eastern Highlands and in south and mid-Argyll. The heartland of the crofting community, then, consists, and always has done, of the islands from Mull and Tiree to Lewis, along with the west and north coasts of the Scottish mainland from Ardnamurchan to the borders of Caithness. In this district, the last bastion of Scottish Gaelic and the culture associated with it, is to be found the greater part of all the land held under crofting tenure. When the crofting community is mentioned, it is usually the people of this area who are referred to. And it is their history that is recounted in what follows.

The 'making' of this book's title refers to the social, economic, cultural and political influences and events which have made the crofting community what it is. And the phrase 'crofting community' has itself been preferred to any obvious alternative because it is in common usage and because it comprehends all the people whose history is to be investigated: cottars or landless people, once numerous now few, as well as crofters in the strict sense of occupiers of holdings. Like any other group or class in society, however, the crofting community cannot be studied in isolation. One of the greatest of modern social historians, E. P. Thompson, contends that the phenomenon of social class occurs only 'when some men, as a result of common experiences . . . feel and articulate the identity of their interests as between themselves and as against other men whose interests are different from, and usually opposed to, theirs'. That is to imply that the development of any social class can be understood only if its relations with other social classes are taken into account. It is for this reason that Highland landlords and their policies loom large in the following pages. Their part is a considerable one, not because this is their history, but because in the western Highlands and Islands, during the period under consideration, landlords constituted the ruling class. They brought crofting into existence. They decided which areas should be occupied by crofters and which should not. And most important of all, the emergence of a feeling of community among crofters was itself a consequence of their recognition of the fact that their interests and those of their landlords were mutually irreconcilable.

Because the conflict between those who owned the land and those who lived and worked on it is a major theme of this book, its approach to modern Highland history is necessarily different from that adopted in most recent publications on the subject. The majority of these – and there have been a lot of them – have been written by economic historians in an attempt to analyse and explain the modernisation of the Highland economy in the hundred years after the Battle of Culloden. Most of the publications in question have been based on the surviving records of Highland estate managements. The consequence has been that, while old simplifications about Highland history have been replaced by scrupulously documented accounts of the way in which the modern economic structure of the region was established, the people upon whom estate managements imposed their policies have been almost completely neglected. In the present century, for instance, there has been only one serious attempt to evaluate the impact of economic change on the Gaelic consciousness – and that by a Gaelic poet, Sorley MacLean*, rather than by an historian.

This situation is in marked contrast to that prevailing in the nineteenth century when, with the exception of the self-justifying volumes produced by one or two landowners and estate managers, accounts of what was then the contemporary history of the Highlands were usually written from a profess-edly popular standpoint. Such accounts were mostly propaganda pieces, produced by radical critics of Highland landlordism when hunger and evic-tion were stark realities or when crofters were engaged in open conflict with their landlords. As propaganda they were brilliantly successful. As history, however, they seem less than adequate to most modern historians simply because they were written by men who were totally committed to one side in the class struggle between crofters and proprietors. Recent writers have consequently tended to dismiss the works of their radically-minded pred-ecessors as the product of what one economic historian, Malcolm Gray, has called 'social prejudice' – and their interpretation of Highland history is usually examined, therefore, only to be refuted. Books which argue the crofting population's case – and which argue it forcefully, lucidly and sympathetically – are available, of course. It is arguable, however, that the modern authors (such as John Prebble and Ian Grimble) who stand closest to the radical tradition of the nineteenth century have, by the very strength of their commitment to it, done it a disservice. Those authors' published histories, for example, are largely made up of refurbished versions of their precursors' books and pamphlets. Thus abstracted from their historical context, the older works are deprived of purpose and effect, their message is distorted and their undoubted weaknesses highlighted – facts that have made it easy for those whose sympathies lie with Highland landlords to

---

*MacLean's pioneering article, 'The Poetry of the Clearances', appeared in the *Transactions of the Gaelic Society of Inverness* in 1939.

damn the few recent writers who have adopted an explicitly pro-crofter stance as, for instance, 'popular historians . . . interested chiefly in the propagandist or sensational aspects' of the Highland past.*

In this book neither of these approaches to the older historical tradition is adopted. It is freely admitted here that the popular view of Highland history is, as has been said on more than one occasion, invariably prejudiced, frequently emotional and sometimes inaccurate. That view is not rejected, however. Instead, a serious attempt is made to understand it and to explain why the crofter's conception of his own past – as preserved in the nineteenth-century books and pamphlets already referred to, in Gaelic poetry, in press and police reports of Highland Land League meetings and, not least, in the collective memory of the crofting community itself – is so radically different from the typical historian's portrayal of it. Such an explanation can be arrived at only by putting the crofter at the centre of his own history. In essence, therefore, this book is an attempt to write the modern history of the Gaelic Highlands from the crofting community's point of view. The recent historians of the region may question the validity of that perspective and the soundness of the conclusions to which it leads. But if it illuminates crofters' attitudes to their own past, the writing of this account of it will not have been in vain.

---

*The phrase in quotes is Philip Gaskell's.

THE END OF AN OLD ORDER

1745–1800

In the world of the eighteenth century, Britain was recognisably unique. In the tumultuous events of the 1640s, it had experienced the first great social and political revolution of modern times. A hundred years later, the country was embarking on the equally significant economic revolution that was to make it the world's first industrial nation. And though its political life was still dominated by a landed oligarchy, Britain's rulers, unlike many of their continental counterparts, were not feudal aristocrats; nor was their king an absolute monarch. In Scotland, admittedly, feudal jurisdictions persisted until the 1740s – an indication, if one was needed, that its earlier history had been very different from that of the larger, wealthier and more populous kingdom south of the Tweed. But in Scotland as in England, the monarchical principles of prior centuries had never recovered from the assaults made upon them in the era of Cromwell and the Covenant. It was as heirs of the previous century's anti-absolutist revolutions, then, that the Whig magnates of eighteenth-century Britain held power. While still given to assessing their personal prestige and influence in terms of acreages owned, Britain's political élite were distinctly unfeudal in outlook. They measured their country's greatness in terms of its trade and commerce. And in their quest for control of global markets, they did not hesitate to wage war in India, in America and on the oceans of the world.

The society which thus supported the beginnings of imperialism was itself increasingly orientated towards the accumulation of wealth. Towns and cities were being built on the proceeds of the slave trade, the tobacco trade and a dozen other forms of commercial enterprise. By the century's end, the construction of other cities was to be financed with fortunes created by that epoch-making invention, the factory. Nor was capitalism's advance confined to Britain's rapidly expanding urban centres. Rural areas, too, were being reorganised on commercial lines. As his fields were expropriated and his commons enclosed in the interests of an economically efficient agriculture, the peasant was vanishing from Britain's countryside. And that countryside itself was being irrevocably altered as 'improving' landlords laid out fields and farms, planted woods and hedges – in short, brought the modern rural landscape into existence.

Beginning in England, those developments soon spread, or were carried, to other parts of the British Isles. In Ireland, the last of the old Celtic society's semi-independent enclaves were overrun during the opening years of the seventeenth century. Thereafter that country was drawn inextricably into England's imperial ambit and its land parcelled out among English landlords. Politically merged with England since 1707, Scotland, for its part, was – by the middle of the eighteenth century if not before – clearly following the example set by its southern neighbour. Having at last gained unrestricted access to England's overseas empire, Glasgow's merchants were showing themselves to be every bit as enterprising and as successful as their counterparts in Liverpool or Bristol – while the lairds and farmers of the Lothians were embarking on their soon-to-be-successful attempt to emulate, indeed surpass, the achievements of more southerly 'improvers'.

By the 1740s, then, the modernisation of British society was everywhere proceeding apace – everywhere, that is, except in the Highlands of Scotland. There an older way of life persisted: a way of life whose social forms were based not on ties of economic dependency, as was increasingly the case in the south, but on the much older bonds of kinship. In the Highlands the descent group, defined genealogically and institutionalised as the tribe or clan, was the focus of all social, economic and cultural activity. Describing a clan was not, and is not, easy. But this mid-eighteenth-century attempt at a definition was a very reasonable one:

> A set of men bearing the same surname and believing themselves to be related the one to the other and descended from the same common stock. In each clan there are several subaltern tribes . . . but all agree in owing allegiance to the supreme chief of the clan or kindred and look upon it to be their duty to support him at all adventures.

In the eighteenth century, kin-based societies of the type thus delineated had long since vanished from the rest of western Europe, and in attempting to enlighten his southern colleagues as to the true nature of Highland society, Duncan Forbes of Culloden, author of that statement and one of the British government's principal representatives in the Scotland of the 1740s, had to contend with a conceptual gulf of considerable dimensions.

Even before Duncan Forbes penned his analysis of clanship, however, there were signs that the gulf between the Highlands and the rest of Britain might soon be bridged. Commercial interchange between the two societies, for instance, was expanding at an unprecedented rate – its most important component being the export of cattle from the Highlands to the south. A part of Highland life since at least the sixteenth century, the cattle trade grew rapidly after 1700, largely because of the increased demand generated by the steadily developing southern economy. Nor were southern influences on the Highlands confined to those associated with trade. Long addicted to dabbling in the politics of the Scottish Lowlands, not to mention those of England and of Ireland, the higher ranks of Highland society were well

accustomed to moving in two cultural universes: that of the Gaelic Highlands on the one hand; that of southern Britain and the rest of western
Europe on the other. This tendency to be involved in southern as well as
Highland affairs was particularly characteristic of the chiefs who constituted the apex of the traditional power structure. In the early eighteenth
century, depending on whether they favoured the Whigs or the Jacobites,
many chiefs were as at home in Edinburgh or Paris as they were in the Highlands, and French or English rolled off their tongues as easily as – perhaps
more easily than – Gaelic. While away from his clan, moreover, the typical
chief – conscious since childhood of his immensely aristocratic status in the
Highland society whence he came – felt obliged to emulate, or even surpass,
the life-style of the courtiers and nobles with whom he mingled. And it was
at this point, significantly enough, that the eighteenth-century chief's two
roles came seriously into conflict with one another. As a southern socialite,
he needed more and more money. As a tribal patriarch, he could do very
little to raise it.

That is not to say, of course, that cash-strapped chiefs did not make the
attempt to find the funds they needed. The criticisms made of a late seventeenth-century MacLeod of Dunvegan by Roderick Morrison, the blind
Gaelic bard and harper known as *An Clarsair Dall*, tell their own story:

Théid seachd trusail air dhàil
air each crudhach as gàirmhor srann;
diallaid làsdail fo'n tòin;
's mór guru b'fheairrd' e srian òir 'na cheann . . .
Cóig ginidhean òir –
gun téid siod ann an cord d'an aid;
lurad eil' oirre féin . . .
Théid luach mairt no nas m
'm paidhear stocainn de'n t-seòrsa 's fearr,
is cha chunntar an corr . . .
Thig e mach as a' bhùth
leis an fhasan as ùr bho'n Fhraing,
Is an t-aodach gasda bha 'n d
m'a phearsa le spéis nach gann
théid a shadadh an cùil . . .

Expenditure on such a scale had its inevitable outcome:

An uair a thilleas e rìs
a dh'amharc a thìre féin,
'n déis na mìltean chur suas,
gun tig sgrìob air an tuath mu spréidh,
gus an togar na mairt
'n déidh an ciùradh 's an reic air féill:
siod na fiachan ag at,
gus am fiarach ri mhac 'na dhéidh.*

*'The equivalent of seven collections are borrowed to pay for a shod, loud-snorting
horse; a lordly saddle under the bottom; and he would, of course, be much the

In the seventeenth century, it must be said, such behaviour was unusual. Indeed there is some evidence that Morrison's *Oran do Mhac Leòid Dhùn Bheagain*, from which these lines are quoted, did something to curb the extravagances of other chiefs. The effects of *An Clarsair Dall's* strictures were neither widespread nor lasting, however. After 1700, the ostentatious extravagance and the commercial outlook which Roderick Morrison had so bitterly condemned became increasingly prevalent.

Thus the Camerons of Locheil involved themselves in the West Indies trade – while Skye's leading chieftains, Sir Alexander MacDonald of Sleat and Norman MacLeod of Dunvegan, sold some of their own clansmen into slavery. In its cynical disregard of the bonds and obligations of kinship, that episode, which occurred in the 1730s, was, as Sorley MacLean has remarked, 'a grim foretaste of the clearances'. But still more indicative of what was to come were contemporary developments on the Campbell lands in Argyll. There, in the late seventeenth and early eighteenth centuries, the Duke of Argyll's need for increased revenues was partly met by a drastic reorganisation of the tenurial relationships prevailing on his clan lands in mainland Argyll, on Mull and on Tiree. The object of this reform was the production of higher money rents. The assumption on which it was based, according to a recent study by Eric Cregeen, was that 'land should produce a revenue . . . like any other capital asset and that it should therefore be allocated, not as a token of kinship, as a reward for allegiance or as a means of maintaining a following, but in response to the operation of competitive-bidding'. As the early twentieth-century historian, R. H. Tawney, commented of a similar shift in aristocratic attitudes to, and beliefs about, land in sixteenth-century England:

> It is easy to underrate the significance of this change, yet it is, in a sense, more fundamental than any other; for it marks the transition from the . . . conception of land as the basis of political functions and obligations, to the modern view of it as an income-yielding investment. Landholding tends, in short, to become commercialised.

The commercialisation of the region's agricultural structure in response to chieftains' financial necessitousness – an undertaking in which the Campbells were eventually joined by every other leading family in the region – is the great fact of eighteenth-century Highland history. From it all else follows. But it was not something that could be achieved within the context

better of a golden bridle . . . Five golden guineas – that is spent on a cord for the hat, and as much again for the hat itself . . . The price of a mart [a cattle beast] or more is paid for a pair of stockings of the best kind, and the change is not counted . . . He comes out of the shop with the latest fashion from France, and the fine clothes worn on his person yesterday with no little satisfaction are tossed into a corner . . . When he returns again to view his own country, though thousands of pounds have already been sent away, a cattle levy is imposed on the tenantry, and so the marts are exported, after being cured and sold at the market. Thus do the debts increase to be demanded from his son after him.' The translation is William Matheson's.

of traditional Highland society. Even the Dukes of Argyll had to temper the dictates of commercialised estate management with those of military security – while chiefs who lacked the Campbells' extra-Highland power base were quite unable to interfere with existing tenurial arrangements to any significant extent. The reason was simple. Prior to the collapse of the last Jacobite rebellion at Culloden in 1746, the Highlands lay outside the effective limits of British jurisdiction. The law and order which were necessary preconditions for the commercial and industrial developments occurring in the south were consequently absent from the area. In England or Lowland Scotland, there had long since passed away 'the turbulent days' when, as Tawney put it, 'lords had ridden out at the head of their retainers to convince a bad neighbour with bows and bills, and a numerous tenantry had been more important than a high pecuniary return from the soil'. In the Highlands, however, a chief's status and even his life still depended on the number of armed men he could command. This truth – encapsulated in MacDonnell of Keppoch's famous remark that his rent-roll consisted of 500 fighting men – was necessarily reflected in the traditional agrarian system.

The essential feature of that system was that it depended on land being laid out to ensure the continued existence of the clan as a socially unified and militarily effective organisation, considerations of agricultural efficiency being of decidedly secondary importance. Most of a clan's territorial possessions were consequently held by tacksmen, an essentially military caste for whom courage and prowess in war were the ultimate virtues. Tacksmen were generally kinsmen of their chiefs to whom they paid only nominal rents for their farms – on the understanding that tacksmen's principal role was to provide chiefs with skilled soldiers rather than with cash. Inordinately conscious of their status as the *daoine uaisle,* or gentry, of the clans they made so crucial a contribution to sustaining, most tacksmen did not deign to soil their hands with the day-to-day tasks of farming. That role was assigned to the subtenants to whom tacksmen sublet the greater portion of their farms – or to the cottars and mailers who, as the subtenants of subtenants, constituted each clan's lowest echelons.

The traditional landholding system thus supported a formidably efficient military machine which was bound together by a chain of command and kinship stretching from the chief through his lieutenants, the tacksmen, to the subtenants and cottars whose function and duty it was to make the apparently undisciplined, but undeniably devastating, charges which were the basis of Highland warfare. Burdened with such an intricate array of tenures and subtenures, the land was clearly incapable, however, of yielding its full agricultural potential. Though a clan could scarcely be bettered as an instrument of war, therefore, its rent-producing capacity was extremely limited. Nor could that capacity be easily increased. The bonds of kinship and mutual obligation on which clans were based effectively precluded the introduction of impersonal money relationships. To even the most casual of eighteenth-century observers, it was consequently obvious that, if a clan's territories were to produce a worthwhile rental for its chief, the multiple gradations of the traditional society would have to be swept away – with a view to clan lands being let directly to men who were willing and able to work those lands efficiently and to pay a realistic money rent for the privilege of so doing. This, of course, was the aim of the Campbell reforms already referred to. The Campbells excepted, however, chiefs hesitated to rent out land competively for fear of alienating the tacksmen upon whom, in the unsettled conditions prevailing in the pre-Culloden period, their own survival depended. In most of the eighteenth-century Highlands, therefore, a chief's conduct had to conform, at least approximately, to the standards of the traditional society – rather than to those prevailing in the commercial world in which he spent a growing amount of his time and to which he was increasingly attracted. As far as his clansmen were concerned, a clan chief could transgress the southern moral code, to say nothing of the Scottish or British government's laws, with impunity. But he could not introduce the apparatus of southern landlordism. To have done so would have been to invite his own downfall. This was a predicament resolved only by the forcible incorporation of the Highlands into the social and political system of Great Britain.

Britain's eventual subjugation of the Highlands was, perhaps, inevitable. The problem of how to pacify the region was one that had taxed successive Scottish governments long before any administration in London was called upon to tackle it. And in the last analysis, it was most improbable that two societies as unlike each other as that of the Gaelic Highlands and that of the rest of Britain could coexist in close proximity for any length of time. That Highlanders were left largely to their own devices for so long was, to some extent, a consequence of their homeland's relative remoteness. More fundamentally, however, it was a consequence of the nature of the southern economy's demands on the Highlands. In the seventeenth and eighteenth centuries, as in more modern times, traditional societies which were felt to stand in the way of English or British interests were habitually destroyed. In Ireland, for example, a Celtic society very similar to that of the Highlands was ruthlessly obliterated, and the native peoples of the eastern part of North America were wiped out even more completely. In both cases, however, the motive was principally that of clearing the way for colonisation. Where such a motive was absent, British commercial interests were quite content to leave traditional societies alone – as long, that is, as they produced such raw materials as the same interests might require.

The Highlands, although part of Scotland and, after 1707, of Britain, were inaccessible and infertile. They consequently offered little to attract the coloniser – while the British economy's main requirement from the area, black cattle, could demonstrably be obtained without incurring the trouble and expense of effectively subordinating Highland cattle-rearers to British rule. Despite the absence of a simple economic motivation for such a development, however, the early eighteenth century was characterised by a steadily growing British military presence in the Highlands. The reasons had little to do with black cattle. They derived from essentially political and strategic considerations turning on the fact that the Highlands were the last great reservoir of Jacobitism in the British Isles.

Why Highlanders should have been so devoted to the cause of the exiled Stuart monarchy is a complex question – and one which has never been satisfactorily answered by the hosts of romantic writers who have dwelt so lovingly on every detail of Highland Jacobitism. What is clear, however, is that a government of capitalist aristocrats – a government which habitually acted in the interests of an increasingly powerful mercantile class and which, for that reason, happily engaged in a protracted struggle with France for control of world markets – was unlikely to tolerate the indefinite existence within its frontiers of a stronghold of an older way of life which could, and did, serve as a convenient springboard for Jacobite and French attempts to renew in Britain the debilitating civil conflicts of the seventeenth century. Successive Jacobite risings were consequently followed by ever more determined efforts to suppress Highland Jacobitism – the final stages of this process being initiated by the amazing successes achieved by the small Highland army which, in a few months in 1745, conquered Scotland and marched to within 127 miles of London. Decidedly shaken by those events, the British government determined to destroy the traditional society of the Highlands – thus ensuring that Highlanders could never again challenge Britain's imperial might. The outcome was Culloden and the bloody and brutal repression which came after it.

From a Highland perspective, the significance of the Battle of Culloden does not lie simply in its having been a catastrophic defeat for Highland arms. There had been such defeats before, and most Highland Jacobites, in 1746, accordingly considered Culloden to be little more than a singularly unfortunate prelude to a future renewal of hostilities. Unlike previous reverses, however, Culloden turned out to be no more than a preliminary to a massive – and highly successful – assault on the social and political institutions of clanship. In 1746 and in the years that followed, then, a concerted attempt was made to integrate – forcibly where necessary – the Highlands into a country from which they had hitherto kept aloof. For example, clansmen, both Jacobite and non-Jacobite, were disarmed finally and completely, the wearing of Highland dress was prohibited, and chiefs' judicial powers over their clans were abolished.

The immediate effect of these events was to accelerate and to enforce the modernising tendencies already at work in the Highlands. The destruction of clans as paramilitary organisations, together with the establishment of law and order as these things were understood in the south, meant that chiefs had no further need for the military services of their clansmen. It also meant that chiefs were divested of their traditional trappings and that their social status would subsequently depend, more than ever before, on the amount of cash at such chiefs' disposal. 'The number and bravery of their followers,' as one eighteenth-century Highlander noted of the chiefs in question 'no longer supports their grandeur; the number and weight of their guineas only are put in the scale'. After 1746, therefore, the incentive to exploit land commercially became stronger. And as a result of the government's post-Culloden policies, the obstacles which the traditional society had put in the way of such exploitation were removed.

As the need for commercial profitability became the dominant influence on estate management, Highland chiefs or landlords, as they now were, fell into an easy and inevitable alliance with the commercial and industrial capitalism of the south: easy, because southern society enabled them to gratify their aristocratic tastes and aspirations; inevitable, because in the south were to be found rapidly expanding markets for their produce. At first, Highland landlords made desultory attempts to promote indigenous economic development. But in the face of natural difficulties and southern competition, native Highland industry was doomed to unprofitability. Such industrial ventures as were launched in the area duly failed, or were abandoned, as their promoters increasingly concentrated on the export of the raw materials needed by urban and industrial Britain.

In the second half of the eighteenth century, therefore, the old semi-independence of the Highland economy was transformed into an essentially neo-colonial subordination to the requirements of the developing industries of England and Lowland Scotland. At first, black cattle, the Highlands' traditional export, continued to be virtually the only saleable product of Highland estates. In the 50 years after 1760, however, the place of cattle was more and more challenged by two new commodities: wool and kelp. The large-scale production of both those materials required a massive transformation of the Highlands' traditional agrarian system. And it was in the course of the consequent changes that crofting, as we know it today on the north-western seaboard and in the Hebrides, came into existence.

In 1773, just 27 years after the Battle of Culloden, Samuel Johnson, then one of England's leading literary figures, came to the Highlands hoping to discover, as he wrote, 'a people of peculiar appearance and a system of antiquated life'. He found, to his evident chagrin, that he had come too late:

> There was perhaps never any change of national manners so quick, so great, and so general as that which has operated in the Highlands by the late

conquest and the subsequent laws . . . The clans retain little now of their original character. Their ferocity of temper is softened, their military ardour is extinguished, their dignity of independence is depressed, their contempt for government subdued, and their reverence for their chiefs abated.

Nearly a century later, Johnson's judgement that the events of the 1740s had destroyed clanship for ever was echoed by the Court of Session, the fount of Scottish legal wisdom:

When all military character, all feudal subordination, all heritable jurisdiction, all independent authority of chiefs are extracted from what used to be called a clan, nothing remains of its essential character and peculiar features.

Although such statements about the demise of clanship are not altogether unfounded, the nature of the historical changes involved in the traditional society's collapse was undoubtedly more complex than was realised either by Samuel Johnson or by the Scottish judiciary of the 1860s. The institutional forms of a society with a continuous history of at least a thousand years were, it is true, destroyed simply by passing and enforcing laws that abolished them. The mental attitudes and beliefs engendered by the Highlands' traditional social system could not be so easily erased, however, The economic transformations outlined above consequently precipitated a crisis of cultural adaption that has left its mark on a great deal of the subsequent history of the Highlands.

Principally because they had been gradually absorbing southern ways and attitudes for many years before 1746, Highland chiefs took to their new roles with alacrity. The British government was able, therefore, to pursue its policy of modernising the Highlands, not by expropriating the Gaelic aristocracy, as had been done in Ireland, but by winning the upper rank of the old order to its side. Only the relatively small number of chiefs who had played an active part in the last Jacobite rebellion were exiled or executed – and even their lands were returned to their families in 1784. Remaining chiefs were left in undisturbed possession of estates of which they were now considered to be the outright owners. All concept of clans or kindreds having an interest in the land which such clans and kindreds occupied was cast aside – while the encouragement thus given to former chiefs to become landlords, on the southern model, virtually shattered the already weakening paternal affection which the traditional chief had felt for his clan.

By the eighteenth century's end any lingering traces of a patriarchal outlook had been strictly subordinated to the pursuit of profit, and Highland 'chieftains' – as the region's aristocrats continued to dignify themselves – were set firmly on the road to becoming the landed and anglicised gentlemen their descendants have ever since remained. In subjecting the dictates of kinship to those of financial expediency, moreover, the Highlands' ruling class, contemporaries agreed, did not experience any undue difficulty:

> The more necessitous, or the less generous, set the example; and one gradually followed another, till at length all scruple seems to be removed, and the proprietors in the Highlands have no more hesitation than in any other part of the country in turning their estates to the best advantage.

That was written in 1805. As far back as 1750, however, a government agent had noted that some Highland lairds had already 'screwed their rents to an extravagant height'. During the next 20 years this 'rage of raising rents' – to use the phrase employed by a 1764 visitor to Lochaber – spread throughout the Highlands. But if the most remarkable feature of the chiefs' response to the commercial order was the ease with which they thus adapted to it, the reaction of the lower strata of the traditional society was significantly different.

First to feel the full force of the wind of change were the tacksmen whom chiefs-cum-landlords not unnaturally wished to transform into business-like farmers of the sort who had already become the mainstay of estate economies in the south. Most tacksmen, however, were unwilling or unable to make the requisite adjustment. Tied to the traditions of their caste, they were usually more concerned to keep up a host of unproductive dependents and retainers than to cultivate habits of industry and thrift. As the military side of clanship passed into history, then, tacksmen began to be regarded by 'improvers' – the term the new breed of modernising and commercialising landlords liked to apply to themselves – as expensive, and not altogether desirable, luxuries. Tacksmen's traditional tenancies were duly curtailed and their lands offered to the highest bidders – developments which tacksmen, who had long considered their lands to be almost as much the inheritance of their families as of the chief from whom they held them, greeted with an incredulity which turned rapidly into resentment. And as a Highland traveller observed in the 1770s, 'Resentment drove many to seek a retreat beyond the Atlantic'.

The extraordinarily complete emigration or migration of the tacksmen is sometimes represented as a catastrophe which deprived the Highlands of its nascent middle class and the region's small tenants of their natural leadership. This Gaelic saying, however, possibly tells a different story:

> Is don an gabhalach,
> Ach don an donuis
> Anns an ath-ghabhalach.*

In the present context, at all events, the significance of tacksmen's decision to take themselves off to America is not that it left the clans' lower orders without leaders, but that it provides a measure of the awesome problem of

---

*'Bad is the tenancy, but the evilness of evil one is in the subtenancy.' The translation is Alexander Carmichael's.

adjustment which other, and lowlier, Highlanders confronted. If tacksmen, individuals who were usually well-educated and who knew something of life outside the Highlands, could not adapt to the situation created by the establishment of commercial landlordism, how could the much less well-equipped commons of the clans make the still greater adjustments required of them?

The answer was simple. They could not. Left to fend for themselves in a strange and hostile environment in which the land of the kindred could be sold for cash and the people who lived on the land treated as an element in a calculation of profit and loss by men 'grown so niggardly', as a Hebridean poet remarked in the 1760s, that they 'would geld a louse if it would rise in value a farthing', much of north-west Scotland's population could take refuge only in a profound sense of betrayal:

> Dh' fhalbh na ceannardan mìleant
> Dh' an robh sannt air an fhìrinn
> Dh' an robh geall air an dìlsean
> Agus cuing air an nàmhaid...
>
> Seallaibh mum cuairt duibh
> Is faicibh na h-uaislean
> Gun iochd annt' ri truaghain,
> Gun suairceas ri dàinhich;
> 'S ann a tha iad am barail
> Nach buin sibh do'n talamh,
> 'S ged dh'fhàg iad sibh falamh
> Chan fhaic iad mar chall e;
> Chaill iad an sealladh
> Air gach reachd agus gealladh
> Bha eadar na fearaibh
> Thug am fearann-s' o 'n nàmhaid.*

The waning of chieftainly prestige, a development underlined by those unsurprisingly bitter verses, was also noted by the vistors the later eighteenth-century Highlands began to attract, in growing numbers, from the Lowlands and from England. Highland chiefs, Samuel Johnson commented in the 1770s, had 'already lost much of their influence and, as they gradually degenerate from patriarchal rulers to rapacious landlords, they will divest themselves of the little that remains'. The accuracy of Johnson's gloomy prediction was inexorably borne out by events until, at the turn of the century, it was possible for another visitor to the region to observe –

---

*'The warrior chiefs are gone who had a yearning for the truth, who had regard for their faithful followers and had a yoke on their foe . . . Look around you and see the nobility without pity for poor folk, without kindness to friends; they are of the opinion that you do not belong to the soil and, though they have left you destitute, they cannot see it as a loss; they have lost sight of every law and promise that was observed by those who took this land from the foe.' The translation is William Matheson's.

both with surprise and with disillusionment – that the native aristocracy of the Highlands, 'instead of being almost adored', were 'in general despised'.

By about 1800, therefore, the tenantry of the Highlands had begun to discard, albeit reluctantly, the duties and obligations imposed on them by their sense of clanship. In the next few years, as those clansmen who did not follow the *daoine uaisle* to North America were converted into crofters, the need for such a coming to terms with the realities of the Highland situation was to become still more pressing. But the consequent emergence of the modern crofting community from the dispirited and demoralised commons of the clans was destined, as ensuing chapters demonstrate, to be a slow as well as an intensely painful process.

2

THE ORIGINS OF CROFTING

1800–1820

Na Caoraich Mora or big sheep, as Highlanders called southern graziers'
blackface and cheviot stocks in order to distinguish them from their own
smaller and wirier breeds, were introduced into Perthshire from the Scottish Lowlands in the 1760s. By 1800, sheep of this new type had largely
replaced black cattle as the main agricultural product of those parts of the
Highlands that lie to the south of the Great Glen. And in the years around
the turn of the century, a time of soaring wool prices, the white tide swept
on northwards and westwards into Inverness-shire, Ross-shire, Sutherland,
and the Hebrides. As was observed by James Loch, business adviser to the
Sutherland family whose estate, the biggest in the Highlands, was soon to
be largely given over to cheviot sheep:

> In this as in every other instance of political economy, the interests of the indi-
> vidual and the prosperity of the state went hand in hand. And the demand
> for the raw material of wool by the English manufacturers enabled the High-
> land proprietor to let his lands for quadruple the amount they ever before
> produced to him.

Even Karl Marx – who was as bitter in his condemnations of capitalism
as Loch was exultant in its praises, and who saw in the events associated
with the introduction of sheep farming into the Highlands a particularly
vicious manifestation of the general process of making 'the soil part and
parcel of capital' – could scarcely have coined a more forceful expression of
the connection between Highland 'improvement', as its promulgators liked
to call it, and southern industrialisation. Industrial demand for wool and
the need for ever larger quantities of mutton to help feed the burgeoning
populations of southern towns: these made the commercial exploitation of
Highland pastureland almost as welcome to southern industrialists as to
Highland landowners. It was for this reason, as the English poet Robert
Southey remarked in the course of a visit to the Highlands in 1819, that
political economists of the time – almost all of them pro-capitalist in their
opinions – had 'no hesitation concerning the fitness [of bringing sheep
farming north] and little scruple as to the means'.

The means, of course, were the clearances. And with them the beginnings of crofting were inextricably bound up. According to Marx and to Donald MacLeod, the Sutherland stonemason who was another of Highland landlordism's early critics, the displacement of whole populations by a few sheep farmers and their shepherds amounted to nothing less than 'reckless terrorism'. Crofters were to take the same view. Their landlords, however, considered the clearances to be a necessary precondition to the establishment of an economically efficient agricultural system in the Highlands, and with regard to sheep farming they were probably correct. As one landlord apologist commented:

> Sheep cannot be cultivated to a profit unless in large flocks . . . Small capitalists cannot thence manage them; and thus arises the necessity of large sheep farms.

The great increase in wealth and production brought about by the arrival of *na caoraich mora*, then, created no opportunities for the native-born tenants who constituted the bulk of the Highland population. Lacking the capital and expertise of the south country graziers who dominated Highland sheep farming from the start, the original landholders were everywhere ousted and dispossessed. Landlords made no attempt to remove such landholders from their estates, however. An obstacle in the sheep farmers' way they might have been, but they retained their usefulness; for without the participation in it of the region's original tenantry, north-west Scotland's kelp industry – an even more profitable enterprise than sheep rearing – could not have got off the ground.

Kelp, an alkaline seaweed extract then used in the manufacture of soap and glass, was first made in Scotland in the 1720s. At that time the industry was confined to the Forth estuary and to Orkney. But in the 1740s it spread to the Outer Isles and, by the mid-1760s, it was firmly established in all the Hebrides and on parts of the north-western coast of the mainland. Until the 1760s, when the average price of kelp first exceeded £2 a ton, landlords were generally unaware of the industry's growth potential and of its possible value to themselves. Most of the early profits from Hebridean kelp were consequently pocketed by a few enterprising tacksmen and by a small band of independent entrepreneurs, most of them Irish. Highland landlords' state of innocence with regard to kelp's importance was of short duration, however. Increasing industrial demand for alkali had the effect of pushing kelp's price steadily upwards. By the 1790s, when imports of Spanish barilla (kelp's main rival as a source of industrial alkali) were cut off by French military action, the average price was in the region of £10 a ton, and even that figure doubled in the nineteenth century's opening decade. Production was accordingly stepped up. Profits rose markedly. Landlords, making up for their initial dilatoriness, accordingly stepped in and took over the industry – establishing legal rights to the seaweed on which it was based and taking control of all its productive and marketing sequences from the cutting of the ware to the unloading of finished kelp on Liverpool and Glasgow waterfronts.

In the opening years of the nineteenth century, between 15,000 and 20,000 tons of kelp were exported annually from the Hebrides. The profits thus accruing to island landowners were estimated to be in the neighbourhood of £70,000 a year – the accuracy of the estimate being confirmed by the size of individual proprietors' takings. Between 1807 and 1809, for example, MacDonald of Clanranald's annual average income from kelp sales was £9,454 – a figure which compared very favourably with his land rental of £5,297 and which amounted, incidentally, to several hundred thousand pounds at today's values. The kelp made on Clanranald's South Uist estate, admittedly, was among the best and most valuable in the Hebrides. But even those landlords whose properties were somewhat less favoured by natural circumstances had little cause for complaint. The kelp produced on Lord MacDonald's North Uist estate was reckoned to be worth 'nearly double' the island's land rent – its sale accounting for the greater part of Lord MacDonald's reputed kelping income of £20,000 a year. Lewis kelp was calculated to be worth £3,500 a year after expenses – and that was a notably conservative estimate made by the trustees of the island's proprietor, MacKenzie of Seaforth, some years after the height of the boom. MacNeill of Barra and the Duke of Argyll – the latter of whom had extensive kelping interests in Tiree – benefited proportionately. And though similar gains were beyond the reach of landlords whose properties were situated on Mull, Skye, or the mainland, areas where seaweed was in less abundant supply, there was scarcely an estate in north-west Scotland where kelp, in the years around 1800, was not an important source of cash.

The enormous revenues thus gained by the region's landowners were secured, in the last analysis, by a labour force consisting of as many as 10,000 families whose members – men, women and children alike – cut, gathered, dried and incinerated the seaweed during the Highland kelping season which began in April or May and continued into August. The seaweeds harvested were principally the deep-sea tangle thrown up on the Outer Hebrides' Atlantic coasts, and the knobbled, black and bladder wracks which cover the rocky shores that are to be found all around the north-west coast of the mainland as well as in the Inner Hebrides and on the eastern seaboard of Lewis, Harris and the Uists. The growing weed – which made much finer kelp than that cast up by the Atlantic – had to be cut from the tidal sounds or rocky islets, where it grew most profusely, by kelpers whose work places were often an island's breadth away from their homes. Once cut, it was dried by sun and wind – a process calculated to occupy no more than three of the dry, warm days which commonly occur in north-west Scotland in early summer. The dried weed was carried in carts and creels to kilns – long low constructions of stone built handily on a nearby beach and filled, prior to each firing, with peat. This peat was next set alight and the mass of seaweed which had been spread across it was reduced, as a result, to ashes – the alkaline residue from the weed accumulating, at the kiln's base, as a glowing, molten mass which cooled into the brittle, bluish material eventually shipped to glass and soap works in England and Lowland Scotland.

Kelping was an arduous occupation. One traveller commented that, compared to the kelpers' way of life, 'the state of our negroes is paradise'. Other observers agreed. Kelpers' working conditions, one of them wrote, were much worse than those of the southern factory hands who were then suffering all the rigours of Britain's industrial revolution:

> If one figures to himself a man, and one or more of his children, engaged from morning to night in cutting, drying, and otherwise preparing the sea weeds, at a distance of many miles from his home, or in a remote island; often for hours together wet to his knees and elbows; living upon oatmeal and water with occasionally fish, limpets, and crabs; sleeping on the damp floor of a wretched hut; and with no other fuel than twigs or heath: he will perceive that this manufacture is none of the most agreeable.

Hardships like these would have been rendered more tolerable by adequate remuneration. But kelpers' returns were extremely meagre – amounting to only a tiny fraction of the gross proceeds of kelp sales.

That the kelper made comparatively little money from his labours was not his fault. Kelping was an ideal trade for a Highland or Hebridean tenant to engage in. The process of production was simple, requiring only a few elementary tools: sickles to cut the growing ware, and the long iron pokers, known as *clatts*, which were used to stir burning seaweed in the kilns. As a result of their own remoteness from southern markets and their landlords' determination to gain control of the industry, however, kelpers were quickly reduced to the status of wage labourers whose earnings bore little relation to the selling price of the material they produced. Varying slightly from one area to another, kelpers' wages generally stood between £1 and £3 a ton – a figure little affected by the rapid rise in kelp prices in the 15 years after 1790. Even when the finished product was selling at up to £20 a ton, Hebridean kelpers were receiving only £2 a ton on average – while their landlords' total expenses, including shipping charges as well as wages, were calculated to amount to about £3.12s. on each ton of kelp produced. The difference between that £3.12s. and the selling price of up to £20 was pure profit.

That landlords were able to reduce their kelpers' share of the proceeds to such an abysmally low level was the consequence of a well-devised and cruelly efficient system of exploitation which turned on the fact that the kelper's connection with the land was deliberately maintained by his employer who was also his landlord. Because the kelper remained an agricultural tenant who lived on the land and who continued to raise cattle and grow crops on that land, his landlord was able to draw on the kelper's labour during the kelping season while leaving him to his own – unpaid – devices for the rest of the year. And as the provider of the land without which the kelper could not survive, the landlord was able to establish a degree of control over his workforce which was quite unmatched by even the most tyrannical factory owner. The first step was to raise rents to a level which, as a Benbecula crofter put it, was quite unrelated to the land's 'intrinsic value'. Unable to pay such rents from the proceeds of their agricultural production alone, tenants were forced into kelping in order to earn the necessary cash. The proprietor consequently recovered a considerable part of his kelping wage-bill in the guise of a land rental; and since he both controlled the industry's raw material and was the sole buyer of the kelp produced on his estate, the landlord was able to direct his tenants to work where and when he liked, and to fix their wages at the level he found most convenient. This level, inevitably, was as low as was consistent with the kelping population's survival.

The one essential prerequisite for the effective enforcement of this method of labour control was that the Highlands' traditional landholding system be reformed in a way that brought all of the region's tenants into a direct tenurial relationship with their landlords. By the eighteenth century's close, to be sure, the number of people who paid rent to a landed proprietor, as opposed to a superior tenant, was already larger than in the past – principally because of the departure of many of the tacksmen who had formerly dominated the agrarian system. Highland farms, however, were still laid out on traditional lines – the typical farm being held in common by the families who were its joint tenants. The latter paid rent to a landlord rather than to the tacksman who had once stood between them and their chief, but they still sublet a considerable part of their holding to a miscellaneous collection of cottars and servants whose plots were held in return for stipulated amounts of labour on the joint farm. Because this system's communal features as well as its array of subtenurial relationships presented a serious obstacle to landlords who were seeking to manipulate rents and landholding in such a way as to provide themselves with large and docile labour forces, there was, by the 1790s, a growing movement in favour of abolishing the traditional agricultural structure and replacing it by a system consisting of holdings occupied by individual tenants – a method of landholding that was at once pleasing to 'improvers' and amenable to the type of manipulation on which a profitable kelp industry depended.

In the years around 1800, it followed, more and more landlords began drastically to reorganise their estates. Old tenures were ended and the scattered strips, or rigs, of arable land which were the basis of the joint farming economy were divided into separate holdings, or crofts, each occupied by a single tenant, or crofter. In the Outer Hebrides, the crofting system thus created was considered an adjunct to the kelp industry. On the mainland

and in those parts of Mull and Skye where its appearance coincided with the handing over of vast tracts of territory to sheep farmers, crofting was seen as a convenient and potentially profitable means of disposing of a displaced population – fishing usually taking the place of kelping in areas where the latter industry had failed to take off. As fishermen, and still more as kelpers, crofters were of huge importance, therefore, to their landlords. And as was demonstrated by the events surrounding the passing of the Passenger Act of 1803, Highland proprietors were accordingly prepared to go to almost any lengths to retain their tenantries on their estates.

In 1799, Lord MacDonald's extensive estates in Skye and North Uist were surveyed with a view to their modernisation and the consequent procurement of a substantial increase in their owner's income from them. The age-old runrig system – 'a careless and slovenly' mode of management, the surveyor called it – was to be swept away, along with the innumerable unfenced and unwalled plots, or rigs, on which it was based. Also destined for extinction were a number of small and chaotically laid-out joint farms which Lord MacDonald's surveyor, whose name was John Blackadder, thought understocked with animals and overstocked with people – characteristics which ensured, Blackadder went on, that landholdings of the traditional type 'never [could] be so profitable to the tenants, or afford such a high rent to the landlord, as large farms'. The more extensive holdings thus to be established were to be let to tenants recruited outside the Highlands – and hopefully in possession of more money and greater agricultural knowledge than such holdings' original occupants. Even on these new holdings, it was envisaged, cattle rearing would continue, at least for the moment. But some of them – and this was a portentous development – were to be stocked with sheep, Lord MacDonald having 'no objection . . . to try one or two sheep farms on a proper scale'. As for the large number of people who would obviously be displaced by these changes, their future was clearly mapped out. Each family would be settled on a single lot, or croft, by the seashore. There, as kelpers and fishermen, they would make a very significant contribution to the estate economy:

> The soil is not only to be tilled but from the surrounding ocean and its rocky shore immense sums may be drawn, equal at least, if not passing, the produce of the soil. As these, funds are inexhaustible, the greater the number of hands employed, so much more will be the amount of produce arising from their labour.

Newly established crofters, it was realised, might not willingly take to a life of kelping and fishing. They were to be forced into it, therefore, by the simple expedient of ensuring that no new croft could provide its tenant with an agricultural return large enough to afford an adequate living for himself and his family. Crofts were thus to be laid out in places where they did 'not interfere with, or mar, the laying out of better farms' and on boggy and rocky land in 'the least profitable parts of the estate'.

In the Skye section of Lord MacDonald's property, then, the mass of the people were to be settled on the coast – with interior holdings being handed over to large farmers. In North Uist, however, a somewhat different mode of proceeding was to be adopted. Instead of being transferred to incoming graziers, as in Skye, that island's runrig farms were themselves to be divided into crofts 'for the encouragement of people who carry on the business of making kelp, which is the first object of the landlord here'. In North Uist, Lord MacDonald's surveyor observed, by way of accounting for his otherwise inexplicable departure from the bigger-means-better philosophy of agricultural 'improvement', kelp was the 'staple' product and 'encouraging a number of inhabitants to settle or remain . . . [was] the sure means of keeping up the advantages and revenue to be derived from the manufacture of that article'. This, to the owner of any kelping estate at any rate, would have been a readily comprehensible argument. 'As you inform that small tenants can afford to pay more rent for farms in Tiree than gentlemen farmers,' the Duke of Argyll wrote to his chamberlain in that island in 1799, 'this determines me to let the farms to small tenants which have been and are at present possessed by tacksmen.' The duke's implication was clear: in the Tiree case, as in the North Uist one, there was more money in kelp than in farming. Previous plans for agricultural improvement were accordingly abandoned and an immediate start made on dividing the Tiree farms into crofts. By 1806, four-fifths of Tiree was occupied by crofters. And on the Duke of Argyll's estates in Mull, where the same principles were applied, practically every coastal farm was similarly made available for crofting settlement.

The major problem confronting the men in charge of such innovations was the innate conservatism of the people most affected by them. To persuade a peasantry to abandon a well-tried method of cultivation is seldom easy. The task of establishing the crofting system was no exception – not least because of a widespread, and justifiable, suspicion that the proposed change would not be for the better. A Harris crofter was subsequently to recall that he had 'seen a woman weeping at being separated from her neighbours by the division of the crofts'. And in parts of Skye the abolition of runrig was said to be widely lamented even 80 years after its occurrence. It is scarcely surprising, therefore, that John Blackadder, in his role as originator of the 'improvements' on the MacDonald estates, should have remarked, in 1799, that 'adherence to inveterate opinions and old uncorrected customs [operated] powerfully against improvements or even alterations'. Among folk who had been tenants and subtenants of old-style joint farms, there was no marked disposition to become crofters. There was, on the contrary, a widespread feeling among such folk that it might be better to leave the estate – indeed Scotland – rather than acquiesce in the proposed changes. As the full implications of the envisaged tenurial upheaval became apparent, that feeling deepened into a profound conviction.

The tenantry of North Uist, Lord MacDonald's chamberlain – or factor – on that island reported in the spring of 1801, were 'equally averse to settle in situations for villages or to take moor crofts for improvement'. They would, he added ominously, 'much rather try their chance in other countries'. A similar antipathy towards the intended reforms was evident in Skye where Lord MacDonald and his agents were bombarded with petitions requesting their abandonment. The MacDonald estate authorities were determined to proceed as planned, however; and in 1801 alone they ordered no fewer than 267 of Lord MacDonald's Skye tenants to quit their possessions. Not unnaturally, removals on such a scale aroused bitter resentment. Tenants at Uig refused point blank to leave their farms. And as the date fixed for the completion of the new arrangements – Whitsun 1803 – approached, it became clear that popular dislike of the new order was about to be translated into mass emigration to America. By April 1803, about two-thirds of the tenants of Strath and Sleat, two of the parishes on Lord MacDonald's Skye estate, had made, or were beginning to make, preparations to emigrate to America. Several parts of those parishes, it appeared, would be completely evacuated.

On Lord MacDonald's tenants making known their intention of taking themselves off to the other side of the Atlantic, the initial reaction of his lordship's advisers was to attribute all such declarations to the activities of the emigration agents who were undeniably active in the Highlands in the early years of the nineteenth century. Those 'worthless itinerant men', it was argued, were spreading 'false hopes' among the people and thus deluding them into deserting their native land. Lord MacDonald's chamberlains in Skye and North Uist were accordingly told to make known that Lord MacDonald viewed with extreme disapprobation the activities of individuals who were 'encouraging the depopulation of the country'. Unfortunately for Lord MacDonald, however, the readiness with which his tenants responded to emigration agents' sympathetic portrayal of America – this land where people 'were not troubled with landlords and factors' – had less to do, as events were to show, with those gentlemen's undoubted propaganda skills than it had to do with conditions which Lord MacDonald was himself creating.

That the current rearrangement of his estates was at the root of his tenantry's evident desire to be off to America was eventually admitted, in 1803, by Lord MacDonald himself. But the strength of their resolve he professed himself at a loss to understand. His people, Lord MacDonald wrote, had been 'invariably treated with kindness'. The proposed increase of 75 per cent in his Skye rental – due to go up from £5,550 in 1799 to £9,690 in 1803 – was, he thought, moderate. As for those of his tenants 'whom it was necessary to remove', the establishment of crofting townships within easy reach of kelp shores and fishing grounds 'secured to them the means of living comfortably in their own country'. Bewildered by what he clearly thought of as his tenantry's disloyalty Lord MacDonald may have been. But he had no intention of risking the depopulation of his estate and the consequent annihilation of his enormous income from kelp. The implementation of the controversial reforms, Lord MacDonald decided, should be delayed until 1804. This postponement, made known in April 1803, had the desired effect. Most prospective emigrants elected to remain at home for another year, no doubt convinced – like Lord MacDonald's factor who thought it 'beneath the dignity' of his employer 'to yield to a few restless, infatuated people' – that they had won a notable victory. But as he must have known when he made it, Lord MacDonald's concession was a sham. Within two months of its announcement, emigration from the Highlands was virtually outlawed by Act of Parliament.

The years immediately before and after 1800 were prosperous ones for British agriculture. Economic growth was proceeding at a rapid rate and, because the practically incessant wars with revolutionary and Napoleonic France had the effect of reducing the level of imports from continental Europe, there was a marked rise in the price of practically every kind of domestic product. Not the least affected commodity was wool, the price of which reached hitherto unprecedented levels in the nineteenth century's opening years. The consequence was that those Highland landlords who had not already turned their estates over to sheep farmers faced almost irresistible pressures to do so – the boom in wool prices being accompanied by a flurry of speculative interest in the sheep-rearing potential of the Highlands' vast tracts of hill pasture. Throughout the Highlands, then, 'the competition for farms,' as one contemporary commentator put it, 'became excessive, and rents were given which were often extravagant'. Enormous expanses of land were made available to southern graziers. And because the need to provide winter grazings for the latter group's sheep stocks rendered it 'compulsory to take from petty agriculture the . . . tracts which are adapted to this purpose', it became 'imperative' to evict the tenants or subtenants who had hitherto occupied such lands. 'Wherever it takes place,' a political economist accordingly observed of the introduction of sheep farming, 'if the country has any inhabitants at all, they must, to a trifle, be expelled.'

And expelled they were: from those parts of Lord MacDonald's Skye estate that were put under sheep at this time as well as from the many other places where landlords enforced a similar change in land use. Parts of Mull were let to sheep farmers in the first year of the nineteenth century, as were parts of the estate belonging to MacLean of Ardgour. Large-scale sheep farming began on Cameron of Locheil's estate at about the same time, with the consequent removal of scores, perhaps hundreds, of tacksmen, tenants and subtenants, especially from Glen Dessary and from the area around Loch Arkaig. 'Families who had not been disturbed for four or five hundred years are turned out of house and home and their possessions given to the highest bidder,' noted the son of one of Locheil's tacksmen. 'So much for Highland attachment between chief and clans.'

Everywhere in the north-west, there were similar occurrences. In Morvern 'the method of uniting farms' was reported to be 'gaining ground in proportion to the avidity for high rents and the rage for sheep stocks'. In Glenelg by the 1790s 'one man often rents a farm where formerly many families lived comfortably'. In Glenshiel and Kintail, cattle were replaced by sheep and farms taken over by incomers. In Lochbroom, 'the engrossing of farms for sheep walks' began in the eighteenth century's last decade. On the Sutherland estate, the first steps towards the establishment of a sheep farming economy were taken in 1799.

The general response to those developments was the same as that encountered by Lord MacDonald in the particular cases of Skye and North Uist: emigration. Towards the end of 1801, for example, MacDonell of Glengarry surveyed his estate 'with the view', as he put it, 'of ascertaining the real value of it, and thus from known data to be enabled to fix the . . . price at which it would be reasonable I should let it to my numerous tenants and dependants'. This price having been determined with reference to prevailing market circumstances, it unsurprisingly exceeded Glengarry's previous rental by a considerable sum. In an attempt to sugar the pill, MacDonnell next made an 'offer to [his] old tenants of remaining upon their lands at . . . 10 per cent below the amount of offers from strangers'. His 'handsome sacrifice' proved insufficient, however, and, in March 1802, he was accordingly 'very much surprised to learn that the tenants for whose comfort and encouragement [he] had proposed to make the above sacrifice . . . had all, with very few exceptions, signed engagements to go to America'.

About Glengarry's experience there was little that was unique. In the 1790s, emigration from the Highlands had been curtailed by war with France. As soon as the Peace of Amiens was signed in 1801, however, emigration 'began to revive', as the gentlemen of the Edinburgh-based Highland Society observed, 'with a spirit more universal than at any former period'. In 1801, about 830 people emigrated from the Highlands. In 1802, at least 11 ships carrying some 3,300 passengers were known to have sailed from the Hebrides and from the west coast north of Fort William. Other ships were believed to have left undetected and, on the basis of preparations in progress when the year began, it was estimated that up to 20,000 people were likely to leave, in 1803, for America. Entire districts, it appeared, were in imminent danger of being completely denuded of their population. No fewer than 150 of the 153 families resident on one small estate were said to be preparing to emigrate. On another larger property, the whole population of about 2,000 was reported to be contemplating a similar course.

This unprecedented exodus was greeted with great alarm by the Highland Society, then something of a landlords' trades union. In July 1801, a special meeting of the society had been called to consider the phenomenon of emigration and a committee under the chairmanship of an Edinburgh lawyer, Colin MacKenzie, had been appointed to investigate it. Like Lord MacDonald, the committee's members inclined to the view that emigration agents were mainly to blame for the Highland tenantry's departure. Their skill in 'the arts of deceit and imposition', it was claimed, enabled these allegedly nefarious characters to dupe 'the ignorant and unwary' into adopting a course that was clearly not in their best interests. Even the Highland Society, however, felt bound to admit that a contributory cause of emigration was 'the removal of many of the tenants from their farms in consequence of a conviction on the part of the proprietors that they would be better cultivated and managed, and pay better rents, when let in large divisions'. This conclusion was affirmed by other observers. The most important single cause of emigration, according to Alexander Irvine, a Highland clergyman who, in 1802, published an inquiry into its causes and effects, was the rapid pace of 'improvement' in the north-west. Whether tenurial rearrangements were intended to facilitate the production of kelp, as was usually the case in the islands, or to pave the way for the introduction of sheep farming, as was invariably the case on the mainland, the consequences were the same:

> This plan of improvement has put the whole Highlands into commotion. They who are deprived of their possessions . . . feel a reluctance in settling anywhere else, conceive a disgust at their country, and therefore prefer leaving it . . . The connection once broken, they care not where they go.

Other pamphleteers agreed. And when, at much the same point, Thomas Telford reported formally to government on what lay behind emigration from the Highlands, he was in no doubt that its 'most powerful' single cause was the conversion of large tracts of territory into sheep farms.

That Irvine and Telford were substantially correct in their diagnoses is indisputable. The emigrations from the estates of Lord MacDonald and Glengarry had their counterparts on all the other properties then being subjected to drastic reorganisations of one kind or another. Locheil's 'improvements', for instance, were accompanied by the departure to Canada of over 600 of his tenants. There, as one such tenant wrote, they considered themselves 'better off to be out of the reach of such unnatural tyranny' – a feeling that was very probably shared by emigrants from Ardgour, Knoydart, Glenelg, Coll, Tiree, Applecross, North Uist, and all the other places where, as the Countess of Sutherland's factor remarked in 1803, 'the people . . . held out a threat of emigration for accomplishing their purposes'.

To Highland proprietors, of course, it was inconceivable that their tenants' 'purposes' should be allowed to prevail over their own. A few Highland landlords, perhaps, retained a trace of their ancestors' desire to be surrounded by a numerous tenantry – while others among them may have shared politicians' evident concern about the effect on Britain's defence capabilities of the departure to America of the Highlands' large reserves of military manpower. An anachronistic paternalism and an anxiety for their nation's security were reinforced, however, by solid financial interests. None of the Highlands' landed gentry wanted to lose the chance of availing themselves of the profits to be made – in a period when military recruitment was a highly lucrative business – from raising Highland regiments. And those west coast and Hebridean proprietors who drew large revenues from kelp had no intention of depriving themselves of such revenues by tamely acquiescing in the decampment of the people who provided them.

It is not at all surprising, therefore, that the Earl of Selkirk, one of Canada's pioneering colonisers and the principal advocate of Highland emigration in the years around 1800, should have found that the most determined and vociferous opposition to his schemes emanated from kelping proprietors. The reasons are plain to see. Not only did kelping require a labour force so vast as to rule out the possibility of seasonal migrations of workers to the kelp estates; it was also, as admitted by Robert Brown, an agent for Clanranald and author (not altogether coincidentally) of an influential critique of Selkirk's arguments in favour of Highland emigration, 'a dirty and disagreeable employment [which] must, if the present race of people were to leave the country, be given up altogether'. Brown's aim stated aim – revealingly enough – was not to limit emigration but to stop it completely; for it was very much in kelping proprietors' interest, he pointed out with more truth than tact, to have as many tenants as possible in order to keep up production and keep down wages.

The government was consequently called upon to act. In March 1802, Glengarry gave it as his considered opinion that 'if the government or the legislature do not speedily interpose, the Highlands will be *depopulated*' – while the Highland Society's committee, faithfully reflecting proprietorial prejudice, was convinced, from the start of its deliberations, that emigration ought, as soon as possible, to be curtailed by legislation. The three reports produced by the committee between January 1802 and March 1803 were quickly placed in the hands of influential politicians – not least Henry Dundas, then the British government's leading man in Scotland. And each successive report reflected committee members' concern about the 'rapidly progressive increase of the evil' by demanding, in ever more strident tones, that measures designed to put an end to emigration be immediately enacted. Having attracted the support of Charles Hope, Scotland's lord advocate or senior law officer, the committee's campaign culminated in Thomas Telford's officially sponsored 'survey of the coasts and central Highlands of Scotland' in the autumn of 1802. A key part of Telford's brief was to enquire into 'the causes of emigration and the means of preventing it'. His investigations demonstrated that emigration from the region was undoubtedly increasing and that the upward trend was likely to be maintained. The House of Commons select committee to which his report was referred accordingly recommended prompt legislation. A Bill was drawn up by Charles Hope and, having passed through parliament without the slightest difficulty, it became law as the Passenger Vessels Act of June 1803.

In campaigning for legislation, Hope and the Highland Society had made a great deal of the sufferings endured by emigrants on the unregulated passenger vessels which then plied the Atlantic. And according to Hope's public pronouncements on the subject, his Act was an obviously humanitarian measure which, with disinterested zeal, laid down a series of regulations designed both to limit the number of passengers carried on any one vessel and to ensure the provision of adequate supplies of food, water and medicine. As Charles Hope admitted in a letter he wrote in 1804, however, the Passenger Act had another, less ostensibly humanitarian, purpose:

> I had the chief hand in preparing and carrying thro' parliament an Act which was professedly calculated merely to regulate the equipment and victualling of ships carrying passengers to America, but which certainly was intended, both by myself and the other gentlemen of the committee [of the Highland Society] appointed to enquire into the situation in the Highlands, indirectly to prevent the effects of that pernicious spirit of discontent against their own country, and rage for emigrating to America, which had been raised among the people . . . by the agents of Lord Selkirk and others, aided, no doubt, in some few cases, by the impolitic conduct of the landholders [i.e., the landlords], in attempting changes and improvements too rapidly.

Hope's desired curtailment of emigration was achieved simply because even the most token compliance with the 1803 Act's provisions entailed an increase in costs large enough to put the price of an Atlantic crossing beyond the reach of most ordinary Highlanders. Before June 1803, the cost of a passage from north-west Scotland to Nova Scotia, the destination of many Highland emigrants, had been around £4. After that date, it rose to £10 or more.

Highland landlords and their agents welcomed the Passenger Vessels Act of 1803 with unconcealed delight – Lord MacDonald's Skye chamberlain reporting that 'the emigration is entirely stopped now from the Act of Parliament which puts it out of the poor people's power to pay the increase of freight', and the Duke of Argyll noting 'that the means of removing to America have been rendered more difficult by the operation of the late Act'. But for those of Lord MacDonald's tenants who had made up their minds to emigrate, the 1803 legislation was an unmitigated disaster. Having sold their stock and having refused to accept the new crofts intended for them, they were left, as Lord MacDonald's chamberlain noted with malicious satisfaction, 'without any situation at all'. Fortunately for such prospective emigrants, however, the unusually high cattle prices of that year enabled them to scrape together the necessary passage money. In October 1803, then, about 100 families left Sleat for North Carolina, the adults paying £12.12s. each for the privilege. 'Their having done so,' Lord MacDonald's chamberlain ruefully remarked, 'shows that no expense . . . if they are able to pay it will deter them from their wandering schemes.'

Emigration, the same man reported in 1804 and 1805, remained as popular as ever. People who had gone to America in 1803 had sent 'very encouraging letters' to their friends at home and a large number of Lord MacDonald's remaining crofters – as most of his tenants had now become – were consequently 'determined' to follow their former friends and neighbours to America 'as soon as an opportunity offers'. Just such an opportunity, in fact, occurred in 1804 – when recruiting agents for a Canadian colonial regiment visited parts of the Highlands and Islands. Volunteers and their families were offered free passages to Canada and promised that land would be made available to them on their discharge from the military. The regiment's recruiting sergeants were astonished by the number of men who enlisted and Charles Hope, who was still keeping a wary eye on the region's affairs, received 'complaints . . . from all parts of the Highlands of the mischief the recruiting agents were spreading among the people . . . Thousands, instead of hundreds, were eager to enlist'.

Such chances to get away were necessarily rare. As Charles Hope, the Highland Society and Highland landlords had intended, therefore, emigration from the Highlands became less and less possible in the years after the passing of the Passenger Vessels Act. Tenants who had not left before June 1803 had mostly to reconcile themselves to staying at home and making the best of the new agrarian system. It was in an attempt to make the latter course more attractive that the government, acting on Thomas Telford's recommendations, initiated the construction both of the Caledonian Canal and a network of Highland roads. The employment thus provided proved a mere palliative, however; for the crofting system then being brought into existence all across the north-west suffered from a malaise too deep-seated to be affected by such superficial applications of government assistance.

With emigration no longer affording prospective crofters an escape route, the years after 1803 were marked by a steady extension of the crofting system. The miserable, overcrowded townships, so characteristic of the agrarian system which was to prevail on the north-west coast of the Scottish mainland for most of the nineteenth century, were established during this period – and settled by people who had been cleared from inland straths and glens in order to make way for sheep. Once established on their coastal crofts, the occupants of these crofts were obliged – few crofts being of a size sufficient to make their occupants full-time farmers – to find new, non-agricultural sources of income. And though kelping was less widely available on the mainland than in the islands, there were high hopes, on landlords' part anyway, of developing the fishing industry. Mainland crofters were consequently compelled to participate in fishing by a method identical to that used to force their Hebridean counterparts to become kelpers: individual crofts were made deliberately small and their rents fixed at a level that was quite unrelated to their productive potential. No longer able to emigrate and in desperate need of a plot of ground on which to build some sort of house or hovel and a patch of land on which to grow potatoes, evicted tenants had no choice but to accept crofts on their landlords' terms. 'These poor people, unable to go to America, are glad to get any sort of plot and hut,' one observer noted in 1813. Many landlords, this same observer added, 'took advantage of their [the crofters'] necessities and tied them down to perform services, to work at fixed prices when called upon, and to turn up a certain space of waste ground annually'. In this way, according to John MacCulloch, a geologist who spent a lot of time in the Highlands around 1820 and who was very much in favour of agricultural improvement as practised by Highland landlords, arable acreages were increased and rentals raised. 'To these advantages,' MacCulloch went on, 'I need scarcely add the clearing out of the pasture farms which the small tenants had encumbered, and the power thus given to the proprietors to occupy them in an advantageous manner.'

From the north coast of Sutherland to the Sound of Mull the pattern was the same. On the Reay estate in north-west Sutherland, clearances began in the nineteenth century's first decade and continued until about 1820. Inland parts of the estate were turned into 'seven great sheep farms' – and the many people thus displaced were settled on the coast. Elsewhere in Sutherland, meanwhile, the clearances executed for the Sutherland family by James Loch, Patrick Sellar and their assistants were, and remain, notorious – although the understandable tendency of most accounts to concentrate on the events surrounding the more brutal episodes, such as Kildonan's *bliadhna na losgaidh* or year of the burnings, has obscured the fact that evictions affected not just a few localities but almost the whole of a very large county. Even in the 1880s, old men could still list the names of 48 cleared settlements in the parish of Assynt alone. Their implicit contention that Sutherland's early nineteenth-century removals were on an unprecedented scale is supported by a large volume of contemporary evidence.

Summarising what he had accomplished on behalf of the aristocratic couple – one of them the former Countess of Sutherland, the other her enormously wealthy English husband – who were his employers, Patrick Sellar wrote in 1815:

> Lord and Lady Stafford were pleased *humanely,* to order a new arrangement of this country. That the interior should be possessed by cheviot shepherds and the people brought down to the coast and placed there in lots [or crofts]

under the size of three arable acres, sufficient for the maintenance of an industrious family, but pinched enough to cause them [to] turn their attention to the fishing. I presume to say that the proprietors *humanely* ordered this arrangement, because it surely was a most benevolent action to put these barbarous hordes into a position where they could better associate together, apply to industry, educate their children, and advance in civilisation.

This was, James Loch thought, 'a policy well-calculated to . . . increase the happiness of the individuals who were the objects of the change [and] to benefit those to whom these extensive but hitherto unproductive possessions belonged'. That the Sutherland family benefited is undoubted. That their tenantry did so is a more debatable proposition. The net effect of what Loch liked to call 'the Sutherland improvements' was to crowd the county's population on to coastal holdings 'of a size to induce every man to engage actively in the prosecution of the herring fishery' – and far too small, therefore, to afford their occupants an adequate subsistence. This was the case even on good land. On poorer soils, crofters' plight was even more unenviable – the terrain involved being quite unsuited, in very many cases, to settlement of any kind. In Farr, on Sutherland's north coast, for example, tenants evicted from Strathnaver were 'thickly settled along the sea coast of the parish – in some instances about 30 lotters occupying the land formerly in the possession of 12, and some of them placed on ground which had been formerly uncultivated'. Around the Kyle of Tongue, meanwhile, land which had been 'occupied by a few' was 'divided among many' – thus becoming 'totally inadequate for the maintenance of all'.

Sutherland crofters, James Loch said to his critics, would easily maintain themselves by fishing and growing potatoes. Unfortunately for his reputation, and much more unfortunately for the people he compelled to become crofters, the one was to prove as precarious a resource as the other.

Developments in Sutherland, meanwhile, were paralleled on more southerly estates. In Wester Ross the introduction of sheep farming led to the establishment of hopelessly congested crofting townships on the coast. Here, too, the fishing industry was thought to be the panacea for all ills. And here John MacCulloch discovered that the consequences of agricultural improvement, despite his frequent assertions to the contrary, were not universally beneficial. In a miserable hut on the shore of Loch Carron, MacCulloch found 'a poor woman cooking some shell fish over a peat fire, attended by two children'. On the hovel's bare mud floor, 'scarcely covered by a wretched supply of blankets, lay the husband, sick of a fever'. Apart from its blankets and cooking pot, the couple's home – if that is the appropriate term – was completely unfurnished. MacCulloch continued:

> We found, on enquiry, that having been ejected from their farm and having no other resource, they [the man and woman in question] had been suffered by a neighbouring farmer to build their hut from his woods, and to graze their only cow upon his waste; and thus, with the assistance of shell fish

which they caught at low water, and some casual labour, they had contrived to live through the portion of the summer which was past. How the winter was to be surmounted it was both too easy and too painful to imagine.

All along the Highland mainland's west coast, evicted families faced similar predicaments. In Glenshiel the establishment of a sheep-farming economy was accompanied by the removal of most of the population to coastal crofts where, as the parish minister put it in the 1830s, they were 'dependent for subsistence on the laborious and uncertain pursuit of the herring fishing'. Those people who had not managed to emigrate from Glenelg at the beginning of the century were herded into ramshackle townships on the Sound of Sleat. MacLean of Ardgour and Cameron of Locheil provided crofts for their displaced tenants on the shores of Loch Eil and Loch Linnhe. In Morvern the interior was depopulated and new and squalid townships established beside the Sound of Mull.

In the islands, too, the number of crofts and crofters was increasing rapidly. On Lord MacDonald's Skye estate, for example, runrig, to which John Blackadder had taken such exception, was virtually extinct by 1811. As had also happened on the mainland, the crofts which took its place were, as Blackadder had planned, invariably small and confined to coastal districts – while the interior pastures, on which MacDonald tenants had long grazed their cattle, were occupied by large farmers. In 1806, the earlier emigration crisis safely behind him, Lord MacDonald had announced his intention 'to introduce some respectable and substantial tenants to his estate from the south country'. Since the latter were sheep producers, their arrival, as Lord MacDonald's factor commented, made necessary the eviction of further groups of subtenants:

> It is no doubt a very hard case to remove a herd of this description, but, on the other hand, it is impossible that a proprietor can receive the same rent . . . if the tenant is to be burdened with a set of needy cottars . . . And were a portion of the grazing to be set aside for their accommodation, such an arrangement would be detrimental to the farm and prevent its being let to the same advantage.

Clearances accordingly went ahead. In the 1830s, as a result, the minister of Sleat, the most southerly parish on the MacDonald estate, was to remark that, of the various changes to have occurred in his district since the turn of the century, the most striking was the extent to which 'lands . . . then possessed by labouring tenants are now converted to sheep farms'.

The inauguration of Skye's new order was not always accomplished without difficulty, however. In 1811, MacLeod of Dunvegan embarked on a series of reforms which included a sharp increase in rents, the introduction of sheep farming, and the establishment of several crofting townships – the latter to be situated, of course, in close proximity to some of the best kelp shores on the Dunvegan estate. One of MacLeod's more substantial tenants, unwilling to pay his new rent, threatened to emigrate and to contribute to the costs of as many lesser tenants as wished to accompany him. 'The common people,' reported MacLeod's factor, 'flocked to his standard.' And it was only after a great deal of energy had been expended by his estate management that the majority of the intending emigrants were induced to remain on MacLeod's property.

That same year, 1811, was also marked by rumours of impending emigrations from MacKenzie of Seaforth's estates in Lewis and Wester Ross. Because it would entail a loss of income from kelp, the prospect of an exodus from Lewis was particularly worrying to Seaforth's agents. And though their anxieties proved groundless, the reasons for them would have been appreciated by the managers of any kelping property, not least by the men in charge of MacDonald of Clanranald's estates in Benbecula and South Uist. Their eagerness to expand kelp production by means of establishing the crofting system on Clanranald's estate was equalled only by their apprehension that 'such an innovation' might not be effected 'without the risk of stirring up a spirit of emigration, or [some] other unpleasant consequence'. On finally getting underway in the summer of 1816, therefore, the creation and allocation of crofts was confined, in the first instance, to Benbecula – 'from the circumstance,' Clanranald's factor reported, 'of an emigration going on in the adjoining island of Barra' which, he feared, 'might extend to South Uist should he attempt to introduce too generally a change to which the inhabitants, from attachment to old habits are very averse'.

At the start of the nineteenth century, crofting had been virtually unknown in the area with which it is now most associated – being confined then to a few parts of Mull and to western Inverness-shire. Twenty years later, however, 'the ancient system of runrig' had 'almost expired' and – all along the mainland's west and north coasts as well as in the larger islands – crofting had become general. Lord MacDonald, MacLeod of Dunvegan, MacDonald of Clanranald, Cameron of Locheil, the Sutherland family: all of them, along with many lesser landowners, had, by the end of the nineteenth century's second decade, settled the coastal fringes of their estates with crofters, large numbers of whom had been evicted from older farms which were by that time under sheep. Even in Lewis, the remotest of all the Hebrides, the division of runrig farms into crofts was recommended in 1800, and commenced about ten years later.

Kildonan and Geirinish in South Uist; Barrapoll, Kenovay, Scarinish, Balemartine, and Crossapoll in Tiree: these and numerous other crofting townships were established simply by dividing the arable lands of a preexisting joint farm into individual holdings. In many places in Sutherland, Skye, Lewis, Harris and elsewhere, however, townships – and such townships' occupants were obviously at a special disadvantage – were laid out on land which had been previously uncultivated. Their differing origins are partly responsible for the wide range of township types still to be found in north-west Scotland's crofting areas. But all crofting townships had, and still have, shared characteristics which generally outweigh the differences between individual settlements. A nucleus of inbye, or arable, land made up of a number of separate smallholdings is almost everywhere surrounded by a tract of hill pasture varying considerably in quality and extent and held in common by all the township's tenants – that particular legacy from the old tenurial system to the new being due less to design than to the fact that, given the number of crofters to be accommodated and the extent to which hill land had been lost to sheep farmers, the principle of division could not be extended beyond each township's inbye.

Although the crofting system as thus established was to experience many vicissitudes during what remained of the nineteenth century, its fundamental features remained, as they still remain, unchanged. At a time when an agricultural revolution was being consolidated in the Scottish Lowlands and a modernised agricultural structure was being established even in the southern and eastern Highlands, therefore, agricultural improvement – as it was understood in the south – made little impact on Scotland's north-west. Improvement's only major achievement there was the sweeping away of runrig. And whatever the demerits of the runrig-based agrarian system thus destroyed, it could not be claimed that the method of landholding which replaced it was any more efficient in an agricultural sense. Mainland proprietors, anxious to put as many acres as possible under sheep and to force croft tenants to assist in developing the fishing industry, encouraged the proliferation of minuscule holdings as a means to these ends – while landlords with kelping interests eagerly followed the same course in order to maximise profits from kelp. Throughout north-west Scotland, therefore, the requirements of an effective arable agriculture were strictly subordinated to landlords' overarching desire to make money by whatever method came to hand.

Considered as a means of creating an almost unlimited supply of cheap labour, however, the crofting system was an undoubted and immediate success. In the 1840s, a Hebridean factor was to remark that 'the kelp trade produced the population' which had been an essential precondition of the same trade's profitability. Demographic statistics bear out the general accuracy of his claim. The population explosion of the late eighteenth and early nineteenth centuries was not confined to the Highlands, and its causes, there as elsewhere, remain a matter of debate. It is no coincidence, however, that while the population of Scotland's northern and north-western counties as a whole rose by 48 per cent between 1755 and 1831, that of the Outer Isles – the principal kelping area and the district where crofting was most widely established in the early nineteenth century – rose by 139 per cent in the same period. On being further broken down, these figures are still more revealing. Thus the population of Harris, an island where not a great deal of kelp was made, rose by 98 per cent during the period in question. But that of North Uist, where kelping was much more important, rose by 141 per cent – while that of South Uist, most productive of all the kelp islands, increased by no less than 211 per cent. This immense growth, as was pointed out in the 1830s, was largely due to the fact that 'the kelp manufacture was . . . so profitable to the landlords that they encouraged the people to remain on their estates' – not least by denying tenants the chance to emigrate. Hence the close connection between population expansion and the establishment of crofting.

Land had long been the be-all and end-all of a Highland tenant's existence, and in the kelp islands, in the early years of the nineteenth century, land was made available to him on terms which were, in some respects, far less restrictive than any he or his predecessors had known. The disadvantages and limitations of subtenancy; the restraints imposed by joint tenancy and the communal management of arable land: these were suddenly and completely removed. The crofter was the sole tenant of his croft and, because the beginnings of crofting (for reasons examined in a subsequent chapter) coincided with the commencement of the potato's long reign as the ordinary Highlander's staple crop and diet, he needed less land than when food crops had consisted – as they had done in the past – of cereals of one kind or another. Besides, to be self-sufficient in food was less imperative than it had been. High cattle prices – the result, before 1815, of wartime scarcities in the south – together with a proliferation of opportunities to earn money as a kelper, or as a labourer on canal and road construction projects, made it fairly easy for crofters to buy the food their diminutive plots could not produce. Directly or indirectly, every one of these developments was related to the introduction of crofting, and every one of them, as it happened, tended to remove restraints on early marriage. With land and money more freely available than ever before, early marriages became, in fact, the rule. And because potatoes with a little fish and milk are a healthy – if monotonous – diet, more children from these marriages survived. As contemporaries observed, therefore, crofting and population growth went hand in hand.

Because crofts were deliberately designed in such a way as to make it impossible for their occupants to be self-sufficient agriculturalists, the subdivision of arable land into tiny units was an integral feature of the crofting system from the moment of its conception. Such subdivision, however, was also accelerated by the population explosion which it had itself helped to produce. Originally encouraged by proprietors who were all too ready to rate profits from kelp more highly than the agricultural wellbeing either of their estates or their tenantries, subdivision soon acquired a momentum of its own and became, as landlords eventually discovered, virtually unstoppable. In conjunction with the development of the kelp industry and other sources of non-agricultural earnings, subdivision meant, as MacDonald of Clanranald's factor pointed out in the early 1820s, that the population soon expanded to a level 'much beyond what the land can maintain'. In Tiree, for example, five farms which the Duke of Argyll had converted into crofting townships in order to cash in on the kelp boom were eventually occupied by a total of 1,080 people. For proprietors thus to encourage – in fact, compel – an essentially agricultural people to become dependent on non-agricultural pursuits, whether kelping or fishing, was a recipe for ultimate catastrophe. Such catastrophe was made all the more likely by the fact that the kelp industry, by its very nature, resulted in the neglect and consequent stagnation of the crofting economy's agricultural base.

The agricultural effects of kelping, contemporaries agreed, were uniformly bad. In a perceptive analysis of Hebridean agriculture published in 1811, James MacDonald, an authority on farming, noted:

> On kelp estates the land is almost entirely sacrificed to that manufacture and is at best, with regard to its agriculture, in a stationary condition . . . In this state of agriculture the land is considered as of no further value than merely to accommodate the kelp manufacturers with some milk, a few carcases of lean sheep, horses, or cattle, and a wretched crop of barley, black oats, and potatoes. Turnips and all other green crops demanding attention in summer, are (excepting potatoes) quite out of the question.

Seaweed, traditionally used to manure the land, was everywhere diverted into the kelp industry. As early as the 1790s, the minister of Harris pointed out that arable land had 'degenerated much through want of the manure formerly afforded by the shores'. And James MacDonald calculated that, during the first decade of the nineteenth century, Hebridean fields were being deprived of no less than nine-tenths of the fertiliser they had previously received. This particular consequence of the kelp industry had been raised as an objection to kelping in Skye in the 1770s. But as the kelp boom developed it was completely lost to sight. Instead, in their scramble for profits, landlords went out of their way to ensure that every scrap of seaweed found its way to their kelp kilns. In 1816, for example, MacKenzie of Seaforth's factor in Lewis was instructed to 'take the most effectual means of punishing any person or persons who may be concerned in cutting, using, or destroying the ware [or seaweed]'. The most efficacious punishment, it goes without saying, was eviction.

The agriculturally debilitating consequences of such a regime were seriously aggravated by the fact that, in the summer months, when his fields were most in need of attention, all a croft tenant's energies had to be devoted to making his landlord's kelp – a situation so obviously fraught with dangers for the future of Hebridean agriculture that it caused at least one estate management a qualm of conscience. As long as kelp was a major source of revenue, Clanranald's advisers commented in 1815, 'it is impossible that the tenants can give that attention to the production of the land which, to secure a decent return, is indispensably necessary'. At the time of year when they 'ought to be labouring and sowing their ground', the same men went on, Clanranald's crofters were 'almost uniformly called off, and that in the best weather, too', to Uist's kelp shores. That his crofting tenants were 'continually distracted' in this way was the reason, Clanranald's advisers believed, for the exceedingly low level of agricultural production on Clanranald's estate. But though they regretted the existence of such a state of affairs, the advisers who made these points could see no alternative to the situation they described. Clanranald's kelp, after all, had to be made.

The kelp boom, although it provided capital which could have been applied to such purposes, and although it proved that massive agrarian reorganisation was not inherently impossible, thus removed any pecuniary incentive north-west Scotland's landlords might have had to establish an effective arable agriculture on their estates. The Duke of Argyll's abandonment of his plans for agricultural improvements on Tiree, and his subsequent adoption of policies which were to make that island one of the most congested and poverty stricken in all the Hebrides, was entirely typical of the times. Throughout the north-west, landlords subordinated the dictates of good estate management to those deriving from their quest for quick and easy profits. This was partly because most Highland landlords, unlike landed proprietors in England or Lowland Scotland, had no interest in their estates or in their tenantries other than as sources of ready cash. Of that state of affairs, early nineteenth-century commentators were highly critical – James MacDonald, for instance, complaining bitterly about 'the non-residence of many of the proprietors who drain the poor Hebrides of their wealth and, too often residing in other parts of the empire, pay little attention to the improvement of their estates'. But such strictures had little effect. 'What Hebridean proprietor lives on his estate that can live elsewhere?' MacKenzie of Seaforth asked in 1823. None did so. By the 1830s, there was no resident proprietor in any of the Outer Isles – while, of the 195 owners of land in north-west Scotland as a whole, only 46 resided even semi-permanently on their properties.

Having adopted the *mores* of a capitalist society in the eighteenth century, Highland landlords had wittingly and willingly embarked on a policy of substituting a commercial rent economy for the familial economy that had gone before. In the process, they had opened the way for an individualistic scramble for land – a scramble reinforced both by population growth and by the proprietorial class's manipulation of the agrarian system as an adjunct to their kelp, sheep and fishing interests. The consequences for the crofting tenants whom landlords had thus brought into existence was that their holdings were too small, their rents too high, and their security almost non-existent.

Crofters profited, to some small extent, from the favourable circumstances of the period around the turn of the century. Their gains, however, were an inconsiderable fraction of those accruing to their landlords – and, after 1820, crofters' overall economic position deteriorated markedly. That deterioration was due, in essence, to altered market circumstances – themselves the consequence of the British economy having entered a period of intermittent crisis which lasted until the 1840s. But crofters were made pitifully vulnerable to the effects of adverse economic change by the fact that the ownership of the land on which they lived had remained the monopoly of a small group of men whose pursuit of easy profits had reduced their tenants to the status of kelping labourers or unsuccessful fishermen. Soon the crofting population's vulnerability and insecurity were to be underlined by new disasters. These took the shape, in part, of increasingly frequent seasons of hunger and distress. But matters were made worse by the extent to which, as fishing proved a broken reed and as the profit indicator swung away from kelp, landlords – looking to get rid of what had become, as far as they were concerned, a surplus population and looking, too, to put still more land under sheep – engaged in a further round of clearances.

3

A REDUNDANT POPULATION

1821–1844

As long as kelping remained a profitable enterprise, crofters were highly esteemed by their landlords and the development of the crofting system was considered an integral and important part of estate management. The possibility that the fishing industry might become an equally remunerative undertaking also entered into proprietors' calculations – especially those of the Sutherland family. But because the majority of crofters were kelpers rather than fishermen, and because the long-held vision of an indigenous Highland fishing industry never really materialised, it was on their role as kelpers that most crofters' usefulness to their landlords depended. And by the 1820s, the kelp industry was in serious trouble.

The turning point in the fortunes of the crofting area's staple commodity occurred at the end of the nineteenth century's first decade. In 1810 and 1811, prices of certain grades of kelp fell to around £10 a ton. By 1815, this figure represented the average price of even the best kelp. And although the position was by no means disastrous, there were indications that it could quickly become so – a particularly ominous portent of future events occurring in 1813 when Newcastle glass manufacturers asked the government to abolish import duties on Norwegian kelp. Scotland's kelping proprietors responded by meeting in Edinburgh and agreeing to put their own case before the government. The Highland interest duly prevailed – but only temporarily. In 1818, further rumours of an impending reduction in duties – this time affecting imports of Mediterranean barilla – produced another crisis meeting and renewed representations to the government. Among the Highland proprietors' ranks, there were now perceptible tremors of panic. To reduce tariffs on kelp, they informed the administration in London, would be to ruin them:

> Many persons have purchased their estates relying on the permanency of kelp, and others have lent money on the security of the annual returns arising from it.

Such was undeniably the case. Even at the height of the wartime boom, the fear had been expressed occasionally that kelp prices, 'supposing a time of peace', might fall as a result of foreign competition. But most proprietors –

and their financiers for that matter – seem to have been blithely unaware of the intrinsically vulnerable nature of the industry. Estates were organised as if the kelp boom was bound to continue indefinitely. And enormous amounts of money were lent to proprietors on the same unfounded assumption. What was not realised was that the industry's profitability was largely a creation of wartime circumstances, and that its days, as a result, were necessarily numbered.

Glass and soap manufacturers – some of whom were soon to be pressing sucessfully for the abolition of the Corn Laws and all the other equally restrictive tariffs which had been put in place at the insistence of Britain's landed interest – saw no point in maintaining artificially high duties on foreign alkali in order to keep Highland landlords in the style to which they had become accustomed. Having failed in 1813 and 1818 to persuade the government to reduce the relevant import duties, the manufacturing lobby merely intensified its campaign and, as chemical processes for the manufacture of alkali from salt were perfected, the same lobby added the abolition of the salt tax to its list of demands. 'Chemistry,' observed MacKenzie of Seaforth in one of his more perceptive moments, 'is the true enemy of kelp and we can only last as long as its advance to perfection is going on.' As something of a liberal in his politics, MacKenzie should also have been aware of the threat to kelp from middle-class industrialists whose advance to political influence was proceeding with a rapidity at least equal to that of the progress of science, and whose demands north-west Scotland's proprietors – lacking the numbers and influence of those more southerly estate-owners whose rents came from grain rather than kelp and who were able to keep the Corn Laws in place for another 20 years – were quite unable to resist. In the early 1820s, import duties on barilla were lowered drastically. This measure was accompanied by a simultaneous reduction in the salt tax and followed, in 1825, by its abolition.

The effects were immediately apparent. The average price of kelp at Liverpool, the main selling centre, fell from £9. 4s. 11d. a ton in 1823, to £6. 16s. 10d. in 1826, to £4. 11s. 5d. in 1827, and, finally, to £3. 13s. 4d. in 1828. As these figures demonstrate, it was in 1827 that the situation became critical. In June that year, a considerable part of the previous season's crop was still on hand in Liverpool, and, as the year advanced, the bottom fell completely out of the market. By December, the best grades of kelp, which had been selling for £6 or £7 a ton in August, were fetching less than £3. That same month, Scotland's kelping proprietors and their agents met in Edinburgh in an atmosphere of understandable gloom. The kelp industry, they resolved, 'has declined and is rapidly declining', a conclusion borne out by their analysis of kelp prices. In the ten years after 1817, the price of prime kelp had fallen by two-thirds and, by 1827, the industry had practically ceased to be a profitable undertaking. In the hypothetical case of an estate on which 600 tons of kelp were made each year – that is, one in the middle range of kelp properties – it was calculated that the profits from kelp would have fallen from an annual average of £2,535 (itself a much lower return than those to be got earlier) in the years between 1817 and 1826, to £695 in 1827 and to only £180 in 1828.

In desperation, the kelp proprietors cast around for ways to revive the industry's flagging fortunes. A reduction in its costs was an obvious expedient. But shipping charges were more or less immutable, and kelpers' wages had never been allowed to rise above a bare subsistence level. Substantial economies thus proved impossible to effect. At the instigation of Clanranald and Lord MacDonald, the landlords who had most to lose from the industry's collapse, various experiments aimed at raising kelp's alkaline content, and thus its value, were carried out in the Uists. All of them, however, proved fruitless – as did appeals for government assistance on the grounds that 'the distress or rather ruin' confronting the kelp proprietors was 'plainly, undeniably, incontrovertibly owing to . . . the repeal . . . of taxes such as those on salt and barilla'.

A more unusual and more ruthless solution to the problem was devised by MacNeill of Barra. Between 1830 and 1833 he built an alkali works on his island estate in order to process his kelp on the spot, thus eliminating transport and agency costs. The project was naturally an expensive one – and, like other Hebridean proprietors, MacNeill was very short of capital. With a view to raising the necessary funds, he divided every croft in Barra in two, charged the same rent for a half-croft as had formerly been paid for a whole croft, and thus doubled the apparent value of the property. About 500 of MacNeill's crofting tenants emigrated rather than fall in with their landlord's plans, their places being taken by several hundred people from elsewhere in the Hebrides – people whom, it was said, 'other proprietors were anxious to get rid of'. Such reckless subdivision did nothing to increase MacNeill's real rental, however. And a chemical works on a remote island could not, in the nature of things, compete effectively with factories in England and southern Scotland. Within a few years of the project's commencement, therefore, MacNeill was bankrupt and Barra's vastly increased population of some 2,300, being unemployed, were unable to pay the inflated rents demanded of them. On his estate being sold to an Aberdeenshire laird, John Gordon of Cluny, in 1841, MacNeill's creditors, by way of making a bad situation even worse, seized almost all the cattle on the island in lieu of unpaid rents. Gordon thus inherited, even by Hebridean standards, an especially impoverished population – most of whom, as will be seen, he was to ship to Canada ten years later.

MacNeill's activities were unusual, however. On most estates, kelping was allowed to go into decline in the later 1820s. By the 1840s, in fact, it had ceased altogether on large stretches of coastline, being effectively prosecuted only on the more productive shores of the larger Hebridean properties. That kelping survived at all was partly due to a continuing, though much reduced, demand for high quality kelp – needed at first for the manufacture of fine glass and later as a source of iodine. More fundamentally, it was a consequence of the fact that the agrarian structure of Hebridean estates had become so inextricably entangled with the kelp industry that kelping could not be abandoned without precipitating a complete collapse of proprietorial finances. Clanranald's South Uist factor summed up the consequent dilemma:

> If the kelp is given up the small tenants cannot continue to pay the present rents, because the work they got [as kelpers] enabled them to pay for portions of ground so small that they could pay nothing from the produce.

Crofting townships, the same factor pointed out, had been laid out with a view to croft rents being paid from kelpers' wages. As long as a crofting population remained on the estate, it followed, some sort of employment would have to be provided – or rents would not be paid at all. As kelping ceased on less productive shores, therefore, large numbers of crofting tenants – many of them working for no wages as an alternative to their being charged rents they could not find – were employed to drain bogs, build roads, seed sand dunes and otherwise improve Clanranald's estate. This was reckoned, by the estate management, to be 'to the great benefit of the property . . . a considerable sum of arrears having thus been recovered which must otherwise have been totally lost'. But such expedients, from an estate management perspective, could not be prolonged indefinitely. As the 1820s advanced, and as kelp became more and more obviously doomed to decline, more radical approaches were accordingly adopted.

The need to solve the problems created by the kelp industry's sudden collapse was made more pressing by the effects of the equally unexpected agricultural depression which followed the ending, in 1815, of the Napoleonic wars. 'During the war,' it was remarked in an 1829 report on Lord MacDonald's estates, 'prices assumed almost an unnatural height. Since the commencement of the peace, they have year after year gradually declined.' This was a sombre, but broadly accurate, assessment of the overall picture – though, in the first instance at least, the fall in prices was rapid rather than gradual. In 1816, for example, the slump in cattle prices was already causing alarm in Skye. Fewer cattle than usual were being exported from the island and crofting tenants on the MacDonald estate and, for that matter, in the north-west generally, were consequently in a 'lamentable and . . . calamitous state'.

The fall in cattle prices, which was not to be reversed until the 1850s, had very serious implications for crofters. Even on kelp estates, where rents were paid largely from wages, steadily rising returns from cattle sales had helped the average crofter, in the years before 1815, to meet the ever rising rent imposed by his landlord and to buy the meal he needed to eke out the scanty produce of his meagre holding. 'Had the prices continued as high as formerly,' Clanranald's factor noted in 1823, 'it is likely that no great sum of arrears would have been lost.' But in the Uists, as in Lewis where 'the constant partial payment of the rents' became a serious problem at the same time, the post-1815 depression was marked both by accumulating arrears and by increasingly frequent seasons of hunger and distress. A broadly similar pattern of events could be discerned throughout the region.

Thanks to the kelp boom and to the period of high agricultural prices which accompanied the wars with France, Highland landlords had been, in the opening years of the nineteenth century, at the crest of a wave of prosperity. The rental of the MacLeod estate in Skye rose by some 220 per cent (from £2,296 to £7,374) between 1800 and 1811 – while that of Lord MacDonald's estate, on the same island, went up by over 150 per cent (from £5,550 to about £14,000) in much the same period. Other proprietors benefited proportionally. The sensible response to the post-war depression would thus have been to reduce rentals in line with the fall in agricultural commodity prices. And this, in fact, was done in the sheep farming sector of the Highland economy – a sector dominated, of course, by tenants who were substantial businessmen ready to pull out at the first hint of trouble. Crofters' ties with the land were of a quite different order, however. There was no way in which they could induce landlords to bring down rents. And landlords themselves, accustomed to a life-style and to an expenditure pattern secured by some 20 years of exorbitant income, were reluctant to cut their coats in accordance with the shrinking quantity of cloth available to them. 'It is impossible I can forego the present rent without extreme inconvenience to my affairs,' Lord MacDonald wrote in 1817. And his was the prevalent attitude.

But for all that rentals remained nominally high, the inescapable realities of economic life made them increasingly fictitious. 'All rentals since 1814 have been a mere joke,' Seaforth remarked in 1823. Other observers agreed – noting that, because of the unwillingness of the landowning class to come to terms with the post-1815 situation, the rents of Highland and Hebridean estates were 'considerably higher than the tenants can afford to pay'. In such circumstances, arrears inevitably continued to accumulate – Seaforth observing, with some asperity, that only those with first-hand experience of it could appreciate 'the difficulty of getting rents from a Highland estate in bad times'. Short of confiscating his cattle, a course which was recognisably disastrous for the future, or evicting him, a scarcely practicable proposition in a situation in which every tenant might be in the same predicament, the landlord had simply to accept the crofter's excuses and allow his backlog of rent to mount up. Allowances of some sort had thus, of necessity, to be made – these usually taking the form of annual abatements of rent. In Skye and Mull in the ten years after 1816, for example, abatements of crofting rent, varying in scale from 10 to 25 per

cent, were commonplace. These reductions were of an essentially temporary character, however; and they were never large enough to cover the
deficiency in crofters' incomes. The inevitable outcome was that crofting
tenants, in addition to all their other difficulties, were everywhere enormously in debt.

The psychological consequences of inexorably increasing indebtedness
were profoundly debilitating. 'When a tenant is sensible he owes his landlord more than he is able to pay,' Clanranald's factor observed in 1823,
'he becomes quite desperate and ceases to make any effort.' The causes of
crofters' desperation, however, derived more from the exigencies of their
tenurial position than from personality defects. Many of them were well
aware that, in the new economic situation, sheep were more profitable than
their traditional stocks of black cattle. But while entire estates could be,
and often were, turned over to sheep production, crofters were quite unable
to effect such a change within their own small confines – simply because
they lacked the necessary capital. Where crofters did acquire a few sheep,
they were invariably the cheapest on the market and were, therefore, 'of
the worst description possible'. Besides, even if a crofter both knew how to
increase his agricultural income and had the cash needed to make the necessary purchases of new stock, there was no point in his doing those things –
for the consequent increment in his income would at once be appropriated
by the factor and set against his arrears in the estate's rent ledger. Apathy
and hopelessness thus ensued – with results described, in 1846, by Hugh
Miller, an author and journalist:

> We have seen whole tracts of country on the north-western coast, in which
> the rents of five whole years hung in one hopeless millstone of debt around
> the necks of the inhabitants. What wonder if, in such circumstances, the
> industrial energies of the Celt should be miserably overlaid?

The same was true of the Hebrides. And in such circumstances there grew
up the myth of the ingrained idleness of the crofter, a myth that was to
persist for many years to come.

———————

Although all Highland estates experienced serious difficulties in the second
quarter of the nineteenth century, the impact of the economic crisis was
greatest on the properties where kelp had been of most importance. Several
Hebridean landlords duly went to the wall during this period, among them
MacKenzie of Seaforth, MacLeod of Harris, MacDonald of Clanranald,
MacNeill of Barra and MacLeod of Raasay. Within the space of about 15
years, then, the whole of the Outer Isles, with the exception of North Uist,
not sold by Lord MacDonald until 1855, passed out of the hands of its
longstanding owners. Several mainland properties changed hands at about
the same time. And the effective demise of so many chieftainly families has,
ever since, been much regretted. The families in question, however, were

themselves mainly to blame for their loss of position. Since the seventeenth century, they had spent vast sums on maintaining what they thought of as their rightful place in southern society. And the loss of income from kelp merely demolished proprietorial finances that had long been subject to serious strain. Besides, the effects of the kelp industry's collapse on its workforce, it needs keeping in mind in this context, were much worse than the same collapse's impact on the folk who had so profited from the boom which had gone before.

Where kelping ceased completely, the consequent loss of wages was a heavy blow. On the Dunvegan estate, by no means a major kelp property, about £400 a year was lost to crofters in this way. And even on estates where – for reasons mentioned previously – kelping was not entirely abandoned or was replaced by some other form of labour, increasing arrears tended to ensure that the crofter received no actual cash in return for work done, his wages merely being credited against the amount of rent he owed his landlord. This was bad enough. But the major consequence of the kelp industry's sudden decline was more profound and more serious – at least as far as crofters were concerned. Originally envisaged by the proprietors who created it as little more than an adjunct to the insatiable labour requirements of a kelping economy, the crofting system, together with crofters themselves, ceased to be of utility to landlords at the moment in the 1820s when kelp became unprofitable. Crofters and their families became, in other words, a burden and a drag on the estates where they resided. They were – in a chilling phrase which was more and more widely applied to them – a 'redundant population' who occupied potentially profitable land for which they were increasingly unable to pay an economic rent. The inevitable outcome was that landlords' earlier commitment to maintaining, indeed increasing, the population of their estates was transformed, within the space of very few years, into an ardent determination to get rid of as many crofting tenants as possible.

On MacDonald of Clanranald's estates in South Uist and Benbecula the initial response to the kelp industry's troubles was, as already mentioned, to provide alternative employment for crofters who were left without work. But by 1827, the year in which it became manifestly apparent that kelp prices would never recover, his estate managers had resolved that it was 'absolutely necessary to arrange Clanranald's . . . estates so as to draw a revenue from the lands altogether independent of kelp'. The most obvious and attractive course, given that sheep farming was now much more profitable than cattle husbandry of the traditional type, was thought to lie in 'parcelling out . . . the estate' into sheep farms. While financially alluring, such a policy was, of course, 'incompatible with the residence of the tenantry'. The answer, according to Duncan Shaw, factor on the estate and a man who only 11 years before had been at pains to keep up kelp production by preventing emigration, was to ship 'at least 3,000 people' to North America.

Since Shaw's scheme involved ridding South Uist and Benbecula of almost half their population, it was not unambitious. As such it appealed to the trustees – most of them Edinburgh-based lawyers – in whom the management of Clanranald's financially imperilled estates had been vested. Obviously, wrote one of the latter gentlemen, large numbers of people would have to be removed from Clanranald's property, for no landowner who had decided to introduce sheep farming on to his estate could afford to 'keep a swarm of lazy, idle tenants for a term beyond his pleasure'. All over the mainland Highlands, the same man pointed out, there were 'hundreds of instances of whole parishes and districts . . . being depopulated to make room for sheep'. And he could see no reason why a similar change should not take place in the Outer Isles.

A switch from kelp to sheep having thus been accepted in principle by Clanranald's trustees, only one problem remained. Clanranald's funds were so depleted as to make it impossible for him to pay for emigration on the scale envisaged – while their growing poverty made it unlikely that his crofting tenants would be able to meet the cost of their own deportation. Government assistance was accordingly sought. The relevant ministers and civil servants in the Colonial Department were unpersuaded, however, by the notion that the interests of Clanranald's estate and Britain's Canadian colonies coincided as exactly as Clanranald's representatives said they did. Neither the estate authorities' appeals nor the petitions from people who had 'received warning to quit their little possessions' succeeded, as a result, in eliciting the public funds needed to finance a really large-scale emigration from Clanranald's properties to Canada. Duncan Shaw, with the trustees' and proprietor's approval, modified his plans accordingly. Since the best kelp produced on the estate was made by tenants in Benbecula, he decided to leave things as they were in that island 'while the kelp [was] at all worth manufacturing'. The northern part of South Uist was to be similarly unaffected, with the 600 or so people who occupied its several settlements – including the townships of Balgarva, Liniquie, Kilaulay and Ardivachar – being left to get on with the task of manufacturing as much marketable kelp as possible. In the central portion of South Uist, however, the kelp industry had become completely unprofitable and people, it followed, superfluous. Four of the district's townships, notably Geirinish and Drimore, were still in the nominal possession of tacksmen – but were, in fact, occupied by large numbers of subtenants. The tacksmen in question, Shaw recommended, should be removed – along with their subtenants and with the tenants of the crofting townships of Grogarry and Stilligarry. The 380 people thus evicted would be accompanied by another 400 who were to be cleared from Howbeg, Snishival, Peninerine and Stoneybridge, and by the 150 occupants of Kildonan, a township whose crofts had been established between 1816 and 1818 in order to make room for the kelpers who had then been so important. Kildonan was to be added to the farm of Milton whose tenant – a sheep farmer who had been in place since 1827 – was willing to give a good rent for the displaced Kildonan crofters' holdings. A similar accommodation was to take place in the southern part of South Uist – where the farm of Askernish had been let to a sheep farmer in 1826. The township of Daliburgh which marched with Askernish would, Shaw concluded, make 'a most desirable addition to it', as would the hill grazings held by the small tenants of Kilpheder.

The inconvenience of evicting about a thousand of his tenants, Duncan Shaw believed, would be offset by the several advantages which would accrue to MacDonald of Clanranald from the adoption of this plan. Because they would not 'emigrate to so small an island without being certain of having a great return for their capital', Shaw pointed out, South Uist sheep farmers' rents would not at first be much higher than the aggregate rents of the crofters they would displace. But farmers' rents could be raised substantially when their initial leases lapsed – and such rents, unlike those of crofters, would be 'well and punctually paid'. As a result of the proposed changes, therefore, 'Clanranald would have a well-paid money rent and a certain income independent of kelp'. His lands, moreover, 'would be well-cultivated and properly managed.' He would also retain on his estate a population which, Shaw thought, would be 'more than sufficient' to work such of Clanranald's kelp shores as were to be kept in production.

Although not executed exactly as planned, Duncan Shaw's 1827 recommendations provided the guidelines for estate policy in South Uist and Benbecula for the next few years – a number of townships being cleared, and substantial emigration occurring, in consequence. The remorseless logic of Duncan Shaw's arguments, moreover, was universally applicable. Developments on Clanranald's estate thus had their parallels throughout the islands. By the 1830s, as a result, crofters were everywhere considered, as one commentator put it, to be 'less advantageous to the proprietors than farmers occupying the same tracts of ground'. People who could afford to emigrate, naturally did so – 'hundreds' quitting one island after another. Between 1826 and 1827, about 1,300 people left Skye for the North American colonies. In 1828, more than 600 folk left North Uist for the same destination, and there were extensive emigrations from Barra at about the same time. On the mainland, meanwhile, there were similar occurrences – further expansion of sheep farming bringing about the emigration of about a thousand people from Wester Ross and western parts of Inverness-shire in 1823 and 1824.

Although the word 'alarming' was applied to them by some observers, there was a vital difference between the emigrations of the 1820s and 1830s and those which had occurred before 1803. Nothing was done to stop them, and they were, on the contrary, 'encouraged very much' by landlords. Throughout Britain the post-war depression had made emigration much more popular than hitherto. To 'shovel out paupers' or, in other words, transport the workless to the colonies was an obvious solution to the country's unemployment problem – and one to which Highland landlords, as already indicated, were by no means averse. Landowners who would formerly have been riven with anxiety at the slightest hint of an emigration which might have deprived them of their kelpers were now convinced that their only hope of financial salvation lay in removing crofting tenants and turning recently created crofts into sheep farms

This policy, as it happened, was strikingly similar to that being pursued in Ireland where the collapse of cereal prices after 1815 had produced a widespread tendency to switch from arable to pastoral farming – the evictions thus necessitated being financed, in some instances, by state-sponsored emigration. The latter, which began in 1822, attracted the attention of at least one Highland proprietor, MacKenzie of Seaforth who, in correspondence with the Chancellor of the Exchequer, suggested that a similar scheme be launched in the Highlands and Islands. Seaforth, however, was too far in advance of his fellow proprietors who, as he remarked with some bitterness, were unwilling to allow, let alone encourage, emigration as long as their tenants' kelping activities were worth anything at all. In a letter which he wrote in 1823, and which was to prove prophetic, Seaforth recorded his conviction that Hebridean landlords would sooner or later have to provide 'for their wretched tenantry either by giving them the means of other employment or of emigrating ere it is too late':

> And convinced I am that, before five years have expired, this they will be driven to under increased difficulties, and then without even the semblance of benevolent and human feeling towards the starving mass of whom in the interval they will make use, so their applications will lose their power and sordid motives will be too justly laid to their charge.

Seaforth's prediction was quickly and amply vindicated. In 1826 and 1827, the years during which kelp prices finally fell through the floor, those who could afford to emigrate were the fortunate few, while landlords who could afford to sponsor emigration were even rarer. The Colonial Department consequently received scores of petitions from the Hebrides and from the Scottish mainland's north-west coast: many of them signed by tenants who had 'suffered from the introduction of sheep into these parts'; all of them asking for assisted passages to Canada. By that time, however, no assisted passages were to be had and each appeal for aid was turned down.

Something was achieved, however. In 1827 the restrictions imposed on emigration by the Passenger Act of 1803 were completely removed – a development which Highland proprietors greeted with a delight that was, perhaps, a little unbecoming in men who had, for allegedly humanitarian reasons, been instrumental in putting the Act on the statute book in the first place. All the wiles of the once despised and castigated emigration agents were now employed on proprietors' behalf with results that were, from the landowning fraternity's point of view, encouraging:

Thig iad ugainn, carach, seòlta,
Gus ar mealladh far ar n-eòlais;
Molaidh iad dhuinn Manitòba,
Dùthaich fhuar gun ghual, gun mhòine.*

The trouble with this type of emigration, as Seaforth's factor remarked in 1827, was that it tended to attract 'the best and most active tenants' – that is, those with most initiative and most money – while 'the poor and weak' were left behind in even worse circumstances than before. To most estate managements, however, any emigration seemed better than none. Everything possible was done, therefore, to encourage it.

By the later 1820s, then, 'informed' opinion – which meant the opinions of landlords, factors, sheep farmers, clergymen and anyone else of higher social standing than crofters – had concluded that overpopulation was the root cause of the social and economic problems confronting north-west Scotland. Quickly elevated to the status of a received truth, this doctrine held sway in landowning and government circles for the rest of the nineteenth century, one of the first signs of its appearance – apart from landlords' sudden discovery of the benefits of emigration – being a marked change in attitudes to the subdivision of crofters' holdings. Blithely encouraged during the kelp boom, subdivision was, from the 1820s onwards, regarded by estate managements as a virtually criminal act which, by making provision for young couples, helped to perpetuate the growth of a population whose economic usefulness was at an end. As Clanranald's factor conceded in 1827, subdivision was difficult to eliminate: 'Marriages cannot be prevented and, of course, parents will not see their children starve'. But plenty of proprietors were willing go to extraordinary lengths to make further subdivision of crofts as difficult as possible. On the MacDonald estates in 1831, for example, it was decreed that any man who married 'without holding lands directly from Lord MacDonald' – before, in other words, he had taken over his father's croft – would be 'forthwith removed from the property'. A similar policy was in force in Coll – while the managers of Sir James Riddell's Ardnamurchan estate thought that the obvious 'remedy for overpopulation' was 'to purge the rent roll, and punish every delinquent, or doubtful character, by immediate ejection furth of the estate'. Such regulations were inherently difficult to enforce, however, and it was generally agreed that the simplest, most effective and most profitable way of dealing with an overpopulated estate was to remove the bulk of its tenants and put the land thus vacated under sheep – an attitude encapsulated in evidence given to a parliamentary committee by the factor of John Hay MacKenzie's estate at Coigach, Wester Ross. Asked, 'If Mr MacKenzie's estate were cleared of the surplus population, what steps would, or

---

*'They come to us, deceitful and cunning, in order to entice us from our homes; they praise Manitoba to us, a cold country without coal or peat.' The translation is Margaret Fay Shaw's.

could, be taken to prevent a recurrence of the evil?' the Coigach factor replied: 'To immediately let the land as sheep farms'. This proceeding, the same man explained, would not only ensure Coigach's continued depopulation but would also result in its owner 'undoubtedly' receiving a 'better rental'. Coigach crofters, in the event, were to be left in undisturbed occupation of their holdings until the 1850s. Crofters elsewhere were not so fortunate.

Among north-west Scotland's landlords, all of them men whose finances were showing signs of strain by the 1820s, none was harder pressed than Stewart MacKenzie of Seaforth, a Galloway laird who had acquired his Highland estates and territorial designation by marrying the last Lord Seaforth's daughter and heiress. To wed such an heiress was not, in the economic circumstances of 1817, the year the marriage took place, the way to gain a fortune, however. By 1819, Seaforth was accordingly convinced that the only way to reverse the decline in his income from his newly acquired properties was to turn them into sheep farms. The Canadian colonies, he believed, were the most convenient receptacle for the people who would be displaced by incoming sheep farmers, and to an influential friend in London he accordingly addressed an urgent enquiry as to whether the government would be willing to subsidise the emigrations he had in mind:

> If it becomes necessary for me, as I fear it will, to carry through the measure of dispossessing a population, overgrown and daily becoming more burdensome, to pave the way for the grand improvement of the introduction of mutton in lieu of man, the numbers almost appal me, and will astonish you when I add that 5,000 souls and upwards, I calculate, may be spared . . . to render the change complete.

Those figures included a number of tenants from Seaforth's estates on the Highland mainland. But it was in the development of the island of Lewis, of which he was the sole owner, that Seaforth was particularly interested. And by the autumn of 1820, the essential features of a plan for its transformation had been committed to paper.

Because no officially subsidised passages were forthcoming, the major obstacle in the way of the successful establishment of a sheep farming economy in Lewis was 'the population and how it is to be disposed of'. The solution arrived at was to establish a number of crofting townships – 'the whole northern part of the island' being thought 'suitable for this plan'. As usual in such cases, the division of traditional farms into crofts was intended to increase the number of people living on a given area of land:

> Whatever grounds are from their nature and situation peculiarly fitted for sheep pasture must be so arranged that the present occupiers may be removed to allotments which are for that purpose to be laid out for them.

The places most obviously 'fitted' for sheep rearing were the parishes of Uig and Lochs – where the low-lying moors that characterise the more northerly part of Lewis rise up to meet the hills of Harris. That Uig and Lochs were 'best adapted for sheep' had been pointed out to Lord Seaforth in 1800. And in 1819, the newly established tenant of much of north-west Harris, a sheep farmer named Alexander MacRae, was casting increasingly envious eyes across Loch Resort to the still sheepless hills of Uig. If the Lewis side of the loch were to be 'planted with sheep', MacRae wrote to Seaforth, he would be delighted to become its tenant. But because the land in question was held by a motley collection of folk whose removal, in his opinion, would greatly enhance the neighbourhood, he would be happy to see Uig 'laid out for sheep', Alexander MacRae continued, 'whoever stocks it'. MacRae's wish was granted by his being made tenant of the Uig farm of Scaliscro. His success in no way mellowed his attitude to the parish's original occupants, however. In 1833, he was writing to Seaforth to complain of the depredations committed on his land and stock at Scaliscro by the occupiers of a nearby, and uncleared, locality. Anxious 'to get rid of so troublesome and disagreeable neighbours', he offered, if they were removed, to take on their lands at a rent which would be, at the minimum, no less than the aggregate rents of the families he wanted out.

Although Alexander MacRae's 1833 letter demonstrates the ease with which evictions could be arranged, the fact that he had to write it shows that Seaforth's plans had not gone as smoothly as Lewis's proprietor had originally hoped. In the spring of 1823, ten years before MacRae penned the letter which sealed the fate of his unfortunate neighbours, Seaforth had intended to remove up to a thousand people from Uig and Lochs and settle them in crofting townships in the parishes of Stornoway and Barvas. The 'violent change' implied by evictions on such a scale alarmed Seaforth's trustees, however. His finances, they pointed out, were in a parlous state – that, after all, was why they had been appointed to take charge of them – and he lacked, therefore, the means properly to establish so many crofts, let alone equip their occupants with the boats and gear they would need if they were to participate effectively, as Seaforth hoped they would, in the fishing industry. Lack of capital, in fact, was the fatal flaw in all Seaforth's plans. But it was a flaw whose existence he could not perceive or was unwilling to admit to. Although forced to accept his trustees' advice, he continued to be possessed of an urge to take what he termed 'decisive steps' in Lewis. Unable to afford the grandiloquent, Sutherland-type clearances which he had planned initially, Seaforth settled for a more gradual chipping away at existing tenurial arrangements. But 'decisive' or not, his measures left an imprint on Lewis.

Even before 1823, a group of Skye farmers had been given a lease, by MacKenzie of Seaforth's managers in Lewis, of the farm of Park in the eastern part of the parish of Lochs. In the following 20 or so years, this

farm was extended steadily until it occupied the greater part of the extensive and hilly peninsula from which it derived its name. During the 1820s
and 1830s, or so a royal commission was informed in 1883, some 28 settlements were cleared and their lands added to Park farm. In the process,
said an old man who had witnessed his own father's eviction from one
of the settlements in question, over 100 families were removed – some
to comparatively nearby townships, others to the neighbourhood of Stornoway. Contemporary evidence bears out the general accuracy of these
claims. Evictions from Park, it seems, began in the early 1820s. And
by 1826 some of the peninsula's former occupants were being settled on
new crofts at Balallan and Leurbost – such new crofts in many instances
consisting of nothing more than roughly pegged-out plots on existing townships' common grazings. Happenings of this kind were to help ensure that
the number of tenants in Balallan grew from 26 at the beginning of the
nineteenth century to 104 in 1888. Back in Park, meanwhile, there were
more evictions. Eishken, Orosay, Shiltenish and Lemreway, all in the Park
peninsula, were cleared between 1833 and 1841 – their tenants, of whom
there were at least 60, being sent to Crossbost, Tong and Tolsta where
former farms of the traditional sort were divided into crofts to make space
for them.

In 1823, Seaforth had remarked that tenants to be evicted from Park
'must and ought to be content with whatever land we can give them' – the
implication being that the setting-up of a soundly based crofting system
was the least of his concerns. In accordance with these instructions, then,
little attempt was made to provide Lewis's new crofters with adequate
holdings – many of those crofters being accommodated in townships situated on land that had never been previously cultivated. One such township was Aird Tunga, the Aird of Tong, a settlement established on waste
land about three miles north of Stornoway. Here a number of Park's former
occupants were installed in 1827. In the following spring, Alexander Craig,
who managed Seaforth's estate at Brahan on the mainland and who had
earlier spent some time in Ireland, had occasion to visit Lewis. To satisfy
his curiosity about recent developments on the island, Craig went to inspect
the new township at Aird Tunga. What he found appalled him:

> Until I saw the actual situation of the new lotters on the Aird of Tong,
> I had no idea of the great hardships and privations that the poor people
> endure who are forced into new allotments without matters being previously
> arranged for their moving. The situation of the new lotters on the Aird of
> Tong at this moment beggars all description. It is worse than anything I ever
> saw in Donegal, where I always considered human wretchedness to have
> reached its very acme.

In a treeless island like Lewis, Craig went on, timber was almost unobtainable and evicted tenants consequently had to transport the rafters of their
old houses to the sites set aside for their new homes. While being disman-

tled and carried northwards, however, many of the timbers – which were often old and rotten to begin with – had been irreparably broken. The consequence was that many of the new houses – if Aird Tunga's ramshackle erections of stone and turf could be graced with such a title – were inadequately roofed. Being too poor to buy new rafters, there was little crofters could do to remedy their situation. But it was a fact, according to Craig, that Seaforth could have provided his crofting tenants with all the timber they needed for a fraction of the legal expenses incurred in evicting them from their original holdings. And if Aird Tunga's houses were bad, Craig concluded, their surroundings were worse. There was no track, far less a road, to the new settlement, and its occupants, therefore, had 'literally to step to their knees in mud the moment they quit their thresholds'.

Craig's protests, like those of the less articulate Lewismen who demonstrated their opposition to the new order by committing 'great depredations' among the sheep stock in Park, seem to have had no effect on Seaforth's policies. All over the southern part of Lewis in the 1820s and 1830s, sheep farming was being consolidated and extended – for sheep farmers, as Seaforth's Lewis factor remarked, 'could be got as fast as the lands could be cleared for them'. In 1826, for example, Duncan Stewart who had been manager of Park farm before becoming factor to MacLeod of Harris – on whose estate, incidentally, he had at once provided himself with a sheep farm – expressed a desire to rent some grazings on the eastern shore of Loch Seaforth, an area adjoining his lands on the Harris side of the boundary between the two neighbouring his estates. Stewart's offer was immediately accepted and the tenants of Aird an Troim – the piece of territory Stewart wanted – were 'duly warned' to remove.

Events in Uig took a similar course. The western part of that parish, especially the area around Loch Roag, had been the main kelping centre in Lewis, and the industry's rapid decline no doubt strengthened the estate management's professed resolve to have the district 'put into large tracts of pasture'. Clearances in Uig began in the 1820s and continued into the following decade – evicted tenants being moved northwards or accommodated in newly laid-out townships on Uig's Atlantic coast. Deprived of their inland pastures, the tenants of these townships were in an unenviable and, it transpired, a precarious position. One of the coastal settlements, Mealista, was soon seen to be suitable for conversion into a sheep farm, and in 1836 a good offer was received for its tenancy. Seaforth's factor accordingly proposed to move Mealista's 16 families to townships in Ness, at Lewis's faraway northern tip. This scheme having foundered – most probably on the expense involved – six of the tenants cleared from Mealista were crammed into the neighbouring, and already congested, township of Brenish. The rest, as a crofter from Uig was afterwards to remark, were 'hounded away' to North America.

'It must be admitted,' declared the authors of a government report of 1837, 'that few cases could arise to which the remedy of emigration on a great scale would appear more appropriate than to that of the Hebrides.' And aided, in some cases, by the government's subsequent decision to make official funds available to meet the expenses of emigration from the Highlands to the Australian colonies, other island proprietors were to show no more hesitation than Seaforth or Clanranald had already shown in switching from kelp to wool and, therefore, from crofting to sheep farming . Entirely typical of a very general process were events in Rum – MacLean of Coll, the island's owner, arranging, in 1826, to have about 300 tenants shipped from Rum to Canada. MacLean spent £5 14s. on each adult emigrant's passage. But the investment from his point of view, if not from that of the island's occupants who were reportedly reluctant 'to leave the land of their ancestors', was an eminently sound one. Rum's pre-1826 rental was about £300 annually. Cleared and let as a single sheep farm, the island brought in £800 a year to its proprietor.

Economic imperatives were everywhere seen to be the same, Lord MacDonald's North Uist factor summing them up in an estate document of 1839:

> The fall in the value of kelp renders . . . a change in the management of the North Uist estate necessary. The tenants have hitherto been accustomed to pay for the greater part of their rents by their labour as kelpers. Kelp is not now a productive manufacture. The population of the estate is greater than the land, the kelp being abandoned, can maintain. The allotments of land held by the small tenants are so small that they cannot maintain their families and pay the proprietor the rents which the lands are worth if let in larger tenements. It becomes necessary, therefore, that a number of small tenants be removed [and] that that part of the estate calculated for grazings be let as grazings.

The former policy of doing everything possible to facilitate the proliferation of crofts in North Uist was accordingly abandoned. Between 1838 and 1843, Lord MacDonald helped around 1,300 people to emigrate from the island – their departure being followed, as all such departures were followed, by the conversion of further tracts of land into sheep farms.

In Harris, where widespread removals began in the 1820s, there were similar developments. Several clearances were instituted by MacLeod of Harris's already mentioned factor, Duncan Stewart, in order to extend his own sheep farming interests. Another beneficiary of Harris's numerous evictions was Alexander MacRae who, like Stewart, was also to have a hand in Seaforth's clearances in Lewis. About 13 settlements on the Atlantic coast between west Loch Tarbert and Kinlochresort were cleared to make way for MacRae's north Harris sheep farm, and their former occupants moved to the island's comparatively barren east coast. Initiated on MacLeod's instructions, these transformations were continued, in the 1830s, by the island's new proprietor, the Earl of Dunmore. By 1837, according to Dunmore's factor, the population had 'in a great measure been removed from the west coast of Harris and other arrangements [were] in contemplation by which what remains of the population [were] very likely soon to be removed'. The nature of the contemplated 'arrangements' became clear in 1838 when the tenant of one of Dunmore's sheep farms refused to renew his lease unless the township of Borve, the largest remaining settlement on the west coast, was added to his lands. About 50 families were accordingly evicted – completing a process by which 'the most fertile farms possessed by small tenants' were 'depopulated and converted into extensive sheep walks'.

In the 1820s and 1830s, then, the fertile machair lands on the Atlantic coast of Harris – lands which had been occupied from time immemorial – were completely cleared and the evicted population settled on the island's eastern shores. This was so bleak and stony a district that, as a Harris crofter observed bitterly, 'beasts could not live' in it. Among the rocks on which they were thus forced to set up home, the newly arrived inhabitants of the eastern part of Harris painstakingly construced the lazybeds or *feannagan* which are still to be seen there and which alone could provide a depth of soil sufficient to raise a crop. More than 100 years later, the pioneer ecologist, Frank Fraser Darling, was to comment of the feannagan in question:

> Nothing can be more moving to the sensitive observer of Hebridean life than these lazybeds of the Bays district of Harris. Some are no bigger than a dining table, and possibly the same height from the rock, carefully built up with turves carried there in creels by the women and girls. One of these tiny lazybeds will yield a sheaf of oats or a bucket of potatoes, a harvest no man should despise.

Such harvests could not support a population used to living on the hugely more productive lands to the west, however, and many Harris people, 'reduced to extreme distress by being crowded into places incapable of affording them subsistence', were duly forced to emigrate. Between 600 and 800 emigrants sailed from Harris in 1828 alone. They were followed by a further 600 in the early 1840s.

Across the Minch in Skye, meanwhile, the clearances which had begun during the nineteenth century's first and second decades went ahead with renewed rigour in the 1820s and 1830s. 'The small tenants have paid wretchedly ill,' MacLeod of Dunvegan's factor reported of the Martinmas rent collection of 1833, 'and since kelp must be given up they will be worse and worse every year unless some other plan is fallen upon to employ them.' Unable to think of any such plan that could be as profitable to MacLeod as the extension of sheep farming, the Dunvegan factor suggested emigration as the best solution to the problem – this emigration to be facilitated, of course, by evictions. Such evictions, in fact, were already occurring on a massive scale as vast tracts of the Dunvegan estate, especially the parts of it contained by the parish of Bracadale, were put under sheep. Bracadale's population in 1821 was 2,103. Ten years later it was 1,769, and the decrease, according to the parish minister, was 'solely to be ascribed to the system of farming which has for some time been adopted, viz., throwing a number of farms into one large tack for sheep grazing and dispossessing and setting adrift the small tenants'. The number of tenants 'set adrift' in this way can be gauged from the fact that, in 1826, no fewer than 229 people from Bracadale, all of whom had received notices of eviction from MacLeod's estate managers, applied for assisted passages to Canada – their applications being accompanied by a similar set of requests from the neighbouring parish of Duirinish. There, by 1841, over 3,000 acres had been converted from arable to pasture.

Sheep farmers naturally welcomed those developments. Of the 384 people on his farm, one of MacLeod's principal tenants complained, only his shepherds were of any use to him. 'The other people' he found 'really an encumbrance'. The presence of the 'poor families' who were 'domiciled in all parts' of another Bracadale farm meant, according to the farm's sheep farming occupant, that 'the quietness of the flocks [was] always subject to disturbance and their safety also put in jeopardy'. If only 'the people [in question] or the greater part of them could be got rid of', it was observed, the farm's rent could at once be raised. The farm was accordingly cleared, and along with tenants evicted from adjacent localities, a number of its former occupants were sent to Glendale, in the north-western corner of the Dunvegan estate, where MacLeod hoped to establish a fishing station. As was usual with such schemes, the fishing station proved a failure. But in order to force the district's crofters to participate in his planned development of the Minch herring fisheries, MacLeod deliberately overcrowded Glendale – employing techniques previously used to coerce Sutherland's crofting population into taking an active part in similarly illusionary enterprises. In the townships of Upper and Lower Milovaig, for example, MacLeod subdivided existing crofts in an attempt to ensure that their occupants – if only to forestall their starvation – could not avoid becoming fishermen.

MacLeod of Dunvegan's overcrowding of Glendale helped sow the seeds of the grievances which were to underlie the eventually triumphant crofters' revolt which broke out there in 1882. At the start of the 1840s, however, that revolt was far in the future, and the crofting population's more immediate prospects were almost as bleak as they could be. A comment made about Applecross summed up crofters' overall plight:

> Of the working class, the ordinary means of subsistence is renting a small croft for about £5, the free produce of which may be £3 per annum, in addition to which they follow the herring fishing, the returns from which are very precarious and sometimes a dead loss.

Deliberately created by landlords who could not bring themselves to remove it even when it had served its exploitative purpose, that yawning chasm between income and rent was, in the second quarter of the nineteenth century, the crucial fact of crofting life. It made saving impossible. It crippled and stifled all initiative and enterprise. Combined with the omnipresent threat of eviction, it ensured the absence of any kind of security. And in conjunction with the smallness of holdings, the other major consequence of landlords' former need to manoeuvre their small tenants into a position of utter dependence and subservience, it pushed crofters into an almost total reliance on one lowly crop, the potato. That root, as the minister of Morvern commented, had everywhere become the crofting population's staff of life:

> Indeed there are many, it is feared, much in the predicament of a little boy of the parish, who, on being asked, on a certain occasion, of what his three daily meals consisted, gave the same unvarying answer, 'Mashed potatoes'. And on being further asked by his too inquisitive inquirer, 'What else?' [he] replied, with great artlessness, but with evident surprise, 'A spoon!'

This almost unrelieved dependence upon a single and inherently vulnerable crop constituted the greatest of all crofters' insecurities. Soon it would result in catastrophe. The poverty stricken Highland emigrants, who were a much commented upon feature of life in the Canada of the early 1840s, were to be joined, as a result, by very many of their compatriots – driven there both by hunger and by clearances more brutal and more sweeping than any that had yet occurred.

4

FAMINE

1845–1850

Famine and scarcity were not novel occurrences in the Highlands and Islands. In the later eighteenth century, the region was estimated to suffer from food shortages in one year out of every three, and there are records of several periods of acute distress. In the spring of 1772, for example, the starving people of Skye were living on the carcasses of cattle which had themselves died of hunger – with other islands being similarly affected. Storms and crop failures brought renewed hunger in the autumn of 1782. And on that occasion a serious famine was averted only by the British government's decision to send more than £17,000 worth of food to the Highlands. Most of this aid consisted of peasemeal, of which the British army – in consequence of the ending of America's War of Independence – had a large surplus. And 1783 was accordingly remembered in the Highlands as *bliadhna na peasrach,* the peasemeal year.

Such scarcities, however, were essentially transient phenomena; the consequence of one bad harvest; inevitable, if tragic, concomitants of a system of subsistence agriculture. The famine which began in 1846 was of a different order of magnitude. A human tragedy on a scale unparalleled in modern Scottish history, it was unprecedented in severity and duration. It was also the culmination of 30 years of growing hardship and despair. In every year since 1815, the government was informed in 1847, there had been 'a gradual deterioration in the position of the people', and each decade had 'shown them more impoverished and less able to meet a season of distress'.

The causes of crofters' declining fortunes are clear enough: the adverse effects of the kelp industry's collapse and of the prolonged fall in cattle prices were aggravated by the loss of two other sources of income as a result of the effective suppression of illicit distillation and the completion of the canal and road construction programme which had begun in 1803. The ensuing drop in crofters' earnings was temporarily offset by a seasonal migration of their sons and daughters to the Lowlands where such migrants helped bring in that area's harvests. But by the 1830s and 1840s, even this sort of employment had become precarious – harvest work having become the virtual monopoly of Irish labourers who, following the inauguration of effective steamer services, could come across to the Lowlands from Ireland more quickly and more cheaply than Highlanders could make their way south.

Their loss of alternative sources of income made crofters increasingly dependent on the land. The land in question, however, was becoming more and more congested and less and less able to support the people living on it. This development has long been blamed primarily on the inexorable pressure of population. And it is certainly a fact that, though growing less rapidly than during the kelp boom, north-west Scotland's population continued, into the 1840s, to expand – except in areas such as Mull where clearances were more than usually widespread and urban receptacles for displaced tenants relatively close. More people, of course, meant more subdivision of holdings that had been too small to begin with. The most important cause of such subdivision, however, is to be found in landlords having put whole districts under sheep. In 1847, for example, it was calculated that some 6,000 of the 16,000 arable acres in Skye were held by just 30 sheep farmers. Almost all this area had been converted from tillage to pasture – leaving Skye's remaining 10,000 acres of arable to support over 4,000 families. Of course, they could not. And in this utterly inequitable distribution of land – something which was to worsen before it improved – is to be found a key cause of crofters' growing proneness to hunger.

Despite population growth, therefore, the Highlands and Islands famine of the 1840s is inexplicable in terms of the sheer weight of numbers alone. The experience of the Hebrides during the kelp boom, as of Ulster during the Highland famine's Irish equivalent, showed that large smallholding populations, and even rampant subdivision, were not in themselves disastrous – as long as money incomes held up and as long, too, as the greater part of the available land remained in smallholders' hands. The Highland famine was thus an economic rather than a biological catastrophe. As such its origins lay in the virtual evaporation of crofters' cash earnings and in the growing tendency to take their land away from them in order to transfer it to sheep farmers – developments which gave an unprecedented importance to crofters' diminishing plots and to their universally dominant crop, the potato.

According to that early Highland chronicler, Martin Martin, potatoes were part of the 'common diet' of the people of Skye as long ago as the 1680s. From other accounts, however, it seems likely that potatoes did not achieve any widespread acceptance in the Highlands until the mid-eighteenth century, a common tradition being that they were introduced into South Uist by Clanranald in 1743. There, as elsewhere, to begin with, they were by no means popular. 'You made us plant these worthless things,' the people of South Uist are said to have told Clanranald, 'but, Virgin Mary, will you make us eat them!' Be that as it may, there is no doubt that the potato made rapid progress in the Highlands during the second half of the eighteenth century. Tolerant of lime deficiency and responding well to manuring with seaweed, it was clearly suited to the region – and, by the early 1800s, was accordingly grown right across the north-west. Because it was the only crop which could support so large a population on what one observer called 'miserable patches of land', the rise of the kelp industry and the consequent development of the crofting system consolidated the potato's position. By 1811, potatoes were reckoned to provide the typical Hebridean crofter with no less than four-fifths of his food. The position was little better on the west coast of the mainland, and everywhere reliance on potatoes was, if anything, to increase during the 1820s and 1830s.

A population used to living on meat, fish, or even bread, can, in times of scarcity, have recourse to humbler foodstuffs. But as was remarked by one of the officials charged with the task of alleviating famine in the Highlands in the 1840s:

> Those who are habitually and entirely fed on potatoes live upon the extreme verge of human subsistence, and when they are deprived of their accustomed food there is nothing cheaper to which they can resort. They have already reached the lowest point of the descending scale, and there is nothing beyond but starvation and beggary.

By the 1840s, then, the agrarian structure of north-west Scotland was, as observed by Norman MacLeod, a Church of Scotland minister who knew the area well, 'in a very hollow and rotten state'. The potato was its only prop. If that prop were to give way, the whole fabric of crofting life would inevitably disintegrate. And as early as the spring of 1817, there were indications of the nature of the cataclysm that, in such circumstances, was certain to ensue.

In 1817, shortages arising from a bad harvest in 1816, together with the further shortages stemming from a failure of the coastal herring fishing, combined to aggravate the already adverse consequences of the post-war fall in cattle prices. And because thousands of Highlanders were returning at that point from military service abroad, greater than usual demands were made upon less than usual amounts of money and food. Only one outcome was possible: as a hard winter gave way to a cold, inclement spring, it became apparent that many people in north-west Scotland, especially in the Outer Isles, were on the verge of starvation. Hebridean proprietors accordingly appealed to the government for assistance – their pleas evoking a remarkably prompt and generous response. Seaforth was sent 2,500 quarters of grain and Clanranald 2,000 quarters – while MacLeod of Harris and MacNeill of Barra got 800 and 600 quarters respectively. Such munificence the landlords in question found somewhat embarrassing – especially when they were asked to foot the government's bill. MacKenzie of Seaforth's share of over £6,000, though eventually halved in deference to his well-founded pleas of poverty, became, for several years, a matter of no little contention between him and politicians in London.

But if island proprietors became thus indebted to government, their tenants, in turn, became indebted to them. For while landlords certainly distributed the grain they received, they did not do so gratuitously. On Lord MacDonald's Skye estate, for example, the price was fixed at the grossly inflated level of two guineas a boll,* payable at Whitsun 1818. Unwilling to add a further large debt to their already accumulating arrears of rent, crofters were naturally reluctant to accept 'assistance' on such terms. Even when 'actually starving', Lord MacDonald's factor reported, they 'always underestimate the quantity they actually need when aware they have to pay high for it'. And as was to be demonstrated in the 1830s, when crofters' financial position was much worse than it had been in the years immediately after the Napoleonic Wars, Lord MacDonald's estate managers were past masters at collecting debts of this kind. In 1837, to alleviate the effects of a particularly bad winter, Lord MacDonald supplied his crofting tenants with seed oats valued at £1,303. Only £81 remained outstanding two years later.

When kelping was all important, such outlays were regarded by landlords as investments, the return on which was an adequately fed labour force and a good kelp crop, and the cost of which could, in any case, be deducted from kelpers' wages. As a Benbecula crofter remarked, therefore, 'there were stores of meal and no destitution in the country while the kelp was going on'. In the 1820s and 1830s, however, grants of meal to crofters brought no bonuses in the shape of increased kelp profits – and not all estate managers were as good at collecting debts as were those employed by Lord MacDonald. Landlords became correspondingly less enthusiastic about assisting their crofters. The latter were thus left increasingly to fend for themselves.

The outcome, made more unavoidable by crofters' deteriorating finances, was that seasons of hardship and scarcity became steadily more frequent. A chronic shortage of meal and of the cash needed to buy it made potatoes quite literally irreplaceable. And every summer there was staged, in the weeks or months between the exhausting of the old potatoes and the digging of the new ones, a miniature rehearsal of what would occur in the event of the staple crop being lost: the shores were ransacked for shellfish; nettles, brambles and any other vaguely edible plants were uprooted, stewed and eaten. In one year, 1836, the potato crop did fail fairly extensively and only governmental and charitable assistance prevented a calamity. The following year brought a good harvest, however, and the 1836 crisis soon passed. The troubles which began ten years later were not so temporary; nor were their effects so easily alleviated.

---

*An old Scots measure a little in excess of a hundredweight.

Although its origins remain obscure, potato blight is now known to be caused by a fungus, *phytophthora infestans,* to which the potatoes of the 1840s had absolutely no natural resistance. Still one of the more serious plant pestilences in the northern hemisphere, blight spreads with astonishing rapidity. Given appropriate weather conditions, notably warmth, moisture and light winds, the spores formed on a single potato plant can infect many thousands of other plants in a matter of days, even hours. To people who had no scientific understanding of its causes, blight was a mysterious and terrifying scourge. And as anyone who has experienced one of the region's typically mild, damp summers will readily appreciate, the Highlands and Islands provided for *phytophthora infestans* an environment that was little short of ideal.

The first major outbreak of blight in Europe occurred in the summer of 1845. But though the fungus was fairly widespread in southern Scotland that year, most of the Highlands and Islands escaped its devastations. Only in Islay and mid-Argyll were serious losses reported. Elsewhere in the region, the crop was healthy and abundant – a state of affairs which enabled some enterprising crofters and proprietors to take advantage of the high prices resulting from scarcities in other parts of the British Isles. No less than 15,410 barrels of potatoes were sent south from Tobermory, and on the Mull estates belonging to the Duke of Argyll and Campbell of Kilpatrick at least £3,158 was received from sales of grain and potatoes to southern dealers – a sum which exceeded those estates' rental by more than £550.

The Highlands, then, were more than usually well prepared for the winter. Nor did the new year bring any immediate change in fortune. The spring of 1846 was mild and pleasant, the early summer warm and dry with the promise of another good harvest. In July, however, it began to rain and with the wet weather came blight. It appeared in Skye in the middle of the month and soon the whole region was affected. In June, the all-important potato crop had been unusually well advanced. In July and August, it was devastated: 'In course of a week, frequently in course of a single night or day, fields and patches of this vegetable, looking fair and flourishing, were blasted and withered and found to be unfit for human food.' Towards the end of August, the *Inverness Courier* sent one of its reporters to Skye, Knoydart, Lochalsh and Kintail. His despatches make depressing reading:

> In all that extensive district he had scarcely seen one field which was not affected – some to a great extent, and others presenting a most melancholy appearance as they were enveloped in one mass of decay.

From each scorched and blackened plot or lazybed there emanated a 'foetid and offensive smell which poisoned the air': the obnoxious, inescapable stench of rotting potatoes.

No area escaped the blight. But losses were greatest in the islands – Skye, where less than a fifth of the average crop was harvested, being fairly typical. On the mainland, the failure of the crop was not quite so universal, but local variations in the blight's incidence and severity were more pronounced. In Glenelg nine-tenths of the usual crop was destroyed. In Ullapool less than half the potatoes were affected. On Sutherland's west coast, the potatoes failed more or less completely, while on the north coast the loss was comparatively trifling. The existence of a few favoured localities did not, however, significantly modify the general picture. As an official report put it: 'The failure is all but universal and complete, the partial exemptions being too inconsiderable to cause any sensible diminution of the tragedy.' At least three-quarters of the entire crofting population of the north-west Highlands and Hebrides, it was estimated at the end of 1846, were completely without food.

The first hint of the coming calamity occurred in Harris in the early summer. The previous year's potatoes having proved inedible when lifted from their storage pits, the island's population were forced to subsist on a diet of shellfish and sand eels. In July and August, as the old potatoes were finished and the new crop blighted, a similar situation began to arise in every part of the region. Norman MacLeod, visiting the islands in August, frequently 'met and conversed with poor people returning from the potato fields, accompanied by their famished children, with empty baskets, and unable to collect what would afford them one meal'. Mull, from which grain and potatoes had been exported 12 months before, was by the end of September completely dependent on imported meal. In Kilmuir, Skye, those crofters lucky enough to occupy larger than average holdings were still managing to eke out their scanty crops of oats. But people with little land, or no land at all, were by October 'reduced to a state of abject famine, and live for the most part on seaweed and scanty supplies of shellfish'.

Crofters were no strangers to scarcity. But its onset in September and October was unprecedented. 'We frequently had bad springs,' one Skye minister wrote towards the end of 1846, 'but this is a winter of starvation.' It was also a winter which set in early and proved cold and stormy, with frequent gales and snowstorms. To the incessant cold and hunger – intolerable enough in themselves – were added sickness and disease. Typhus and cholera broke out in several places. The shellfish scavenged from the beaches caused diarrhoea when eaten. And even when a little meal was added to such a diet it remained, in the absence of potatoes, seriously deficient in essential vitamins. One outcome was that scurvy reappeared in districts where it had been unknown for more than a century.

To quantify human suffering is impossible; even to try is probably undesirable. All that can be done to give some idea of the appalling conditions endured by crofters and their families in the winter of 1846–47 is to quote from a single, but by no means untypical, report made by a member of a clerical deputation which visited the Skye parish of Strath on Christmas Day, 1846:

> We found the condition of very many of them miserable in the extreme, and every day, as they said, getting worse. Their houses, or rather their hovels, and persons the very pictures of destitution and hopeless suffering. A low typhus fever prevails here in several families who seemed to be left to their fate by their neighbours. In one most deplorable case, the whole of the family of seven persons had been laid down, not quite at the same time, in this fever. The eldest of the children, a son about 19 years of age, had died just when his mother was beginning to get on foot. No one [for fear of infection] would enter the house with the coffin for the son's remains. It was left at the outside of the door, and the enfeebled parent and a little girl, the only other member of the family on foot, were obliged to drag the body to the door and put it into the coffin there, whence it was carried by the neighbours with fear and alarm to its last resting place.
>
> When I entered the wretched house . . . I found the father lying on the floor on a wisp of dirty straw, his bedclothes, or rather rags of blanket, as black nearly as soot, his face and hands of the same colour, never having been washed since he was laid down; and the whole aspect of the man, with his hollow features and sunken eyes, and his situation altogether was such as I had never beheld before. In a miserable closet, beyond the kitchen where the father lay, I found the rest of the family, four daughters from about 11 years of age to 17, all crammed into one small bed, two at one end and two at the other. The rags of blanket covering them worse, if possible, than those on the father; their faces and persons equally dirty, the two youngest having no night clothes of any kind. One of these poor girls was very ill and was not likely to recover. The others had the fever more mildly, but had not yet been so long in it.
>
> The effluvia and stench in this place, and indeed in every part of the miserable dwelling, were such that I felt I could not remain long without great risk of infection, as there was no means of ventilation whatever, and not even of light. The poor woman said she had got a stone or two of meal, she said she did not know from whom, which had barely served to make gruel for the unfortunate patients. The family had no means whatever of their own.

In the midst of such a disaster there was relatively little people could do to help themselves. 'The flocks of the large sheep-owners,' the minister of Duirinish in Skye had written some years before the coming of the blight, 'are annually thinned by those who feel the pinching of famine.' In 1846, as in immediately subsequent years, such 'thinning' was particularly drastic – while some North Uist crofters' plan to take forcible possession of 'a certain portion of wheat' was thwarted only by the efforts of a local minister. Such windfalls as were gathered in were supplemented with shellfish and other makeshift substitutes for potatoes. And oatmeal was bought by crofters with such small savings as they possessed. All those alternative sources of food were inherently limited, however – while the obvious substitute for potatoes, fish, was largely unobtainable because of the way in which the fishing industry had developed, or failed to develop, since the days when

James Loch and his fellow 'improvers' had envisaged the wholesale trans-formation of crofting tenants into fishermen.

Because of their low incomes and high rents, crofters were unable to accumulate the capital needed to purchase the relatively sophisticated boats and gear required for deep-sea fishing. The lion's share of the profits made in west coast waters went, therefore, to better equipped and more highly skilled fishermen from Scotland's east coast. Crofters were left with little but the summer herring fishing in the sea lochs – an essentially precarious resource which, as observed at the time, 'served only to eke out the insuf-ficient subsistence derivable from the soil'. Although 'ostensibly a fishing population', crofters, as the government's 1846 enquiries revealed, were 'so poorly skilled and so ill-provided with means that . . . they [did] not possess the ability to pursue the occupation with effect'. This, it was concluded, rather than any innate Celtic indolence of the sort to which southerners regularly attributed the crofting population's failings, lay behind crofters' otherwise incomprehensible neglect of 'the stores apparently within their reach'.

Apart from emigration overseas, the cost of which was now beyond their unaided resources, the only other course open to the crofting population was to move south in search of employment – a procedure whose unpopu-larity, for reasons already touched on, was commonly put down to High-landers' supposedly ingrained laziness. The real reasons for crofters' reluc-tance to move to the Lowlands, even temporarily, were the language diffi-culties they – as Gaelic speakers – confronted there, the risk of falling ill far away from home, the obstacles in the way of making adequate provi-sion for one's family when at a distance and, not least, what one observer called 'the tenacity of [crofters'] attachment to their native soil'. Despite the prevalence of such feelings, seasonal migration was by no means unknown, however. In 1846, it was undertaken on an unprecedented scale, with crofters themselves joining the younger members of their families in the trek to the Lowlands where – helped by a demand for labour generated by that year's railway construction boom – many of them succeeded in obtaining employment.

Like stealing sheep or collecting shellfish, however, this type of migra-tion could only alleviate, or delay the onset of, the tragedy which blight had made inevitable. Only outside assistance could avert catastrophe, and for the necessary help the Highland people could look only to three agencies: the government, their landlords, and private charity.

As the dimensions of the Highland calamity became apparent during the summer of 1846, politicians were made aware of it in a variety of ways. At the end of July, the Marquis of Lorne, son of the Duke of Argyll, wrote to Sir George Grey, home secretary in Lord John Russell's administration, to ask if, in the event of the potato harvest being lost, government ministers would 'extend to Scotland the advantage they have given to Ireland under the same affliction'. Three weeks later, reporting the crop's 'total failure', the marquis informed Grey that 'a very unusual calamity' was likely to occur in the Highlands if steps were not at once taken to forestall it. Soon similar warnings of catastrophe, together with appeals for aid, were pouring into the Home Office. Skye's principal landowners met in Portree on August 18 and resolved to ask for government assistance. Sir James Riddell wrote to Grey from Ardnamurchan on August 24, requesting immediate government intervention in the developing crisis. A public meeting at Glenelg passed resolutions to the same effect. So did a meeting in Argyll of representatives of the Free Church of Scotland – a denomination which had come into existence just three years before but which, for reasons explored in a later chapter, included many crofting families among its members. Noting the prevalence of 'extreme destitution' in much of Argyll, the Free Church representatives in question decided, on September 3, 'to make immediate representations of [the] . . . sufferings of the people to the government . . . praying that means may be devised by the government for administering relief to the suffering poor'.

On receipt both of these communications and of a letter from the lord advocate, the government's senior representative in Scotland, warning about the possible occurrence of a 'great, general, and urgent . . . calamity' in the Highlands, politicians in London acted with commendable alacrity. The delays and vacillations which had characterised their policy in Ireland, where the potato harvest had failed in 1845, were not repeated in the case of the Highlands – largely because the machinery for dealing with distress was already in existence. Responsibility for the prevention of famine in north-west Scotland, as well as in Ireland, was given to the Treasury and, more specifically, to that department's powerful assistant secretary, Sir Charles Trevelyan, already 'the director and virtual dictator of Irish relief'. By September 2, Trevelyan had decided that one of his subordinates should at once be despatched to conduct an enquiry into the Highland situation and, if necessary, take charge of famine relief operations in the region. A few days later, this task was formally allocated to Sir Edward Pine Coffin.

Almost at the end of a military career which had begun during the Peninsular War and which had taken him to corners of the globe as far apart as Mexico and China, Coffin – in spite of his inauspicious name – was a kindly, painstaking man of marked ability. Since January 1846 he had been in charge of famine relief in the remote and impoverished south-west of Ireland, an experience which had earned him his knighthood and given him an understanding – unmatched among that era's public servants – of the numerous problems confronting the underdeveloped Celtic fringe of the British Isles. This understanding Coffin was to put to good use in the Highlands and Islands. Most men in mid-nineteenth century public life –

and Coffin's coldly efficient superior, Charles Trevelyan, provides as good an example as any – were, in their attempts to deal with the Irish and Highland famines, unable or unwilling to rise above the economic conventions and perspectives of their time. To that rule, Coffin was the outstanding exception.

Pausing in Edinburgh to confer with Sir John MacNeill – the official charged with the administration of the poor law in Scotland – and with the agents of several Highland landowners, Coffin reached Oban in mid-September, and immediately began a four-week voyage of investigation along the north-west coast and among the islands. His findings confirmed the worst reports already received. The crofting population undoubtedly stood in need of immediate and massive assistance – assistance which clearly would not be provided, as the government had originally hoped, by Highland landlords. Landowners' obligations to their tenants, 'if not very frequently acknowledged', were not, Coffin admitted, denied. But while professing 'an inclination to provide for the wants of their dependants', most Highland proprietors declared 'an utter inability to effect it from their own resources'. The validity of such excuses was of no great importance. True or false, Coffin wrote, 'they serve to show that the moral obligation supposed to attach to the landowners cannot be relied on to secure the people from destitution'. In accordance with Irish precedent, it was consequently decided to establish two meal depots in the area – one at Tobermory, the other at Portree. For even if Highland landlords could be cajoled into buying provisions, local 'commercial enterprise', Coffin thought, was 'hardly to be trusted for a regular and sufficient supply'. In mid-October, therefore, work began on fitting out two naval frigates as depot ships – while three of the British admiralty's mills, together with two privately owned mills, commenced 'grinding night and day' with a view to turning out the necessary meal.

Such a gross interference with free market principles – principles by which Victorian governments set immense store – could not be lightly undertaken, however. Instructions were accordingly given that no meal was to be issued from the Portree and Tobermory depots until 'all available resources . . . from the produce of the late harvest or otherwise' had been exhausted. Nor should anything be done, it was insisted, which could in any way be construed as impeding the development of local commerce. There was thus to be no question of a gratuitous distribution of meal. A 'fair price' was to be charged. That, however, was easier said than done; and the determination of the fair price thus became one of Coffin's constant preoccupations. Highland meal prices were those of a few small dealers, completely unable to cope with the massive demand engendered by the famine and exacting exorbitant rates from those fortunate enough to be able to compete for their scanty stocks. In Tobermory, for example, oatmeal which sold for around 16s a boll in normal years was fetching 26s a boll by

November. To have adopted such prices, Coffin wrote, 'would have been either to tantalise the hungry with the sight of food which they were unable to purchase, or to convert a professedly beneficent measure into one of usurious profit'. Deliberately to undersell local dealers, on the other hand, would have been to destroy their trade – a step which no Victorian politician could countenance.

Although such dilemmas were partly resolved by adopting a rate based on current Liverpool and Glasgow prices, 'with a proper addition for the expense of conveyance, etc.', Edward Pine Coffin, in short supply of everything except letters from London, continued to find the Treasury's instructions about prices 'the hardest to reconcile with the humane consideration due to the objects of relief'. Because Liverpool and Glasgow meal prices were invariably higher than those prevailing in Dundee and Aberdeen where some Highland merchants obtained their supplies, those hardy entrepreneurs made extravagant profits simply by charging the same as the government depots. And as winter set in, the price problem was further aggravated by a general scarcity resulting from shortages of grain in the rest of Britain and Europe. By the new year, Coffin felt such 'great alarm at the continuing advance of prices' that he dared to question the soundness of Treasury policy: 'At such rates as we ought to charge . . . it is impossible for men to maintain their families above the level of starvation on the ordinary wages of labour'. Trevelyan, however, was adamant. 'We cannot,' he insisted with all the fervour of a devout free trader, 'force up the wages of labour, or force down the prices of provisions, without disorganising society.'

In the autumn of 1846, those bureaucratic wrangles lay in the future. The depot ships did not arrive at their stations until December. And throughout October and November, therefore, as the few remaining potatoes were consumed and the beaches cleared of shellfish, the only people in a position to provide assistance to their starving tenantries were Highland landlords. Not unappreciative of the latter's financial difficulties, the government instructed Coffin to draw their attention to the Drainage Act – a recently passed measure which was intended to help solve the Irish crisis by providing official funds for estate improvement and, therefore, for employment of the destitute. Highland proprietors, it was hoped, would follow their Irish counterparts' example, take advantage of the Act's provisions, and employ large numbers of crofters as ditchers on their estates. But to this plan, Coffin discovered, landlords were unwilling to conform. Most of them did not even apply for a loan until around the new year. This delay, coupled with various technical difficulties, completely nullified the Drainage Act's potential impact on the immediate crisis. In the short term, therefore, such aid as the crofting population received came from their landlords' unaided resources – more especially from the resources of the few proprietors who rose promptly to the exigencies of the situation.

In a circular issued in December 1846, MacLeod of Dunvegan acknowledged his 'duty to see that there was a sufficiency of good wholesome food in the country' and promised that no exertion would be spared on his part to prevent starvation and alleviate distress. This pledge, MacLeod faithfully kept. For the rest of the winter, almost all the able-bodied men on the Dunvegan estate were provided with regular employment. And by the early spring of 1847, MacLeod was feeding some 8,000 individuals – a total which included not just his own tenants but many people from the estates of neighbouring, and less generous, proprietors. The average weekly cost of this endeavour was between £225 and £300. But he would rather, MacLeod wrote, face ruin than let his people starve – a sentiment which was unique in the Highlands of the 1840s.

MacLeod's dedication to his tenants was unequalled. But the second Duke of Sutherland, disregarding James Loch's advice to leave his tenants' sufferings to be alleviated by the mechanisms of supply and demand, spent £18,000 on famine relief, most of it on the provision of meal and seed for overcrowded crofting townships on Sutherland's west coast. In terms of sheer expenditure, however, the lead was easily taken by Sir James Matheson, the tea and opium baron who had bought the Lewis estate from the bankrupt MacKenzies of Seaforth in 1844. Matheson's Lewis improvement programme – which he had begun in 1845 and which involved drainage schemes, road construction works and a variety of other measures – was stepped up to deal with the crisis caused by the blight, and, by 1850, Lewis's new owner had spent some £329,000 on his island. Only a tiny proportion of that vast sum (equivalent to many millions) found its way into crofters' pockets. But the employment generated by Matheson's expenditure undoubtedly helped to protect Lewis from the worst of the famine.

The proprietors of one or two smaller west Highland estates played similar, if less grandiose, roles. Lord Lovat, for example, did a lot to help his tenants in North Morar. And MacLean of Ardgour's estate near Fort William was, according to Coffin, 'quite a model of good management' – MacLean showing his crofting tenants how to cultivate peas, carrots, cabbages and other substitutes for potatoes, as well as providing them with the food they needed to get through the worst of the winter. The success attending MacLean's efforts, it was observed, constituted 'an unanswerable reply to those who are always exclaiming against the inveterate indolence and incorrigible obstinacy of the Highlanders'. To blame the famine on its victims' shortcomings remained, however, a convenient excuse for doing nothing about it. And all such excuses were widely seized – the endeavours of the few humanitarian landlords who did exist being, from the outset, quite exceptional.

Always much more reluctant than Edward Pine Coffin to call landowners' motives into question, Charles Trevelyan suggested that 'the backwardness of some of the proprietors in their preparations for meeting the crisis was, in some cases, owing to their not being sufficiently alive to the grave and extensive character of the emergency'. But even Trevelyan did not doubt that Highland landlords' lack of urgency was a fact. Many proprietors – expecting the British government to provide aid on a massive scale and optimistically ignoring ministers' repeated declarations that no 'general system of relief' would be set up – did nothing at all, in the hope of forcing the administration's hand. That their expectations were unfounded was a truth that dawned only very slowly – with some landlords' agents travelling more than once to Sir Edward Pine Coffin's Oban headquarters in the hope of eliciting a promise of financial support. 'With regard to assistance to proprietors,' reported MacLaine of Lochbuie's factor after one such inter-view in January 1847, 'he says he has but one answer: take money under the Drainage Act. From government nothing else is to be got.'

Because it was originally intended to be an Irish measure, the Drainage Act was not altogether suited to Highland conditions. The drainage schemes instituted under its provisions on several Highland estates did little perma-nent good – while, as far as crofters were concerned, its effects were posi-tively detrimental. Where drains were dug, it was not crofters' holdings that benefited, and, in accordance with their usual custom, those proprie-tors who borrowed government money in order to finance improvements simply passed the financial burden on to their crofting tenants. Even 40 years after the famine, crofters in Skye, Tiree and other areas were still paying the resulting 'drainage money' over and above their rents.

Landlord-organised drainage schemes, however ineffective, would have been better than nothing in the circumstances of 1846. But as one of their more prominent critics remarked at the time, the famine 'appears rather to have paralysed than aroused the possessors of the soil'. On the majority of Highland estates, crofters and their families were left to their own devices – Coffin confessing himself 'deeply grieved and disappointed' by landowners' evident indisposition to take steps to alleviate their tenants' sufferings. 'It is a mistake,' he told Trevelyan at the beginning of 1847, 'to suppose that all the proprietors are yet doing what we consider their duty.' And among the most negligent he included John Gordon of Cluny, the recent purchaser of Barra, South Uist and Benbecula.

Reports of a critical situation on Gordon's island properties began to reach Coffin in December 1846. In January, he sent one of his subordinates, a Captain Pole, to discover the true position. Gordon, Pole wrote, had provided some employment on road works in the early summer of 1846. But in August, despite the advent of blight, these projects had been aban-doned and the tenants working on them dismissed. Informed by his factor that at least 8,000 bolls of meal would be required to prevent widespread destitution, Gordon – who lived in Aberdeenshire and who was one of

Victorian Scotland's richest men – had made arrangements to send 900 bolls. In January, none of these had yet arrived, and Pole consequently found 'greater wretchedness and privation' on Gordon's estate than on any of the other Highland or Hebridean properties which it had been his 'painful duty' to inspect. So desperate, for example, was the plight of the inhabitants of Eriskay, a small island lying between Barra and South Uist, that even the herbs and grasses growing on the island were divided into plots, each one of which was allocated to a crofter and his family – an action which would lead Eriskay's people to recall the famine with the words: 'Bhiodh 'ad a' roinn a' bhloinigein an uair sin'*. In Barra, where Pole found 'few families with any food at all', the situation was equally ghastly. Everything that could be eaten, including the seed corn set aside for spring sowing, had been eaten; and the island's population were subsisting on a debilitating diet of shellfish. Dysentery, typhoid and cholera were even more widespread on Barra than elsewhere in the region. And although most of the many deaths in north-west Scotland that winter were officially attributed to disease, rather than to the hunger which had made disease so prevalent, there not surprisingly occurred in Barra the only two deaths which even the poor law authorities were forced to put down to starvation.

Horrified by his discoveries, Pole found it 'an awful reflection . . . that, at this moment, the wealthy heritor [proprietor] of this island is not employing the poor population'. If Gordon did not at once take action, Pole believed, 'scenes will occur in South Uist, Barra, and Benbecula, which would be disgraceful to his name, and injurious to the reputation of Great Britain'. Sharing those opinions, Coffin at once addressed a fiery letter to Gordon, threatening 'to interpose in favour of the sufferers . . . leaving to parliament to decide whether or not you should be legally responsible for the pecuniary consequences of this just and necessary intervention'. Coffin's threat had the desired effect. Road works were restarted and Gordon's tenants supplied with quantities of meal which, even if they did not come up to Edward Pine Coffin's expectations, were considerably in excess of the amounts which Gordon had planned originally to despatch.

The predicament of crofters in Barra and South Uist was paralleled by that of crofting tenants on properties in every part of north-west Scotland. In January 1847, Sheriff-Substitute Fraser of Fort William was sent to report on the situation in western Inverness-shire and Wester Ross. In every part of that large district, he found 'a considerable population . . . bordering on starvation'. One of the places visited by Fraser was Glenelg, bought in 1837 by Baillie of Dochfour. Already the owner of an extensive estate at the eastern end of Loch Ness, Baillie, like his factor, was an absentee. The one had not been in Glenelg for several years, it was noted. The other

---

*'They were dividing wild spinage at that time.' The translation is John Lorne Campbell's.

came only to collect the rent. Because of its sheltered situation and relatively good soil, Glenelg is one of the more fertile parishes in the north-
west Highlands. In the nineteenth century's opening decades, however, the
greater part of the parish – including the previously cultivated straths of
Glenmore and Glenbeg – were put under sheep and the bulk of the population removed to a few ramshackle and grossly overcrowded townships on
the coast. 'Such a collection of wretched, filthy, smoky, unglazed, and in
every respect comfortless hovels, I have never seen, even in Ireland,' one
visitor remarked. In Glenelg, perhaps more than anywhere else, the famine
thus served to point to the single most tragically ironic consequence of
the clearances: 'Fertile land lying waste at one end of a glen and people
starving at the other'.

On Lord Cranstoun's Arisaig estate, where no fewer than four-fifths of
the entire population were in need of assistance, the position was equally
bleak, Cranstoun and his factor having no more interest in the property
than their Glenelg counterparts: 'The one lifts the rent and the other carries
it off and consumes it; and this comprehends the whole of the relation
between landlord and tenant in Arisaig.' Baillie had at least provided his
crofting tenants with a little meal before abandoning them to the government. But Cranstoun did not make even this gesture, complete catastrophe
being averted only by the heroic efforts of Arisaig's priest, Father William
MacIntosh, assisted, it should be noted, by a local tenant farmer.

Examples of this sort of proprietorial apathy could be multiplied endlessly.
One Ross-shire laird expressed his regrets about his tenants' virtual starvation, but added that he could do nothing to save them 'till a more convenient season'. An Inverness-shire landowner, meanwhile, kept all the meal
on his estate locked up in a store which, as one of Coffin's men remarked
bitterly, 'might as well be in China'. And if north-west Scotland generally
was unlucky in its landlords, the Hebrides were particularly unfortunate.
In Mull, according to Tobermory's sheriff, the proprietorial class's conduct
was 'with a few honourable exceptions . . . extremely remiss and impolitic'.
In Skye, it was reported by Major Haliday, the officer in charge of the
government's Portree meal depot, 'MacLeod of MacLeod is the only thoroughly active and good landlord of the larger class and Mr. MacLennan
of Lyndall of the smaller.' Of Skye's other landowners, Haliday singled
out Lord MacDonald for particular censure. Confronted with a destitute
population of about 14,000, he had agreed to employ 400 of them on a
government-funded drainage project – which he had abandoned within a
few weeks of its commencement. As for Lord MacDonald's crofting tenants
in North Uist, they were most assisted by the shipwreck of a vessel that
chanced to be laden with £15,000 worth of flour and other provisions.

In the face of the landowning fraternity's unhelpful stance, official
attempts to coerce reluctant landlords into purchasing supplies for their
tenants met with little success. Lord MacDonald's factor, for example,

bought a considerable quantity of meal in Liverpool. On pausing to consider, however, he decided that he could not transport it to Skye 'without being forced to sell it at a great loss'. The meal was consequently resold in Liverpool – and since prices were steadily rising the MacDonald estate management made 'a handsome profit' on the transaction. The upshot, as the Portree meal depot's Major Haliday remarked caustically, was that Lord MacDonald's crofters had to come to Portree 'every week, often distances of 30 or 40 miles from the extreme points of the island, to procure the food which he or his factor would not import for them'.

Because of proprietors' evident lack of enthusiasm for the role which the government had optimistically assigned to them, the pattern of events on Lord MacDonald's estate was repeated throughout the north-west. An early ruling that the two meal depots' wares be sold only to landlords – to be redistributed by them in the form of wages to crofters employed on drainage projects – was, of necessity, revoked. Instead meal was sold directly to its consumers. In townships, and occasionally in groups of townships, crofters duly clubbed their meagre savings together to raise the cash needed for the minimum quantities of meal that depot regulations allowed them to buy. Long, tedious and sometimes dangerous journeys had to be made to Portree and Tobermory from districts separated from these places by many miles of bad roads and rough seas. At the end of it all, crofters had bought £24,000 worth of government meal – as against the £12,000 worth purchased by their landlords. Although Coffin's assertion that his measures had 'saved the people from inevitable starvation' is consequently unchallengeable, the cost to the crofting population was immense. One inevitable outcome was that the spring of 1847 found crofters without the cash required to buy the seeds needed if that year was to provide any kind of harvest.

Seed potatoes had been destroyed by blight. Stocks of seed oats, especially important because of the obvious risk of renewed potato crop failures, were generally low and, in some areas, such as Barra, the Uists and Arisaig, non-existent – for the simple reason that they had had to be eaten during the winter. The government refused to supply the necessary seed on the somewhat dubious grounds that to do so would be to subsidise landlords. And Coffin's immediate priority became the task of persuading proprietors to make good the deficiency. Despite a government offer to cover transport costs, however, Highland landlords were no more eager to supply their crofters with seed than they had been to provide them with meal. Lord MacDonald, for example, refused to sell seed corn to his tenants except at prices 'which their present necessities deprive them of the power of taking advantage of'. And suspecting that grants made to their impoverished tenantries would never be recovered, many other proprietors adopted a similar stance – with the result, as Emily MacLeod, MacLeod of Dunvegan's sister, pointed out, that 'many a crofter had the misery of seeing his land lie fallow'. By the spring of 1847, in fact, even Dunvegan's laird was becoming dispirited. Engaged 'in discouraging the cultivation of land for which the crofters [were] unable of themselves to buy seed', he was, he wrote, 'getting very low about it all' and wished himself 'away from this scene of wretchedness'. Although Coffin's exhortations, supplemented by some charitable funds from the south, did something to encourage both MacLeod and several other proprietors to further exertions, the spring sowing was neither as large nor as early as it should have been.

In view of the magnitude of crofters' troubles and the generally lackadaisical attitude of their landlords, it was perhaps fortunate that the British government was not left to shoulder all the responsibility for famine relief in the Highlands. First to come to the government's aid was the Free Church whose Argyll Synod began to collect funds and distribute food in September and October 1846. In November, with the appointment of a Free Church Destitution Committee, the Argyll Synod's endeavours were extended to the whole of Scotland. More than £15,000 was quickly raised, and the Free Church schooner, *Breadalbane*, built to carry ministers around the Hebrides, was used to ship provisions to the more destitute islands. Although many such islands were Free Church strongholds, the church's response to the famine was notably and laudably free of sectarianism – nobody speaking more highly of its efforts than the Catholic crofters of Moidart and Arisaig. But charitable feeling was not, of course, a Free Church prerogative. At public meetings in Edinburgh and Glasgow on 18 December and 6 January, influential and wholly undenominational committees were formed to raise funds for Highland famine relief.

To the government's harassed officials, those developments were a godsend. Edward Pine Coffin believed that the various relief organisations represented the Highlands' only chance of averting a catastrophe similar to that occurring in Ireland. And Charles Trevelyan – who was of the opinion that the Irish crisis had 'proved to demonstration that local distress cannot be relieved out of national funds without great abuses and evils, tending, by a direct and rapid process, to an entire disorganisation of society' – treated the emergence of the Edinburgh and Glasgow committees as a glorious opportunity for government to extricate itself from the Highland morass. Declaring it to be obvious that 'the temporary evil [of famine] ought to be met by the temporary expedient of private charity', Trevelyan instructed Coffin to furnish the two committees 'with all the information . . . calculated to direct their exertions into useful channels'. Under government pressure, therefore, the Glasgow and Edinburgh groupings were quickly unified as the clumsily entitled Central Board of Management of the Fund for the Relief of the Destitute Inhabitants of the Highlands. This body held its first meeting in February 1847, its members being assured by the Treasury that they could 'depend upon receiving all the countenance and assistance which it is in our power to give'.

Although the Central Board of Management took overall responsibility for fund-raising and food distribution, its component parts retained a considerable degree of independence – the Glasgow group, or 'section' as it now became, taking charge of the board's operations in Argyll, western Inverness-shire and the Outer Isles, while the Edinburgh Section was entrusted with Wester Ross, Skye, the eastern part of the mainland and the Northern Isles. Answering to each section were committees appointed in each parish or district from lists of names supplied by local clergymen. Those committees were entrusted with the actual distribution of meal to the hungry – the stipulated allowance being one-and-a-half pounds of meal per adult male per day, with women receiving three-quarters of a pound and children under twelve a half-pound. Although calculated to do no more than prevent starvation, this ration, by contemporary standards, was not ungenerous. When the potatoes failed in Lewis in the spring of 1837, for instance, the estate authorities' allowance to crofters had been only half-a-pound of meal per adult male per day – even a pound being considered 'far too high' by MacKenzie of Seaforth's factor. And in Ireland, as Trevelyan informed the Central Relief Board, 'one pound of good meal, properly cooked' was thought 'amply sufficient for an able bodied person'. For crofters and their slowly starving families, however, there was understandably little comfort in such comparisons. Each weekly or fortnightly distribution of 'destitution meal' was thus a most cheerless affair:

> At the appointed time and place the poor creatures troop down in hundreds, wretched and thin, starved and wan. Some have clothing, some almost none, and some are a mass of rags. Old and young, feeble and infirm, they take their stations and await their turn. Not a murmur, not a clamour, not a word – but they wept aloud as they told of their miseries.

The Central Relief Board's appearance, then, by no means signalled an end to the crofting population's sufferings. Its immediate achievements, nevertheless, were remarkable. In the spring and early summer of 1847, the particularly hazardous period before the new harvest, the board supplied the greater part of the Highlands' emergency provisions – the Glasgow Section alone despatching 7,047 bolls of wheatmeal, 5,696 bolls of oatmeal, 1,980 bolls of peasemeal and 690 bolls of indian corn meal, or maize, in the first three months of its existence. All this was made possible by a veritable flood of contributions. By April 1847, the Relief Board's resources amounted to £138,175 – and they eventually totalled more than £250,000. Most of these funds were raised in Scotland. But large donations were also received from England and from Scottish emigrants in Canada and the USA – the latter sending several thousand barrels of meal, flour and beef as well as cash. And although the strange new cereals – such as maize – which now put in an appearance in crofting areas were viewed with some initial suspicion, even by people who had nothing else to eat, crofters and their families soon adapted to life without potatoes: making good use of the seeds sent them by the Relief Board as partial substitutes for their former staple crop. By the summer of 1847, 'flourishing crops of the most useful roots and other vegetables . . . some of them previously unknown in the country', were to be seen all over the Highlands. And the government – by no means alone in crediting the board with the prevention of many thousands of deaths from starvation – had decided that it could safely end its 'unnatural' intervention in Highland affairs. Coffin's meal depots were accordingly closed and their remaining stocks sold to the Relief Board which thus inherited the task of warding off renewed famine.

The Relief Board's original intention had been that its operations should last for only one season – ceasing 'as soon as the harvest will enable the people to have their wants supplied by the new crop'. As the summer of 1847 advanced, these optimistic expectations were encouraged by the prospect of an unusually good harvest. In Mull, for example, 'there never was . . . in the memory of the present generation, so luxuriant and promising a crop.' The board's calculations, however, turned out to be based on a false premise – for, even if the harvest had come up to expectation, insufficient food would have been provided. Only about one-sixth of the usual quantity of potatoes had been planted, and replacement crops of oats and barley could not possibly make good the resulting shortfall since, on a conservative estimate, it took at least three acres of grain to equal the food value of one acre of potatoes. Although crofters who occupied larger than average holdings were at something of an advantage, almost all crofters were bound to run short. As Edward Pine Coffin remarked before leaving the Highlands in September, 'the only point undetermined was the probable extent of the deficiency'. The nutritional value of the forthcoming harvest, Coffin believed, would be between 50 and 75 per cent of normal. And even that estimate proved unduly optimistic. In the early autumn, the weather broke and, for several weeks the whole of the north-west was swept by almost incessant rain and gales. Crofters' corn was flattened and practically destroyed, while a new outbreak of blight decimated the already scanty crop of potatoes.

Having suspended its food distributions as planned, the Relief Board soon found itself pressed to resume them. Norman MacLeod, who visited the Outer Isles in August and who was particularly horrified by what he saw on John Gordon's island properties, was certainly in no doubt about the need for renewed assistance:

> The scene of wretchedness which we witnessed as we entered on the estate of Col. Gordon was deplorable, nay heart-rending. On the beach the whole population of the country seemed to be met, gathering the precious cockles . . . I never witnessed such countenances – starvation on many faces – the children with their melancholy looks, big-looking knees, shrivelled legs, hollow

eyes, swollen-like bellies – God help them, I never did witness such wretched-ness!

As the summer of 1847 gave way to a wet and windy autumn, moreover, it became clear that hunger and malnutrition were not confined to a few unfortunate localities. In Skye, the potatoes had 'absolutely gone' by November, and destitution was reported to be 'fast increasing'. The entire population of Wester Ross was in serious difficulty by December, and not a few families were 'on the verge of starvation'. In those areas, as in Arisaig, Tiree, Barra, the Uists and Harris, where the position was 'so deplorable as to cause serious apprehension', the situation was, if anything, worse than it had been a year before. The Relief Board's eventual decision that it would have to resume its duties, therefore, was something of a foregone conclusion.

The board's assumption of a role that was more permanent than the one originally envisaged for it by its members and supporters was accompanied by its adoption of a mode of management which, if more efficient than that which it replaced, was also more autocratic and, it followed, less in touch with the people for whose benefit the board's funds had been provided. Their local committees, board members felt, had been unhealthily demo-cratic. Some committees had included crofters who were themselves in receipt of relief. And all such committees, it was commented, had shown a lamentable tendency to act as 'the representatives and advocates of those seeking relief . . . rather than [as representatives] of the relieving party'. That crofters should have even this meagre influence over their own fate was something that the Highlands' ruling class was not prepared to concede. It is no coincidence, then, that from landlords, factors, sheep farmers and other 'respectable people' the Relief Board's representatives heard 'the same tale about the indolence and worthlessness of the people, and how poor ignorant lotters were sitting in committee distributing meal to them-selves'. Which of the two sides in north-west Scotland's rapidly intensifying social conflict had most influence over the board was made clear by its instructions concerning the appointment of the paid staff of inspectors, sub-inspectors, relief officers and overseers who, it was decided, should replace local committees: 'They must be men of intelligence and firmness, who will do their duty as representing the board, and not by sympathising with the people.'

Within a few weeks of its formation, Sir Charles Trevelyan had made clear to the Central Board exactly how he expected its operations to be conducted:

> Next to allowing the people to die of hunger, the greatest evil that could happen would be their being habituated to depend upon public charity. The object to be arrived at, therefore, is to prevent the assistance given from being productive of idleness and if possible, to make it conducive to increased exer-tion.

In accordance with those instructions and in accordance, too, with then standard theories as to the purpose of poor relief, the board had initially tried to ensure 'that money or labour shall be extracted from those supplied with food' by ordering local committees to provide employment on road construction works and similar projects. This the committees had signally failed to do, their general attitude being summed up in the reply received by a poor law official who had 'expressed surprise [to one committee] that relief was ever given without requiring labour'. 'There is no work to give them,' he was told, 'and they cannot starve.'

In order to ensure that such old-fashioned humanitarianism should not continue to triumph over the economic and moral assumptions of the Victorian governing order, the Relief Board began its new season by introducing what it liked to refer to as its 'labour test'. The meal ration remained the same as before – although an adult male's one-and-a-half pounds could now be reduced to a pound 'as a penalty upon idleness'. But meal was only to be distributed in return for eight hours' work a day, six days a week. The recipient of such aid received an automatic allowance for each child under twelve years of age. But older children got meal only 'in return for such work as they can give', while wives and mothers were required to take up knitting and spinning in order to qualify for assistance. Charles Trevelyan, of course, approved. Others were less appreciative, the editor of the *Inverness Advertiser* arguing, for example, that 'The cruel and demoralising principle has been to exact a maximum of labour for a minimum of wages.'

That wages – paid in meal or in tokens which could be exchanged only for meal – were low was unchallengeable. For three of the four years during which the Relief Board's 'test' was in operation in the Highlands the price of meal was one penny a pound. A married man with six children (large families being the rule) thus received for his week's work the meal equivalent of under three shillings. The lowest wages paid on the open market at this time were about six shillings a week, with even those crofters labouring on the Duke of Sutherland's privately organised famine relief projects getting about a shilling a day. And if the plight of a family man forced to labour on Relief Board schemes was bad, that of a single man was worse. For his six days of often backbreaking work such a man received exactly ninepence worth of meal. That this was a pittance, even Relief Board members admitted. But their object, they added, was to make relief 'necessarily unpalatable', 'a test of destitution', a last resort.

The Relief Board's much vaunted 'labour test', then, aroused widespread discontent and bitterness – emotions intensified by the fact that it was administered by a well-paid staff. Emily MacLeod summarised the prevailing mood:

> [Crofters] feel the injustice of being paid at a very low rate out of what they
> not unnaturally consider their own money, and are exasperated at seeing

gentlemen living in comfort on what they know was subscribed for them, while they have to walk, often without shoes and always in insufficient clothing . . . to the source of labour where, after working for eight hours, they receive the value of 1½d.

That many crofters preferred to endure their 'many privations' rather than submit to the degrading indignity of the Relief Bord's 'test' is not really surprising. Still less surprising is the fact that the Free Church's Synod of Argyll, which had taken the initiative in raising the relief fund, should feel moved, because of 'the inadequacy for the comfortable support of human life of the [Relief Board] allowance', to 'memorialise the Central Relief Board to represent to them the necessity of distributing with a more liberal hand the funds placed at their disposal by a generous public'.

To such appeals, as to more immoderately worded allegations that the half-starved recipients of relief were collapsing on the roads they had been ordered to construct, board members paid little heed – even when they received corroboration of the validity of their critics' complaints from their own staff. 'The people are very willing to work,' the Relief Board's Lochalsh inspector reported, 'but so much are they weakened by insufficient food that much work cannot be got out of them.'

The Relief Board's new system of management, according to one journalist, consisted of 'a huge staff of stipendiaries on liberal pay, and multitudes of starving supplicants receiving a modicum of meal'. It was, a Skye minister observed of the same system, 'nothing more' than a means of 'spending the fund of the charitable [while] starving those for whom it was intended'. The board's members, however, were well satisfied. Expenses admittedly were higher. In 1847, for example, relief operations in Skye had been administered by eight committees, each one consisting of a number of unpaid volunteers. In 1848, an inspector, 13 relief officers and a dozen overseers were required to do the same job, and their wage bill alone amounted to about £100 a month. In an analysis of the amounts of meal distributed over the two years, however, is to be seen the effect of the 'test' and the cause of the board's gratification. Despite 'an equal amount of destitution', the average fortnightly allowance of meal to Skye crofters fell from 1,280 bolls in 1847 to 330 bolls in 1848. In Wester Ross the corresponding figures were 938 and 254 bolls respectively. And in Tiree, although there was – as between 1847 and 1848 – 'much more destitution' and a consequent increase in the number of recipients, a similar reduction was achieved.

As in the previous year, the Relief Board's operations were temporarily suspended in September. But prospects for the winter of 1848–49 were even more dismal than those of 12 months before. The potato harvest failed more or less completely, and the grain crop was so late that in many areas it remained uncut. In Wester Ross, for instance, crofters' corn was still green when the first snow fell in October. Matters were made worse by an 'unusually unproductive' herring fishing and by a falling away in demand for labour in the south – a development which meant that temporary migration to the Lowlands no longer provided crofters with a way out of their troubles.

While not unwilling to recommence its activities in the autumn of 1848, the Relief Board was uncomfortably aware that its resources, though still considerable, were not unlimited – especially since it was now called upon to extend its operations into areas such as Lewis and Sutherland whose proprietors, tempted by the prospect of getting something for nothing, had overcome original scruples about the damage that might be done to their carefully cultivated 'improving' images by a tacit admission that charitable aid was needed to bail out their tenantries. In 1849, therefore, the board changed direction yet again – its aim, on this occasion, being to make the Highlands and Islands more self-sufficient and thus to prepare crofters for the eventually inevitable cessation of external assistance.

The board's new policy depended on the development of north-west Scotland's economic infrastructure and on getting the region's landowners to take an active interest in that development. This policy had its origins in a Relief Board's decision, of February 1848, to provide a Wester Ross estate management with half the £2,500 required for the construction of a road along the southern shore of Loch Maree – the sum in question being made available on condition that the landlord benefiting from it provided his crofting tenants with work on his road construction project. This 'system of co-operation', as it became known, neatly met all the board's requirements: it involved proprietors in famine relief projects, allowed the board to reduce its staff and, theoretically at least, helped to develop the Highlands' natural resources. On a less favourable view, it was 'a monstrous malversation of a charitable fund . . . giving largesse to noblemen and gentlemen who . . . have improved their estates by means of public subscription'. But either way, the new mode of management was as popular with Highland landlords as it was with the Relief Board. In 1849, when every proprietor in Gairloch and Lochbroom received funds for road construction and when the board agreed to meet half the cost of a 34-mile road from Lairg to Loch Laxford on the Sutherland estate, the 'system of co-operation' was extended to most parts of the north-west mainland. About a thousand people were employed on Wester Ross roadworks during 1849, and by 1850 the area's landlords were in possession of a 90-mile network of new roads, linking Ullapool, Poolewe and Gairloch to Dingwall.

Those 'destitution roads', as the highways in question became known, were the Central Relief Board's great practical accomplishment – its other developmental efforts making little tangible impact on the Highland scene. Between 1848 and 1850, admittedly, the board made a strenuous attempt to modernise the region's fishing industry by building a number of piers and jetties and by supplying fishermen and crofters with boats, gear and free instruction in deep-sea fishing techniques. But despite these investments, no general increase in efficiency and productivity was reported. The board's piers, according to the fishery authorities, were 'spoken of slightingly'. This was hardly surprising if the jetties built in Loch Torridon and in Loch Kishorn were typical of the rest:

> Both of them were small and insubstantial erections. The first, it was said by the fishermen, had been erected too far up the loch to be of service to them. The second had been left unfinished.

Attempts to establish a hosiery industry in Skye were scarcely more encouraging. Having originated as a suitable female employment under the infamous 'test', the industry got off the ground in 1848 when the Relief Board entered into a marketing contract with an Aberdeenshire businessman. At a cost of over £1,500, the businessman in question was provided with a spinning and carding mill in Portree. By 1850, ten women were employed in the mill itself, while over a thousand outworkers were turning out more than 1,600 pairs of stockings a month. To fulfil their production quotas the crofters' wives and daughters who were thus employed had to 'knit along the road, oftentimes with their creels full of peats on their backs . . . Thus a good knitter may earn, with diligence and industry, something less than one penny a day'. This, on any basis, was the grossest of exploitation. It was made all the more unacceptable by the fact that the Aberdeenshire entrepreneur who was its sole beneficiary had not even been obliged, thanks to the board's generosity, to capitalise his venture.

The Central Relief Board's developmental policies, then, made little impression on the overall Highland situation which, instead of improving, showed every sign of deteriorating still further. 1849 brought even more poverty and hunger than 1848 had done – as was indicated by the position in Skye where, 'notwithstanding a management even more strict . . . than that of [the previous] year', the number of people receiving relief rose from 5,559 to 8,162. That summer a deputation from the Relief Board's Glasgow Section visited the Outer Isles to see the effects of famine for themselves. They found islanders 'living in miserable hovels, not a few miserably clad, children looking half starved and prematurely old – in short, misery, wretchedness and destitution in many a form'. A better harvest and a more successful herring fishing meant that the winter of 1849–50 was a little less bleak for crofters. But the crisis was by no means over when, in September 1850, its funds exhausted, the Relief Board suspended its operations for the last time.

At the start of the Highland famine, Sir George Grey, then in charge of the Home Office, had expressed a hope that 'permanent benefit may ultimately be derived from the calamity by the introduction of a better system of agricultural management and by a consequent improvement in the social condition of the people'. The same hope underlay the Central Relief Board's original statement of its objectives:

> To improve the condition of the people and to develop the resources of the country; to prevent the recurrence of so great a calamity and convert the sufferings of the people into the germ of their future amelioration.

Those goals the board had manifestly failed to achieve. An official enquiry into the Highland situation in the spring of 1851 concluded that 'no sensible progress has been made, and the state of the population continues to decline'. The consequent, and very prevalent, sense of disillusionment was summed up in an *Inverness Courier* editorial: 'The result of this splendid fund has altogether been so unpopular and so unproductive generally . . . that we are convinced no such subscription will ever again be raised for the Highlands.' As events in the 1880s and the 1920s were to show, that last prognostication proved unduly pessimistic. But that it could be made at all is a measure of the Relief Board's inability to measure up to its own aspirations.

One reason for the board's lack of success was that its programme was simply too ambitious. Such an organisation, no matter how enthusiastically conceived and managed, could not bring about the social and economic revolution which it envisaged. Even within the limits of the possible, however, the wrong objectives were often pursued. Road construction, on which so much money was spent, provides a case in point – not least because the board's roads were usually undertaken with landlords', rather than crofters', needs in view. Thus the principal function of the road from Lairg to Loch Laxford was to open up the remote southern and western portions of the Duke of Sutherland's Reay deer forest – its completion being quickly followed by the erection of shooting lodges at Stack and at Lochinver. And in an underdeveloped economy of the Highland sort, as was pointed out by a critic of Sir James Matheson's roads in Lewis, the last people likely to benefit from an expanded road network were crofters: 'The tangible benefits in the shape of improved communications do not come home to those who . . . wish nothing to be brought to them, and have nothing to send away.' As was remarked by the editor of the *Inverness Advertiser*, more permanent good would have been done by injecting much needed capital into crofting townships through a concerted effort to improve access roads, provide agricultural instruction, and encourage draining, fencing and other improvements. But far from changing crofting agriculture for the better, the Central Relief Board's activities often served merely to aggravate the damage already done to it by famine and by negligent land management.

In charge of board policies were a small group of Edinburgh and Glasgow lawyers and businessmen, 'with an admixture of small Lowland proprietors'. Those individuals knew very little about the Highlands and still less about crofting. But on the subjects of poverty and poor relief, they possessed all the prejudices of the classes to which they belonged. The inevitable outcome was that, instead of taking a wide and sympathetic view of the situation confronting its representatives in the Highlands, the Central Relief Board – encouraged and supported by Treasury officials, most notably Charles Trevelyan, whose views were equally circumscribed – subjected crofters to a regime based on what one irate Skyeman referred to as 'petty workhouse rules'. A classic example of the idiocies that resulted is provided by one of the board's 1848 directives:

> Parties who possess means of their own, or who have not consumed the produce of their ground or stock, or whose property is sufficient to enable them to render their credit available, are not [to be considered] destitute until their means are exhausted.

Crofters' attempts to conserve seeds and stock were thus nullified. They were compelled to eat the former and sell the latter before being granted relief. And although this particular rule was eventually rescinded, most of the board's regulations – often enforced by utterly unimaginative officials, and consequently as 'unalterable as the laws of the Medes and the Persians' – proved quite immutable. Crofters who worked their own holdings instead of labouring on the board's projects were refused meal and in many instances, therefore, starving tenants had virtually to abandon their crofts in order to obtain food for themselves and their families. The hostility engendered by the board's 'labour test' was thus increased, and their ensuing bitterness made crofters understandably unwilling to co-operate with the board's officials on fishery development and other more sensible aspects of board policy.

Because Relief Board rules forced crofters to sell their cattle and to convert their few savings into food, board policy had the effect of completing what had been well begun by three decades of steadily growing poverty: the crofting population was bereft of almost all capital resources. One consequence was that many of the marginally more affluent crofters, folk who could once have raised the funds needed to emigrate, were no longer able to afford even this way out of the dilemmas facing them.

The Relief Board's members, to be fair, were not entirely unaware of the importance of the Highland economy's agrarian base. But they could do very little to promote the better utilisation of the land without the whole-hearted co-operation of the men who owned it. This fact was recognised by no less a personage than Sir Robert Peel – who responded to the Highland famine by expressing the hope that Highland landlords would show sufficient 'public spirit . . . and enough of sympathy with the position of their crofting tenants' to take the lead in a programme of agricultural improvement. Peel, however, did not know his Highland landowners. The area's landed proprietors, Relief Board members declared in one of their more exasperated moments, showed 'an entire want of faith in the possibility of improving the position of the people, or any desire to aid in the attempt'. Supported by sheep farmers who, as Edward Pine Coffin had discovered, were only too eager to oppose any scheme 'which promises to have the effect of confirming the people in the tenure of land which they would prefer to see in their own occupation', Highland landlords consistently refused the Relief Board's pleas to grant leases to crofters – not least because most such landlords were engaged in the wholesale eviction of their crofting tenants. In the absence of crofting leases, the board, for its part, felt unable to encourage crofters to carry out improvements which might well be followed by the improver's ejection from his holding. Some sort of security of tenure, declared one of the Central Relief Board's more intelligent inspectors, was 'the keystone to every exertion on the part of the crofter' – an opinion shared by a leading economist of the period, G. Poulett Scrope, and one that received striking confirmation in the spring of 1849 when a reluctant Lord MacDonald promised one of the board's representatives that he would grant eight-year leases to crofters who – in return for standard allocations of board meal – improved their holdings by draining and enclosing them. As the Relief Board's Edinburgh Section was informed by its delighted inspector in Skye:

> The immediate effect of this new annunciation was the betrayal of an enthu-siasm so long and unexceptionably dormant that there was a general doubt of its existence, but which took the true and practical direction of a general change, from vegetative apathy and stagnant indifference, to the bustle and industrious business which new hopes, opening prospects, confidence, and self-interest engendered. I myself, in the course of an eight-mile drive . . . found that the people were at work, without superintendence, from before six in the morning, until the shades of evening fell, and I counted something more than 100 new drains opened on the second day of the new system in the same district.

But while most other Skye proprietors entered into similar contracts in 1850, these arrangements were never extended to other districts. Even in Skye, moreover, the agreements made between landlords and their crofting tenants were so hedged about with unnecessarily complicated conditions that they were easily broken when the Central Relief Board's inspectors had departed for the last time. Lord MacDonald's own estate was to be the scene of some of the most extensive clearances of the 1850s. The enthu-siastic activity of the spring of 1849 thus remained only a momentary glimpse of what might have been: a forgotten precedent for the widespread improvements which followed the true security of tenure that crofters were finally to gain in 1886.

5

FEWER PEOPLE, LESS LAND

1850–1857

Far from bringing about a regeneration of the crofting economy, as Central Relief Board members and some politicians had hoped in their more sanguine moments, the famine of the 1840s served only to intensify Highland proprietors' hostility to the crofting system and to make 'redundancy of population' an even more 'prominent topic of lamentation' in landowning circles. A tenantry that could scarcely prevent its own starvation was unlikely to produce a worthwhile rental, and it seemed to landlords, therefore, that the famine had conclusively demonstrated the complete bankruptcy of crofting as a way of profitably organising their estates. If a very large number of people were not at once removed from the Highlands, warned MacLeod of Dunvegan's factor in 1850, several well-known lairds would 'very soon bid adieu to their properties' and join the growing list of landed families who had already sunk in a sea of debts. Of the risk they ran of being added to that list, many of the region's landowners were only too well aware, and the immediate effect of the famine on land management policies was thus to accelerate and to intensify an already existing tendency to make sheep farming the main prop of estate economies in districts where kelping, and therefore crofting, had once been dominant – a development necessarily accompanied by further clearances. In a consequent reversal of long-established demographic patterns, the total Highland population, which had been growing for at least 100 years, began to fall – the immediate cause of the decline being a new wave of emigration.

Landowners' conviction that emigration was the answer to their problems stemmed from their belief that it would free them 'at once and forever', as was said at the time 'from the care of their burthensome dependents'. And the cost, it was hoped by the more optimistic spirits among them, would be minimal – because 'any large plan of emigration must become a national undertaking, and therefore be conducted at the public expense'. To interest the government in such a scheme, it was necessary to argue that massive emigration from north-west Scotland would be simultaneously of benefit to Britain's overseas colonies and to the crofting population: by adding to the talents at the disposal of the former, and by removing the latter from a life that had little to offer but poverty, hunger and distress.

Highland landlords' propaganda skills were accordingly deployed to this end almost from the moment that the famine began. But for men professedly concerned solely with their tenants' welfare, they showed a rather suspicious tendency, it was commented, to maintain 'against all assurances and evidences to the contrary' that the colonies 'afforded an unlimited field for the reception of an emigrant population without discrimination of age, sex, or capacity', while simultaneously denying that the industrial areas of southern Scotland offered more than the most transient and unattractive prospects. Edward Pine Coffin, who noted this phenomenon with wry amusement, drew his own conclusion:

> As it is plainly the desire of those who press for a reduction of numbers that the emigrant . . . should not have the power of returning, their indisposition to promote that form of removal which gives him the option leaves room to doubt the entire disinterestedness of the motive.

By the end of the 1840s, to give a specific instance of why it was that promotion of emigration made such excellent sense to landlords, Lord MacDonald's debts amounted to no less than £218,000 – and his creditors were becoming increasingly impatient. The MacDonald family fortunes, it was clear, could be saved only by fairly massive borrowing. But the necessary loans proved difficult to raise – not least on account of Lord MacDonald's bankers objecting to his rental being 'spread over such a number of small tenantry'. It was left to Lord MacDonald's factor to draw the obvious conclusion. During the preceding 40 years, he pointed out, those sheep farms which had been enlarged by the simple expedient of evicting such crofters as lived beside them had gained greatly in value – thus demonstrating 'the immense advantage to the proprietor of encouraging the system of clearing croft farms adjoining the larger possessions'. Lord MacDonald's chaotic finances, his lordship's factor believed, could best be repaired by a more widespread and thorough application of the same principle. And since much the same could be said of every estate in northwest Scotland, mass emigration – which, as one commentator shrewdly remarked, 'they never regarded as beneficial to their tenants until it began to appear advantageous to themselves' – came to be more and more assiduously canvassed by the landed class.

Highland sheep farmers, whose industry was entering a period of unprecedented profitability, adopted a similar stance – thus ensuring a further diminution of their standing among the crofting population. Of one Lochcarron sheep farmer 'it was commonly reported among the people that he never saw a green spot of earth but he coveted it as his own'. And that characterisation, if unduly unkind, was by no means unfounded – immoderately expressed opinion to the effect that 'the larger farmers of the Highlands . . [were] the scourges of the people' being supported by a considerable weight of more sober testimony. Thus Edward Pine Coffin 'constantly' heard from sheep farmers that emigration was 'the sole remedy for the distress of the country'. Their 'evident aim', he reported of such farmers, was 'to depopulate the districts which they occupy'. And because their rents constituted the largest and most dependable part of their landlords' incomes, sheep farmers could exercise influence out of all proportion to their numbers – influence increased by the fact that they, unlike crofters, had the ear of estate managements. The typical factor was invariably of the same social standing as the sheep farmers on the estate he administered, had many friends among them and was willing always to heed their views. In many instances, indeed, factors – Patrick Sellar being one such – farmed sheep on their own account, their greatest source of earnings often consisting of the favourable lease granted them by the landlords who were their employers. Since crofters' feelings counted for next to nothing, all those who mattered on Highland estates were in favour, then, of clearance and emigration. But while there is thus no reason to doubt the judgement of the Skye factor who subsequently declared that 'the great rise in the value of sheep' was 'the real cause' of the widespread evictions of the mid-nineteenth century, there was another important reason for landlords' and farmers' all-too-evident desire to be rid of the crofting population: the working of the new Scots Poor Law.

Throughout north-west Scotland, the aid available to paupers from official funds was – before the passing of the new Poor Law in 1846 – so small as to be almost negligible. Poor rates being unknown, annual allowances to the poor were sometimes as low as two shillings, and seldom exceeded ten shillings, even in cases of special necessity. Persons classified as paupers thus depended on the charity of friends and relatives who, though by no means affluent themselves, adhered to the traditional view that the destitute had a natural right to food and clothing – speaking of a person in need, not as a beggar, but as someone *ag iarraidh a'chodach*, seeking or asking his portion. Such communal solidarity, however, held little attraction for Victorian poor law reformers. In 1846, therefore, the Highlands were treated in exactly the same way as the rest of Scotland, a legally enforced poor rate taking the place of the voluntary contributions on which the poor had previously relied. Crofters derived considerable benefits from this change. But landed proprietors and sheep farmers – who had been united in opposing it – were forced, as the only ratepayers of consequence in much of the Highlands and Islands, to shoulder a new and unwelcome burden which immediately became all the heavier with the onset of famine. By the early 1850s, the poor rate in three of the parishes on the MacDonald estate in Skye amounted to 15 per cent of the gross rental and the local rate had become one of the subjects meticulously enquired into by prospective buyers of the many Highland properties then coming on to the market. In Skye and the Outer Hebrides as a whole, it was calculated in 1852, the poor rate stood at around 2s. 8d. in the pound as compared to a Scottish average of under two shillings. And much worse, it was feared, was to come.

On the Central Relief Board's final withdrawal from the Highland scene in the autumn of 1850, the government received numerous, sometimes frantic, appeals for renewed assistance. These, however, were rejected on the grounds, first, that the aid made available in the 1840s had not produced 'any permanent improvement in the condition of the people' and on the grounds, second, that the time had come for Highland expenditure to be met from Highland resources. In the implementation of such a policy, the poor law seemed destined initially to play little part – for the simple reason that, under its provisions, the victims of famine and destitution counted as 'able-bodied' and 'occasional' poor who were not entitled to assistance. No doubt prompted by the government, the Scottish poor law authorities had determined by 1851, however, to take advantage of the provisions made by the 1846 Act for the 'temporary relief' of such persons. Under those provisions, Highland poor law boards were informed, they had to accept responsibility for famine relief and they were duly instructed to extract from landlords, farmers and other ratepayers 'the largest amount of assessment' which the latter were 'able to pay'. This highly dubious interpretation of the 1846 Act was eventually to be challenged successfully in the courts. But by that time the damage had been done. An analogous decision that Irish landlords should help to meet the cost of famine relief had been a major stimulus to clearance and eviction in Ireland. And the imposition of a heavy Highland poor rate, combined with the threat of still heavier rates in the future, undoubtedly contributed to the same result in north-west Scotland.

As had been the case since the Highland clearances began some 50 years before, evictions and removals had their apologists among some of the most influential sections of southern public opinion. In the Highlands as in Ireland, declared *The Economist,* the famine had shown that 'the departure of the redundant part of the population is an indispensable preliminary to every kind of improvement.' And though mid-nineteenth-century Scotland's small band of pro-crofter pamphleteers could take some comfort from the writings of the one or two economists – notably G. Poulett Scrope and W. P. Alison – who were prepared to argue that the Highlands' economic salvation lay not so much in the deportation of crofting tenants as in the development of a reformed crofting system incorporating greater security of tenure and other incentives to agricultural betterment, it was the more orthodox viewpoint of *The Economist* that found most favour at an official level. At that level, by the 1850s, a rapid reduction in the region's population was widely seen as the only way of permanently improving Highland prospects.

This attitude was in marked contrast to that prevailing in 1846 and 1847 when, despite the pleas of MacLeod of Dunvegan and other proprietors, there had been no question of paying for emigration out of public funds. The change of front is partly attributable to the disillusionment caused by the Relief Board's obvious failure to do more than prevent the actual starvation of the crofting population – a disillusionment which, by 1849, had led to some of the board's own members advocating the deployment of a part of the famine relief fund in the emigration sphere. Although the board subsequently assisted 1,155 people to make their way to Canada, it did so only on condition that crofts vacated by emigrants were used to enlarge neighbouring holdings – aid being refused, for example, to Gordon of Cluny on the grounds that lands relinquished by Uist and Barra emigrants were being added to sheep farms. To its own satisfaction at any rate, the Central Relief Board thus succeeded in squaring its advocacy of emigration with its obligations to the crofters for whose benefit its funds had been collected. But the Board of Supervision, the body charged with the task of administering the Scotland's poor law, had to contend with no such scruples. Impressed by the Central Relief Board's lack of success and convinced – with a zeal that would have done justice to characters in a Dickensian satire – that generous assistance to the poor was more debilitating than poverty itself, the poor law authorities had, by the early 1850s, become firmly attached to the idea of emigration. They decided, to put the matter bluntly, to starve crofters into emigrating. And their determination to make the Highland poor law boards responsible for the relief of destitution in their own areas was in part designed to make such emigration still more likely.

That the government shared poor law administrators' views was borne out, in January 1851, by the appointment of Sir John MacNeill, chairman of the Board of Supervision, to conduct an enquiry into the state of the Highlands and Islands. MacNeill's pro-emigration views were well known, and Highland landlordism's few public critics immediately forecast that the result of his investigations would be more emigration – this emigration to be paid for, very possibly, by the taxpayer. The same critics considered MacNeill, who was the third son of the then laird of Colonsay, to be little more than a landlords' spokesman – an opinion scarcely modified by his conduct of the enquiry over which he presided. The bulk of the evidence taken into account by MacNeill's team was provided by Highland proprietors or their representatives – and, to the openly expressed disquiet of, among others, the Free Church Destitution Committee, and the Edinburgh economist, W. P. Alison, emigration, in fact, turned out to be the only remedy for Highland distress which Sir John felt able to propose.

The legislative consequence of John MacNeill's recommendations was the Emigration Advances Act. Introduced into the Commons on 22 July 1851, the Act had an unopposed and unusually rapid passage through both Houses of Parliament, receiving the royal assent on 7 August. Highland problems, according to its preamble, were most likely to be 'relieved by affording facilities for the voluntary emigration of a portion of the population', and the sums needed for this purpose, the Act's authors added, could readily and appropriately be deducted from funds originally voted under the Drainage Act. Emigration, in short, was deemed to improve an estate in much the same way as ditching it. And though the Act came too late to affect some of the major emigrations from Highland properties, it set the seal of official approval on landlords' policies – no doubt helping to quieten any remaining qualms of conscience among landowners about what they were doing to the crofting population.

In the summer of 1847, a year or so into the famine, the Duke of Sutherland helped 380 of his tenants to emigrate. And during the next ten years at least 16,000 more people were similarly assisted – by their landlords, by the government, or by public subscriptions raised for the purpose – to leave north-west Scotland for North America and Australia. Some further families emigrated at their own expense. And many thousands of crofting folk made their own way south to the Lowlands.

How many of these departing Highlanders were forced to leave? How many went voluntarily? These are difficult questions – not least because the distinction they embody is, in many respects, unreal. Starvation and poverty, no less than eviction, imply some degree of compulsion. And the issue is further confused by the fact that it was in the interest of those who favoured emigration, whether landlords or the officials of central government, to represent the people affected by it as being in favour of it also. But there is no reason to suppose, it should be acknowledged, that crofters as a class were completely opposed to emigration. America was their traditional refuge from poverty and oppression, and the traumatic experience of the famine not unnaturally awakened a new interest in escaping to the other side of the Atlantic. As early as October 1846, one of Edward Pine Coffin's subordinates reported that 'the lower orders' were 'turning their hopes to emigration', and the subsequent deterioration in their circumstances made many crofters and their families only too eager to get away. In 1848, for example, several families left the MacLeod estate for the United States – and lots more, it was said, were prevented from accompanying them only by their lacking the necessary funds. The one obstacle to mass emigration, apart from crofters' poverty, was crofters' hope that something might be done to improve their position at home. That hope, however, was finally dashed by the winding up of the Central Board and by the government's subsequent refusal to resume its own relief operations. As the Board of Supervision's secretary remarked with obvious satisfaction, there was 'reason to believe' that, because of the latter decision, 'the reluctance of the people to emigrate [had] greatly diminished, and will probably be altogether overcome by a just appreciation of the hopelessness of their prospects'. This was borne out by a crofter from Creich in Mull telling Sir John MacNeill, in 1851, that 'not one in three would remain if they could find the means of emigrating'. And Sir John himself calculated that more than half the population of some crofting parishes would emigrate 'if they could find the means'.

Finding the means was no easy task. Assisted passages, it is true, did exist – for, as a consequence of an acute labour scarcity in the Australian colonies, colonial funds had been set aside to help pay the fares of certain classes of emigrants. Administered by a body known as the Colonial Land and Emigration Commission, those funds, however, were doled out only sparingly – prospective emigrants having to advance a deposit whose size was determined by the extent to which they met the colonies' requirements. A single man paid £2 and a single woman £1 – wives being in short supply. A married couple under 45 years of age paid £2 – with ten shillings being added for each of their children. People who were over 45 paid between £5 and £11. And all emigrants, irrespective of age or status, were required to provide a suitable outfit for the voyage and to make their own way to the nearest port of embarkation. Intending emigrants thus needed considerable capital. For much of the 1840s and 1850s, therefore, most crofters were prevented from taking advantage of the Emigration Commission's terms by the more or less absolute poverty to which the famine had reduced them. In 1849, for example, people who were willing to emigrate from Skye could not afford to make their way to Greenock, the nearest port from which the Commission's transports sailed, far less find the deposits demanded of them. And financial considerations apart, Highlanders were less than enthusiastic about going to Australia. Earlier emigrants to New South Wales had sent back letters which 'did not at all give a favourable account of the place'. And since information from such sources received more credence 'than anything written in newspapers or sent from England', the widespread preference for North America, the traditional destination of Highland emigrants, was never completely overcome – despite the widespread dissemination of semi-official propaganda of a decidedly pro-Australian nature.

So acute were their sufferings by the early 1850s, however, that many crofters wanted only to shake Highland dust forever from their feet – their ultimate destination being relatively immaterial. The potato harvest continued to be regularly blighted. And conditions along the north-west coast and in the islands remained, as a result, deplorable – a not untypical plight being that of the evicted family who lived, or at least existed, at that time in a makeshift lean-to of boards and sailcloth on the outskirts of Portree and who depended for survival on 'a few ha'pence from the steamer'. In the winter of 1850–51, the now commonplace hunger and distress were aggravated by the absence of any relief measures. The following winter brought conditions that were, if anything, even worse. By 1852, then, it was possible to observe of north-west Scotland that 'the great bulk of the population in those parts . . . are . . . on the verge of pauperism, with no immediate visible prospect of their distresses being alleviated'. In Skye that summer, there was said to be 'more squalid misery and positive starvation' than at any time since 1846, an Emigration Commission representative who visited the island in June reporting:

> Any description that can be given must fall short of the sad reality. It is not too much to say that many of the swine in England are better fed and better housed than are the poor of this island.

Conditions on Lord MacDonald's estate, this emigration agent went on, were particularly appalling. He had been forced, he wrote, to turn down appeals for assisted passages from several MacDonald tenants because they had 'suffered so much from starvation'. And from Sir Edward Pine Coffin – revisiting, in the summer of 1852, the scene of his endeavours of five or six years before – there came further confirmation of the seriousness of the crofting population's predicament:

> Nothing convinces me so much of the present poverty of the people as the general falling off in the state of their clothing. In 1846 and 1847, I scarcely saw any, however ill off for food, who were not on the whole better dressed than our peasantry in the West of England: while now . . . rags are no longer uncommon, and many declare that they have only the covering in which they stand.

Despite the overwhelming and inescapable misery of their lives, Portree's sheriff reported, crofters were still convinced that their prospects could be dramatically brightened 'by properly devised remedial measures'. But by 1852, he added, they had come to 'despair of such measures being adopted'. Their savings and other resources having long since been converted into food, crofting families had come to look on emigration as affording 'the only sure means of escape' from an otherwise hopeless situation – and had even ceased to care whether or not they were being removed to make way for sheep. But while many crofters were willing, therefore, to accept assisted emigration as a preferable alternative to starvation, it was clear – as was remarked by several contemporary observers – that, if their departure was to help solve Highland problems, it would have to be accompanied by the enlargement of the holdings occupied by such crofting tenants as chose, or were permitted, to remain. That vacated land be utilised for such purposes had been a condition, as already noted, of the Central Relief Board's sponsoring of emigration. And because the arguments in favour of such a procedure were both so obvious and so overwhelming, it was one to which landlords felt obliged to pay lip-service. Implicit or explicit in all the pro-emigration propaganda which emanated from Highland proprietors and from official and semi-official sources, therefore, was the contention that emigration would benefit crofters by relieving congestion and by making possible the creation of bigger, and thus more viable, crofts.

The more outspoken enemies of Highland landlordism – such as Donald Ross, a Glasgow advocate and pamphleteer, and Hugh Miller, editor of *The*

Witness newspaper – were quite unconvinced of the genuineness of such pronouncements, and accordingly declared that the landed class's advocacy of emigration had its origins in the same class's desire to extend and consolidate the sheep farming system. By 1849, a year which, according to Hugh Miller, 'added its long list to the roll of Highland ejections', such men were convinced that an all-out assault on crofting was under way. Their views were backed by the MP and economist, G. Poulett Scrope, when he toured the Highlands that summer. As something of an authority on Ireland's agrarian structure, Scrope was not given idly to invoking Irish parallels. But in many parts of north-west Scotland, he reported, 'ejectments and house levellings' were 'almost as frequent as in Clare or Galway'.

Clearances on such a scale implied that little, if any, more land was being made available to crofters – an inference borne out, in the 1860s, by the results of an unofficial but painstaking enquiry into the effects of emigration on Highland agriculture. In most instances, it was concluded, 'the lands of emigrating tenants are added to some existing sheep farm and the small tenants, whose holdings are altogether inadequate for their support, are left just as they were'. Later, and much more detailed, analyses were to confirm that verdict. And it was one from which crofters themselves never dissented:

> I have never seen that emigration gave more room to people, though it did to sheep. The tendency has been to add more families to places already over-crowded.

Thus the Free Church minister of Kilmuir in 1883. And thus a crofter from Lochalsh:

> Emigration has not, in any case we know, improved the condition of . . . those who remained in the country. The reverse was the result . . . They were reduced to poverty, their lands being added to sheep farms.

A Skye crofter's conviction that tenants were never 'removed from townships for the purpose of bettering the condition of those who [were] left behind', was echoed by the son of a crofter from Sutherland:

> Those emigrations were not carried out in order to effect an improvement in the condition of the crofters. They were carried out in order to convert the land into sheep farms.

With such contentions, the first royal commission of enquiry into crofting matters saw little reason to disagree. What commission members called 'the residuary population,' gained, the same men concluded, 'little benefit from . . . emigration' – because most emigrants' holdings were given to sheep farmers rather than to crofters. That such was indeed the case is evident from even the most cursory examination of the events of the 1840s and 1850s.

Sir James Matheson helped 1,771 people to emigrate from his island estate between 1851 and 1855. His treatment of those emigrants was, by the standards of the time, decidedly generous – a model to other proprietors according to immigration officials in Quebec. But his attitude to those of his tenants who were unwilling to exchange their crofts for an uncertain future in Canada was notably less benevolent. In the spring of 1851, for example, it was announced that any crofter who owed more than two years' rent and who rejected Matheson's offer of a free passage to Canada would be 'served with a summons of removal at Whitsunday and deprived of his lands'. The subsequent evictions were accompanied by the wholesale clearance of several townships. At least 48 crofters were removed from Reef and Carnish in 1851 alone And in the next few months there were extensive evictions from the island of Bernera, on Lewis' west coast, as well as from the township of North Tolsta, a settlement established in the wake of Seaforth's clearances in the 1820s. Evicted tenants were moved into other, uncleared, townships – thus adding to the already serious problem of congestion and overcrowding. As had been the case in Seaforth's time, the parish of Uig was particularly badly affected. Its population had more than doubled in the preceding hundred years, but its crofters had, by the 1850s, been deprived of almost half the land their fathers and grandfathers had occupied.

A Lewis crofter once remarked with justifiable bitterness that, for all Sir James Matheson's enormous expenditure on his estate, not 'one single shilling was spent in improving our crofts and houses'. But because he had equipped his emigrating tenants with the funds they needed to establish themselves in Canada, Matheson, in the 1850s anyway, enjoyed an excellent reputation in all but the most anti-landlord circles. The same cannot be said of his fellow purchaser of Hebridean islands, John Gordon of Cluny. The latter, commented Sir Charles Trevelyan, by no means an intemperate critic of Highland proprietors, was 'notorious . . . for his indifference to the feelings and interests of those connected with him'. And his notoriety, it was generally acknowledged, stemmed from the circumstances surrounding the transportation of no fewer than 2,715 of Gordon's crofting tenantry to Canada in the years between 1848 and 1851.

Of all the many thousands of folk who left north-west Scotland during the famine years, none were more brutally driven out than the people of Barra, South Uist and Benbecula. Prospective emigrants who refused to board the transports which Gordon had chartered for the occasion were hunted down with the aid of dogs, bound up and despatched willy-nilly. The miseries endured by the men, women and children who were the victims of these proceedings can now only be guessed at. But something of them is preserved in the recollections of Catherine MacPhee from Iochdar, South Uist. MacPhee, when a girl, had witnessed the events she afterwards so graphically described:

Many a thing have I seen in my own day and generation. Many a thing, O Mary Mother of the black sorrow! I have seen the townships swept, and the big holdings being made of them, the people being driven out of the country-side to the streets of Glasgow and to the wilds of Canada, such of them as did not die of hunger and plague and smallpox while going across the ocean. I have seen the women putting the children in the carts which were being sent from Benbecula and the Iochdar to Loch Boisdale, while their husbands lay bound in the pen and were weeping beside them, without power to give them a helping hand, though the women themselves were crying aloud, and their little children wailing like to break their hearts. I have seen the big strong men, the champions of the countryside, the stalwarts of the world, being bound on Lochboisdale quay and cast into the ship as would be done to a batch of horses or cattle . . . the bailiffs and the ground-officers and the constables and the policemen gathered behind them in pursuit of them. The God of life, and He only, knows all the loathsome work of men on that day.

As Catherine MacPhee indicated, such emigrants' troubles did not end with their eviction. When South Uist emigrants were landed at Glasgow, *en route* for Quebec, in the summer of 1848, they were so destitute that they had to bivouac in the open for several nights. Subsequent groups fared no better. George Douglas, the medical officer in charge of the Grosse Île quar-antine station in the St Lawrence river and a man who had coped with repeated influxes of refugees from the Irish famine, wrote of one contingent from Gordon's estate that he had never seen 'a body of emigrants so desti-tute of clothing and bedding'. Children 'of nine and ten years old', Douglas went on, 'had not a rag to cover them'. And because such children's parents were almost all 'without the means of leaving the ship, or of procuring a day's subsistence for their helpless families', Canada, George Douglas feared, offered them little prospect of immediate betterment.

To Highland landlords and to the British government's officials in London and Edinburgh, the departure of the 'surplus population' from north-west Scotland was self-evidently beneficial. The Canadians who were in daily contact with crowds of ragged, starving Highlanders, able to speak only enough English to beg for bread, found it easier to doubt the wisdom of the policy which had brought them there:

We have been pained beyond measure for some time past, to witness in our streets so many unfortunate Highland emigrants, apparently destitute of any means of subsistence, and many of them sick from want... There will be many to sound the fulsome noise of flattery in the ear of the generous land-lord who has spent so much to assist the emigration of his poor tenants. They will give him the misnomer of *benefactor,* and for what? Because he has rid his estates of the encumbrances of a pauper population.

The *Dundas Warden,* the newspaper which printed those sentiments, is most unlikely to have come to the attention of John Gordon of Cluny. But the main burden of its editor's complaint – that Highland emigrants were 'often so situated' as to make their emigration 'more cruel than banish-ment' – was taken up by Alexander Buchanan, a Quebec immigration official, in a letter to Gordon's factor. 'The mere transfer to this port of an indigent tenantry,' Buchanan pointed out, 'gives no reasonable grounds for expecting their subsequent successful progress.' Besides, Buchanan added, those who had already arrived in Canada would naturally make 'unfavourable representations' to their friends and relatives at home and the result would be a general 'disinclination to follow'. Buchanan's letter was not received in the Uists until the controversial emigrations were over. And it is, to say the least, doubtful if Gordon's estate management would have taken any heed of its contents even if it had arrived some months before it did – John Gordon having already declared that he considered himself 'neither legally or morally bound to support a population reduced to poverty by the will of providence'. In the long run, however, at least one of Alexander Buchanan's prognostications proved correct. When, in the 1880s, emigration was again canvassed as a solution to the crofting problem, the suggestion – unsurprisingly – was greeted with particular hostility in Benbecula, South Uist and Barra.

Had the miseries endured by such emigrants or by the parties of people – 'lately expelled from the island of Barra' – who arrived, 'in a starving state', in Edinburgh and Inverness during the winter of 1850–51, been compensated for by a generous redistribution of the land they relinquished, the events of these years might have been remembered with less resentment in the islands where they took place. In practically every case, however, the emigrations from Gordon's Hebridean properties were accompanied by renewed clearances. The Benbecula townships of Balivanich, Aird, Uachdar, Griminish and Torlum lost arable and pasture lands to the large farm of Nunton. The South Uist sheep farms established by Clanranald in the 1820s and 1830s were further extended and consolidated, Askernish and Milton being the principal beneficiaries. And in Barra, where there had been relatively few clearances hitherto, at least ten townships were obliterated prior to a third of the island being put under sheep.

Although Gordon's clearances were unrivalled in their sheer nastiness, they were not unparalleled in scope. Lord MacDonald's estate managers' commitment to clearance has already been noted. Predictably, therefore, the shipping of over 2,500 of Lord MacDonald's tenants to Canada and Australia between 1849 and 1856 was accompanied by extensive removals and evictions. On the MacDonald estate in North Uist, there were, in 1830, well over 350 tenants. By 1854, there were only 243 and the 36 crofting townships of a quarter-century before had been reduced to 20 – the greater part of the island, including most of the best land, having been converted into sheep farms in the process. On Lord MacDonald's Skye possessions, for reasons previously examined, sheep farming was of much longer standing. But in Skye as elsewhere, the famine was interpreted to mean that the time had come for it to be expanded. In the parish of Sleat, Lord MacDonald's factor wrote in 1851, 'many of the croft farms by the removal of the people might with great propriety be added to the tacks-men's [meaning farmers'] possessions'. There promptly followed – both in Sleat and in the adjoining parish of Strath – a series of evictions which, in the words of the then minister of Sleat, were 'attended with circumstances of heartless cruelty'. Not the least notorious of these clearances involved the removal, in 1853, of the tenants of Boreraig and Suisnish. Witnessed by a pioneer geologist, Archibald Geikie, it was described by him as follows:

> I had heard some rumours of these intentions, but did not realise that they were in process of being carried into effect, until one afternoon, as I was returning from my ramble, a strange wailing sound reached my ears at inter-vals on the breeze from the west. On gaining the top of one of the hills on the south side of the valley [of Strathsuardal], I could see a long and motley procession winding along the road that led north from Suisnish. It halted at the point of the road opposite Kilbride, and there the lamentation became loud and long. As I drew nearer, I could see that the minister, with his wife and daughters, had come out to meet the people and bid them all farewell. It was a miscellaneous gathering of at least three generations of crofters. There were old men and women, too feeble to walk, who were placed in carts; the younger members of the community, on foot, were carrying their bundles of clothes and household effects, while the children, with looks of alarm, walked alongside . . . Everyone was in tears . . . When they set forth once more, a cry of grief went up to heaven, the long plaintive wail . . . was resumed, and . . . the sound seemed to re-echo through the whole wide valley of Strath in one prolonged note of desolation.

Boreraig and Suisnish were converted into a sheep farm consisting of 2,761 acres of hill grazings and 183 acres of formerly arable land. The latter, it was subsequently noted, was 'of fair quality' while the hill pasture was 'of good quality and some of it may be described as superior'. Several of the families evicted in order to establish this eminently desirable holding emigrated to Australia. The remainder – about 120 people in all – were moved to other townships, principally Isleornsay, Drumfearn, Tarskavaig and Breakish, where already small crofts were subdivided further to make room for them.

Developments at Boreraig and Suisnish were accompanied by the clear-ance of several townships which had the misfortune to march with Lord MacDonald's deer forest – the bulk of those townships' tenants being moved into the already overcrowded settlement of Sconser which became, as a result, one of the most congested and unhealthy locations in Skye. The parish of Kilmuir, whose 'numerous small tenantry' Lord MacDonald's factor considered a 'scourge', was similarly affected – several of its sheep farms being extended at crofters' expense. But despite one of MacLeod of Dunvegan's farming tenants having looking forward, at this point, to 'the emigration mania' bringing about the clearance of Glendale, there were, in fact, few further evictions on the MacLeod estate – the main reason being that most MacLeod land suited to sheep farming had already been devoted to exactly that purpose. On smaller Skye properties, however, Lord

MacDonald's activities were assiduously emulated. Extensive evictions on the Strathaird, Greshornish and Lynedale estates were accompanied by the clearance of a number of settlements on Raasay. Several townships in the southern part of that island were converted into a sheep farm and the 63 crofting families who had formerly occupied them were forced either to emigrate to Australia or to remove themselves to other parts of the estate. Raasay's departing emigrants, one eyewitness recalled, left 'like lambs separated from their mothers', and with them, it was reported, they took handfuls of the soil which covered their people's graves in the island's churchyard. Those who stayed behind gained none of the land the emigrants had given up. Several families were settled on subdivisions of already meagre holdings. Others were moved to the neighbouring island of Rona, a place that the Scottish Land Court would afterwards describe as 'suitable for nothing else than a grazing for a very limited number of sheep'.

To the people affected by them, all such clearances were utterly overwhelming catastrophes whose effects – psychological as well as physical – were profound and long-lasting. But while these effects are susceptible to analysis of the sort provided here, it is impossible to convey – in retrospect and in cold prose at any rate – the nature of the Highland Clearances' immediate impact on the crofting population. To give details of all the removals of the 1840s and 1850s would consequently be to reduce many thousands of intensely personal tragedies to a catalogue of superficially similar events. The following paragraphs are intended, therefore, to do no more than make the point that almost no part of north-west Scotland escaped experiences of the type already described.

The emigration of over 400 people from Harris in the early 1850s was accompanied by renewed clearances. Most of Coll was cleared at about the same time. And from Tiree, in 1849, the Duke of Argyll shipped almost 600 people to Canada. Cholera broke out on the transports that carried the Tiree people across the Atlantic and, on their arrival in Quebec, they could not afford to move on into the interior to look for work or land. With the city's immigrant sheds already crammed with the human debris of the Irish famine, the Tiree folk could obtain no shelter from the weather and, huddled together on the wharfs, many of them died of exposure and disease. These and subsequent emigrations from the island were accompanied by scores of evictions, the duke himself admitting to 40. Half of Tiree was thus taken out of crofters' hands – a development paralleled on the Duke of Argyll's property in the Ross of Mull and, indeed, on practically every other estate in the latter island.

In Mull, it was reported in 1849, the 'poverty and misery' caused by the famine were 'being daily added to by the evictions taking place'. Dozens of ejected families settled themselves in 'wretched hovels' which sprang up in the neighbourhood of Tobermory, and there they supported themselves on shellfish scavenged from nearby beaches. Other families, both from

Mull and from the smaller islands in its vicinity, emigrated or moved to the Lowlands at this time. Among the clearances which precipitated their departure was that of the small island of Ulva, off Mull's west coast. A premier kelping property, Ulva, in the 1830s, was occupied by 88 crofters settled in 16 townships. The kelp industry's decline had been accompanied by a drastic fall in the island's rental. And in the 1840s, spurred on by the famine, Ulva's owner, in the words of one of his admirers, made 'a decided stand against crofting' – proceeding, as Sir John MacNeill discovered in 1851, 'to warn off a certain number yearly and to convert the vacated lands into grazings, until, in four or five years, the population was reduced from 500 to 150'. Soon even that small population had been removed – leaving Ulva in the occupation of its landlord, his shepherds and two or three labourers.

The owner of Ulva's conviction that 'the crofting system cannot be made an advantageous mode of occupying property in this part of the country' was shared by landlords whose estates were situated on the Highland mainland's west coast. From the north-western corner of Sutherland, where tracts of crofting land were added to sheep farms in the 1840s and 1850s, all the way to Ardnamurchan, a district where 'great advantages' were reported to have arisen from 'small possessions being thrown into sheep walks', emigration and clearance went hand in hand. In Kintail, Lochalsh, Arisaig and Moidart, there were numerous evictions – the expropriated tenants' lands being added to sheep farms in almost every case. In Glenelg, the local proprietor's motives in providing his crofters with free passages to the colonies are revealed by the fact that such passages were only made available to people who agreed to pull down their houses before leaving the district. In Knoydart, where its owner's death when his son was still a minor led to MacDonnell of Glengarry's estate being placed under the management of trustees, there were very similar occurrences.

On discovering that a part of the property was occupied by a number of crofters who had paid scarcely any rent since the onset of the famine, the Glengarry trustees decided to eject the crofters in question and to let their lands to a sheep farmer. Over 300 people accepted the offer of a free passage to Canada. By way of ensuring that their holdings remained vacant, their houses were demolished. In August 1853, a few weeks after the emigrants had sailed, those Knoydart crofters who had refused to go to Canada were evicted, and their houses, too, were destroyed. Some newly homeless families were taken in by friends and relatives. But about 30 people who had nowhere else to go had the temerity to erect makeshift huts and tents among the ruins of their homes. 'With a view to compel them to remove,' Sir John MacNeill reported in 1854, 'their temporary shelters were pulled down, in some instances more than once.' Although some of the refugees were still squatting on the estate in the summer of 1855, their unequal struggle both with the elements and with landlordism had eventually to be given up. When the Knoydart estate was sold in 1857, it was almost all under sheep. There remained – in an area where hundreds of families had once lived – only one small, congested township of about a dozen crofters whose holdings consisted of a few acres of shallow, rocky soil on the shore of the Sound of Sleat.

In 1852, as if Highland landlords and the British government between them were not doing enough to facilitate emigration, charitable endeavour, in the shape of the Highlands and Islands Emigration Society, stepped into the fray. This organisation – responsible for the greater part of Highland emigration after 1852 – had its beginnings in Skye in the previous autumn when, on the initiative of Sheriff Fraser of Portree, a committee of all Skye's resident proprietors and farmers had been set up to disseminate information about emigration and to help finance the departure of such crofters as were desirous of leaving the island. When fund-raising committees were established in Edinburgh and London in the spring of 1852, however, it became clear that control of the emigration society was not destined to remain for long with its originators, the committees being presided over by Sir John MacNeill and Sir Charles Trevelyan respectively. The latter, within a very few weeks, assumed overall command of the organisation thus provided for him – with MacNeill becoming his willing lieutenant, and with Fraser and his colleagues being quickly relegated to a distinctly subordinate position.

No single event better illustrates the trend of official thinking on crofting issues in the years following the famine than this take-over of an emigration association by the two civil servants who had been, since 1846, most closely connected with Highland affairs. They hoped, in Trevelyan's words, to bring about an outflow of people that would match the 'wonderful exodus' from Ireland and, in the process, effect 'a final measure of relief for the Western Highlands and Islands by transferring the surplus of the population to Australia'. The number of people 'whom it would be necessary to remove from the islands and [from] the west coast' was estimated to be in the region of 40,000 souls. And the society, it was agreed, ought to meet two-thirds of the cost (this proportion to be repaid by emigrants themselves after they reached Australia) of each emigrant's departure – with the emigrant's landlord paying the remainder.

While thus recognising that emigration was much to the advantage of Highland proprietors, the Highlands and Islands Emigration Society, in its public pronouncements at any rate, made a great deal of the well-worn argument that the 'emigration of a part' was 'necessary for the welfare of the whole' – Trevelyan going to great lengths to deny that his organisation had been founded to 'facilitate landlords' clearances'. When proprietors or their agents were being addressed in confidence, however, rather different arguments were adopted. The society's activities, it was pointed out, were less likely than those of individual landowners to give rise to the 'clamours and complaints of evictions that tend very materially to render Highland property unpopular as an investment'. And with the society's assistance, it was further suggested, 'the superabundant population' of Highland estates could 'be transferred to Australia at a cost to the proprietors calculated not to exceed £1 per head'. This, from any Highland landlord's standpoint, was an attractive prospect, and it is not at all surprising, therefore, that all north-west Scotland's crofting landlords – with the exception of Gordon of Cluny, on whose estate clearance had already been pushed to its limits – gave financial support to the Highlands and Islands Emigration Society.

That the ostensibly charitable grouping he had founded should have become entangled with evicting landlords was not, to Sheriff Fraser of Portree, a pleasing development. The sheriff suggested, therefore, that the emigration society should dissociate itself from them – if only to the extent of ceasing to employ their factors as its agents. This idea Trevelyan treated with undisguised contempt. 'Fraser aimed only at administering a small charitable fund,' he wrote to MacNeill, 'but the matter has now assumed the character of an extensive social operation.' Besides, the end of depopulation, Charles Trevelyan believed, justified the means:

> Considerable estates belonging to the MacLeod and MacDonald families are in the market, but nobody will buy them while they are occupied by swarms of miserable tenants who can neither pay rent nor support themselves.

But for all that the Highlands and Islands Emigration Society succeeded in sending nearly 5,000 Highlanders to Australia in the five years of its existence, Trevelyan's more far-reaching ambitions remained unfulfilled, principally because 1852, the year of the society's formation, brought a harvest more productive than any since 1845. Blight was practically absent. Cattle prices began to rise. And renewed economic expansion in the south meant that migrant labourers were once more in demand. By the standards of immediately preceding years, therefore, 1853 was 'a season of universal prosperity' in the crofting areas. And although 2,605 people had sailed for Australia before the excellence of the crop became apparent, its ingathering was followed by an immediate and dramatic decline in the number willing to join them. A bad harvest in 1854 brought a temporary regression to near-famine conditions. But subsequent years produced better crops and better fishings as well as the Crimean War – which imposed something of a check on every type of emigration from the British Isles. Trevelyan having consequently concluded that crofters were now 'able to live comfortably at home', and his society having in any case run short of funds, emigration from the Highlands to Australia was suspended in 1857. And because the depression which began in the United States and Canada in the same year made transatlantic destinations less attractive also, emigration from the

Highlands to the North American colonies tended to peter out at much the same time.

The crofters of the later 1850s were not living quite so comfortably as Sir Charles Trevelyan suggested – an official enquiry concluding, in 1857, that, 'on the whole, the Highland population must be considered . . . poorly fed'. But the worst, it is true, was over. In the ten years after 1846, the crofting population had plumbed the depths of deprivation. Driven from their homes by their own poverty and by their landlords' determination to find more profitable uses for their land, many thousands of crofters had left north-west Scotland for the colonies and for the Scottish Lowlands. The position of those crofters who remained had not improved in consequence. On every side, crofters' lands had been taken from them. Whole townships had been obliterated. The common grazings of others had been drastically curtailed. Throughout the Highlands and Hebrides crofting had become an activity of only marginal agricultural and economic importance, and, by the region's landlords, its remaining practitioners were openly regarded as little more than a nuisance. In spite of everything, however, the crofting population had retained a presence – no matter how precarious – on the land. And for the first time in more than 40 years, crofters' prospects were improving. The fury of the blight was spent. The prices of produce, especially cattle, were rising. Prospects of remunerative employment were better than at any time since the failure of the kelp industry.

But of even more importance than those material improvements were indications that crofters were becoming aware of common interests, common objectives – and that they were becoming capable of uniting in pursuit of them. The latter development makes it possible to write, from this point forward, of a 'crofting community' – a phrase implying the existence among crofters of social cohesion of a sort that had hitherto been lacking. The significance of this cohesion is underlined by the way in which the historical initiative, in consequence of the crofting community's emergence, started to shift away from landlords – whose decisions dominated the early years of crofting – and to move towards crofters themselves. That such a decisive transformation was occurring was not at all apparent in the 1850s – and it did not, in fact, become so until the 1880s. Its origins are nevertheless to be found in the early nineteenth century. It is with those origins that the following chapter is primarily concerned.

6

THE EMERGENCE OF THE
CROFTING COMMUNITY

In all the extensive literature about the Highland Clearances, no feature of
them attracts more comment than crofters' lack of resistance to evictions –
the consequent absence of violence, terrorism and intimidation being in
quite striking contrast to their prevalence among Irish peasants whose situation was not dissimilar to that of their Highland counterparts. That the
existence of this relatively peaceful state of affairs in the Highlands was an
important reason for official neglect of the region's problems is undoubted.
It was the endemic violence of the Irish countryside, as is remarked in the
course of one study of Ireland's rural history, 'that made it difficult for the
governing classes to ignore the poverty of the majority of the Irish people'.
But in the Highland case, as the normally pacific Hugh Miller remarked in
the famine year of 1846, there was no such stimulus to concern:

> They [the Irish] are buying guns, and will be by-and-bye shooting magis-
> trates and clergymen by the score; and parliament will, in consequence, do a
> great deal for them. But the poor Highlanders will shoot no-one . . . and so
> they will be left to perish unregarded in their hovels.

This passiveness should not be exaggerated. In some respects, in fact, it was
more apparent than real – many of the clearances mentioned in preceding
chapters having been violently resisted by the crofters who were affected by
them. Attempts to evict some 600 people from the townships of Dunskellor,
Mallaclete, Middlequarter and Sollas on Lord MacDonald's North Uist
estate in the summer of 1849, for example, were vigorously opposed by
the crofters concerned. Evicting parties of sheriff-officers and estate officials were, on three separate occasions, driven away by crowds of people
who pelted them with stones and other missiles. And in order finally to
serve summonses of eviction, a force of about 30 policemen had to be
deployed. Other clearances produced numerous instances of the same sort
of response, and in some cases, as at Borve in Harris in 1839, crofters so
successfully 'defied and severely maltreated' the officers sent to evict them
that troops had to be called in to restore order.

These and many other instances of a similar kind have been copiously
described elsewhere, and it is not proposed to re-examine them here. In
form and intent they conform to the normal pattern of rebellion in pre-

industrial societies. And the recurrence of many of their common characteristics in the course of the much more highly organised uprising of the
1880s should not, in itself, be taken as an indication that the early protests
marked the beginnings of a full-scale crofters' revolt. All such protests
were spontaneous and isolated acts of defiance, born out of utter desperation and condemned to failure before they began. In every case, the boundaries of township and locality represented the outer limits of the protesters'
political universe, and there was consequently no worthwhile attempt to
raise the standard of revolt among the crofting population at large. All this
was in marked contrast to the situation prevailing in the 1880s, as was the
virtual absence of links, prior to that later decade, between crofters and the
outside world. Contacts between crofters and southern radicals were not
exactly unknown in the early nineteenth century. But where they existed,
they were extremely tenuous – with none of the radically inclined and
vociferously anti-landlord propagandists who wrote so pungently and effectively about the clearances of the 1840s and 1850s making any attempt to
organise a resistance movement among crofters themselves.

That such a movement did not appear was not due to an absence of
causes for a crofters' revolt. Indeed such causes, as previous chapters have
amply demonstrated, were so numerous, and the misery and degradation
of crofting life so overwhelming, that it is difficult at first sight to see why
no revolt occurred. As has been well said by historians of rural protest in
nineteenth-century England, however:

> Human beings do not react to the goad of hunger and oppression by some
> standard and automatic response of revolt. What they do, or fail to do,
> depends on their situation . . . on their environment, culture, tradition and
> experience.

In order to understand why there was no social and political uprising in the
Highlands until the clearances were only a memory, it is to 'culture, tradition and experience', then, that reference must be made.

Until the eighteenth century was well advanced, a man born in north-
west Scotland lived his life in much the same way as his father or grandfather – the essential continuity of past and present encapsulated in genealo-
gies and traditions which often spanned several centuries. Then, within
the space of just one lifetime, all was changed. The crofter, working his
single holding and labouring for a wage as a kelper, was – in the Highland
context – a pioneer, and, like his landlord, had little use for much of what
had gone before. The early nineteenth-century crofter had not been born
into a culture familiar with the capitalist order in which he found himself,
for that order had come from outside: insidiously, through the operation of
economic forces of which crofters had no comprehension and over which
they could exercise no control; violently, through military conquest and the
deliberate and systematic destruction of the Highland people's traditional

way of life. In attempting to cope with the situation created by commercial landlordism, then, crofters were at an acute disadvantage, not least because they were complete strangers to the social antagonisms which are an integral part of capitalism.

The traditional society of the Highlands, like all societies based on kinship, was by no means an undifferentiated or homogeneous mass. It was, on the contrary, highly stratified and contained several distinct layers of rank and position. It was, nevertheless, a highly unified society, for although a great gulf was fixed, and was known to be fixed, between the chief and his tacksmen on the one hand, and the lowly commons of the clan on the other, both sides – for reasons of military security if for no other – had an interest in maintaining all sorts of bridges across this chasm. Economic inequalities were consequently transcended by an egalitarianism expressed in terms of blood relationship, however remote, and enshrined in the right of every clansman to shake the hand of his chief. Class conflict between feudal lords and peasant masses, an important feature of the history of pre-capitalist Europe, was thus unknown in the Highlands – where it was only under the impact of capitalism and the associated imposition of a commercialised agricultural structure that a peasantry, in the usual sense of the word, was created from the lower strata of the traditional society.

The crofter inherited, therefore, no popular tradition of resistance to feudal oppression and exploitation. Instead he inherited a folklore concerned with conflict between clan and clan, locality and locality – traditions which hindered rather than helped the creation of a sense of unity among crofters as a whole. To the stultifying influence of such a folklore, there was added the confusing fact that, initially at least, most Highland landlords were the descendants of the area's clan chiefs. That a nineteenth-century MacDonald of Clanranald, MacKenzie of Seaforth or MacLeod of Dunvegan was a landowning aristocrat rather than a tribal patriarch may be obvious to historians. As far as nineteenth-century crofters were concerned, however, the weight of loyalty due traditionally to clan chieftains rendered more difficult their appreciation of social and economic transformation than would have been the case if the Gaelic aristocracy of the old Highlands had, like that aristocracy's Irish counterparts, been expropriated and swept into oblivion. Even in the 1880s, when a radical critique of Highland landlordism had been fully developed, there was still said to be, 'on the side of the poor, much reverence for the owner of the soil'. Something of that is evident in a Gaelic proverb:

Ge dona an t-uachdaran
'S e tha truagh am bàillidh.*

---

*'Though bad be the proprietor, it is the factor who is really bad.' The translation is Alexander Carmichael's.

This reluctance to attribute ill-intent even to men who had ordered the eviction of hundreds of families was very widespread. It can be seen – surprisingly enough – in the work of Mary MacPherson whose Gaelic poetry was easily the most forceful to emerge from the land agitation of the later nineteenth century, but who was unwilling or unable, in that poetry, to criticise the longer established landowning families of her native island of Skye.

The undermining of such beliefs – given expression in comments to the effect that 'if our landlord knew our circumstances well, he would give us justice' – was, perhaps inevitably, an immensely slow process which had its origins in the eighteenth century and which is by no means complete even today. Hastening on this process in the early nineteenth century, however, were the clearances which, in their stark inhumanity and their terrible disregard for the traditions of clanship, embodied all that Highlanders found alien and wrong in landlordism:

> Mo mhullachd air a' chaora mhór
> Càit bheil clann nan daoine còir
> Dhealaich sinn nuair bha sinn òg
> 'S mas robh Dùthaich 'c Aoidh 'na fàsach.*

In that and many other poems, there is to be found the awful anger that marked the beginnings of an effective anti-landlordism among crofters. Here, by way of a further example, is part of Derick Thomson's translation of one of the most penetrating of all the poetic condemnations of what was done to Highlanders by their former chiefs, Iain Mac a' Ghobhainn's *Spiorad a' Charthannais,* the Spirit of Kindness:

> They handed over to the snipe
> the land of happy folk,
> they dealt without humanity
> with people who were kind.
> Because they might not drown them
> they dispersed them overseas;
> a thraldom worse than Babylon's
> was the plight they were in.
>
> They reckoned as but brittle threads
> the tight and loving cords
> that bound these freemen's noble hearts
> to the high land of the hills.
> The grief they suffered brought them death
> although they suffered long,
> tormented by the cold world
> which had no warmth for them.

---

*'My curse on the big sheep. Where are the children of the kindly folk? We parted when we were young, before MacKay's country had become a wilderness.' The translation is John MacInnes's.

Does anyone remember
in this age the bitter day
of that horrific battle,
Waterloo with its red plains?
The Gaels won doughty victory
when they marshalled under arms;
when faced with strong men's ardour
our fierce foes had to yield.

What solace had the fathers
of the heroes who won fame?
Their houses, warm with kindliness,
were in ruins round their ears;
their sons were on the battlefield
saving a rueless land,
their mothers' state was piteous
with their houses burnt like coal.

While Britain was rejoicing,
they spent their time in grief.
In the country that had reared them,
no shelter from the wind;
the grey strands of their hair were tossed
by the cold breeze of the glen,
there were tears upon their cheeks
and cold dew on their heads.

Although such poems have best survived the test of time they were, throughout the nineteenth century, supplemented by the personal recollections of those who had seen, or been involved in, evictions. 'I think I hear the crying of the children till this day,' a Lewis crofter said in 1883 when recalling the Uig clearances of the 1850s. A comment made at the same time about Sutherland's early nineteenth-century clearances is to the same effect: 'The accounts of old men living in Aird, and in the different townships about, are more graphic and vivid and harrowing than anything that has ever been written on the subject.' And implicit or explicit in all such accounts was a comparison of the kind made in 1805 by the Earl of Selkirk when he drew attention to the contrast between those responsible for 'the frequent removal of the ancient possessors of the land' on the one hand, and the 'very opposite behaviour of [those people's] former chiefs' on the other.

Theories of lost rights, of a past and happy state, are common to the history of many communities and societies. The Fall of Man, the Golden Age, the legend of the Norman Yoke which was supposedly imposed on the Anglo-Saxons by William the Conqueror and which was so influential in the radical politics of seventeenth-century England: all express a belief that inequality, injustice and the exploitation of man by man have a historical origin; and all embody a hope that the better and fairer society preserved in the popular imagination will one day be restored. The myth of the clan past – the commonly held notion that 'the old population of the country lived in some condition of arcadian bliss, founded on the relation between Celtic clansmen and their chiefs' – was of this type. And in the nineteenth century it became 'very prevalent' in the Highlands. Apparent as early as the 1820s, it tended, in the later part of the century, to take the form given to it by Peggy MacCormack from Lochboisdale in South Uist:

> How we enjoyed ourselves in those faraway days – the old as much as the young. I often saw three, and sometimes four, generations dancing together on the green grass in the golden summer sunset: men and women of four-score or more, for they lived long in those days, dancing with boys and girls of five on the green grass. Those were the happy days and the happy nights, and there was neither sin nor sorrow in the world for us. The thought of those young days makes my old heart both glad and sad, even at this distance of time. But the clearances came upon us, destroying all, turning our small crofts into big farms for the stranger, and turning our joy into misery, our gladness into bitterness, our blessing into blasphemy, and our Christianity into mockery. *O a dhuine ghaolaich, thig na deoir air mo shuilean le linn smaoininn air na dh'fhuilig sinn agus na duirb thainig sinn 'roimhe.* O dear man, the tears come on my eyes when I think of all we suffered and of the sorrows, hardships, oppressions we came through.

Embodied in all such evocations of the past – especially in claims that, in the old Highlands, 'the cattle were fat and plentiful and the land produced abundance for man and beast' – was a great deal that is obviously unhistorical. 'When enquiry is made as to when these happy times were,' declared *The Scotsman* in one of the editorials which made it the most widely hated newspaper in the Highlands of the 1880s, 'they are found to recede further and further back . . . The truth is, of course, that the land never did flow with milk and honey.' Highland landlords, not unnaturally, were of the same opinion. And most historians would agree with them. It should be noted, however, that the uniformly crushing poverty of the early nineteenth century – a poverty epitomised in the famine of the 1840s – was worse, and potentially much worse, than anything that had gone before. The new order – this order of crofts and of clearances – had been imposed, moreover, in a manner which entailed the destruction of the social and cultural unity which had characterised the pre-Culloden era and which had compensated, to some extent, for that era's other deficiencies and drawbacks. When crofters spoke of the 'old people' as 'men of a very independent noble spirit, who were on the most cordial and friendly terms with their chiefs' and who 'looked upon their chief as their father and had no feeling of awe such as they have of proprietors nowadays', they did no more than speak the truth.

But to dwell thus on the facts of Highland history is, as already suggested, rather to miss the point that folk like Peggy MacCormack were endeavouring to make. What *The Scotsman* and most landlords failed to realise – and what some historians have apparently failed to realise, too – is that the enduring significance of crofters' view of the past is not to be found in its historical accuracy or lack of it, but in the fact that it enabled crofters to set the grim realities of the nineteenth-century present against a vision of an older order in which material plenty was combined with security and social justice. Crofters were thus provided with an effective, if unsophisticated, critique of the social and economic system which was necessarily associated with commercial landlordism. Like their longstanding beliefs about the nature of their rights to the land, beliefs examined in a later chapter, the myth of the clan past, though ostensibly backward looking, enabled crofters, therefore, to define and articulate their by-no-means-conservative demands in a language that all of them could understand. Among contemporary observers of the nineteenth-century Highland scene, only one member of the Napier Commission of 1883 seems to have grasped the importance of that fact:

> The tendency to paint the past in attractive colours will not easily be abandoned, nor is it likely to be obliterated by contemporary education or political training. A comparison of the present with the past is a favourite and effective instrument for stirring popular aspirations for enlarged rights . . . [Crofters'] delegates have accordingly not failed [in the course of their evidence to us] to bring all the features of distress and dependency in their actual existence into marked contrast with the happier conditions and higher privileges they believe to have prevailed in a preceding age.

But if such beliefs helped crofters come to terms with, and seek to change, the situation created by commercial landlordism, the existence of those beliefs does not, in itself, explain how the crofting community, considered as a social and cultural entity, was created from the commons of the clans. Nor do such beliefs explain how it was that crofters eventually gained the control over their own destinies which they so conspicuously lacked at the time of the clearances. In this process of shaping a community of feeling among crofters, it is clear, a large part was played by evangelical Presbyterianism – still an important element in crofting life and, in the past, one of its vital components. For although the crofting community's decisive victories were won in the 1880s by means of political action and well-organised social protest, crofters – like many other people whose traditional way of life has been destroyed by capitalist civilisation – initially sought relief from the frustrations and sufferings of their new existence in the sphere of religious experience.

Until the eighteenth century, most Highlanders had little interest in Protestantism of the Presbyterian variety. Its individualist ethic was not calculated to appeal to a people for whom work and war were necessarily communal activities. Only in the heartland of Clan Campbell, already aligned with the Whig and Hanoverian ascendancies and thus with Scotland's Established Church, was there a properly inducted and popularly accepted Presbyterian clergy in the years immediately after 1700. Outside the Campbell pale – and outside the belt of Catholic predominance which traversed the region from the southern part of the Outer Isles to Arisaig, Morar and Lochaber – episcopalianism, like the Jacobitism with which it was usually associated, had survived both the Glorious Revolution of 1688 and the attempts made, in that revolution's wake, to impose Presbyterian forms on all of Scotland. To put down episcopacy was, it followed, the eighteenth-century Scottish Kirk's main mission in the north. In a Highland context, therefore, the Established Church, like the Whig state whose support it enjoyed, was uncompromisingly modernist – committed not just to rooting out religious and political dissent, but committed also to destroying the society which underpinned such dissent. Opening with the formation of the Society in Scotland for Propagating Christian Knowledge (SSPCK) in the century's first decade, and intensified after each Jacobite rising, the Presbyterian offensive reached its climax in 1746 when many episcopal chapels and meeting houses were destroyed by Hanoverian troops and the episcopalian creed officially proscribed. Thereafter, episcopacy ceased to be an effective force in the north-west and, by the 1790s, the Episcopal Church retained significant numbers of Gaelic-speaking adherents only in a narrow belt of territory stretching along the eastern shore of Loch Linnhe from Appin, through Duror, to Ballachulish.

But for all that Presbyterians were in undisputed control of Highland pulpits by the eighteenth century's end, there was little sign of popular enthusiasm for, or attachment to, the Established Church. The latter, admittedly, laboured under immense difficulties. As the church's general assembly was informed in 1760, many parishes in the north-west were 'so extensive as to render the charge of them resemble a province, requiring the labour of a body of clergy'. And everywhere there was a chronic shortage of church buildings – many people whose homes were remote from their parish church, or whose parish church had been allowed to fall into a ruinous condition, being forced to worship 'in the open fields'. Not until the 1820s, when public funds were made available for the construction of a number of so-called 'parliamentary churches', was a serious attempt made to come to grips with this problem. And even by the 1830s, it had by no means been solved completely.

But while it would be uncharitable to discount these and other problems, notably of finance, it must be said that many Highland ministers regarded the difficulties of their situation, not as spurs to action, but as convenient excuses for doing nothing. Whatever its performance elsewhere in Scotland, not a great deal was achieved by the kirk in the Highlands during the period – starting in the eighteenth century and continuing into the nineteenth – when the Church of Scotland was controlled by anti-evangelical clerics known as 'moderates'. John Buchanan, whose accounts of his travels in the north-west in the 1780s contain a number of passages on the region's ecclesiastical affairs, drew a picture of a neglectful and apathetic clergy, out of touch and usually out of sympathy with ordinary people. Not a few Hebridean ministers tenanted substantial farms or tacks, and, 'like some other tacksmen', were 'too prone to treat their subtenants with great severity'. Nor, in this respect at least, did the nineteenth century bring any improvement. In the 1820s and 1830s, several Skye ministers were also sheep farmers and some of them actually acted as factors – something scarcely calculated to enhance their popular appeal. While the more extreme allegations made against such ministers by their evangelical critics have to be treated with some caution, there seems no reason to doubt the general accuracy of the contemporary opinion, as stated to the general assembly in 1824, that the clergy of the north-west were for the most part 'inattentive to the interests of religion' – at least insofar as 'religion' was understood to incorporate a sense of evangelising mission. Several of the area's clerics, it was reported, did not even possess a working knowledge of Gaelic – a state of affairs which, in itself, placed an impenetrable barrier between them and their congregations.

The irritating effects of such abuses were aggravated by the tendency – a tendency reinforced, of course, by some clerics doubling as factors – for the Established Church to become identified, in the popular mind, with the interests of the landlord class. In the pre-1746 Highlands, ministers had mostly been recruited from among tacksmen and, like tacksmen themselves, had occupied something of an intermediate position in the region's social hierarchy. In the Highlands of the early nineteenth century, however, the clergy were often drawn into the society of farmers, factors and proprietors – a development which served to distance them from the crofters who constituted the overwhelming bulk of their congregations. It followed that ministers who objected to the Highland Clearances were few and far between. One or two, notably Lachlan MacKenzie who was minister of Lochcarron from 1782 to 1819, earned a lasting popularity among the crofting population by denouncing evictions. But ministers who adopted such a stance were invariably evangelicals who felt landlords' control of church patronage to be a threat to their own position, and their views were not shared by the moderates who occupied most Highland pulpits. Donald MacLeod, the Strathnaver stonemason, may have been exaggerating when he claimed that Sutherland's ministers threatened 'the vengeance of heaven and eternal damnation' on anyone presuming 'to make the least resistance' to the organisers of evictions. But there is no doubt that most Established Church clerics gave at least tacit consent to landlords' policies, and that their role during the clearances has, ever since, haunted the reputation of the Church of Scotland in the Highlands.

Disorientated and demoralised by social and economic change and bereft of their traditional leadership, the generality of the tenantry could not look, then, to the Established Church for guidance and assistance. And the religion to which they eventually adhered so passionately was not, in fact, the religion of the establishment, certainly not the religion of the kirk's moderate ascendancy. It was, on the contrary, a fervent evangelicalism which, in a series of dramatic 'revivals', swept through north-west Scotland during the opening decades of the nineteenth century – finally carrying the greater part of the region's people into the Free Church. As already suggested, the origins of this 'deep and stirring religious awakening', as Highland revivalism was afterwards dubbed, are to be found in the social and psychological consequences of the collapse of clanship. The 'spiritual destitution' which nineteenth-century evangelicals discerned in the Highlands was very real. It was the inevitable outcome of the absence – since the mid-eighteenth century – of any real sense of social cohesion or framework of moral reference. The evangelical faith helped make good this deficiency. It provided new beliefs and new standards. It created a new purpose in life and in an insecure world it gave some sense of security. A people, whose former way of life had been destroyed, found in a particularly fervent brand of Christianity both 'a place to feel at home'* and a way of coping with the problems inherent in the commercial world into which they had been propelled.

In parts of the eastern Highlands, especially Easter Ross, evangelicalism gained a foothold in the seventeenth century. In the north-west, however, the spark had to come from outside, its main bearer in the first instance being the Society for Propagating the Gospel at Home, formed in Edinburgh in 1798 and dominated by two congregationalist brothers, Robert and James Haldane. The society's object was 'to supply the means of grace wherever', as its founders put it, 'we perceive a deficiency'. And since the Highlands seemed particularly lacking in grace as in much else, its missionaries at once turned their attention northwards. Soon their efforts had been rewarded by a religious revival in southern Perthshire – the first, as it turned out, of a northwards and westwards spreading series.

The Established Church's reaction to the Society for Propagating the Gospel at Home was predictably hostile. In 1799, the general assembly adopted a resolution prohibiting 'all persons from preaching in any place within their jurisdiction who are not licensed', and, in a pastoral admonition, condemned the doctrines of 'false teachers' who assumed 'the name of missionaries'. This Church of Scotland stance had its origins in the widespread resentment generated by Haldanite attacks on what were called 'the false doctrines of unfaithful ministers'. It had its origins, too, in fears that the revivalist movement might be socially subversive; for, while the Haldanes were no friends of the Jacobin-led revolution which had shortly before occurred in France, their congregationalism did have a mildly demo-

---

*This phrase is borrowed, incidentally, from a study of directly analogous developments in Africa.

cratic aura, and there hung about the popular nature of the movement they initiated enough of an egalitarian taint to make it more than slightly suspect in the neurotically repressive political atmosphere of the late 1790s. By its enemies, the Society for Propagating the Gospel at Home was observed to have turned into missionaries men who were 'mechanics' and 'artisans'. And in 1797, Neil Douglas, a former member of the Jacobin-inspired Friends of the People – acting independently, it should be acknowledged, of the Haldanes – preached in Argyll. It is hardly surprising, therefore, that it should have been remarked:

> Some of these reformers of religion, as they wish to be considered, intermix their spiritual instructions with reflections on the incapacity and negligence of the clergymen of the Established Church, and on the conduct of the land-lords, whom they compare to the taskmasters of Egypt.

David Stewart of Garth, author of that comment, deplored the spread of new-fangled ideas among Highlanders with all the considerable ire of which his romantic Toryism was capable. The blame for this development Stewart laid squarely on the shoulders of itinerant preachers – those 'ignorant and fanatical spiritual guides', he called them – to whom Highlanders were increasingly turning. Even more significantly, there seemed to Stewart to be an obvious connection between the itinerants' success and the discontent engendered by economic change:

> Wherever the people are rendered contented and happy in their external circumstances by the judicious and humane treatment of their landlords . . . no itinerant preacher has ever been able to obtain a footing.

Much the same point was made by James MacDonald in the perceptive account of Hebridean agriculture which he published in 1811. Here is part of what MacDonald had to say about island crofters:

> The bond of connection and the ties of clanship which lately subsisted between these tenants and their landlords . . . are dissolved. In many cases, indeed, they are replaced by a spirit of jealousy and hatred. Discontent and a desire for change are almost universal. The ancient attachment to church and state is grown very feeble . . . Without fixed or definite ideas concerning any failure in duty of their clergy, they gradually relax in their respect for them, and have no small hankering after the pestilent fellows who, under the name of different sectaries, swarm over these neglected regions. Without any original tendency to bigotry or, indeed, any serious attachment to or predilection for any specific articles of faith, they frequently indulge in a disputatious vein of religious controversy. This, with political speculations, some of which would astonish a man not accustomed to the amazing powers of the common Hebridean in conversation, interlarded with reflections upon the character and conduct of their superiors, and upon the hardships of their own condition, fills up their leisure hours. They have an idea that they deserve a better fate than that which has fallen to their lot . . . They always suspect that they are peculiarly ill-treated, and live under an ungrateful government and oppressive landlords. In support of these charges, they mention . . . above all . . . the dearness of land, and the shortness or absolute want of leases.

On occasion, therefore, the connection between religious revivalism and social dislocation was manifested not only in the fact that crofting tenants – many of whom had been subjected to eviction – were particularly susceptible to the new religion, but also in the fact that the doctrinal proclamations of the revivals' originators and adherents embodied some part of the social and other aspirations beginning to be voiced by crofters. Thus in one early revival:

> Many of the converts became emaciated and unsociable. The duties of life were abandoned. Sullen, morose, and discontented, some of them began to talk of their high privileges and of their right, as the elect few, to possess the earth . . . The landlord was pronounced unchristian because he insisted on his dues.

This was to engage in millennial talk of the sort that peasants elsewhere in Europe had been engaging in for centuries. But such talk, of course, was a wholly novel phenomenon in the Highlands. There it appealed, in the 1790s and subsequently, to the social group conjured into existence by clearance and eviction – the social group consisting of folk who had been dispossessed of their landholdings by their landlords. Although the number of crofting tenants attracted by the notion that they might, after all, have a 'right . . . to possess the earth' is, in the nature of things, impossible to estimate, millenial movements could clearly be significant locally. Around 1800, for example, such a movement was initiated in the Great Glen 'by certain religious itinerants':

> [They] addressed the people by interpreters and distributed numerous pamphlets calculated, as they said, to excite a serious soul concern. The consequence was that men who could not read began to preach, and to influence the people against their lawful pastors . . . They next adopted a notion that all who were superior to them in wealth or rank were oppressors – whom they would enjoy the consolation of seeing damned.

Haldanite influence extended into north-west Sutherland, and, in 1805, John Farquharson, an itinerant associated with the Haldanes, preached for some months in Skye. But for the most part, the north-west was still outside the Haldanite sphere of influence when, towards the end of the nineteenth century's first decade, the Society for the Propagation of the Gospel at Home fell victim to its own doctrinal dissensions. Almost at once, however, its evangelical mission was taken up by another body, the Gaelic School Society founded in Edinburgh in 1811. Although that society, as its name suggests, was primarily concerned with helping Highlanders become literate in their own language, it was also interested in the propagation of the gospel and seems often to have employed men imbued with evangelising fervour. Gaelic School Society teachers consequently played a prominent part in the religious life of the communities in which they were stationed, not the least of their contributions to that religious life being found in the use they made of the Gaelic bible, the only book used in the society's schools.

The task of translating the scriptures into Gaelic was completed in 1801 and, during the next 25 years, 60,000 Gaelic bibles and 80,000 new testaments were distributed in the Highlands by the SSPCK and by the British and Foreign Bible Society. The bible was thus the first – and, for long enough, the only – book to be widely available in Gaelic. Its appearance coincided with the highly successful literacy campaign launched by the Gaelic school movement. And its importance to the nineteenth-century crofting population can hardly be overestimated.

Until about 1800, the vast majority of people in the north-west were dependent for their knowledge of the bible on the clergy of the Established Church. They alone had access to Christianity's written sources and their interpretation of those sources was, in consequence, almost impossible to dispute. After 1800, that situation changed totally as more and more crofters became able to read the bible, for themselves, in their own language. In itself, this development was bound to enhance the self-confidence of crofting tenants. More important, however, were the discoveries they made as a result of their bible-reading: the discovery that the established kirk's clergy were not necessarily infallible; the discovery that the bible appeared to have much to say that was relevant to their own predicament, not least to the land question; the discovery, in short, that the fundamental principles of Christianity could be applied to their own lives in a way that was very different from that usually suggested to them by their moderate ministers. It is no accident, therefore, that religious revivalism in the north-west coincided with the spread of the Gaelic bible and the growth of Gaelic literacy.

Being well aware of this connection, moderate ministers looked on the Gaelic schools with some disfavour; and many of the Gaelic School Society's teachers consequently found themselves hauled up in front of church courts on charges of irregular conduct of one kind or another. A note in the 1829 minutes of the Presbytery of Mull summarises one such incident:

> Two teachers of the Gaelic School Society of Edinburgh stationed in the parish of Ardnamurchan have assumed to themselves the office of public exhorters and are in the stated practice of abstaining from public worship . . . The presbytery find themselves called upon to put an effective stop to such practices – practices subversive of all established order and so calculated to produce the most pernicious consequences.

Curtailing the Gaelic School Society's activities was easier to contemplate than to achieve, however. In 1830, several of the society's teachers in the area under the Mull presbytery's jurisdiction were reported to be persisting in 'schismatic and irregular practices'. They were refusing to attend Established Church worship 'on the ground that the gospel [was] not preached' by Church of Scotland ministers. They were also 'in the regular habit of publicly exhorting and expounding, [thus] exhibiting an example in all respects pernicious . . . engendering dissension among the people... and a spirit of disaffection towards all those in authority over them'.

Elsewhere there were similar happenings. In the township of Back in Lewis, for example, a Gaelic School Society teacher conducted worship every Sunday. His activities, the minister of Stornoway complained, 'alienated the people from me in a great measure, so that on the Sundays I preached at Back they would in droves that day pass me on the road'. Much the same result was produced by the society's endeavours in Wester Ross, and there a few of the local men employed as catechists by the SSPCK appear quickly to have joined the movement the Gaelic School Society's staff had initiated. Thus John Davidson, an SSPCK catechist in Lochcarron, set himself up as a 'public expounder of scripture' and attracted a mass following:

> [On a Sunday in March 1820] he assembled the greater part of the population of Lochcarron to a place within sight of the parish church, and there, while public worship was conducting regularly by the parish minister and such of the parishioners as were with him . . . [Davidson] employed himself in reading, lecturing, and praying with his congregation.

Such occurrences indicates that, although the revivalist faith came initially from outside the region, Highland revivalism very soon developed an impetus, and produced a leadership, of its own. Thus one result of John Farquharson's 1805 visit to Skye was the conversion to the evangelical faith of Donald Munro, a local man who, despite his being a catechist in the pay of the Established Church, was more renowned for his ability as a fiddler than for his devotion to Christianity. Under Farquharson's influence, Munro put away his fiddle and began to conduct prayer meetings at various places in the northern part of Skye. The eventual outcome of his activities is best described by a more or less contemporary account of it:

> In the year 1812, by means of these meetings, an uncommon awakening took place among the people, which was attended with distress and trembling of the body . . . Some persons came under convictions when attending these meetings, others when they came in contact with awakened persons who attended them . . . These were days of power and of sweetness to as many as had spiritual taste and discernment, so that frequently when they met they were reluctant to part.

A similar revival took place in Lewis during the 1820s, and at least one of its initiators, John MacLeod, a Gaelic School Society teacher in Uig, had been involved in the events of 1812 in Skye. But in Lewis, too, local preachers quickly emerged. In 1823, as a result, Lewis's Church of Scotland clergy began to complain of the 'religious frenzy which [had] become so prevalent of late', and of the activities of 'the blind, daring fanatics who [had begun to] infest this island . . . disseminating wild unscriptural doctrines'. The extent of the growing divergence between the popular religion and the Established Church was demonstrated at a communion service in the parish church of Lochs, in the south-eastern corner of Lewis, in August 1823. When the parish minister, Alexander Simpson, a man who – or so evangelical tradition insists – was a drunkard as well as a moderate, began his sermon, he was interrupted by several 'fanatics' who challenged the validity of the doctrines being propounded from the pulpit. On being asked to leave the church by Simpson, the 'fanatics' refused to budge and had to be 'dragged off'. Not a whit intimidated, they then began to 'sing and expound scripture and read it among themselves in the neighbourhood, so near that their singing seemed meant to disturb the service'. Angered by this calculated defiance of his authority, Loch's parish minister, with the support of the presbytery of Lewis, lodged a formal complaint with the civil authorities. Five men who had played a prominent part in the August 1823 disturbances were promptly arrested and shipped to Dingwall where they were jailed for a month – a proceeding which did nothing to quell the revival but which had the effect, as one of MacKenzie of Seaforth's Lewis correspondents remarked, of setting Church of Scotland ministers firmly 'on the fair road to damn their popularity in the Lews'.

Such events were not confined to Skye and Lewis. In Harris, a revival commenced in the early 1820s under the leadership of John Morrison, a Rodel blacksmith better known by his Gaelic nickname, *Iain Gobha*. By 1829, 'fanaticism and sectarianism' were reported to be 'making rapid progress' on the island – where Murdo MacLeod, another 'lay-preacher or exhorter' was said to have 'exerted all his influence to prevent the parishioners from attending divine worship in . . . established churches'. From North Uist, meanwhile, came reports of people following 'divisive courses' and organising their own Sunday services. In Mull, dissent had 'proceeded to an alarming extent'. And in Lochcarron, by 1825, the leadership of the popular movement had devolved upon John Finlayson, another blacksmith, who was accused by his local presbytery of 'following divisive and schismatic courses, absenting himself from attendance on the public ordinances of religion [and] collecting crowds at his house during divine service upon the Lord's day.'

The emergence of the class of lay-preachers made up of John Finlayson, Donald Munro, John Morrison and their fellows was one of the revivalist movement's most important features, not least because those preachers – known as *na daoine*, 'the men', in order to distinguish them from the ordained clergy – constituted the first leadership of any sort to emerge from the crofting population's own ranks. Although they had a long history in those parts of the eastern Highlands where evangelical Christianity had been implanted in the seventeenth century, it was only in the early nineteenth century that *na daoine* – defined by one church historian as a 'definitely recognised but ecclesiastically unofficial order of evangelical laymen who won public veneration by their eminence in godliness' – made their appearance on the north-west coast and in the islands. In some cases, as in that of Donald Munro in Skye or that of John Davidson in Lochcarron, *na daoine* had some previous connection with the Established Church or with the SSPCK – organisations which had long maintained a staff of lay cate-chists whose duty it was to assist the ministers of larger parishes. For the most part, however, *na daoine* seem to have been ordinary men drawn from the lower strata of Highland society. Usually they were crofters. Occasion-ally they were craftsmen – blacksmiths seem to have been especially promi-nent. But their distinguishing features consisted mainly of their strength of character and the profound conviction of their religious beliefs: qualities which enabled them to preside over the popular religious movement from the start; conducting prayer meetings, holding services; presiding at the huge, open-air 'fellowship meetings' which were to become a feature of the Friday before communion throughout the evangelical Highlands.

Well aware of their status in the localities they served, *na daoine* culti-vated a distinctive appearance, wearing their hair long and, in some areas, adopting a recognised 'uniform'. On the northern mainland, this consisted of 'a camlet coat and a spotted handkerchief tied over the head' – while in Skye multi-hued nightcaps were favoured. *Na daoine*, then, are not to be imagined as precursors of the sober-suited clerics one finds in crofting areas today. They were an infinitely more colourful breed. And their fervour had its counterpart in the emotional, often hysterical, nature of the move-ment which they led – a movement in which there can be discerned at least some trace of those vast and mysterious upsurges of chiliastic and millen-nial fervour which occasionally gripped the imagination of the masses of medieval Europe and which have more recently erupted in widely separated parts of the Third World. Thus one contemporary observer, noting that it was 'known to everyone conversant with the Highlands that the recent degradation and misery of the people have predisposed their minds to imbibe these pestiferous delusions to which they fly for consolation under their sufferings', went on to describe how revivalism's adherents, as he put it, 'see visions, dream dreams, revel in the wildest hallucinations'. There is plenty of other testimony to the same effect. In Skye, for example, many people – especially women – were said to have become 'fanatical' and fallen prey to fits of religious ecstasy. In Lewis, too, people were 'seized with spasms, convulsions, fits, and screaming aloud' – with the result that *bliadhna 'n aomaidh*, the year of the swooning, was long remembered in the island.

The millennial character of Highland revivalism had its counterpart in *na daoine*'s religious teaching. Their theology was of the most elemental type, combining a harsh and pristine puritanism with a transcendental mysticism that had less to do with nineteenth-century Presbyterianism than with an altogether older faith. Visions of heaven and hell, prophetic utterances, intensely personal conflicts with the devil and his angels: these were integral to *na daoine*'s creed and a common part of their experience. In *na daoine*'s preaching, it was noted, homely illustration was combined with mysticism and allegory. And while *na daoine* were often fully literate, knowing their bibles 'as few besides have known them', they did not hesitate to introduce into their Christianity concepts which were clearly derived from the neo-pagan heritage of the Highlands. Many of *na daoine*, for example, believed themselves to have the power of second sight, and even Lachlan MacKenzie of Lochcarron, one of the earliest of the evangelical ministers who were afterwards to become such a force in the Highlands, was thought a prophet by his congregation.

Na daoine were no primitivists, however. They had, on the contrary, a very low opinion of much of the traditional culture of the Highlands. Indeed, their onslaughts on that culture were to go a long way to destroying it. What is not generally recognised in all that has subsequently been written about the devastating effect of Highland puritanism on Gaelic song and Gaelic tradition, however, is that the society which had supported such song and tradition had effectively been overthrown in the eighteenth century. In expressing an unyielding hostility to much of what had been derived from the past, therefore, *na daoine* can be regarded as trying, more or less consciously, to come to terms with the realities of a social and economic system dominated by landlordism rather than by clanship. It is of interest, in this connection, that revivalism's social and political teachings were arguably more relevant to the actual situation of the early nineteenth-century crofting population than were the social and political perspectives embodied in the secular poetry of the period – much of which, in the opinion of at least one authority, Sorley MacLean, is dominated by a weak, romantic nostalgia for the old order. As early as the 1760s, for example, Dugald Buchanan of Rannoch – perhaps the greatest evangelical poet to write in Gaelic – included in *An Claigeann,* The Skull, a telling indictment of the commercial landlordism which was then just beginning to make its mark on the Highlands. Several bitter verses are devoted to a rack-renting laird who flays his people and thins the cheeks of his tenants by his excessive exactions. If the rent is delayed, the cattle are seized, no heed being paid to the cries of the poor. Before this landlord, there stands an old man, his head uncovered in the bitter wind. His pleas and petition are ignored by his laird. For striking down such a tyrant, Buchanan concludes, death is to be praised.

Here, then, is no anachronistic reluctance to admit the exploitative role of the former chief. And, in fact, Buchanan's tirade marked the beginning of a long association between Highland evangelicalism and anti-landlordism. Alexander Campbell, the leader of an early secessionist movement in Argyll, thought it worthwhile to record his 'testimony against covetous heritors that oppress the poor'. And not least among the faults of the moderate clergy, according to *na daoine,* was that they 'dined with the laird' and generally associated with the upper strata of Highland society. Some of *na daoine* went further still, the social protest contained in the vision of hell accorded to David Ross from Ferintosh, Ross-shire, being so explicit as to require no elucidation:

> In one spot David saw a poor soul surrounded by busy devils. 'There is a rich miser for you,' said the angel [who served as Ross's guide to the underworld]. 'They are pouring buckets of molten gold down his throat. There again,' said he, pointing to another, 'There is a laird who has been driving out tenants from their farms, squandering his means after strange women, rendering poor people miserable and himself so miserable that at last he had to take away his own life. He is now for ever doomed to be alternatively bitten by serpents and have his wounds licked over by hell hounds. Poor fellow! Little did he think during his moments of heartless pleasure and dissipation that he was sowing for himself the seeds of such an eternity of woe.'

Na daoine and their movement thus posed a threat to all those whose interest lay in maintaining the social and economic status quo in the Highlands – whether moderate ministers, landed proprietors or sheep farmers. As far as the Church of Scotland was concerned, only its evangelical ministers – whose own beliefs at least approximated to the tenets of the popular religion – had anything approaching a cordial relationship with *na daoine*. Of such evangelicals, always a tiny minority in Highland and Hebridean presbyteries, the most popular were Roderick MacLeod, or *Maighstir Ruairidh*, minister of Bracadale in Skye, and Alexander MacLeod, minister of Uig in Lewis. These men's churches were regularly filled to capacity with evangelicalism's converts – many of them tramping to such churches each Sunday from parishes where moderates remained in charge. But for the most part, *na daoine* and their followers, as already indicated, took next to nothing to do with the Church of Scotland. In Skye in the 1820s, for example, there were only two parishes – one of them Roderick MacLeod's Bracadale and the other the neighbouring parish of Duirinish – in which there was no 'meeting held for social worship on the Sabbath distinct from that carried on in the parish church'.

In view of *na daoine*'s obvious leanings towards anti-landlordism, it was inevitable that the Established Church's animosity towards them was encouraged by landowners and by their associates. Not only did *na daoine* articulate crofters' growing dislike of landlords, a profoundly popular movement equipped with its own leaders clearly constituted, simply by virtue of its existence, a threat to the landlordism's hitherto undisputed dominance of the Highlands. The opinions of the minister of Barvas in Lewis – a man who thought it 'easy to see that no good can come to society from the raving effusions of . . . ignorant men who, with consummate effrontery, assume the character and office of public instructors' – were accordingly echoed and endorsed by many landed proprietors. 'No gentleman,' it is recorded, 'associated with Donald Munro'. At his meetings and those of his fellow lay-preachers, there might be seen, among hundreds of crofters and their families, 'an occasional sheep farmer, if a native of the district, but never a factor'. It is wholly unsurprising, therefore, that Lord MacDonald's estate manager considered *na daoine* to be 'an evil influence'. MacLeod of Dunvegan – who thought 'the influence of lay preachers . . . injurious to the people' – was of exactly the same view. So were those Skye sheep farmers who reacted to revivalist gatherings on the island by making representations to Lord MacDonald, 'soliciting his lordship's power and authority to suppress these meetings and to proceed against those who held them'.

In the context of the history of the popular religious movement in the Highlands, the so-called Disruption of the Church of Scotland in 1843 was a largely fortuitous event. The internecine conflict between evangelicals and moderates – leading eventually to the former's secession from the kirk and to the formation of the Free Church – had nothing to do with Highland affairs, and was, on the face of it, of little interest to the mass of the crofting population. As the ecclesiastical crisis approached, however, the evangelical leadership in the Lowlands made a determined effort to win support in the north. Pro-evangelical pamphlets were translated into Gaelic and put into circulation across the Highlands. Evangelical deputations toured the region. Most important of all, the Highlands' few evangelical ministers – men like Roderick MacLeod – strenuously endeavoured to win to their side of the developing church conflict both *the men* and their adherents.

In making this attempt to gain popular backing, evangelical ministers had many advantages. They were the only clerics for whom crofters felt any respect or affection, and they were consequently able to draw on a fund of good will built up over many years – with M*aighstir Ruairidh*, for example, easily managing to attract enthusiastic crowds to the pro-evangelical meetings he staged in the winter of 1842–43. Moderates, for their part, possessed no such advantage. For them there was only a deeply felt dislike. It was predictable, therefore, that *na daoine* should have adhered unanimously to the Free Church and that, throughout north-west Scotland, the 1843 secession of evangelical sympathisers from the Established Church amounted to 'a tidal wave which . . . carried the population *en masse*'. The situation in Lewis, where fewer than 500 people out of a population of some 20,000 remained in the Established Church, was typical. There as elsewhere, parish churches were 'swept bare of worshippers', their congregations being reduced to a handful of sheep farmers and their shepherds. When, on the first Sunday after the Disruption, Durness's church bell was muffled by the help of an old sock and a dead dog was hung over the pulpit in Farr, the symbolism was very apt. The Established Church had ceased to have any claim to authority over the crofting population.

The immediate cause of the evangelicals' withdrawal from the Church of Scotland having been their opposition to landlords' longstanding right to appoint ministers to Church of Scotland pulpits, the Free Church held decidedly anti-landlord views. Landlords, it followed, were intensely suspicious of the new denomination, their antipathy towards it manifesting itself in a campaign of obstruction and harassment which usually took the form of refusing to sell to the Free Church the sites it needed for church buildings. Although not confined to the Highlands, this practice was more widespread and effective there than anywhere else – because the sheer size of Highland estates enabled their owners to deny the Free Church access to whole parishes and, in some cases, to entire islands, even counties. In one famous episode caused by Sir James Riddell's persistent refusal to provide a site for a Free Church place of worship at Strontian, the problem was overcome by the provision of a floating church which was moored in Loch Sunart. Elsewhere persecution was more difficult to counter. In Mull, a Free Church congregation was obliged to worship in a gravel pit below the high-water mark – while Lord MacDonald, owner of the most extensive estate in the Hebrides, refused sites to no fewer than seven congregations. When, during the winter of 1845, the people of Paible – on the MacDonald estate in North Uist – attempted to build a Free Church meeting house on the township's common grazing, the building was promptly pulled down by the estate management and nine of the crofters involved in its construction evicted. A subsequent attempt to hold services in the lee of a large rock on the same common grazing was countered by the simple expedient of ploughing and sowing the ground around it.

Visiting north-west Scotland five years after the Disruption, Robert Somers, a journalist, made the following comments about it:

[In the Highlands] there are only two ranks of people, a higher rank and a lower rank, the former consisting of a few large tenants . . . and the latter consisting of a dense body of small lotters [or crofters] and fishermen . . . The proverbial emnity of rich and poor in all societies has received peculiar development in this simple social structure of the Highlands. The clearances laid the foundation of a bitter animosity between the sheep farmers and the lotters, and, as these violent changes were executed by the authority of the lairds, they also snapped the tie which had previously, amid all reverses, united the people and their chiefs. One link still bound the extremities of society in formal, if not in spiritual, union. The parish church was a common centre where all classes met . . . But even religion . . . was converted at the Disruption into a new fountain of bitterness . . . There is thus a double point of collision between the two ranks – an ecclesiastical as well as an agrarian enmity. It is consequently almost impossible to find an individual in the upper rank who has not a grudge against the people, either on the score of their Free Churchism, or on the score of their hostility to the sheep walk system.

Although the link between social conflict and religious dissent went back further than Somers realised, his remarks contain an essential truth. In the Highlands, the Disruption was not just an ecclesiastical dispute. It was a class conflict. Its battle line was the line of class demarcation, the line between crofters on the one hand, and sheep farmers, factors and landed proprietors on the other. In that fact is to be found the explanation of what is otherwise inexplicable: the intensity of proprietorial opposition to the Free Church.

Highland landlords' experience of the popular religious movement had done little to convince them that its institutionalisation in a church founded on an essentially anti-landlord principle would be to their advantage. The Free Church, declared Sir James Riddell, proprietor of Ardnamurchan, would lead the people 'astray from the ministrations of the regularly ordained clergy who were placed over them for their spiritual good and edification', making them, in the process, more than ever dependent on 'the teaching of illiterate laymen'. Besides, Riddell added, and the argument must have seemed a powerful one in the politically troubled world of the 1840s, once one part of the established order had been successfully challenged, there was no knowing where such challenges might end. Already, Riddell thought, the Free Church had 'bid defiance to the powers that be' and 'broken up society from its very foundations'.

Such expectations were exaggerated. Ultimately dependent on the urban middle-class of Lowland Scotland rather than on the crofting population of the Highlands, the Free Church was inherently unlikely to sanction a serious challenge to private property in land or in anything else. The real threat posed to landlords' interests by the Free Church was thus more subtle – though nonetheless serious in the long term – than the red revolution feared by Sir James Riddell in his more fevered moments. It was, as was pointed out by Hugh Miller, a leading evangelical journalist as well as one of the most effective and influential of Highland landlordism's early critics, that the Free Church threatened to end crofters' political isolation: 'to translate their wrongs into English', as Miller observed, 'and to give [such wrongs] currency in the general mart of opinion'.

Broadly speaking, this was what occurred. Among the Free Church's southern membership, there immediately appeared feeling to the effect that 'the enthusiastic adhesion' of the crofting population to their cause imposed upon that membership special responsibilities with regard to this same crofting population. Feeling of that sort made possible the generous financing, from Lowland sources, of Free Church efforts in the Highlands. It also went a long way to account for the extraordinarily generous donations made by Lowlanders to the charitable funds raised to combat the Highland famine. At the same time, and very much through the medium of the Free Church, which one of Scotland's historians has described as 'the bulwark of the Scottish Liberal Party', the first concrete links were established between the incipient agrarian radicalism of the crofting population and the mainstream of Scottish liberal and radical politics. It is not without significance, therefore, that the crofting population – acting in concert with an important section of southern public opinion and in concert, too, with Scotland's Liberal and evangelical press – was able, through the medium of a parliamentary enquiry which unreservedly condemned the landlords' conduct, to force site-refusing proprietors to give way and to make available the building plots needed by the Free Church. The passing in 1886 of the first Crofters Act was the outcome, by no means coincidentally, of a very similar sequence of events.

Of more immediate importance, however, was the fact that, in north-west Scotland, the Free Church came into existence as a profoundly popular institution, the heir to a long tradition of religious dissent. It was, and would long remain, the church of the mass of crofting tenants, and it was, in a very real sense, their creation – a victory for their interests over those of their landlords. It was in this way, above all, that the achievement of 1843 contributed to the more important victory of 1886 – for the Disruption and the revivals which preceded it were largely instrumental in welding a disparate collection of crofting tenants into a community capable of acting collectively and possessing, for the first time, something like a shared outlook. That the future of the Gaelic language can be said, in the 1970s, to be bound up with the fate of the Free Church is no accident. Nor is the fact that even the socialism and anti-clericalism of a modern Gaelic poet like Sorley MacLean is expressed in language reminiscent of that of the evangelical revivals. Evangelicalism and the emergence of the modern crofting community are inseparable phenomena, if only for the reason that it was through the medium of a profoundly evangelical faith that crofters first developed a forward-looking critique of the situation created in the Highlands by the actions of the region's landowning class. And for all that the principles at stake in 1843 were ostensibly religious, they reflected the deep-seated social antagonisms which eventually erupted in the more explicitly political conflict of the 1880s. In 1843, a majority of the crofting population stood up to their landlords for the first time. And they won. Not even the famine and the clearances which followed it could obliterate the significance of that victory.

7

YEARS OF RECOVERY

1858–1880

During the famine years of the 1840s and 1850s, Highland proprietors and central government became convinced that the solution to the problems of Scotland's north-western fringe lay in a drastic reduction of the region's smallholding population. The ostensible aim was to ease congestion and to enlarge crofters' holdings. The real objective, as far as landlords at least were concerned, was to consolidate and extend the sheep farming system. Hence the clearances and forced emigrations of the later 1840s and early 1850s. The inevitable result of those events, as a royal commission discovered some 30 years later, was that crofters were everywhere 'confined within narrow limits' – with congestion and overcrowding, it followed, being as bad, if not worse, than they had ever been. This state of affairs was the logical outcome of the developments outlined in the first part of this book; the crofting community's long struggle to break free of it constitutes the theme of the remainder. Before that theme is taken up, however, it makes sense to give some account of crofting society as it emerged from the terrible years of the mid-century.

By the 1850s, both on the Highland mainland's north-west coast and in the Hebrides, sheep farmers occupied most of the best hill grazings as well as a good deal of the land which had formerly been in cultivation. Although decidedly detrimental from a wider crofting standpoint, this situation had the paradoxical effect of bestowing an unforeseen degree of security on such crofting families as had escaped eviction in the famine's immediate aftermath. Once those families ceased to require assistance to keep them alive, their removal from the 'inferior and exhausted soil' which they almost invariably occupied would have caused their landlords sufficient trouble and expense to outweigh such profits as might have been made from putting still more land under sheep. The resulting tendency to leave crofters in undisputed occupation of their meagre plots and scanty grazings was enforced, towards the end of the 1860s, by a falling away in sheep farmers' profits. While there were, in that decade, a few more instances of the once prevalent practice of adding crofters' common grazings to sheep farms, these were exceptional, and when, in the 1870s, Highland sheep farming – encountering, by that point, low-cost competition from overseas –

158

entered a period of severe depression, clearances of the early nineteenth-century sort ceased completely.

In the 1850s, therefore, an era of crofting history came to an end. Since its beginnings, crofting had existed in a state of flux. Whole populations had been uprooted and removed. Evictions and expropriations of every kind had gone on more or less continually. Poverty, endemic from the first, had worsened year by year. The 1860s and 1870s, in contrast to all of that, were a period of unprecedented stability. Not only had the clearances ended, but crofters' incomes were rising for the first time since 1815. The British economy was once more expanding. Agriculture was booming. And though crofters did not do as well as their sheep farming neighbours, many of whom amassed substantial fortunes in the early 1860s as the price of wool soared to record heights, they did experience a fairly rapid expansion of their agricultural returns. Crofters benefited, above all, from a steady rise in cattle prices – for though crofters had been deprived of most of the pastures on which the eighteenth century's huge herds of black cattle had been reared, the proceeds from the sale of its cattle beasts still made up the greater part of such revenue as was derived from the typical croft.

By the early 1880s, for example, crofters' stirks – worth less than a pound a head in the 1840s – were being sold for between £6 and £9, with two-year-olds fetching up to £10 and three-year olds worth a further four or five pounds. Few crofts were large enough to grow the winter fodder needed in order to take advantage of the higher prices fetched by more mature animals. But most croft holdings were capable of raising one or two stirks a year – the importance of the latter to the crofting economy of the time being attested to by a common contemporary saying to the effect that 'the stirk pays the rent'. Nor were crofters wholly excluded from the sheep farming economy. When compared with the flocks maintained by sheep farmers with thousands of acres at their disposal, the sheep numbers to be found on the average croft were, of course, tiny. But even in Lewis, where the crofting population was most congested, the average crofter owned about eight sheep, one or two of which were sold each year. Although worth less than those reared by sheep farmers, the three-year-old wedders most commonly marketed by crofters were usually capable of fetching around 35 shillings apiece.

Despite steadily rising stock prices, however, crofters – apart from the fortunate occupants of the one or two large crofts to be found here and there on the mainland – remained part-time agriculturalists, as dependent as their fathers and grandfathers had been on earnings obtained away from their holdings. Kelping, the industry originally responsible for this most enduring feature of the crofting life, was, in most places outside the Uists, little more than a memory by the 1860s. With the exception of the few remaining kelpers and those tenants who combined the management of their crofts with a trade such as blacksmithing, joinery work or shoemaking, crofters had to leave home to find work. Some crofters – and more sons and daughters of crofters – still went south each summer to look for casual employment as harvesters on Lowland farms. 'It is by their work in the south country that they are making a living,' it was said of such folk in Skye in the 1880s. A more permanent stake in the southern economy was represented by the growing number of crofters' daughters who left home to enter domestic service of one kind or another. The Skye crofter who remarked that he had 'three daughters at service and they always assist me at the term' was by no means unique. Many rents (most of them falling due on the Martinmas 'term-day' to which the Skye crofter quoted here was referring) were paid, and many bills settled, with money earned in the prosperous middle-class households of Glasgow and other southern cities.

The sporting estates that began to proliferate in the Highlands in the 1870s provided similar opportunities – the stalkers and ghillies who staffed them often being either crofters or crofters' sons. And on the sheep farms, too, there was work to be had – especially in autumn when sheep were 'smeared'. Smearing, the precursor of the modern practice of 'dipping' sheep in pesticides, involved working a mixture of butter, tar and grease into the fleece, in an attempt to give protection against vermin. Since one man could smear only about 20 sheep a day and since a quarter-of-a-million were smeared annually in Inverness-shire alone, labour, at the critical time, was obviously much in demand – and much of it was supplied by crofters. During the 1860s and 1870s, moreover, the wages paid for casual work of this type rose steadily – more or less doubling between 1850 and 1880.

Important though those sources of income were, they were completely dwarfed in size and significance by the fishing industry. Members of the Napier Commission, whose 1883 enquiry into crofting conditions is the single most important source of information about the social and economic situation in the Highlands in the later nineteenth century, were of the opinion that crofters derived a larger annual income from the sea than they did from the land – a state of affairs which, in view of what was said about the Highland fishing industry in earlier chapters, seems little less than astounding. The cash that fuelled the fishing industry's eventual take-off, however, did not come from the crofter descendants of the folk James Loch and Patrick Sellar had tried so hard to turn into fishermen. The crofters of the 1860s and 1870s, though better off than their predecessors, still possessed no more than a fraction of the capital needed to develop a successful fishery. That capital came from outside the crofting community, and crofters shared only indirectly, therefore, in the fishing industry's profits. Although they received greater rewards for their labour, their position was not dissimilar, in fact, to that of their kelping forebears – in that crofter-fishermen were as disastrously vulnerable to market fluctuations as their kelper grandfathers had been. That would only become fully apparent in the 1880s, however. In the 1860s and 1870s, as the typical crofter's returns from his maritime activities expanded even more markedly than those from his work on the land, the fishing industry seemed the secure financial prop that crofting had always previously lacked.

As far as crofters were concerned, the fishing industry was divided into two quite separate branches: the white fishing and the herring fishing. The first of these, the coastal fishing for cod and ling which went on during the winter months, was given a new lease of life after the mid-century when the introduction of regular steamer services between west coast centres and the Clyde helped secure new markets. Substantial funds were injected into the industry, at this point, by curers who established themselves in places like Castlebay and Stornoway. In Stornoway, for example, there were, in 1853, only some half-dozen persons engaged in the curing business. By the 1880s, there were around 50. As well as purchasing fishermen's catches, such curers advanced the money needed to buy boats and gear. The result was that, by the 1880s, there were between 500 and 600 Lewis boats engaged in the winter fishings off the island – a total which had doubled since the 1850s and which was made up of boats usually two or three times larger than those of the earlier period. Returns to crofters, admittedly, were limited by the impossibility, in the absence of adequate rail links, of transporting fresh fish to southern markets – as well as by the control exercised over the industry by curers. The latter operated a credit system of payment which, by ensuring that fishermen were almost as perpetually and deeply in debt as kelpers had once been, made it easy for curers to keep down prices and otherwise manipulate the market to their own advantage. Despite the difficulties under which they laboured, however, it was possible for crofters to derive a reasonable income from the cod and ling fishings. In Lewis in the 1870s, for example, the six or eight men who made up a boat's crew could clear £15 to £20 apiece in a good winter – besides providing themselves and their families with fish for consumption. Such returns were seldom equalled outside the Outer Isles, the industry's main centre, but in most of the north-west, especially in Tiree, Skye, Wester Ross and Sutherland, crofters were assured of at least some income from the winter fishings. It was to the summer herring fishings, however, that they looked for real financial rewards.

Between 1850 and the early 1880s, the west coast herring industry experienced a spectacular expansion, the average annual total of barrels cured at west coast ports rising from under 80,000 in the period 1844–53 to over 180,000 in the ten years after 1874 – by which time herring landings at Stornoway were exceeded only by those at major east coast ports like Wick, Fraserburgh and Peterhead. Crofters, it is true, were even less directly involved in the organisation of the herring fishery than in its cod and ling equivalent, the herring business being the preserve of east coast fishermen who alone possessed the technical sophistication and the capital equipment – in the shape of boats and nets – needed to make a financial success of deep-water herring fishing. When east coast drifters arrived in the Minch each May, however, they almost all took on one or two local men as extra crew members. And though crofters from the Outer Isles got the lion's share of these jobs, it was not uncommon for crofters to travel to Castlebay and Stornoway from Skye, or even from the mainland, in order to obtain employment.

The west coast herring season lasted for six to eight weeks, the crofters hired for its duration earning from £7 to £10 on average. But this was only a beginning. When the drifter fleet followed the migrating herring shoals to the North Sea in July, thousands of west Highlanders and Hebrideans went with them to provide the temporary labour force that was required to man the huge number of boats engaged in the much more extensive herring fisheries which then got underway around the Northern Isles and in east coast waters. Originating in the early nineteenth century, when crofters from Sutherland, Wester Ross, Skye and Lewis began to spend a few weeks in Wick each summer, this seasonal migration grew rapidly in size after 1850. By the 1870s, practically the whole adult male population of some districts participated in the summer exodus – in Lewis, for example, 'only a few old men and boys' being left behind. Crofters from the Outer Isles, particularly Lewis, had a greater stake in the east coast fishings than tenants elsewhere. But though some Skye crofters favoured the summer fishings off the Irish coast, others went east in 'hundreds' each July, and it is probable, therefore, that the annual influx of Gaelic-speaking Highlanders experienced by fishing ports from Fife to Caithness included crofters from almost every township in north-west Scotland.

As the herring industry boomed throughout the 1860s and 1870s, so demand for labour increased – wages rising by leaps and bounds. In the 1850s, average earnings at the east coast fishings were in the region of £3 to £3.10s per person per season. By the 1880s, the corresponding figure was at least £12 – and it was not uncommon for a Lewis crofter to come home in September with £20 or £30 in his pocket. In the 1870s and 1880s, too, a growing number of women and girls, most of whom obtained their initial training in Castlebay and Stornoway curing stations, began to travel to the east coast with their menfolk in order to get work as herring gutters – their gross seasonal earnings, of around £4 or £5 per person, contributing a further boost to family budgets.

The steady rise in income from such sources – coupled with the fact that, outside a few rack-rented properties of which the Kilmuir estate in Skye was the most glaring example, rents remained at their old levels – meant that the typical crofter of the 1870s was much better off than his father had been. Once blight died down in the 1850s, potatoes again became the most important foodstuff. But dependence upon them was everywhere less complete than before the famine, the staple diet of boiled potatoes being supplemented by fairly large quantities of fresh and salted fish. And though meat was still a rarity, because sheep and cattle were too valuable to be slaughtered for food, a chicken or two might be put on the table on a special occasion, while milk and eggs were usually quite plentiful. Grain crops were generally used as winter fodder for cattle. But when crofters' potatoes ran out in spring and early summer there was usually enough money available to buy meal – imports of which rose steadily between the 1850s and 1880s.

Expanding cash incomes meant that more money could be spent not only on necessities like meal but also on all kinds of 'shop produce', crofters' name for manufactured goods. During the 30 years after 1850, therefore, manufactured clothes and shoes steadily replaced homemade varieties, while tea, sugar, jam and tobacco ceased to be almost unobtainable luxuries. Until the mid-nineteenth century, tea, for example, had been an infinitely rare and expensive beverage in north-west Scotland, and members of a crofter's family would have counted themselves lucky to have one cup each a week. But by the 1880s, when 'the poorest houses' in districts where tea had been virtually unknown before the famine brewed a pot of it 'twice a day at any rate', the *strupag* was already institutionalised as a vital component of the crofting household's existence. And the dramatic rise in tea consumption is but one obvious example of a much wider change in the crofting way of life – a change reflected in Lewis crofters' habit of spending up to £30 a year on imported goods. Their predecessors of 30 years before could not have found a sixth of that amount.

Facts such as these, as the minister of South Uist remarked in 1883, show that after the famine the crofting community shared 'in the general progress of the country'. It should not be forgotten, however, that crofters seemed prosperous only because they had recently lived in penury and that, although crofting conditions were very much better in the 1860s and 1870s than they had been in the first half of the nineteenth century, crofters' living standards did not compare at all favourably with those prevailing elsewhere in Britain. That this was the case is most apparent from Highland housing conditions, which were as bad, if not worse, than those to be found in all but the most wretched urban slums. In fact, to a stranger, as the following passage from the autobiography of a South Uist schoolmaster makes clear, crofters' houses could be almost unrecognisable for what they were:

> I shall not forget the shock I had, after a mile or so searching the road right and left for dwelling houses, and only seeing in the fast failing light what I took to be large isolated heaps of stones or earth, lying well back some hundreds of yards or so from the road we were travelling. I burst out: 'But where are the houses?' Pointing to one of the . . . heaps I had noticed, my companion replied, 'These are the houses!'

Such were one man's first impressions of the black houses in which, in the 1870s, the bulk of the crofting population still lived.

Varying somewhat in design from one locality to another, the black house's principal architectural feature was an enormously thick outer wall made by building two drystone dykes, the one inside the other, and filling the space between with earth and rubble. Seldom more than six or seven feet high, the walls were as many feet in breadth at the base but tapered slightly towards the top. On them was raised a framework of rafters, often consisting – especially in the Outer Isles where timber was almost unobtainable – of a nondescript collection of old oars, masts and pieces of driftwood. The rafters were covered with 'divots' or large turfs and those, in turn, were thatched with straw from the householder's corn. The thatch was secured by heather ropes weighted with large stones, and the roof as a whole rested on the inner edges of its supporting walls, the absence of eaves ensuring that the roof could not be blown off by Atlantic gales.

Long and low, the crofter's house, according to one observer, resembled nothing so much as a potato pit – a resemblance most striking in the case of the more lowly hovels which were constructed of turf rather than stone and which were propped up by the simple expedient of piling earth against their walls. Nor was the unprepossessing outward appearance of the black house compensated for by inward comfort. The floor was of earth and, because of the absence of eaves, the walls were perpetually damp. In the 1870s, admittedly, the availability of a little more money led to the appearance – in Skye and on the mainland at least – of black houses equipped with windows, floorboards, more than one door, a modicum of decent furniture and, perhaps, two apartments. The older type of dwelling – still much as it had been in the 1830s or, for that matter, in the 1770s – had none of these refinements, however, and in the 1870s and 1880s it was still to be found all over north-west Scotland, especially in the Outer Isles where its predominance was almost completely unchallenged.

Houses of this sort had no windows and no chimney, the smoke from the peat fire which burned day and night, winter and summer alike, being left to find its way out through the thatch. Furnished with some planks and barrels, a few three-legged stools, and a box bed which was often roofed over to shelter its occupants from the sooty rainwater which dripped from the thatch, the archetypal black house consisted of a single apartment. The crofter and his family lived at one end; their cattle inhabited the other; and, as if that were not diversity enough, the crofter's hens roosted in the rafters above the fire. Animals and humans entered by the same door and only rarely was any attempt made to erect an internal partition between their respective halves of the dwelling – the only general concession to sanitation consisting of an effort to incline the earthen floor towards the byre, or cowshed, in the hope that dung and urine, if not the stench they emitted, could be confined to that end of the house. Dung was seldom so confined, partly because of droppings from the hens in the rafters, partly because the interior midden was removed only once a year – when it was spread on the fields in spring. In winter, when the weather was wettest and when cattle were confined for long periods, conditions were particularly appalling. A newspaper correspondent who visited Lewis in January 1878 reported that, in crofters' houses, 'cows stand . . . knee deep in a dung heap'. And five years later a Free Church minister in the same island told the Napier Commission that, when visiting members of his congregation, he frequently knelt in mud while praying with them. Damp, dark, and dirty inside, crofters' dwellings were usually surrounded by domestic refuse of all kinds, the general squalor and discomfort being added to by the frequent non-existence of paths and approach roads as well as by crofters' enforced habit of building their homes in the least attractive and often wettest part of their holdings in order to conserve their all too precious arable land.

The unhealthy effects of dampness and insanitation were aggravated by the tendency – especially prevalent in more congested townships – for one croft's midden to foul the well of the holding beside it. In such conditions, a poor law official remarked in 1885: 'It is not surprising that . . . typhus and typhoid fevers and other forms of disease . . . should be of frequent occurrence; it is more surprising that any person should escape.' Typhoid continued, therefore, to be fairly common among the crofting population in the Outer Isles even at the end of the nineteenth century – by which time it had more or less been eliminated from the rest of Scotland. Tuberculosis, too, remained a crofting scourge. As late as the 1920s, for instance, the tuberculosis mortality rate in Lewis, where the black house lingered longest, was two-and-a-half times the Scottish average. Often contagious disease was kept in check only by the relative isolation of many communities or by the traditional practice of shunning its victims. And even when it was absent, conditions were far from ideal. The health of children, in particular, was poor. Thus the logbooks of the state-run schools established in the Hebrides after the Education Act of 1872 record a great deal of sickness and ill-health among their pupils. And the report of a newspaper correspondent who visited Skye in December 1877 makes the point more adequately than any statistics:

> At the top of the village [of Torrin], gathered in a listless way on a bit of moss land before an almost ruinous cottage were a dozen children – as squalid and as miserable as any that could be produced from the innermost dens of the Cowgate [one of Edinburgh's more notorious slums] . . . What I saw at Torrin I have seen at many places since: children, not the bronzed, healthy urchins such as one meets in Lowland country districts, but puny, uncombed, bleareyed, shivering little objects . . . This sorrowful index to the condition of the crofter forces itself very strongly on a stranger's notice as he passes through this island.

Although standards of living were rising, the crofting community was not, therefore, in a position that could be described as satisfactory. And even the economic situation was not one of unimpeded progress, higher stock prices and increased incomes being at least partly offset by the deteriorating capacity of crofters' arable land. 'For the last 54 years I have been continuously cropping the same ground,' a North Uist crofter told the Napier Commission in 1883. 'And how,' he asked, 'can you expect good crops out of that?' The answer, as crofters were only too well aware, was that you could not. Yet in many townships the same tiny plots had been incessantly cultivated since individually occupied crofts had taken the place of the periodically reallocated, and sometimes fallowed, rigs which had been central to pre-crofting husbandry. Crofters, it needs stressing in this context, were not unaware of the benefits of allowing land to go occasionally out of cropping. In one township in North Uist, for example, crofters made strenuous efforts to practice a rotation which permitted regular fallowing. But so small were their holdings that if they left more than about one-tenth of their arable land out of cultivation, they could not produce the fodder needed for their cattle. Everywhere, crofters were similarly situated, the common predicament being articulated thus by tenants of Connista in the Trotternish district of Skye: 'The smallness of the crofts renders it imperative on us to till the whole of our ground from year to year, and by so doing the land is growing inferior and less productive.' In those circumstances, a steady decline in the land's productive capacity was inevitable. While it remained possible, with the aid of lavish applications of seaweed and manure, to obtain as many as seven or eight returns on potatoes in a good year, returns on cereal crops fell to almost ludicrously low levels.

In the parish of Kilmuir, a district containing some of the most fertile land in Skye, crofters' fields were reckoned in the 1880s to yield only two or three returns of oats – meaning that for every grain sown as few as two were harvested. In one more than usually prosperous township near Portree, ten or 11 bolls of oats cropped for every five bolls sown was considered a fair return, and was achieved only by changing seed every two years – more often than most crofters thought necessary. In areas where the land had deteriorated even more markedly, or where it had not been so good to begin with, yields were even more pitiful – with the result that, in the 1870s and 1880s, many crofters expected little more than a single return on the corn sown on their desperately impoverished holdings. And since poor harvests were the rule even in good years, a wet summer meant no harvest at all. In the spring of 1877, for example, the 20 crofters in the township of Earlish, just south of Uig in Skye, sowed 77 bolls of oats. That autumn they harvested 20 bolls.

Few crofts, as stressed previously, had ever been large enough to produce all the food needed by the families living on them. But the marked decline that occurred in their productive capacity in the nineteenth century's third quarter meant that crofters had to spend a steadily growing proportion of their incomes on meal and other provisions. In the early 1880s, for example, many Skye crofters had to buy as much as £12 worth of meal every year. And throughout the north-west there were individual crofters who had to set aside £20 or more annually in order to purchase the food their holdings could not grow. The experience of one Barra crofter was typical. Over 35 years, he brought home more than £500 from the east coast fishings. As he told the Napier Commission, however, he 'spent the whole of that on meal and on other things to support the family, all for want of land'.

Despite their increased incomes, therefore, crofters remained unable to accumulate any capital. They were, on the contrary, in debt to meal dealers and to merchants and travelling salesmen of every kind. 'Our liabilities are so great that, supposing we sold all our cattle, we would still be left in debt,' crofters at Carinish, North Uist, declared in 1883. 'The property that we have does not belong to ourselves,' a South Uist crofter remarked. 'It belongs to the men who supply us with food and clothing.' This was universal. In the parish of Snizort in Skye, by the early 1880s, one township of seven tenants owed £54 to their meal suppliers, while larger townships of around 30 tenants owed between £150 and £300 to the same men. Almost everywhere in the Highlands and Islands, then, the crofting community's new-found prosperity rested on shaky foundations. Much of it depended on credit. And crofters' credit was good only as long as wages and stock prices continued high. As a Skye crofter pointed out in 1883: 'Want of success at the fishing, or other work we go to, for even one year, means either ruin or starvation.'

Despite large-scale clearance having ceased, his insecurity, therefore, was still the dominant fact of the crofter's life. In part, that insecurity was financial; in part, it derived, as it had always done, from the natural difficulties of his situation. Either way, as the Napier Commission pointed out, each and every crofter was 'exposed to unusual risks and vicissitudes':

> A good harvest or a good haul may make him comfortable for a season. A blight, an early frost, a wet autumn, a long winter, a gale of wind, a wayward movement of the herring, may deprive him of food for his family, funds for his rent, and seed for his ground.

As stressed at the start of this book, however, frost, gales and the like were acceptable hazards. Far less tolerable were problems arising from human action. And many of the difficulties confronting the late nineteenth-century crofting population were deemed, by crofters anyway, to be in this latter category. Thus the crofter's tenurial position, far from encouraging him to make some attempt to overcome the obstacles in his way, acted as a powerful disincentive to betterment of any kind. Not for nothing did at least one early nineteenth-century traveller, an Orcadian by the name of Samuel Laing, remark on the huge difference, in this regard, between crofters and their Norwegian counterparts. The latter laboured under climatic conditions that were even worse than those confronting tenants in the north-west of Scotland. But their ownership of the land and the fact that they received 'the advantage of their own exertions', gave them, or so Laing thought, an interest in effecting all sorts of improvements. Not only were their small farms better cared for, their houses – in contrast to the 'dark one-room hovels' of the Highlands – were commodious residences with several apartments, wooden floors and glass windows. In Norway, Samuel Laing concluded, one saw 'the Highland glens without the Highland lairds'.

Landlords and their apologists, of course, blamed the many obvious deficiencies in crofters' conditions on their alleged idleness and conservatism. The charge of laziness was a slur that can readily be dismissed. As Frank Fraser Darling was to acknowledge in the 1950s, however, the accusation of conservatism cannot be so readily rejected:

> It does not matter to the Gael that a changed practice will reap him a bigger material reward. That is not recompense for having to that extent placed himself outside his group. If the material reward is real, he will be envied by his fellows, and that is not a good state to be in, even for one growing season. If the reward is illusory, he will be ridiculed, and that is not good either in a society where there is no privacy.

But constraints of this kind operate in practically every rural society on earth, and though they produce a situation in which 'progress' is less of a self-evident good than in urban societies, they do not make it impossible. Their innate reluctance to embrace innovation, then, does not, in itself, explain why, for example, crofters lagged so far behind their peers in Norway. The real explanation of that state of affairs, as many nineteenth-century writers and many more crofters suggested, and as is indicated by what followed the Crofters Act of 1886, is to be found in those tenurial arrangements which have already been mentioned – arrangements as agriculturally adverse as they were socially unjust.

'If you give a tenant a rock in perpetuity, he will make it a garden before long,' Arthur Young, an eighteenth-century agriculturalist, remarked. 'If you give him a garden for a limited time, it will become a wilderness.' The relevance of Young's comment to nineteenth-century crofting circumstances would have been immediately apparent to the parish minister of Glenshiel in Wester Ross:

> The lotters [or crofters] holding their lands only from year to year, having no meliorations allowed them, and having learnt from experience that to improve their houses or lots, instead of producing any permanent advantage to themselves is only holding out an inducement to others to offer a few shillings of additional rent, and to deprive them of the fruit of their labour, are discouraged from attempting improvements.

Made in 1836, that complaint was to echo and re-echo through the 50 years that followed. 'If we had the assurance that our rents would not be raised, or ourselves removed,' a Skye crofter told the Napier Commission, 'we would have encouragement to improve our holdings better than we do.'

But as things stood, he went on, 'if I should improve my holding, the land-lord can have my improvements valued to increase the rent, and if I don't pay such a rent, I will be warned and sent off at the May term.' That crofter spoke from personal experience. And as was afterwards attested by Sheriff David Brand, the man put in charge of the judicial tribunal* eventually established with a view to remedying such injustices, his experience was by no means unique:

> Again and again I have had cases brought under my own observation where old men were able to give the history of successive holdings occupied and improved by them, but taken away after a certain term of years and the benefit of the improvements passed on to someone else or to the landlord.

Equally debilitating was the constant serving of eviction summonses on crofting tenants. These, as a Lewis crofter remarked, awaited anyone who dared to 'transgress the laws of the chamberlain [or estate manager]' – for they were, to cite David Brand again, 'the ordinary and normal mode of bringing a crofter to book for some real or supposed shortcoming on his part'. Between 1840 and 1883, 1,740 such notices of eviction – affecting some 7,000 families – were issued in Skye alone. Most were intended to enforce the payment of rent arrears and the majority were not acted on – if they had been there would have been no crofters left on the island. But their effect can well be imagined in a society where attachment to, and dependence on, the land was such as to make eviction – to borrow Prime Minister William Gladstone's famous utterance on the Irish land question – 'equivalent to a sentence of death'. Estate managements, however, seldom took their tenants' susceptibilities into account. In 1874, when the factor on Sir James Matheson's Lewis estate served eviction notices on no fewer than 56 crofters in Bernera, he considered his action 'a little detail . . . too small a matter to bother Sir James about'.

Occasionally, voices were raised in criticism of such policies. Thus the author of an 1858 treatise on Highland estate management noted that he had 'met with hundreds of instances of the earnest desire crofters have to improve if they have fair opportunity'. Urging landlords to interest them-selves in their crofting tenantry's welfare by granting leases, modernising houses, and giving instruction in scientific agricultural techniques, the same author went on:

> We have a peasantry in the Highlands whom we lodge in hovels of mud, whom we drive out of their native glens and straths . . . and [whom we] crowd into these parts that are not so capable of supporting sheep. We extort rents for the miserable plots allotted to [crofters], give them no stated employ-ment, leave them as ignorant as cattle, and then abuse them because they are not all that we wish them to be.

---

*The background to the establishment of this tribunal, the Crofters Commission, is explored later.

Other writers made similar points. But their recommendations, like those made by the Central Relief Board during the famine, were ignored. Assured of massive incomes from the then booming sheep farming sector, most landlords, throughout the 1860s and 1870s, wished only to forget about the crofters whose expropriation had made such incomes possible. In the few cases where leases were offered to crofting tenants they seem to have been designed, therefore, to weaken rather than to enhance the latter's position. Thus the leases offered to some Lewis crofters in the 1870s contained no less than 54 separate regulations, the infringement of any one of them immediately cancelling the rights of the lessee. An old man from Ness summed up the general feeling. He could not, he said, keep ten commandments for a mansion in the heavens, far less 54 for a black house in Lewis. The leases were accordingly turned down.

Because they had no security, crofters made few improvements to their homes and holdings. Their landlords, whether from lack of interest or from meanness, made none either. Here and there, admittedly, crofters were helped and encouraged to build better houses. But such enlightened actions were exceptional. And the few crofters who dared to commence improvements on their own account ran the risk of losing not only the benefit of those improvements, if removed, but also the capital invested in them – for landlord were not legally obliged to compensate evicted tenant for the loss of such investments as they might have made in holdings from which they were ejected. Some landlords paid a little compensation – but never enough. Others paid nothing at all – the history of John Gillies, a crofter on the Kilmuir estate in Skye being, in this respect, quite typical. On being turned out of one holding he 'got £7 as the value of the house' he had been forced to abandon. 'The wall of that house cost me £15 to build.' Gillies said. 'At the next place from which I was removed,' he continued, 'I quarried all the stones for the house which I built and I got no compensation for it'.

Nor did landlords evince any interest in combating the causes of agricultural backwardness among the crofting community. This was a pity because crofters could not, as one commentator put it, 'drink in agricultural theories from the clouds'. And if their landlords gave them no help in this regard, no one else was likely to make good the deficiency. As was observed of North Uist in 1799:

> To carry on the business of improvements in this island to advantage, it will be necessary to set a proper example. The greatest part of the people have never been out of the island and are altogether unacquainted with agriculture or improvement of any kind whatever, and without some instruction it cannot be supposed that they will do anything out of the common road.

That advice was never acted on by the landowner, Lord MacDonald, to whom it was addressed. And the proprietors of other crofting estates adopted an identical stance – with most estate managements making absolutely no effort to promote more effective utilisation of crofting land. Seeds, in consequence, were not changed more than once in a dozen years, and what crofters knew of crop rotation they had picked up for themselves. Drains were seldom dug; fences seldom built. To have done such things would have been to risk a rise in rent, perhaps eviction if the additional rent could not be found or if the landlord's factor was looking for a better-than-average croft with which to reward someone to whom he owed a favour.

Because of the general lack of boundary walls and fences, there was little to differentiate each crofter's skimpy plot from those of his neighbours. In Lewis, for example:

> A few small stones erected at intervals form the only divisions, so that in autumn when the crop is housed and the potatoes pitted, one common stretch of barren looking land, over which the cattle and sheep roam at will, surrounds the various cottages.

Such a system, of course, favoured the most traditionalist and least progressive crofters – for if a man did improve his holding by a judicious application of seed or fertiliser, he was quite unable to protect his improvements from the ravages caused by his neighbours' straying stock.

The autumnal dreariness of the typical township was added to, in the opinion of outside observers at least, by the ubiquitous lazybeds, those ineptly named and laboriously constructed mounds and ridges of earth which were thrown up in rocky and marshy land in order to supplement the produce of crofters' tiny fields. A visiting newspaperman penned this description of lazybeds at Keose in Lewis:

> Of every shape and size, these grave-like patches give the place on a dull day an almost sepulchral appearance. Some of them, two or three yards in breadth, run in straight lines from the road away up the hillside, divided from one another by trenches more than a foot deep and several yards in width; others curve round corners in crescent form; a [third] kind straggle about in serpentine fashion; yet another variety have an irregularity worthy of the most neglected country churchyard. All speak to not a little labour on the part of the occupants.

Essentially a response to an environment that was frequently uncongenial to normal modes of cultivation, lazybeds or *feannagan*, as that account of Keose suggests, varied in design according to the terrain – while their numbers varied in inverse proportion to the quantity of more naturally fertile arable land at the disposal of particular townships. In townships situated on the machair land of the Outer Isles' Atlantic seaboard, therefore, lazybeds were few and far between. In districts such as the south-eastern corner of Lewis and eastern Harris, on the other hand, they constituted almost all the crop-bearing land available to crofters.

On lazybeds and in fields alike, the main crofting crops were oats and potatoes – the latter giving way gradually to the former as rising cash incomes made it possible to buy alternative foodstuffs and as higher stock prices made cattle rearing, and thus fodder production, an increasingly attractive proposition. Irrespective of what it carried, however, land was mostly cultivated with the help only of spade and *cas chrom*, the traditional agricultural implement of the Gael. Although frequently despised by external observers of the crofting scene, the cas chrom, or foot-plough, arguably produced better crops than the mechanical ploughs of more modern times – by virtue of its enabling crofters to make the best possible use of intrinsically marginal land. Turning over the ground by hand – whether with spade or cas chrom – was nevertheless a laborious task, and one that was made all the more unpleasant by the speed with which it had to be performed. So weak and shallow was the soil, so heavy and persistent the winter rains, that crofters could not cultivate their holdings in winter – as was the custom further south – without causing serious erosion. All the work on the land had consequently to be done in the few brief weeks between the winter's end and crofters' departure for the herring fishings. For the crofting tenant, therefore, the spring was an acutely difficult time. If he planted his crops too early he chanced losing them in a cold, wet April and May – while, if he delayed too long, they might not ripen at all. Once made, however, his decision ushered in a busy and – in some ways cheerful – time for the crofter and his family. With the help of his wife and children, he carted the winter's accumulation of dung from his byre to his fields, adding to this dung his share of the tangle thrown up on any half-way accessible beach and adding to it also the soot-impregnated thatch and turf taken – prior to its annual rethatching – from the roof of his house. Then, with spade or cas chrom, the crofter worked his precious fertilisers into his famished land.

The relatively unsophisticated nature of the crofter's system of cultivation was paralleled in his stock rearing activities. In most crofting districts the quantity of stock owned by a tenant was determined by estate managements who fixed a so-called 'souming' for every holding. In order to determine soumings, still very much a feature of crofting life, the 'carry' of a township's common grazing – that is, the numbers of cattle, sheep and other stock which it could pasture – was first established. From the total township stocking thus arrived at, a fixed proportion was allocated to each tenant, individual soumings being calculated with reference to the wintering capacity of a croft's arable land or with reference to the rent paid for it – the two, in theory at least, being closely related. Since they involved a whole series of equations in which, for example, one horse equalled eight foals or two cows, while one cow equalled eight calves, four stirks, eight sheep, twelve hogs or sixteen lambs, souming regulations were inherently difficult to enforce. Hence the 1912 verdict of the officially appointed body eventually put in place to handle such matters: 'The greatest source of trouble in the crofting area has been, and is, the management, or rather mismanagement, of common grazings'. Even today, despite the existence of a veritable host of parliamentary Acts and Orders on the subject, souming regulations are frequently ignored or abused. In the nineteenth century, needless to say, that was still more common. Over-stocking was rampant and, combined with the effects of declining soil fertility, produced a situation in which there was seldom enough winter fodder to go round. The outcome – except in unusually open winters – was that spring found crofters' cattle in very poor condition.

The principal cause of over-stocking and kindred sins was ignorance rather than cupidity. And during the 1860s and 1870s, such practices began to be offset as the beginnings of agricultural enlightenment started to be evident among crofters. By the 1880s, for example, crofters' cattle and sheep were generally better cared for than they had been some 20 or 30 years before – a fact which accounted for a considerable part of the higher prices obtained for them. Most crofters, however, still knew very little either of the principles of stock management or of advances in breeding techniques. And even when the necessary knowledge was available it was seldom applied – since crofters, being far from wealthy, usually yielded to the 'almost irresistible' temptation to sell their best and most valuable animals rather than retain them for breeding purposes. Little attention was thus paid to the quality of bulls and still less to the quality of tups – for if crofters were not greatly concerned about the pedigrees of their cattle, they were, as one observer remarked, 'still less careful in the management of . . . sheep [consisting, for the most part, of] a nondescript class of blackface'. The result was that common grazings, which if pastured by the proper number of correctly-bred stock would have been capable of yielding fine animals, were generally grazed by sheep and cattle of obviously indifferent quality – something all too apparent in the difference between the market price for crofters' stock and that fetched by animals reared on sheep farms.

The crofting community's many difficulties notwithstanding, the 1860s and 1870s, in comparison both with what had gone before and with what was to follow, were a prosperous period. From the foregoing account of their circumstances, however, it is clear that crofters had little cause to be satisfied with the conditions in which they lived. Their houses were little more than hovels. They had no security of tenure. On being deprived of their holdings, they received no compensation in respect of such improvements as they might have made to these holdings. They depended for their livelihood on wages earned far from home. Above all, they did not have enough land. In the 1880s, when crofters at last launched a concerted attack on Highland landlordism, all these grievances came very strongly to the fore. And all of them, especially the lack of land, stemmed ultimately from the agrarian system which commercial landlordism had itself created.

In the decade prior to the land war which began in north-west Scotland in 1882, the region's agrarian structure was dominated, as it had been since the eighteenth century, by great estates. Some of these were of quite gigantic proportions. Many sizeable islands were entirely owned by a single individual – while one mainland property, that of the Duke of Sutherland, occupied the greater part of a county. The proprietor of Lewis, Sir James Matheson, owned 424,560 acres – valued, in 1872, at the rental equivalent of £19,488 a year. Lord MacDonald and MacLeod of Dunvegan, owners of the two largest estates on Skye, had been forced – by their reduced financial circumstances – to sell off large tracts of their ancestral possessions in the years around 1850. Some 20 years later, however, the former still owned 129,919 acres worth £11,614 a year, while the latter had at his disposal a grand total of 141,679 acres, thought capable of bringing in an annual income of £8,464. Properties of comparable size were to be found on the mainland's west coast – Alexander Matheson's estates in Kintail and Lochalsh extending to 220,433 acres, and those of Cameron of Lochiel in northern Argyll and western Inverness-shire amounting, in all, to 125,754 acres. But large though such possessions were, they were completely dwarfed by the colossus of the Sutherland estate which, in the early 1870s, extended to 1,362,343 acres worth £68,398 a year.*

Although fairly small estates – small in this context meaning from five to twenty thousand acres – were to be found here and there, especially in Mull, Morvern and parts of Skye, the general pattern was, therefore, one of a few wealthy landlords controlling vast expanses of territory. The whole of the Outer Isles from the Butt of Lewis to Barra Head, for example, was divided into only five estates. The islands of Tiree and Iona were relatively small components of the Duke of Argyll's 168,315 acre domain – as was the Ross of Mull. And though Skye in the 1880s was parcelled out among ten landlords, four of these – Lord MacDonald, MacLeod of Dunvegan and the proprietors of the Glendale and Kilmuir estates – owned about 90 per cent of the island's land surface, leaving only 10 per cent, or 38,000 acres, for the remaining half dozen.

The rate of absentee landlordism was high throughout north-west Scotland. And it was invariably highest on large estates. In Skye in 1882, for example, the five resident proprietors owned 24,045 acres between them. The rest of the island, 365,762 acres in all, was owned by absentees. Such absenteeism was, as it still is, a highly emotive issue. But in some respects, it was of no immediate matter to nineteenth-century crofters. Crofting tenants had little contact with their landlords, whether resident or absentee. And while the former probably reinvested a greater proportion of their rentals in their properties than the latter, it was sheep farmers – from whom Highland lairds derived the bulk of their revenues – rather than

---

*For comparative purposes, this last figure is worth more than £2 million at late twentieth-century values.

crofters who were most likely to be the beneficiaries of such reinvestment. As a gross and highly visible violation of the typically Victorian notion that property had duties as well as rights, absenteeism, however, attracted a great deal of adverse comment from nineteenth-century radicals of every hue. And by highlighting the immensity of the gulf between their own lives in north-west Scotland's all too often squalid townships and the lives lived by their landlords in London or the south of France – where Skye's Lord MacDonald, for instance, seems to have spent a lot of time – absenteeism may have done something to foster discontent among crofters themselves. But it made little direct contribution, as far as can be ascertained, to fuelling the fires of rebellion.

Since landlords could not effectively manage their properties from a distance, absenteeism did have the important effect of enhancing the role of estate factors – men who, as a Tiree crofter remarked bitterly, 'had all the power in their own hands'. In his 1813 publication, *A General View of the Agriculture of the Counties of Ross and Cromarty*, one Highland landlord, George MacKenzie of Coull, commented:

> There can be no doubt that the less a factor has to do with the management of an estate the better. The temptations to which he is constantly exposed, when full powers are given, are sometimes greater than a man of ordinary virtue and fortitude can resist.

Mostly, such strictures went unheeded. Factorial abuses multiplied accordingly, such multiplication being hastened by the fact that – in a society composed of a handful of resident proprietors, a few sheep farmers and a multitude of crofting tenants who were considered beyond the pale of social respectability – factors easily, indeed inevitably, accumulated into their own hands practically every one of the public offices in the districts they administered. In his estate management capacity, for example, Donald Munro, who was factor on the Lewis estate from 1853 until 1875, brought complaints against crofters to the attention of the legal authorities. Then, as Stornoway's procurator fiscal, Munro initiated prosecutions of the crofters whose alleged misconduct he had reported to himself. Another Hebridean factor, Alexander MacDonald – who was known to crofters as the 'uncrowned king of Skye' and to civil servants in London by the less flattering soubriquet of 'Pooh-Bah' – simultaneously managed no less than five of Skye's estates, thereby holding sway over 85 per cent of the island's population. MacDonald's factorial functions were combined with his activities as a bank agent, with his role as Skye's only lawyer, with his official duties as Skye's principal collector of rates and taxes, with his clerkship of six parochial school boards and with his captaincy of the Portree volunteers.

The power and influence wielded by such men was immense and, as far as crofters were concerned, quite unchallengeable: 'He who is factor, banker, farmer, JP [Justice of the Peace] and so forth,' as was observed in

1876, 'has very little sympathy to spare for those whom he considers in his way'. Rank injustices could thus be perpetrated with impunity. Donald Munro – 'a name,' it was remarked in 1960, 'still spoken of with loathing in Lewis' – distinguished himself by annually appropriating a specified number of hens from each household, hence Munro's nickname, *Domhall Ruadh nan Cearc*.* Other estate managers, for their part, favoured petty tyrannies of a still more bizarre nature. There are, for instance, authenticated cases of factors whose policy it was to increase crofters' rents by sixpence on every occasion that crofters omitted to touch their caps or otherwise show respect for them. Corrupt, inefficient, riddled with favouritism and nepotism, dependent at a local level on so-called 'ground-officers' drawn from among the crofter class and consequently more despised than the factor himself, Highland estate managements were both hated and feared by the crofting community. 'Na'm bu tig a' la dh'eireas tu-sa as a sin,' a Hebridean crofter is said to have remarked at a factor's graveside.† And a verse composed at another estate manager's funeral reflects the same very general sentiments:

> Cuiribh air! Cuiribh air!
> 'S e chuireadh òirnne;
> 'S ma dh'éireas e rihist,
> Cuiribh e 'n còrr oirnn!‡

It was thus no coincidence that, during the troubles of the 1880s, those proprietors who managed their own estates were said to have experienced considerably less 'inconvenience' than landlords whose properties were looked after by factors.

Most of the estates presided over by Donald Munro, Alexander MacDonald and their fellows shared the same broad characteristics. On the mainland, it is true, there were one or two properties, such as the Knoydart estate in western Inverness-shire, where the clearances had been pushed to their logical conclusion and almost all the available land put under sheep. And there were other areas – Morvern, Glenelg, and parts of Mull and Skye, for instance – where crofters' share of the land was so minute as to be almost negligible. The parish of Bracadale on the MacLeod estate in Skye was one of these. Described by a Skye crofter as 'practically a desert', it consisted almost entirely of six sheep farms, three of which, Glenbrittle, Talisker and Drynoch were enormous holdings whose tenants, in 1883, paid annual rents of £1,800, £1,575 and £1,260 respectively. More typical of the north-west coast and the Hebrides, however, were those districts where the

---

*Meaning, Red (Munro having been red-haired) Donald of the Hens.

†'May the day never come when you'll rise out of that!' The translation is Alexander Nicolson's.

‡'Heap on him! Heap on him! It's him that would put on us, and if he rise again, he'll just put more on us.' The translation is Alexander Nicolson's.

effects of clearing extensive tracts of land and cramming evicted tenants into the less desirable corners could be observed side by side. Four such localities were the widely separated, but by no means untypical, parishes of Farr in Sutherland, Uig in Lewis, Duirinish and Waternish in Skye, and the islands of South Uist and Benbecula.

The aggregate land rental of the parish of Farr was £6,492. And in Farr, as elsewhere, the proportions paid by the various classes of agricultural tenants provide a fairly accurate guide not only to the value of the lands occupied by them but also to the nature of the social and economic system which the land supported. Of the total rental of £6,492, then, seven farmers paid £5,810 and 293 crofting tenants £682. Of the latter group, none paid more than £10 a year in rent, five paid between £6 and £10, 160 paid between £2 and £6, and the remainder paid under £2. The smallest farm was valued at £290 a year, the largest croft at £7.16s. And while almost 300 crofters occupied holdings whose aggregate value was only £682 a year, a single sheep farmer – who was not even resident in the district – held lands for which he paid an annual rent of £1,688. Such was the end result of the much vaunted 'improvements' on the Sutherland estate. The parish which had witnessed the clearance of Strathnaver now contained, as the Napier Commission observed, 'the extremes of subdivision and consolidation; there is a striking absence of intermediate positions; the small farmer and the substantial crofter disappear entirely'.

The total land rental of the parish of Uig, in the south-western corner of Lewis, was £3,698. Although less far-reaching than those in Sutherland, the clearances in Uig had been far-reaching enough. As a result, the tenants of two deer forests – which, by the 1880s, were replacing sheep farms all over the Highlands – held lands valued at £1,120 annually. Four sheep farmers whose annual rents were over £100 apiece, paid £887 a year to the estate. And two farmers whose rents were below the £100 mark, paid £170. The total annual rent of the 420 crofts in the parish was £1,521. Five crofters occupied fairly substantial holdings worth between £10 and £30 a year. A further 22 held crofts valued at between £6 and £10. But the vast majority, 393 in all, had to be content with holdings worth less than £6 a year. Because clearance had been less complete, the social and agricultural extremities were not, therefore, so far apart as they were in Farr. As the Napier Commissioners pointed out, however:

> Two small farms below £100 in annual rent and five crofters' holdings between £10 and £30, out of an aggregate number of 426 agricultural tenancies, is a miserable representation of that system of substantial and graduated tenancy so desirable in a community of which the vast numerical majority are associated with the cultivation of the land.

In Duirinish and Waternish, as in Benbecula and South Uist, the situation, though different in detail, was similar in kind, and particulars need not be provided here. What needs stressing, however, is the picture of north-west Scotland's agrarian system that can be derived by combining information drawn from all four study areas.

The aggregate land rental of the four districts was £22,180. Of this amount, 28 sheep farmers and two tenants of deer forests paid £13,982. Half-a-dozen tenants whose holdings were classified as small farms – that is, they were worth between £30 and £100 a year – paid £345. The 2,090 crofting tenants whose holdings were worth less than £30 a year paid a grand total of £7,853, which represented an average croft rent of £3 15s.1d. per head, as compared with the sheep farmers' average of £488. Of the 2,000-plus crofting tenants, only 56 whose holdings were worth more than £10 a year could be considered substantial crofters. A further 256 occupied moderately sized holdings for which they paid between £6 and £10 a year. But the overwhelming majority, 1,778 in all, paid annual rents of under £6 for what were, at best, insufficient holdings and, at worst, mere scraps of sterile land.

The total population of the four areas under examination was 15,816, and was made up of 3,226 families of whom 3,091 were the families of small agricultural tenants. Of the latter, as already mentioned, six held small farms; 56 (under 2 per cent of the total population) held substantial crofts; 256 (or 8 per cent of the total) occupied moderately sized crofts; 1,778, (55 per cent of the total) were the tenants of small crofts; and the remaining 825 families, who paid no rent at all, must be considered land-less cottars and squatters. Taken together, these figures show that, in our four parishes, sheep farmers and deer forest tenants, who numbered only 30 in all and constituted less than 1 per cent of the population, paid 63 per cent of the aggregate rental – while crofting tenants, who made up almost 90 per cent of the total population, paid only 35 per cent of the rent. At the same time, and even more significantly, *the 30 tenants in the first category occupied nearly two-thirds of the available land leaving little more than one-third for the other 3,061.*

These figures are italicised because they encapsulate the consequence of the clearances – a consequence which underlay the discontent which erupted into violence in the 1880s. On one side, a large population lived on tiny holdings in conditions of acute congestion and deprivation. On the other, a few wealthy men occupied vast emptinesses on which they grazed sheep or stalked deer.

Nor can it be argued that crofters, being cultivators of land as opposed to sheep-rearing pastoralists, were not so badly affected by this situation as might at first appear. The amount of pasture available to a crofting township was, and is, of crucial significance to its occupants – for crofters, considered as agriculturalists, were, and are, pastoralists first and foremost. And not only had crofters lost the bulk of north-west Scotland's hill pastures to sheep farmers, they had lost the best and most desirable portions of these pastures. In Uig, for example, the cleared areas incorporated some of the parish's best wintering ground, including all the machairs except those of Valtos and Kneep. Uig crofters, then, were left in occupation only of the East Loch Roag and Carloway districts – less attractive to sheep farmers because their grazings are of a poor, boggy type. As *The Times* remarked on the day following the publication of the Napier Commission's report, then, the Highland Clearances had reduced northwest Scotland to 'an economical condition scarcely consistent with agrarian content and social stability', and the many ill effects of this state of affairs were seriously aggravated by the region containing lots of absolutely landless families.

In the four parishes mentioned in preceding paragraphs, about a quarter of all resident families were classified as landless and subsumed under the generic titles of cottars and squatters. The former, in technical terms, were the inhabitants of dwellings built on holdings whose officially recognised occupants were usually close relatives of the cottars concerned – while the latter usually lived in houses built on the edge of a township's common grazings. Cottars generally cultivated a part of the croft on which they resided and occasionally paid a share of the rent. Squatters, however, paid no rent, despite the fact that they had frequently brought a part of common pasture into cultivation. Because their position was utterly insecure and their very existence a violation of estate regulations, precise numbers of cottars and squatters are difficult to determine. Equally hard to determine is the point at which the lowlier crofters became cottars – a fact which led the Napier Commissioners to observe, correctly, that the distinction between the two groups was 'more easily felt than delineated'. About the origins of landlessness, however, there was no debate. It was the consequence of congestion and subdivision pushed to their ultimate conclusion: when holdings became too small to be further divided, and when there was no land on which new holdings could be created, some unfortunates were necessarily left without any land at all. The dictates of the kelp and fishing industries, combined with the effects of clearances and population pressure had begun the process. And though these had ceased to be operative by the 1860s and 1870s, except in Lewis where the population maximum was not reached until the early twentieth century, the landlessness created before the mid-1850s remained. Locally, in fact, it was still tending to increase, if only for the reason, as an Arisaig crofter put it, that it was 'a hard thing for any man to rear a family and expel them . . . It is the young people who support the old.'

Predictably, the problem of landlessness was most acute in areas where the crofting population was at its most dense. On the mainland and in Mull, therefore, cottars and squatters were fairly few and far between. On Skye, where the MacDonald estate alone contained 122 cottars in 1883, they were more numerous. And in Tiree and the Outer Isles, it was not uncommon, as the Napier Commission noted, to find 'crowds of squatters who construct hovels, appropriate land, and possess and pasture stock, but pay no rent, obey no control, and scarcely recognise any allegiance or authority'. In Tiree, for instance, the Duke of Argyll's policy of consolidating crofts at every opportunity – while benefiting those lucky enough to become the tenants of the holdings thus enlarged – led to the frequent dispossession of the families of deceased crofters. Having nowhere else to go, they joined the landless population originally created by the Tiree clearances of the 1850s. By 1904, as a result, Tiree contained over 200 cottars and squatters. In Barra, South Uist and Benbecula where, in 1883, there were at least 400 landless families, the situation was equally bleak. But while the ratio of cottars to crofters was also high in North Uist and Harris, it was in Lewis – the only part of the Highlands and Islands, as already observed, where population growth continued in the post-1850 period – that landlessness took on the dimensions of a major social and agricultural catastrophe.

The population of Lewis rose from 19,684 in 1851 to 29,352 in 1911. In 1883, there were over 800 cottar families on the island and so rampant was the consequent subdivision that in the course of the 50 years following 1844, the Matheson estate management was forced to recognise that, without any resettlement, the number of holdings had increased from 2,110 to 3,105 – 483 of them being little more than allotments worth under £1 a year. Many crofts were divided between two, three or even more occupants in the manner outlined in the following description of a holding in the township of Keose:

> On an uneasy, undulating site there was apparently erected by the original holder a primitive hut with windowless walls . . . Alongside the father's hump-backed hut, there had been run up by the elder son a second dwelling in all respects identical with the old family nest to which it joined so as to do away with the need for one of the side walls. Then, again, there has been swung out behind this pair of cottages a third low-walled house which grows in a crooked way out of the stonework of its neighbours, and there another member of the family has taken up residence.

The occupants of these dwellings, like cottars and squatters everywhere, were economically dependent on the fishing industry or on some other form of casual labour. And having – by definition – little or no land on which to fall back in hard times, they were particularly vulnerable to downward fluctuations in money incomes from such sources. During the famine period, for instance, many of the crofters from whom landless families obtained their potato patches had put the whole of their crofts under corn – causing cottars to be especially susceptible, as they were to be again when economic conditions deteriorated once more in the 1880s, to hunger. The obvious way out of their predicament, as cottars and squatters saw it, was for them to be given crofts of their own. They could then, they contended, raise their own crops and regularise the position by which – in defiance of souming regulations – they pastured numbers of cows, stirks and sheep on township common grazings. In a society in which the occupation of land was the be-all and end-all of everything, this was an inevitable aspiration. It was one that was particularly strong, perhaps, among cottars and squatters whose forebears had occupied much loftier social positions than they did.

There were innumerable cottars whose families, like that of Ronald MacDonald, a cottar at Hynish, Tiree, had occupied a recognised holding 'from time immemorial and paid the rent' only to be 'evicted to make room for sheep.' And there were plenty who could look back, like John Matheson, a cottar at Achnahannait on the MacDonald estate near Portree, to a time when their people had been the comparatively prosperous joint tenants of a traditional farm. In the course of the evidence he gave to the Napier Commission in 1883, Matheson said:

> My . . . great-grandfather was a tenant in Achnahannait, and had a fifth part of it . . . My grandfather succeeded him and had a fifth part . . . My father succeeded my grandfather and had an eighth part of the land, and in his lifetime he came to be reduced to a sixteenth of the land. My father had six sons of whom I am the eldest, and not one of them would get a sod from Lord MacDonald.

In the 1880s and in subsequent decades, men like Ronald MacDonald and John Matheson were – not at all surprisingly – prominent in raids on, and seizures of, land from which their fathers and grandfathers had been cleared. But while land hunger was most acute amongst cottars and squatters it was not confined to them. Among the crofting population generally, as the Napier Commissioners discovered, 'the principal matter of dissatisfaction' by the 1880s, was 'the restriction in the area of holdings'.

Crofters possessed no statistical analyses of their position. Their grievances were entirely personal and subjective – deriving from their own experience of their own particular situations. But as is illustrated by the statement made to the Napier Commission by the crofters of Tarskavaig, a township in the Skye parish of Sleat, those grievances were none the less real for that:

> A good number of years ago, but within the memory of some of the oldest inhabitants, Tarskavaig was inhabited by only four tenants . . . They were in a pretty comfortable condition . . . Subsequently, as evictions and clearances became prevalent throughout the parish, sheep farming got the preference, and people evicted from other townships began gradually to crowd in upon us till, at the present day, our township is inhabited by 40 tenants, occupying patches of ground varying from one and a half acres to three and a half acres. It therefore stands to reason that, out of such a small portion of land, it is an utter impossibility to make a livelihood . . . What we desire . . . is a reasonable share of the land, whereof we can make a livelihood, without being obliged to go to distant parts of the country to earn a living . . . There

is sufficient land to distribute, and land formerly cultivated by tenantry, but of late converted into sheep farms.

What was true of Tarskavaig was true of practically every township in north-west Scotland, and the 'question of the restriction of crofts', as the Napier Commission's chairman remarked, was consequently the 'capital grievance' of crofters everywhere. 'The place in which we are is so straightened,' complained the tenants of Glashvin on the Kilmuir estate in Skye:

> We are crowded into a space of one mile between two tacks on which there are 23 families of us without land . . . There are 36 crofters besides on that strip of a mile and the place must needs be poor.

The township of Husabost on the western shore of Loch Dunvegan, its tenants declared, had, until 1838, been 'held in common by eight tenants, paying a yearly rental of £8 each'. By the 1880s, however, 'the third and least profitable part' of it was 'overcrowded by 26 crofters paying yearly rents varying from £1 to £6'. Castlebay, Barra, a 60-year old cottar commented in 1883, was, in his 'first recollection', tenanted by ten families:

> They kept a stock of from two to seven cows each family . . . Now they have only about the fourth part of that place, and there are 22 families paying rent in it. There are 30 families in addition to these without land at all allocated among them.

In these circumstances, to obtain more land and thus to reverse the clearances – 'to return to the land which my father tenanted', as one South Uist crofter put it – was, for crofters, an ambition so natural as to be almost instinctive. 'The peasant,' it has recently been observed of nineteenth-century Russia, 'naturally saw the root of all his difficulties in the shortage of land, his only salvation in an increase of land.' Exactly the same could be said of the crofting population of the same period:

> This is the cause of it all: that we see the land which our fathers had brought under cultivation by the sweat of their brows put under [sheep farmers] or, as they should more properly be called, desolators of the land, and ourselves heaped upon one another upon small patches of the very worst portions of the land, and many without any land at all, while upon the land which they [the sheep farmers] possess as grass from one year's end to the other my father saw fourteen oat crops raised in succession . . . Now, insofar as I can understand the mind of the people, and especially of the younger portion of them, I fear that there is a danger that they may rise as the clans of old rose, if they don't get a hold over the land of which they are deprived . . . If some will say it is not right that we should be seeking these things, I shall not regard these as the poor man's friend; for if it is unlawful for us to ask [for the land] now, it was quite as unlawful for them to deprive us of it formerly.

The sentiments contained in that statement by Donald Martin, a crofter at Back in Lewis, were universally held. 'The only thing that would remedy our ills,' a Skye crofter said, 'is that we should get more land.' 'If we had plenty of land,' another averred, 'there would be no poverty in our country' – an opinion endorsed by the North Uist crofters who believed that, if more land were made available to them, 'there would be peace and plenty instead of living from hand to mouth and contracting debts'. All that a Harris crofter wanted, he told the Napier Commission, was 'more of the land which God created for man to take his living out of' – while crofters in Uig, Lewis, stated that they had 'no hope' of their condition being improved 'except by getting enlarged holdings'. Everywhere this sort of craving for more land was given force and direction by the fact that each overcrowded crofting township was typically hemmed in by huge and practically uninhabited sheep farms – all of them, as a landless Skyeman observed, containing 'green places on which crofters lived before'.

Throughout the north-west Highlands and islands, the Napier Commission's chairman wrote in 1885, 'the vacant land' and 'the starving multitude' were to be found side by side. A then common Gaelic saying put the matter succinctly:

> Na biasta mor ag itheadh nam biasta beag,
> Na biasta beag a deanamh mar dh'fhaodas iad.*

A particular example of the general situation is provided by conditions in the township of Solitote on the Kilmuir estate in Skye, a visitor to that 'miserable place' discovering, in the 1880s, that:

> The patches of ground which the tenants cultivate vary in size from three roods to two acres. The township has no right of grazing. There are 17 families in the township and only three cows, and two of these are fed with grass purchased from the tenants of Conista, while the third picks up its living at the roadside.

Given these circumstances, it was unsurprising that the tenants of Solitote 'pointed to the green fields of the . . . farms lying around, and asked why they should be huddled together while so much of the best land in Skye was under sheep'. Not every township, admittedly, was so constricted and so depressed as Solitote. But there were few localities which knew nothing of the problems and frustrations of its tenants. 'When I open my door,' a Lewis crofter remarked, 'there is no place within the range of my sight except where there are big sheep.' And those sheep, as one of his neighbours pointed out, grazed on 'land which our fathers had'.

Like Lord Napier, all the crofters quoted – and lots more could be quoted to the same effect – had grasped the contradiction inherent in the situation created in north-west Scotland by the clearances: the hemming in of congested townships by vast tracts of empty, uncultivated and often fertile land. So profound were the social tensions created by such a pattern of land use that, even if it had existed quite unaltered for a hundred years or more,

---

* 'The big beasts eating the little beasts, the little beasts doing as best they can.' The translation is Alexander Carmichael's.

some sort of uprising would not have been improbable. And because it had not so existed, rebellion was practically unavoidable. The sheep farms laid out in Park and Uig in Lewis in the 35 years after 1820; the farms created on South Uist in the aftermath of the kelp industry's collapse; the farms established on Tiree in the 1840s and 1850s; the farms formed or enlarged on Lord MacDonald's estates in Skye and North Uist at the same time: these are but a few of the farms designated by crofters as suitable for resettlement by themselves. All of them, as can be seen by referring to earlier chapters, had been brutally and forcibly cleared of their original occupants. Of that fact and of its significance, the crofters who – in the 1880s and again in the early twentieth century – laid claim to the lands in question by forcibly reoccupying them, were well aware. In the 1880s, after all, many witnesses and many victims of the clearances of the famine period were still alive. And where living memory failed, there were the carefully preserved traditions of earlier expropriations. In north-west Sutherland in the 1890s, for example, 'the names of the townships . . . from which the people were driven' in the nineteenth century's opening decades were widely remembered – as were clearance songs and stories in South Uist in the 1930s. In the folk memory, then, the sense of expropriation was undoubtedly vivid and strong. And even if that memory lapsed, which it seldom did, the tangible evidence of removals and evictions, was, and still is, there for all to see. 'Standing on any one of the great heights,' a hillwalker of the 1870s observed, 'you see on every side of you the green slopes marked with the old ridges.' These, together with the other signs of relatively recent habitation discernible on practically every sheep farm in the Highlands, constituted, as the Napier Commission stated, a record of the clearances which was 'written in indelible characters on the surface of the soil'. And where there had been crofting tenants or their predecessors before, it was not unreasonable to suppose, there could be crofting tenants again.

During the 1860s and 1870s, the comparatively good times brought by the cessation of the clearances, and even more so by the steady rise in crofters' incomes, ensured that the discontent engendered by the Highlands' agrarian order remained below the surface. But while actually broken on only one occasion – by the disturbances that following an attempt to evict a number of Lewis crofters in the spring of 1874* – the social peace of these decades was both fragile and precarious. Even a modest deterioration in crofters' financial circumstances was bound, for reasons examined in this chapter, to precipitate a new crisis in crofting society – a crisis whose effects would be all the more unsettling because of its following a period

---

*This was the so-called Bernera Riot. For an excellent account, see Joni Buchanan, *The Lewis Land Struggle: Na Gaisgich*, Stornoway, 1996.

of rising living standards and of correspondingly enhanced expectations on crofters' part. Most affected by any such crisis, it might readily have been predicted, would be the generation which had grown up since the famine. Unaccustomed to the absolute poverty of the past and used, instead, to a situation in which each year was a little easier, a little more rewarding, than its predecessor, this generation was most unlikely to take kindly to any threat of a return to the conditions that had prevailed in the first half of the nineteenth century. Younger crofters, moreover, were much better equipped to defend their interests than their fathers and grandfathers had been. Not only had they inherited that growing feeling of community whose emergence has already been examined, they were also developing a political consciousness of a type never before seen in the Highlands. Better educated and more aware of the outside world than their predecessors, and possessing an unprecedented confidence both in themselves and in their abilities, they had taken, for example, to reading newspapers – newspapers, it was noted, of a radical and anti-landlord kind. Most prominent of these was *The Highlander*, published in Inverness where it had been founded, in 1873, by John Murdoch – the man to whom, more than to anyone else, there belongs the credit for arousing the crofting community to a sense of its own potential.*

Born some miles to the south of Inverness in 1818, John Murdoch was brought up in Islay where he acquired a deep and enduring interest in Gaelic culture and an equally enduring hatred of Highland landlordism. In the course of a long and varied career in the revenue service, Murdoch observed and was influenced by a number of radical political movements – not the least important of his experiences being his involvement, during several years spent in Dublin in the 1850s and 1860s, in the politics of Irish nationalism. In Ireland, John Murdoch discovered Fintan Lalor's analysis of that country's land question – an analysis which gave pride of place to the peasantry as the main agent of agrarian change and one which Murdoch himself elaborated in a series of articles in *The Nation,* the principal vehicle of Ireland's home rule aspirations. When he retired to Inverness to launch *The Highlander*, therefore, it was the concept of creating a Highland land reform movement rooted securely in the crofting community that was uppermost in Murdoch's mind. The task was a formidable one. But Murdoch's contribution to its successful accomplishment was decisive and twofold: first, he persuaded Lowland Scotland's urban-based Gaelic and Highland societies – usually composed of middle-class Gaelic revivalists who, though often the sons or grandsons of crofters, had formerly taken little real interest in crofting affairs – to align themselves behind the crofting population in its struggle for a more equitable agrarian order in

---

*A more detailed account of Murdoch's career can be found in J. Hunter, *For the People's Cause: From the Writings of John Murdoch*, Edinburgh, 1986.

the Highlands; second, he encouraged, exhorted and cajoled crofters themselves into taking the initiative in that struggle.

Murdoch's objective, then, was to 'awaken' among crofters 'an intelligent and vigorous public spirit and afford opportunity and encouragement to the inhabitants of the Highlands to be heard on their own behalf'. This he achieved, not only through the columns of his newspaper, but also by tireless campaigning, on the ground, in crofting areas where, in the 1870s, the distinctive figure of *Murchadh na Feilidh** became increasingly familiar and influential. His kilt – a garment which, in the 1870s as much as in the 1970s, was more identified with the synthetic Celticism of Highland lairds than with the genuine Gaelic culture of the crofting community – was emblematic of Murdoch's endeavour to 'encourage the people to set a higher value on things pertaining to their country and particularly to their race, lore and language'. And that, in turn, was but one of the ways in which he attempted to increase crofters' self-confidence and to inspire them to action on their own behalf. Such action, his Highland expeditions showed him, was much needed:

> As I went along, I saw something of the poverty of the people: the poor land they held and in such small quantities, while there were so many large and good farms... and the poor congested just to make room for these. Then their husbandry was slovenly, their houses uncomfortable, and their crops, they could be nothing but poor on such land.

To get crofters to protest about their conditions was far from easy, however. Thus in South Uist, Murdoch noted, 'the poor people were in such a state of slavish fear' of the estate management that they dared not attend his meetings, let alone act on his advice. But on his finally obtaining a captive audience at a 'clipping' at Iochdar, John Murdoch – whose listeners, on that occasion, were obliged to hear him out because they could not abandon the sheep whose fleeces they were removing – succeeded in persuading the tenants of several townships to embody their more important grievances in a petition to the proprietor:

> I took care in the course of it that I was not teaching them, not telling them what to do, not putting grievances into their heads, not exciting their discontents . . . Small though these proceedings were they were the breaking of the first links in their chains.

From such an occurrence to effectively challenging the entire basis of Highland landlordism was a long and fateful step. But in 1881, the year during which *The Highlander* succumbed to the last of a long series of financial crises, this step was about to be taken.

---

*The nickname meant simply Murdoch of the Kilt.

8

THE HIGHLAND LAND WAR: BEGINNINGS

1881–1883

The 1880s in the Highlands were a decade of severe, occasionally chronic, agricultural depression. As wool prices collapsed, sheep farmers' profits and landlords' rentals fell back sharply from the heights they had reached in the balmy years of the 1860s and early 1870s. Confronted by diminishing revenues and by a growing number of sheep farmers who refused to renew their leases, landowners sought financial salvation in a massive shift in land utilisation patterns which – because it turned on the wholesale transformation of sheep farms into deer forests – involved a radical reshaping of the agrarian structure established in the early nineteenth century. But while sheep farmers could pull out of the Highlands and while the region's landlords could look for new and equally profitable uses for the grazings thus vacated, the crofting community, more prone to the effects of a recession than were either of those groupings, could do little to protect its own position – little, that is, that was within the generally accepted norms of economic and political behaviour.

As far as crofters were concerned, the 1880s began with a sharp reminder of their continued vulnerability to sudden crises. The Highland harvest of 1881 was uniformly poor, and though the following summer began with the promise of an unusually abundant crop, it ended with crofters' potatoes being more completely destroyed by blight than at any time since the 1850s. To this loss of the potato crop were added the still more disastrous consequences of an unremunerative east coast herring fishing. The 4,000 or more Lewismen who spent the summer on the drifters came home in September with only about £3 apiece, while some Skyemen thought themselves lucky to return with £1 in their pockets. Then, on 1 October, matters took yet another turn for the worse. Crofters' corn, most of which had remained unharvested because of prolonged rain in August and September, was largely flattened and destroyed by an exceptionally severe southerly gale. All the islands and the entire north-west coast of the mainland were affected by the storm which, as well as adding to the agricultural havoc already wrought by blight, caused no fewer than 1,200 boats to be damaged or destroyed and brought about the loss of an immense quantity of nets and other fishing gear.

The inevitable outcome of this series of calamities was that, in the winter of 1881–82, the crofting population was plunged into conditions reminiscent of those which had prevailed during the famine of the 1840s. By New Year, the effects of scarcity were everywhere apparent, especially in Lewis where 'numerous families in every district of the island' were reported to be 'in absolute want'. And though mainland areas suffered a little less severely than the Hebrides, no crofting district escaped unscathed – the general misery being aggravated by the price of meal, much in demand as a result of the potato failure, soaring to exceptionally high levels. To obtain the funds needed to buy meal, then, many crofters, for reasons reminiscent of those which had impelled similar actions more than 30 years before, had either to add to their already crippling debts or sell their cattle – cattle which were themselves suffering because of a severe shortage of fodder.

As the seriousness of north-west Scotland's situation became apparent, appeals for aid were again launched in the south – where, during the early months of 1882, over £10,000 was collected for distribution to crofters and their families. From government, however, no assistance was forthcoming. The Scottish poor law authorities admitted the existence of unusual distress among the crofting population but did nothing to alleviate it. In parliament, meanwhile, William Gladstone's Liberal administration refused to countenance proposals that crofters be supplied with seed oats and seed potatoes at taxpayers' expense – a private member's Bill incorporating such provisions accordingly failing to be passed into law. Those sections of the press which reflected the opinions of the political establishment were equally unsympathetic. The Liberal *Scotsman* believed that crofters should at once be 'disabused' of any notion that they were 'entitled to government aid', and joined with the Tory *Times* in commending a 50-year-old answer to Highland problems: emigration. In the centres of political power and and influence, it thus appeared, there was little interest in, and less understanding of, the crofting community's difficulties. But at the very moment when their prospects seemed bleaker than for many years, crofters, by their own initiative, at last forced their grievances on the attention both of Britain's decision-makers and of the country's wider population.

In the 1880s, as had been the case for most of the nineteenth century, crofters' troubles were paralleled by those affecting tenants in Ireland – where the agrarian structure approximated to that of north-west Scotland. The winter of 1879–80 had brought near-famine conditions to a large part of the Irish countryside. And the ensuing distress had greatly facilitated the remarkable rise of the Irish Land League, a tenants' movement founded, in 1879, by Michael Davitt, Irish nationalist, ex-Fenian and, not insignificantly, the son of a smallholder evicted from an estate in County Mayo in 1852. The Land League had as its president and principal parliamentary spokesman, Charles Stewart Parnell, then at the start of his meteoric career as leader of the pro-home rule Irish Party in the House of Commons. The league's strength, however, lay not so much in its considerable parliamentary representation as in its mass following in rural Ireland where rent strikes and other forms of direct action organised by the Land League quickly threatened to undermine, or even destroy, the enormous power of the Irish landlord class. Having failed to crush the league by the deployment of all the coercive apparatus at its disposal, Gladstone's administration, on the prime minister's initiative, responded to its challenge by resolving to reform the Irish agrarian system – the outcome being the Irish Land Act of 1881. Although not a final solution to the Irish land question, the Act was a landmark in agrarian legislation. It conceded several of the Land League's demands, notably those for security of tenure and judicially determined rents, and was, in sum, a scarcely less than revolutionary attempt to remedy Irish tenants' grievances at their landlords' expense.

Irish unrest and its legislative consequences did not go unnoticed in the Highlands. The government's publishers received an order for a copy of the Irish Land Act from a remote part of Lewis. And at least one group of Skye crofters, on 'hearing of good news from Ireland', expressed an inclination, as they expressed it, 'to turn rebels ourselves in order to obtain the same benefits'. Their reaction can scarcely have been unique. For after 1881, as one of the crofting community's spokesmen was subsequently to observe:

> It was impossible that the intelligent crofter should not contrast his condition with that of the Irish tenant and ask to what the difference was due – whether it was due to violent agitation in the one case, and to peaceful, quiet, law-abiding habits in the other.

It is no coincidence, therefore, that, in the winter of 1880–81, when the no-rent tactics of the Irish Land League were receiving wide publicity in the press, the crofters of Valtos and Elishader on the Kilmuir estate in Skye intimated their intention to cease paying rent to their landlord.

The 46,142 acre Kilmuir estate, bought from Lord MacDonald in 1855 by a Nairnshire gentleman, Captain William Fraser, was a place where crofters could claim to suffer, like their Irish counterparts, from rackrenting. Under Fraser's ownership, the crofting rental of the property had almost doubled – despite a substantial reduction in the amount of land available to crofters – and the rents of some crofts had risen by more than 160 per cent. As early as 1877, a visitor to Skye had commented that the repeated increases in their rents had led to widespread murmurings of discontent among Fraser's tenantry, and it is not at all surprising, therefore, that the crofters of Kilmuir proved particularly receptive to the lesson implicit in events in Ireland. Their new departure was not matched by any sudden change in estate policy, however – the initial response of Fraser and his factor to the Kilmuir rent strike being that traditionally associated with Highland landlordism when confronted with the slightest hint of crofting insubordination. A petition calling for a rent reduction was rejected by the

Kilmuir estate management and summonses of removal taken out against crofters who had dared to put their names to it. But then, in the spring of 1881, and for reasons that remain obscure, the Kilmuir estate authorities switched from a coercive to a conciliatory policy. Rents in Valtos and Elishader were reduced by 25 per cent, on the ostensible grounds that Fraser had discovered an error in their soumings.

In the wider world, these small beginnings of effective direct action by crofters passed practically unobserved. Before 12 months had elapsed, however, crofting issues had become matters of national concern.

The crofting townships of Gedintailor, Balmeanach and Peinchorran which constitute the district known as Braes or the Braes are situated on the east coast of Skye about eight miles south of Portree. Braes – of whose setting a press reporter wrote in 1882 that it 'would be difficult to imagine anything more romantic' – is a fairly typical, if slightly isolated, crofting community delineated to the south by Loch Sligachan, to the east by the Sound of Raasay and to the west by a ridge of hills of which the highest is Ben Lee. Though unspectacular by the standards of an island containing the Cuillin, Ben Lee effectively separates Braes from Glen Varragil which carries the main, and nowadays very busy, road from Kyleakin to Portree – thereby ensuring that Braes can be easily approached only by a narrow, winding road that runs southwards from Portree. In 1882, as will become apparent, that fact was of some importance. But of more importance was the status of Ben Lee itself.

Like most other hills in the Highlands and Islands, Ben Lee, which was capable of carrying between 1,200 and 1,400 sheep, had once been part of the common pastures of the townships at its foot. That much was generally agreed. All else, however, was in dispute. The representatives of Lord MacDonald, whose estate included both Braes and Ben Lee, admitted that until 1865, when the hill was leased to a sheep farmer for an annual rent of £128, the Braes crofters had been allowed to graze their stock upon it. But since the reorganisation of the MacDonald estate in the early nineteenth century, they added, Ben Lee had been outside the recognised boundaries of the Braes townships whose tenants, therefore, had had the use of the hill 'merely . . . on sufferance', had 'no right or claim to it', and were not entitled to any abatement of rent because of its loss. Braes crofters took a more straightforward view of the situation, one of them summing up their stance thus:

> I and my father before me, and my grandfather, great-grandfather, and great-great grandfather have been living in the township of Balmeanach, and the hill of Ben Lee was all that time connected with our township.

In 1865, the Braes crofters – whose account of events was eventually recognised as the correct one – had submitted, as had many thousands of other crofting tenants before them, to the loss of their grazings. That they raised the issue again in the autumn of 1881 owed something to the fact that the current lease of the hill was about to expire, and a good deal more to the passing of the Irish Land Act – the MacDonald estate factor's contention that 'there was no combination [in Braes] till after the Irish affair', being borne out by comments voiced by the Braes crofters themselves. 'What made us raise the question just now,' one of them remarked, 'is that we were hearing that there were new laws passing about lands.' Nor was their knowledge of Irish events derived exclusively from newspapers – several Braes crofters having been employed, in the summer of 1881, on fishing boats working out of ports in south-west Ireland. The extent of those crofters' contacts with their Irish counterparts is impossible to estimate, but they almost certainly saw something of the conflict raging in the Irish countryside and from it drew their own conclusions. On their return to Skye, at all events, the Braes men who had been in Ireland were instrumental in drawing up a petition which demanded Ben Lee's restoration to them as of right. Signed by almost all the tenants of Gedintailor, Balmeanach and Peinchorran, this petition was presented to Alexander MacDonald, Lord MacDonald's factor, in November – only to be at once rejected.

Less bold spirits might have accepted the rejection of the Ben Lee petition as final. But it was, in fact, at this point – which occurred just a few weeks after Parnell, issuing his No-Rent Manifesto from his cell in Dublin's Kilmainham Jail, had called on Irish tenants to 'choose . . . between the Land for the Landlords and the Land for the People' – that the Braes crofters took a decision as brave as it was crucial. They announced they would immediately cease paying rent to Lord MacDonald. A few days later, on the Martinmas termday of 1881, the tenants of Braes marched together into Portree, halted outside Alexander MacDonald's office and informed him 'that their rents would not be paid that day, or any other day, until Ben Lee was returned to them'.

Crofters at Valtos and Elishader had already made effective use of the rent strike, a fact of which the Braes men could not have been unaware. On the Kilmuir estate as in Ireland, however, a refusal to pay rents had been used solely to force a landlord to reduce rents. And that, in relation to the Highland and Islands as a whole, was a tactic of limited value, if only for the reason that relatively few crofters suffered from grossly extortionate rents of the kind levied by Kilmuir's proprietor. As emphasised in the previous chapter, however, almost all crofters suffered from a scarcity of land. And by recognising that a rent strike could be used not merely to enforce a rent reduction but to coerce a proprietor into giving more land to crofting tenants, the Braes crofters had adapted the principal weapon of the Irish Land League to Highlands and Islands circumstances. They initiated a movement, therefore, which, if at all successful, was bound to appeal to crofters everywhere.

The significance of events at Braes was not lost on Skye's landlords. Obsessed by Irish precedent, they feared, at best, some kind of legislative intervention on the crofters' side and, at worst, agrarian revolution. Strenuous attempts were accordingly made to have a number of Braes crofters arrested on charges of intimidation. And when these failed from lack of evidence, the bulk of the collected testimony having served simply to demonstrate the Braes tenants' unanimous and almost entirely voluntary adherence to their cause, it was decided to evict a number of crofters on the grounds that, as a result of their rent strike, they had fallen into arrears. Summonses of removal were consequently taken out against a dozen of Lord MacDonald's tenants at Braes. And on 7 April 1882, a sheriff-officer left Portree to serve the eviction orders which, though entirely in accordance with the law as it then stood, were clearly designed to intimidate their recipients. This they equally clearly failed to do. At Braes, the luckless sheriff-officer was accosted by a crowd of about 150 people and assaulted. Although he was not seriously injured, the summonses were taken from him and burned on the spot. The crime of deforcement – the name given in law to an attack made upon a sheriff-officer or any other legal official in the course of his duties – had thus been committed. And since the names of five of the crofters who had taken a prominent part in the proceedings of 7 April were known to the authorities, warrants were immediately issued for their arrest.

The forcible destruction of eviction notices – the cordially hated symbol of their landlords' virtually unrestricted power over them – was a traditional response of Highland tenants to attempts to remove them from their holdings. But in the past, as noted in an earlier chapter, such actions had been little more than desperate gestures of defiance in the face of effectively irresistible force. At Braes in the spring of 1882, however, the crofters' campaign was well organised and was, moreover, offensive, rather than defensive, in origin and conception. Its circumstances being thus entirely novel, the Braes crofters' resistance to their landlord and to the law did not at once collapse as had that of their predecessors at Kildonan, Borve, Sollas and a dozen other places between the 1790s and 1850s. The Braes folk's morale, on the contrary, remained high. They posted sentries on the hills overlooking the road from Portree and sat back to await developments.

Until April, the tenants of Braes had conducted their campaign in an entirely peaceable manner. Their deforcement of a sheriff-officer, however, made it possible for the authorities to move against them. This opportunity was especially welcomed by William Ivory, Sheriff of Inverness-shire, whose instinct it was to crush the crofters' movement – an objective which was to preoccupy him for the next six years. Because Inverness-shire did not possess a police force large enough for the type of action he thought necessary in Skye, Ivory appealed for assistance to the local authorities in Glasgow, home of Victorian Scotland's largest constabulary. With what seems, in retrospect, surprisingly little fuss, his request was granted. Before dawn on 19 April, a day of cold, incessant rain, a detachment of over 50 policemen, most of whom would have been much more at home in the streets of the British Empire's second city, marched from Portree with Ivory at their head or, to sacrifice drama to truth, at their rear – the sheriff always being one to exercise discretion in such matters.

This 19 April expedition, whose task it was to apprehend the men wanted in connection with the deforcement of 12 days before, passed through Gedintailor without encountering any resistance. And though the police were met outside Balmeanach by a crowd of about 100 men, women and children, the Braes crofters, who had not expected to be raided at such an hour and on such a day, were not so well prepared as they might have been. Guided by a local ground-officer, a police contingent was consequently able to arrest the wanted men without undue exertion. While the arrests were being made, however, the Braes people had gathered in some strength and, as the police attempted to withdraw towards Portree with their captives, they were surrounded, stoned and otherwise assaulted. About a dozen constables were more or less seriously injured and, on the police drawing their batons and repeatedly charging the crowd in an attempt to regain control of the situation, one or two crofters and their wives were severely cut about the head. For a few minutes it seemed as if the captured crofters might be rescued by a detachment of their comrades who had occupied the Portree road at a point where it traverses a hillside rising almost sheer from the sea – the place is known locally as An Cumhang. But in the end the police were victorious. A final desperate charge took them through the encircling mass of crofters and, at a run, they escaped towards Portree through a last barrage of mud and stones.

Such, in outline, were the events which passed into history and folklore as 'The Battle of the Braes' – events whose immediate effect was to give unprecedented publicity to crofters' grievances. Within a few days of the Braes confrontation, there were in Skye no fewer than 11 journalists, representing newspapers as far apart geographically and politically as *The Scotsman*, the *Inverness Courier*, the *London Standard* and the *Freeman's Journal* of Dublin. Their reports, not least their descriptions of the conditions in which Hebridean tenants lived, undoubtedly helped to swing public – and especially radically inclined – opinion in the crofting community's favour. But public opinion would not, of itself, have moved the government to make concessions to crofters. That was achieved only by further agitation and, above all, by the development of a crofters' political organisation.

In April 1882 that organisation had yet to be formed. But in the aftermath of the Braes affair, John Murdoch's long campaign for a political union between crofters and the adherents of the Gaelic revivalist movement then flourishing in the south at last began to bear worthwhile fruit in the emergence of a pro-crofter coalition headed by: John Stuart Blackie, professor of Greek and passionate Celticist; Dr Roderick MacDonald, president of the Gaelic Society of London; John MacKay, a member of that society and a prominent Gael; Angus Sutherland, president of the Glasgow Sutherland Association; Alexander MacKenzie, a founder member, in the early 1870s, of the Inverness Gaelic Society and editor of the influential *Celtic Magazine*; and G. B. Clark, a Scottish doctor residing in London where he was to have a long career in left-wing politics. This increasingly effective pressure group had as its parliamentary spokesmen: Dr Charles Cameron, a Glasgow Liberal MP and the chairman of the Federation of Celtic Societies; Charles Fraser-MacIntosh, Liberal MP for Inverness and a leading Gaelic scholar and antiquarian; and Donald H. MacFarlane, Irish nationalist member for County Carlow but a Highlander by birth. Here then, was the nucleus of a potentially powerful political alliance. But though Cameron, Fraser-MacIntosh and MacFarlane at once set about the task of bringing the Highland land question to the attention of the House of Commons, they laboured under the difficulty of having no very strong links with crofters themselves. That particular problem, as it happened, was soon to be overcome. Until it was, however, developments on the wider political stage and those occurring in the Highlands and Islands proceeded in virtual independence of each other – a state of affairs which did not, admittedly, prevent Highland landlords and other upholders of north-west Scotland's agrarian status quo from attributing the unrest in the region to a Dublin-based conspiracy whose principal agents were held to be the Glasgow branches of the Irish Land League. That the latter took an active interest in Highland discontent is undoubted. But the cool reception accorded to their emissary to Skye indicates that while crofters were willing to draw on the Irish example they were not, at this stage anyway, prepared to encourage direct Irish involvement in their affairs. The supposedly subversive 'agitators' – Irish or otherwise – who, it was widely suggested at the time, were responsible for disturbances in crofting areas, prove, on inspection, to have been no more and no less than the mythical creations of understandably frightened members of the possessing classes.

In Skye itself, meanwhile, the movement launched at Braes was – without any assistance from Ireland or anywhere else – attracting growing support among the island's crofting population. Some months before the dramatic happenings of 19 April 1882 had drawn the attention of the outside world to Peinchorran, Balmeanach and Gedintailor, crofters in the north-west corner of the island had commenced their own campaign of protest. The districts affected by it were the Husabost and Glendale estates: the former a small property on the western shore of Loch Dunvegan; the latter a 35,022-acre estate centred on the fertile strath of Glendale which runs southwards into the hills of Duirinish from the head of Loch Pooltiel. Glendale was owned by the trustees of the recently deceased Sir John MacPherson MacLeod who – some 30 years before his death in 1881 – had bought the property from a financially stricken MacLeod of Dunvegan. Husabost, an estate of around 5,000 acres which had passed out of MacLeod of Dunvegan's hands at about the same time, was owned by a Dr Nicol Martin who, though a resident landlord and a native of Skye, was held in little esteem by his tenants – largely because his management of the property was principally distinguished by his maintenance of quasi-feudal services of a type long obsolete elsewhere in Britain. Ten days' unpaid labour was required each year from crofting tenants on Martin's estate, and failure to answer the landlord's summons – which usually came at seed-time or harvest when crofters were busiest on their own holdings – was punished by 'fines' of 2s. 6d. a day.

But while the situation on Martin's property was clearly such as to heighten the discontent produced by crofters' universal grievance, lack of land, it fell to the Glendale estate management to arouse the district's crofters to action. In January 1882, the factor on the Glendale estate, himself a sheep farmer, issued a series of edicts designed to promote local sheep farmers' interests at the expense of those of the crofting population. Crofters were forbidden, for example, to keep dogs and ordered to cease collecting driftwood on the seashore – a practice which, it was claimed, involved them in trespassing on sheep farmers' lands. Announced at a time when news of the rent strike at Braes was no doubt sweeping across Skye, those impositions had the effect of inducing a group of Glendale crofters to call a public meeting at which their grievances, new and old, were discussed. Attended by crofters living on Martin's estate as well as by most of the Glendale tenantry, this meeting was a resounding success. Pledging themselves to present a united front to their landlords, those present resolved that tenants of the various townships on the two estates should at once draw up petitions embodying their respective complaints and send those petitions to Martin and to the Glendale trustees.

Martin's tenants not unnaturally requested the abolition of 'the slavery called day's work' as well as asking 'that the hill ground . . . taken from us be now duly restored'. But the demand for more land was common to Husabost and Glendale. Crofters at Skinidin, for example, demanded the restoration to them of two islands in Loch Dunvegan – islands which had been added to a sheep farm in the 1840s but which, as an 80-year old crofter remarked, were 'ever since my recollection . . . looked upon as part of the grazing belonging to the township'.

Just like those made by the Braes folk with regard to Ben Lee, all such requests were turned down by the estate authorities to whom they were addressed. A letter to Donald MacDonald, the Glendale factor, encapsulated the crofters' reaction to this development:

Sir . . . We received a letter from the trustees from whom we were expecting to obtain pleasure for our petitions, but misfortunately we were disappointed . . . We conclude that you shall be without the rents until we receive what we are wanting, and that shows you that we are all the same as one man. Certainly you need not put any to the trouble of going out with summonses. None shall quit the estate until all demands are arranged. We are, yours respectfully, the tenants of Milovaig and Borodal, including all the Glendale tenants.

Although the rent strike thus announced affected the entire area encompassed by the Glendale and Husabost estates, tension was highest in the townships named in the crofters' letter, Upper and Lower Milovaig and Borodal. The tenants of those townships had asked the Glendale trustees to let to them the nearby sheep farm of Waterstein, the lease of which was due to expire at Whitsun 1882. But their request having been refused, the farm – almost by way, one might think, of adding insult to injury – was handed over to the Glendale factor, Donald MacDonald. The latter, while not declining this excellent opportunity to add to the extensive lands he already occupied, felt his position to be so dangerous that he armed himself with a revolver. The Milovaig and Borodal crofters, for their part, declared that, at the Whitsun term, they would occupy Waterstein with or without permission. Convinced that their threat was a serious one, the late proprietor's trustees visited Glendale at the beginning of May and urged their tenants to give them a little more time to enquire into the situation on the estate. The reply the trustees received summed up the spirit and significance of the entire revolt in Skye in 1882:

We told them that our forefathers had died in good patience, and that we ourselves had been waiting in patience till now, and that we could not wait any longer – that they never got anything by their patience, but constantly getting worse.

By the end of May, Milovaig and Borodal crofters' stock was being pastured on Waterstein.

From the Court of Session in Edinburgh, the Glendale estate's trustees obtained an order instructing offending tenants to remove their animals from the disputed grazings. But the order was ignored, and the factor's shepherds threatened with violence should they make any attempt to clear the farm. On exactly such an attempt being made in November, a shepherd was, in fact, severely mauled by crofters. But for all that warrants for the arrest of 25 of his assailants were subsequently issued by the authorities, the wanted men remained at large – for the simple reason that, in the re-run of the Braes battle likely to be produced by an attempt to apprehend them, the small force of police then stationed in Skye (from which the contingent of Glasgow constables had long since been withdrawn) would be no match for Glendale's crofters.

Less dramatic than events on Waterstein farm, but equally indicative of the strength of feeling among the Glendale and Husabost tenantries, was the outcome of the Martinmas rent collection on the two properties. No rents at all were paid at Husabost. At Glendale only five of the estate's 500 crofting tenants came forward to settle their accounts – the feeling of the overwhelming majority being demonstrated, in December, by the burning of a corn stack belonging to one of the crofters who had broken faith.

While these developments were occurring in Glendale, the crofters who had borne the brunt of the authorities' first clumsy attempt to quell the growing unrest in Skye remained every bit as uncowed as their Glendale counterparts. Of the five Braes crofters arrested in April, two were fined 50s. and three 20s. by an obviously sympathetic court in Inverness. They came home to a heroes' welcome and, thereafter, events at Braes closely paralleled those in Glendale – the Braes crofters driving their cattle on to Ben Lee in the month that Waterstein was similarly invaded, and Lord MacDonald's estate managers, like their Glendale equivalents, obtaining a Court of Session order which instructed the Braes folk to desist from actions which, in the court's judgement, were entirely illegal. Copies of this latest order, which was to be served on no fewer than 53 of Lord MacDonald's tenants, were entrusted to a messenger-at-arms who arrived at Braes on 2 September. Since most of the locality's menfolk were away at the east coast herring fishings, the defence of the Braes townships devolved, this time, on their wives and daughters. The latter rose appropriately to the occasion. 'Howling in a frightful manner', and with their shawls pulled over their faces to prevent their identification, they pelted the messenger and his party with stones and other missiles – forcing all the officials concerned to retreat precipitately to Portree.

Graham Spiers, sheriff-substitute at Portree, had been of the opinion, since the first hint of violence at Braes in the spring, that Skye could be satisfactorily pacified only if the police received military assistance. Subsequent developments, he thought, had served only to confirm the accuracy of his original prognosis. By September, Spiers was convinced that, unless troops were at once deployed on the island, law and order would not be restored – with the result that there would then be nothing to prevent 'feeling in Skye', or so Spiers commented, 'coming to the climax which Ireland has got to'. With this view, the sheriff-substitute's superior, William Ivory, was in full agreement. On 21 September, Ivory accordingly asked the government for 100 troops 'to act as a protection and aid to the civil authorities in serving . . . the interdicts and other orders of the Court of Session'. Although J. B. Balfour – who, in his capacity as lord advocate, was the foremost Scottish minister in Gladstone's administration – supported Ivory's request, the majority of the prime minister's cabinet colleagues, with their Irish experience fresh in their minds, had no desire to become embroiled in yet another agrarian uprising. Ivory's appeal for aid was thus turned down. Instead of applying for help from the army, it was suggested to him, the Inverness-shire authorities should immediately set about strengthening their own police force. This they agreed to do. In November, 50 constables were added to the county constabulary – a step which brought its total strength up to 94 men.

While showing that the crofters' movement was being taken more and more seriously, those developments did little to solve the problem confronting the authorities in Skye. Any police force, a Highland sheriff was to observe on a future occasion, was likely – and the point is one with which revolutionary tacticians of modern times would instantly agree – to prove 'quite insufficient to prevent resistance to the law . . . where the sympathy of the people is against the enforcement of the law'. In Skye, in the autumn of 1882, the truth embodied in that remark was becoming rapidly apparent. On 24 October, for example, the forces of law and order in the shape of a messenger-at-arms, a police inspector, a superintendent and nine constables were prevented from entering Braes by a large and 'determined' crowd. For Lord MacDonald's agents, who had hitherto demanded that 'prompt steps' be taken to put down what they referred to as the 'illegal combination' at Braes, this particular incident was the last straw. Concluding that 'the law is no longer respected in Skye', they decided that the advantages of an immediate settlement at Braes outweighed the risk of a continuing conflict. In December they consequently agreed to lease Ben Lee to the tenants of Braes in return for an annual rent of £74.15s. The Braes crofters were soon to conclude that they had been more or less duped into paying a hefty rent for ground which, as they continued to reiterate, 'was part of their holdings in time past'. The December 1882 agreement thus proved to be no more than a temporary truce. But in forcing Lord MacDonald to come to terms with them, the Braes tenantry seemed, at the time, to have won something of a victory – as indeed they had done. They accordingly called off their rent strike, and brought Braes' year of troubles to an end.

As tranquillity returned to Braes, the authorities turned their attention to Glendale where, behind a cordon of sentries posted on the narrow and winding hill road which crosses into the glen from Dunvegan, the district's crofters were reported to be preparing to defend themselves against an expected police incursion with crude but effective pikes consisting of scythe blades lashed to poles. Reports of these weapons' existence may or may not have been mere rumours. But it was all too manifestly obvious that Glendale had effectively passed out of civil and criminal jurisdiction: in January, after all, the crofters who had assaulted the Glendale factor's shepherd in November were still at large. For Ivory and his subordinates to have indefinitely countenanced such an admission of their own helplessness would have been unthinkable. On 16 January, an attempt was accordingly made to station a police sergeant and three constables at Hamara Lodge in the centre of the Glendale estate. The estate's crofting population, however, were quite determined to prevent any arrests and, if possible, to preserve the virtual autonomy which they had recently won for themselves. Alerted to the approach of the police detachment by the sound of horns blown by their sentries on the hills to the east of the glen, Glendale's people gathered in strength, and, about a quarter of a mile short of their destination, the four policemen were set upon by a crowd of about 500 men, many of them armed with stout sticks. Knocked down, kicked and beaten, the sergeant, his constables and the inspector who was accompanying them were driven like cattle to the estate boundary and left to make their own way back to Dunvegan. On the following day, by way of consolidating their command of the situation, the Glendale crofters deforced a messenger-at-arms and drove him off the estate. And on 20 January, several hundred men carrying sticks, scythes, graips and other weapons marched from the glen to Dunvegan – with the aim of forcing the police to completely evacuate the district. This was achieved with spectacular case. Some hours before the well-drilled and well-armed column of Glendale crofters reached Dunvegan, the police abandoned the village and fled across the hills to Edinbane – some miles to the east.

––––––––––

Initially limited to a refusal to pay rents, the crofters' movement – as events in Skye make clear – had grown spectacularly in scope in the nine months which followed the first clash between crofters and police at Braes in April 1882. Lands had been seized, the courts defied, officials manhandled and substantial areas closed to the police. Skye's troubles, in short, had assumed something of the status of a revolutionary challenge to the existing social and agrarian order in those localities where they had begun. But even more worrying, from the landlords' point of view at least, were signs that crofting unrest was unlikely to remain for long confined to just one or two spots. In the closing months of 1882, for instance, crofters on the Kilmuir estate began a new rent strike, and the tenants of several townships on Lord MacDonald's property threatened to withhold their rents until hill pastures which had long since been added to sheep farms were restored to them. Still more significant, perhaps, were increasingly numerous manifestations of discontent in districts outside Skye.

In 1880, John Murdoch, Angus Sutherland and several kindred spirits had hailed as a glorious opportunity to launch a Highland land reform movement an attempt to evict a number of crofters from Leckmelm – a township situated on the north shore of Loch Broom not far from Ullapool. On that occasion, little had come of their endeavours. But as the autumn of 1882 gave way to winter, there were indications that such a movement, sparked off by events in Skye rather than by paragraphs in the radical press, might at last be about to take shape. An attempt to evict a crofter at Rogart in Sutherland was resisted by a crowd armed with sticks. At Lochcarron, a sheriff-officer was deforced while trying to serve summonses of removal on two crofting tenants. Tiree crofters petitioned the Duke of Argyll for a reduction in their rents, and the tenants of one of the island's townships, Balephuil, demanded the restoration of pastures – on Ben Hynish – which the duke's managers, years before, had added to a neighbouring farm. Crofters on Barra made identical requests in respect of sheep farms which had similarly been enlarged at crofters' expense. And the tenants of several townships in Uig, Lewis, began to hold public meetings with a view to ventilating analogous grievances. The hardships suffered by them, they declared in a January 1883 letter to Lady Matheson, widow of Sir James Matheson and owner of the island, stemmed ultimately from the existence of 'huge possessions in the hands of sportsmen and [farmers]'. They had 'no desire at present', the Uig people added, 'to follow the example of the Skye crofters'. But they could not 'vouch for the course the crofters of Lewis may pursue, judging from the views expressed at their recent meetings'.

The proliferation of events such as these, Home Office civil servants concluded in February 1883, showed that there was 'much discontent and excitement' in widely separated parts of north-west Scotland. What the Home Office called 'intimations' had been made 'to various proprietors' that, 'if demands put forward by crofters for additional lands are not voluntarily conceded, forcible possession of the lands will be taken'. Given the sheer extent of such threats, it is not surprising that, in the opening months of 1883, Britain's government intervened actively in crofting affairs for the first time since the famine of the 1840s.

The expulsion of the police from Glendale had, as was remarked by J. B. Balfour, the lord advocate, 'brought matters to a crisis'. By the end of January, therefore, the cabinet had been persuaded to accede to Sheriff William Ivory's repeated requests for troops. The military's immediate objective was to be the apprehension of five Glendale crofters – all of whom were to be charged with offences arising out of the recent affrays in that area. As a conciliatory gesture, however, it was decided that a final attempt should be made to persuade the wanted crofters to surrender themselves voluntarily – the man charged with this delicate task being Malcolm MacNeill, the official in charge of administering the poor law in north-west Scotland. MacNeill was duly conveyed to Loch Pooltiel in a gunboat, and, on 9 February 1883, he met about 500 crofters in Glendale's Free Church. A prolonged debate ensued. And though MacNeill's participation in it was greatly facilitated by his being fluent in Gaelic, his mission at first seemed likely to end in failure. All Glendale's crofters, MacNeill was informed, had participated equally in the events of the previous few months, and, while they were ready 'to go in a body', to jail they were not prepared to give up just five of their number. In order to avoid a potentially bloody and obviously unwinnable confrontation with the army, however, the Glendale crofters eventually agreed to adopt the course advocated by Malcolm

MacNeill. The five wanted men consented to stand trial in Edinburgh where, on 15 March 1883, they were sentenced to two months' imprisonment.

For the moment, therefore, military intervention was avoided – something for which government ministers at least were duly grateful. But as a means of putting an end to crofting protest the sentences imposed on 'the Glendale martyrs', as the five imprisoned crofters were soon dubbed, were a failure. In Glendale itself, for instance, the crofters' rent strike remained solid – an attempt to break it by evicting 45 crofting tenants failing, on 10 April, when the sheriff-officer charged with delivering the necessary summonses of removal was deforced and driven off the estate by a large crowd. Neither he nor any other officer could be induced to make a second attempt. And since, in order to take effect at the Whitsun termday, eviction summonses had to be served before 15 April, Glendale's crofters thus won another victory.

Against the backdrop of such skirmishing, meanwhile, the political campaign launched by the crofting community's parliamentary allies began to gain both in momentum and in effect – assisted, no doubt, by the fact that the unprecedented publicity given to crofting affairs had resulted in the emergence of what J. B. Balfour subsequently called 'a considerable body of vague and floating sentiment in favour of ameliorating the crofters' condition'. At the parliamentary level, the pro-crofter feeling thus described by the Liberal lord advocate was strongest among more radically inclined members of his own party. In January 1883, Charles Fraser-MacIntosh was accordingly able to get some 20 Liberal MPs to put their names to a House of Commons motion calling for a royal commission of enquiry into crofters' grievances. Earlier moves in this direction had been frustrated by the government's initial inclination to avoid Highland entanglements – Gladstone having responded to a November 1882 request for a royal commission by informing Donald H. MacFarlane that 'no such question' was 'under the consideration of her majesty's government'. In the opening weeks of 1883, however, events in Glendale, coupled with growing parliamentary pressure, of which Fraser-MacIntosh's Commons resolution was the most notable example, forced a change of policy. On 26 February, the government announced that it would, after all, set up a royal commission 'to inquire into the condition of the crofters and cottars in the Highlands and Islands of Scotland'. On 8 May, this commission, under the chairmanship of a Borders peer, Lord Napier, began taking evidence from crofters at Braes.

The setting up of the Napier Commission, though clearly a considerable victory for the crofters' cause, did not at the time seem quite so momentous an event as it does in retrospect. Suspecting that the commission was merely a delaying tactic and that its activities would be confined to the few areas where violent outbreaks had already occurred, many of the crofting community's southern sympathisers regarded its appointment as a reason for more, rather than less, agitation. It was with this object in view that they founded in London, during February 1883, the unwieldily named but politically portentous Highland Land Law Reform Association (HLLRA). The association's programme was loosely modelled on that of the Irish Land League. But to league demands for 'fair rents, durability of tenure and compensation for improvements', the HLLRA added a call for 'such an apportionment of the land as will promote the welfare of the people throughout the Highlands and Islands' – this last point being explicitly intended to remedy the lack of land which, as stressed earlier, was the crofting population's most deeply felt grievance.

To begin with, the HLLRA was simply an institutionalised version of the more informal crofting lobby which had been in existence for some time. This was reflected in its choice of office-bearers. Donald H. MacFarlane was elected HLLRA president, and among his numerous vice-presidents were prominent Gaelic revivalists such as John Stuart Blackie, Charles Fraser-MacIntosh, Roderick MacDonald and John MacKay, as well as radical land reformers like G.B. Clark. Donald Murray, a London solicitor who was also a Gaelic-speaking Highlander from Shieldaig in Wester Ross, became the HLLRA's secretary and its headquarters were established at his chambers in Westminster.

Had the HLLRA remained thus confined to London, its impact – from a Highlands and Islands standpoint anyway – might have remained relatively muted. Instead the association declared itself 'open to all who approve of its objects and subscribe to its funds' – thus opening the way to the HLLRA becoming, as it very shortly did, the principal means of organising crofting protest at a grassroots level.

The HLLRA could not, in the nature of things, instantly rally the crofting community around its banner. But while Donald H. MacFarlane and his colleagues were setting up shop in London, the Napier Commission – which included several estate owners among its members and which was accordingly thought by the HLLRA leadership to be grossly biased in favour of landlords – was having the unexpected and unintended effect of galvanising crofters into action on their own account. Until the Commission's emergence, a crofter afterwards remarked, 'We were afraid we would be persecuted if we should speak out'. As is illustrated by an exchange between Lord Napier and his commission's first witness, a Braes crofter by the name of Angus Stewart, such fears were both real and very general.

Asked by Lord Napier to state 'the hardships and grievances, if any, of . . . the people whom you represent', Stewart memorably replied:

> I would wish that I should have an opportunity of saying a few words before I tell that, and that is that I should have the assurance that I will not be evicted from my holding by the landlord or factor, as I have seen done already . . . I want the assurance that I will not be evicted, for I cannot bear evidence

to the distress of my people without bearing evidence to the oppression and high-handedness of the landlord and his factor.

Under heavy pressure from Lord Napier, Lord MacDonald's factor and most of his counterparts elsewhere in the Highlands and Islands agreed – though almost always with some reluctance – to provide assurances of the sort Angus Stewart demanded. Crofters were consequently enabled, even exhorted, publicly to voice their thoughts for the first time. In advance of the Napier Commission's evidence-taking tour of crofting areas in the spring and summer of 1883, many such areas were visited by land reformers like John Murdoch and Alexander MacKenzie who repeatedly urged crofters to take this tremendous opportunity 'to give expression to their own opinions'. But possibly more decisive in their impact were the actions of the Napier Commission itself. In every crofting district, for instance, there were posted up impressively official notices which instructed tenants to meet and elect delegates to the commission. At the mass meetings held for this purpose, as well as at the commission's numerous sessions in crofting townships, discontents were discussed and aspirations articulated in a way that was quite new. Crofters who had been hitherto uninvolved in the movement initiated in Skye thus gained their first – and undoubtedly intoxicating – experience of organising themselves in an attempt to better their own conditions. Crofters accordingly grew in self-confidence. They also began to be aware of their own power to shape, even to control, events – for was not the Napier Commission itself a direct outcome of crofting agitation in Skye? Gradually, therefore, the crofting population became attuned to the idea of marshalling itself for a wider and more far-reaching struggle than that originally envisaged by tenants at Braes and Glendale – a crucial stage in this process being reached, in August 1883, when some 2,000 crofters, gathered at Fraserburgh for the summer's North Sea herring fishery, met to discuss the land question. On their return home, those crofters resolved, they would set up 'Land Law Reform Associations . . . in their various parishes'.

The effect of the Fraserburgh resolution, news of which featured widely in crofters' letters to their wives, was reinforced in the autumn by support from the editorial columns of the *Oban Times* – which had recently acquired, in Duncan Cameron, a young, intensely radical editor who was passionately devoted to the crofters' cause – and by the HLLRA's decision to begin issuing Gaelic and English circulars urging crofters to organise themselves under its auspices. One typical circular declared:

> The object of the HLLRA is to effect, by unity of purpose and action, such changes in the land laws as will promote the welfare of the people . . . The cause has many friends . . . but the success of the movement must necessarily depend upon the unity and determination of the Highland people . . Unity is might and, with might on their side, the people will soon succeed in obtaining their rights.

In order to be affiliated to the wider association's London headquarters, a local branch of the HLLRA had to have a membership of at least 20, each member paying an annual subscription of one shilling to central funds and also helping to meet any expenses incurred by his own branch. Control of the branch was vested in an eight-man committee headed by a chairman, secretary and treasurer – all of whom, like the rest of the committee, were elected by the branch's members. To establish an HLLRA branch was, therefore, a simple process, requiring no more effort than had been needed to elect delegates to, and prepare evidence for, the Napier Commission. And in those areas where crofters were already engaged in active confrontation with their landlords the procedure was even more straightforward: all that was needed was the adoption of the title HLLRA by one of the regular mass meetings which crofters had themselves evolved in order to supervise rent-strikes and other activities of that kind.

The ground having been well prepared for it, the success of the HLLRA's initiative was more or less assured. The association's first Highlands and Islands branch was constituted at Glendale on 5 December 1883. Two months later, the *Oban Times* was able to report that 'branch societies of this new mode of agitating crofter grievances are now in full swing in most parts of Skye'. And for all that landlords, factors and several clergymen joined in denouncing the HLLRA as a 'Fenian fraternity', other crofting areas quickly followed suit. The crofters' movement found itself equipped, as a result, with an organisational framework which rapidly made it possible for crofters to transcend the limitations previously placed on their efforts by geographical and other barriers to region-wide action. In 1884, then, the Highland land war entered a new and more decisive phase.

9

THE HIGHLAND LAND WAR:
IS TREASA TUATH
NA TIGHEARNA*

1884–1886

The Napier Commission, by arousing expectations of immediate legislation on the crofting question, had the effect of temporarily stilling the troubles which had preceded its appointment – a development reinforced, in the particular case of Glendale, by the estate management's decision to let one-third of Waterstein farm to the crofters of Milovaig and Borodal. When crofters began to get home from their summer jobs in the Lowlands and on east coast herring drifters in the autumn of 1884, however, it began to be suspected that an officially imposed solution to crofters' problems was far from imminent. Unrest accordingly manifested itself once more. On the Glendale and Kilmuir estates, rent strikes were consolidated and intensified. The part of Waterstein still held as a sheep farm was reoccupied by crofters. Other lands were seized near Hamara, Glendale, and in the neighbourhood of Garrafad on the Kilmuir estate – attempts to remove tenants who took a leading part in these proceedings failing when the sheriff-officers charged with the task of delivering their eviction orders were assaulted and deforced in what was rapidly becoming the standard manner. Elsewhere in the Hebrides, meanwhile, there were similar developments. The tenants of several Tiree townships began a rent strike and threatened to occupy grazings on Ben Hynish and Ben Hough. In South Uist, farmland was seized in the neighbourhood of Stoneybridge. North Uist crofters petitioned the island's proprietor for more land, and a sheep farmer's grazings at Melbost in Lewis were occupied by crofting tenants.

But if the Napier Commission had delivered no instant solution to crofting problems, its report, when published in April 1884, had proved, as G. B. Clark for one admitted, 'more sympathetic . . . and more advanced in its recommendations than was generally expected'. By comprehensively exposing the many glaring iniquities inherent in north-west Scotland's agrarian structure – as well as by recommending a fairly sweeping reform of that structure – the Napier Commission, then, had given the crofting community's cause a considerable boost. The commission's attempt to

---

*Gaelic proverb and land reform slogan, usually translated as 'The people are mightier than a lord'.

devise specifically Highland remedies for what its members saw as specifically Highland grievances – this attempt turning on proposals to give legal status to the traditional institutions of the crofting township and on a planned phasing out of all holdings under six acres – was not at all to the liking, however, of crofters themselves. Most of them had set their hearts on legislation along the lines of the Irish Land Act of 1881. At mass meetings throughout the crofting area, the Napier Commission's recommendations were duly condemned as complicated, impractical and, above all, inadequate.

By the summer of 1884, therefore, the optimism engendered by the establishment of the Napier Commission had largely faded away – a development hastened by the Liberal government's evident lack of anxiety to pass, or even seriously contemplate, crofting legislation of any kind. Some understandably exasperated crofters in Glendale were heard to remark that the only way to obtain a Highland Land Act might be to follow the Irish example and shoot a few landlords. If that suggestion – for better or worse – was not meant to be taken very seriously, the same was not true of the underlying intention to step up direct action. At a mass meeting held before their departure for the summer herring fishings, the Glendale men resolved that, if no governmental gesture was forthcoming by the autumn, more sheep farms would be forcibly appropriated.

As crofting discontent increased, so did the prestige and influence of the HLLRA. By June 1884, the association was able to boast a paid-up crofter membership of around 5,000, and a vigorous recruiting drive organised by the HLLRA's recently appointed 'lecturer', John MacPherson, acknowledged leader of the Glendale crofters and one of the 'martyrs' of 1883, was bringing in more members almost daily. Declaring that 'the time had now arrived that crofters should unite together and agitate their cause for freedom and more land', MacPherson spent the summer addressing meetings and helping to establish HLLRA branches in Skye, Mull, north Argyll and the Outer Isles. His tour was everywhere wildly successful – in Barra, for example, he was escorted from township to township by a procession of some 600 crofters. And those members of the HLLRA's executive who joined their representative in the islands in the early autumn were quickly caught up in the general enthusiasm. Thus D.H. MacFarlane, a man with much direct experience of Ireland's land reform movement, considered:

> [Irish] feeling upon the subject was weak and vacillating in comparison with the determined spirit of the people of the Highlands. The Highland people are convinced that their cause is just, that their demands are just, and they are determined to seek redress.

The HLLRA's star being undeniably in the ascendant, MacFarlane's heady optimism was amply justified by events. The association's membership was soaring. Its contention that the Highlands' agrarian order was archaic and unjust had been acknowledged – to put the matter no higher – by a royal commission. And speaking in Edinburgh in August, William Gladstone had at last personally and publicly pledged his government to legislate on crofting issues. It was in an atmosphere of enthusiasm bordering on euphoria, therefore, that the HLLRA convened its first annual conference at Dingwall in September 1884. The conference was attended by crofters' delegates from all over north-west Scotland and its principal outcome was the HLLRA's adoption of a manifesto soon to be known to the crofting community as the Dingwall Programme.

This programme, while welcoming the Napier Commission's report, largely rejected the commission's suggested reforms in favour of a more radical approach – predicated on the contention that each and every crofter, irrespective of his holding's size, should be granted both security of tenure and a statutorily guaranteed right, should he relinquish his tenancy, to compensation for improvements made by him to his croft. But security of tenure and compensation for improvements were but two of the Dingwall Programme's several demands. The programme insisted, for example, on the establishment in the Highlands and Islands of 'a land court with judicial and administrative functions' – a measure incorporated in the Irish Land Act of 1881 but ruled out, in a crofting context, by the Napier Commission. Such a court, the HLLRA envisaged, would determine fair rents and be empowered to 'enlarge crofting townships and form new townships . . . on any land which the court may consider suitable'. It would, in other words, redistribute land in the crofting community's favour.

The Dingwall Programme, dismissed by *The Times* as 'a piece of pernicious nonsense', was thus a very radical document which, not content with proposing a drastic modification of landlord-tenant relationships, went on to propound a scheme of compulsory land settlement – a concept which one cabinet minister thought 'attended with far-reaching and . . . dangerous consequences'. The HLLRA programme, then, represented a considerable advance even on Gladstone's Irish Land Act of 1881, a measure which – though stopping short of redistribution – had itself been widely condemned as a gross and unacceptable interference with the rights of landed property. But of almost as much significance as the HLLRA's aims were the methods which the association now adopted with a view to securing those aims. Appended to the Dingwall Programme was an HLLRA announcement to the effect that the association's members, at the next general election, would 'only support parliamentary candidates for the northern constituencies who approve of this programme and promise to support a Bill to give it full legislative effect'. In conjunction with the imminence of the Liberal government's Third Reform Act, the measure which gave crofting tenants votes for the first time, this declaration amounted to a knell of doom for landlordism's long dominance of Highland politics.

Although the electoral effects of the challenge thus thrown down to the Tory and Liberal Parties in the Highlands did not become apparent until the end of 1885, the months immediately following the Dingwall conference were marked by a rapid escalation of the conflict between the crofting community and its landlords. At HLLRA meetings in Tiree it was demanded that 'the land be justly divided' and, both in Tiree and in South Uist, wire fences around sheep farms were clandestinely destroyed. In November, moreover, South Uist crofters resolved, at a mass meeting, to pay no rent to their proprietrix, Lady Gordon Cathcart, who had inherited the estates which had once belonged to her father, John Gordon of Cluny, until she instituted a general rent reduction and restored 'the arable and pasture land forcibly and unlawfully taken . . . to enlarge big farms'. Since no rent reductions or land redistributions were forthcoming, crofting tenants on South Uist and Benbecula paid almost none of the rents due at Martinmas 1884. And in accordance with another resolution adopted at their November meeting – 'that unless the land be justfully divided at the New Year the nearest tacks [or farms] will be taken possession of and appropriated' – the crofting tenants on the two islands marked the commencement of 1885 by occupying lands from which their forebears had been evicted 30, 40 or more years before.

Typical of such seizures of land was one conducted by crofters from Stoneybridge in South Uist. With a total disregard for the dire warnings emanating from the estate authorities, they took possession of lands on Ormaclett farm – a substantial holding from which some of them had once been evicted – allotted their illegally-occupied fields among themselves, and started to prepare their new 'crofts' for cultivation by spreading seaweed on them. A subsequent attempt to serve 42 of the offending tenants with court orders instructing them to withdraw from Ormaclett led only to the deforcement of the sheriff-officer concerned.

Elsewhere in the Outer Isles there were identical occurrences. Barra crofters met to demand more land. North Uist tenants pegged out new 'crofts' on Balelone and Balranald sheep farms. In Lewis, crofting rents were withheld, farm fences destroyed and lands seized. The Shawbost branch of the HLLRA, for example, organised the occupation of part of Dalbeg farm, the branch secretary's announcement of their action summing up the general feeling of Hebridean crofters in that eventful winter:

> We have put up with these grievances for a long time, but now we venture to lay hold of that piece of our old grazings with the strong hand of the people united for their rights . . . Now the fence is broken down in several places and our sheep and cattle are feeding on our old possessions.

In Lewis, too, a sheriff-officer was deforced. But there, as elsewhere in the islands, the really distinctive feature of this new wave of unrest was the increased use by crofters of intimidatory tactics of one kind or another. The overnight destruction of fences and dykes became commonplace. In South Uist, telegraph wires were cut and a boat belonging to a farm manager destroyed. In that island and in Lewis, boulders were placed on the roads in order to harass farmers, factors and landlords – the only people who could afford to travel by carriage. And at the same time, the boycott – the social ostracisation which the Irish Land League had developed into a formidable weapon of agrarian conflict – made its appearance in the Highlands and Islands. Crofters in Skye and South Uist were instructed by their HLLRA branches to do no work for sheep farmers. And it was made abundantly clear that anyone who dared to occupy the holding of an evicted tenant would be made to feel the displeasure of his fellow crofters in no uncertain fashion. Nor was this latter threat, as was demonstrated by events, an idle one. In Kilmuir, for example, a boat belonging to a crofter who refused to take part in HLLRA activity was destroyed, his windows smashed and his byre burned down. The corn stacks belonging to two North Uist crofters who refused to join the HLLRA were similarly sabotaged and their cattle mutilated.

By the end of 1884, therefore, the crofting population of north-west Scotland, so long quiescent in the face of oppression and exploitation, were actively engaged in a campaign of subversion, of which 'agrarian crimes' – as the authorities labelled incidents of the North Uist or Kilmuir type – were merely a small, if particularly striking, component. To landlords, the spectacle was a decidedly alarming one. Their views, as always, were faithfully reflected in the leader columns of *The Scotsman*:

> Throughout the Hebrides men are taking what does not belong to them, are setting all law at defiance, and are instituting a terrorism which the poor people are unable to resist . . . Rents are unpaid, not because the tenants cannot pay them, but because in some cases they will not, and in some cases they dare not.

If law and order were not quickly and firmly restored, *The Scotsman* concluded, 'the condition of the islands will soon be as bad as that of Ireland three years ago'. As it happened, the intimidation thus condemned by Scotland's leading Liberal newspaper was genuinely deplored by the HLLRA's urban leaders. But there was little the latter could do to control the association's Highlands and Islands branches whose members' struggle with their landlords and with the law had long since assumed a quite unstoppable momentum of its own. Estate owners and the police – who did not need the clarion calls of *The Scotsman* to arouse them to the seriousness of the situation they faced – were equally helpless. The picture of a few evil and unscrupulous 'agitators' engaged in terrorising a fundamentally law-abiding population whose fervent desire it was to be allowed to pay rent to their landlords was one that had no reality outside the fertile imaginations of leader-writers in Edinburgh. The vast majority of the crofting community sympathised quite openly with fence breakers and land raiders. The inevitable result, as the owners of one Hebridean estate complained, was that 'the perpetrators of these crimes could not be discovered'.

As was always the case in the early years of the land war, unrest was most acute in Skye where, in the autumn of 1884, crofters occupied several sheep farms on the Glendale and Kilmuir estates. Intimidation having been reported to be particularly rampant on the latter property, an attempt was consequently made, towards the end of October, to station a police superintendent and ten constables inside the Kilmuir estate boundary. All 11 men were driven off the property by a large crowd. And at the beginning of November 1884, therefore, Kilmuir's crofting tenants were the unchallenged masters of their landlord's estate – a position which, it seemed, they were reluctant to give up. That is evident from a report made to the Home Office, by the increasingly distraught chief constable of Inverness-shire, on 9 November:

> [The Kilmuir people] have for the past week been assembled in hundreds, day and night, armed with sticks for the purpose of assaulting an expected body of police, and declare that they will attack any number of constables . . . At present a reign of terror exists in the district, and nothing short of government aid or [military] protection for the police in restoring order and maintaining the law will suffice.

In September, the Inverness-shire authorities had asked to be allowed to arm their Skye constables, and they had subsequently received 50 service revolvers and 1,000 rounds of ammunition from the War Office. Confronted with what was, from their point of view, an unsupportable situation in Kilmuir, the same authorities now decided to march a detachment of 40 armed police on to the property. Contemporary press reports that some of the crofters guarding the approach roads to the Kilmuir estate were armed with rifles, as well as with the more usual cudgels and sticks, may have been erroneous. But there is every reason to suspect, nevertheless, that a bloody confrontation might easily have resulted from an incursion of newly armed and recently recruited policemen into a district where tension was high, tempers frayed and the police detested. It was probably as well, therefore, that the government at last agreed to make troops available for duties in Skye.

The outcome of that decision was the arrival off Skye, in mid-November 1884, of a small flotilla consisting of a gunboat, a troopship carrying 300 marines, and the civilian steamer, *Locheil* – the latter chartered from its owners, David MacBrayne Ltd, to serve as a mobile police barracks when it became apparent that none of the island's innkeepers were willing to take the undoubted risks involved in providing accommodation for policemen. On being informed of the nature of their mission, the *Locheil*'s captain and most of her crew resigned – while Kilmuir crofters, for their part, reacted to the government's display of force by announcing that they would not rest 'until they got justice done and until the iniquitous land laws [were] reformed'. Having issued this defiant statement, however, the Kilmuir men prudently resolved to refrain from confronting the marines. Partly, this decision was taken with a view to avoiding a battle crofters knew they could not win. Partly, it reflected the fact that crofters' hatred of the police – who, as a government minister observed, they 'regarded . . . as the agents of the landlords rather than as part of the constituted authorities of the country' – did not extend to the military who, in the event, were very cordially received.

Crofters' professions of non-resistance notwithstanding, the redoubtable Sheriff Ivory was determined to make the fullest possible use of the troops who had at last been placed at his disposal. He accordingly began the task of pacifying Skye by marching 250 fully armed marines around the northern part of the Trotternish peninsula from Uig to Staffin – a route carefully chosen to take in some of the most disturbed parts of the Kilmuir estate. Sadly for Ivory, the outcome of his endeavours was a propaganda triumph for the crofters. The marines' manoeuvres, a *Times* correspondent reported, 'were intended as an imposing military spectacle to overawe the natives':

> Few of these, however, were stirring and those that were abroad seemed to be amazed rather than intimidated by the display . . . Taken as a whole, today's proceedings can only be described as an extravagant display of force, the effect of which was to excite the astonishment, and mirth even, of the crofters but not to cow them.

The government took a similar view, Ivory being curtly informed that the home secretary, Sir William Harcourt, was 'somewhat surprised' at the scale of his initial operations. But though they made Inverness-shire's luckless sheriff their scapegoat, Ivory's difficulties were largely of government ministers' own making. They constitute, therefore, important testimony to the vacillating and indecisive nature of the Liberal administration's Highland policy.

Because Gladstone's cabinet did not wish to offend the crofting community's numerous sympathisers on the Liberal Party's radical wing, the troops sent to Skye towards the close of 1884 were not, on Harcourt's instructions, allowed to perform duties normally carried out by the police. They could not, for example, be used to escort sheriff-officers engaged in the serving of eviction orders. When such officers were deforced, as they almost invariably were, the military were consequently forbidden to intervene, except as police escorts, in any subsequent attempt to apprehend the deforcers. Thus, while it undoubtedly convinced both the wider crofting community and the political leadership of the HLLRA that the Liberal government was not to be trusted, the military presence in Skye did absolutely nothing to help the island's landlords enforce their will on their increasingly rebellious tenantries.

In the last week of December 1884, to give only one example of a common pattern of events, sheriff-officers were deforced while attempting to serve summonses of eviction on crofters in Kilmuir and in Glendale. But a full month elapsed before any attempt was made to arrest the crofters concerned – the atmosphere in which the arrests were eventually made being illustrated by the fact that the police involved had to be protected by marines who, at one stage, were ordered to fix bayonets in order to ward off an angry crowd.

The persistence of this sort of situation had a predictable outcome. An attempt to evict crofters who had occupied lands on Nicol Martin's Husabost estate failed, in January 1885, because a sheriff-officer, for whom no military escort could be provided, decided that he could not serve summonses of removal on Husabost 'without great risk of personal injury'. Following further deforcements in the spring, refusals by sheriff-officers to serve writs, court orders and eviction notices became commonplace. Renewed appeals for a strong line were accordingly made to the home secretary by landlords and their allies. But Harcourt – who, for all his desire to maintain law and order, had no wish to lay himself open to the charge of aiding and abetting Highland landlordism – made it clear, once again, that there was to be no military involvement in the serving of eviction notices. The result – since equipping sheriff-officers with police escorts usually provoked, rather than prevented, disturbances – was that such notices, together with other legal documentation, remained, for the most part, unserved. Court proceedings against crofters thus became, for all practical purposes, valueless.

With such military protection as was extended to them, the police in Skye were able to regain access to areas from which they had recently been excluded. But as a means of putting an end to rent strikes and other manifestations of crofting discontent, military intervention in Skye affairs was, for reasons just outlined, a costly failure. At the Martinmas rent collection on the Kilmuir estate, the area where the marines were most active, almost no rents were paid by crofters. And from Glendale and Kilmuir the no-rent movement spread, in November and December 1884, to the rest of Skye. In township after township it was resolved that no rents would be paid until grievances were redressed. Thus crofters at Sconser demanded that lands which had been added to Lord MacDonald's deer forest during the clearances of the 1850s be restored to them. At Braes, a new rent strike was instituted, the tenants of Balmeanach, Gedintailor and Peinchorran now demanding that the additional rent being paid by them for Ben Lee should immediately be cancelled. In Sleat, a district previously unaffected by unrest, crofters petitioned Lord MacDonald for more land. At Elgol, on the Strathaird estate, rents were withheld and fences around sheep farms were destroyed. On the Dunvegan estate, too, the winter brought indications of still more trouble – with some of MacLeod of Dunvegan's crofting tenants commencing their own rent strike.

That rents were withheld on such a scale was partly due to the damage done to crofters' domestic economies by the steep fall in cattle prices which began in 1884 and continued for several years. By the later 1880s, stirks which would have fetched £7 or £8 in 1883 were worth only about £1 10s – and many could not be sold at all. Prices for more mature cattle fell proportionately – while crofters' wedders declined in value by about 50 per cent. After 1883, therefore, the happy state of affairs in which 'the stirk paid the rent' came to an end. Within two or three years, the returns on cattle sales had fallen so drastically that they did not even cover the cost of the winter fodder many crofters bought to supplement the grain produced on holdings which, as already emphasised, were invariably incapable of yielding much in the way of crops. Debts thus increased and credit became more difficult to obtain. But though one poor law administrator – with all the insensitivity which made his a detested profession – remarked that the solution to the crofting community's financial problems lay in crofters learning to curb the 'extravagant habits' they had contracted in the relatively prosperous 1870s, the crofters of the mid-1880s were in no mood to hand over to landlords, by way of rent, money they desperately needed to maintain their own families. A letter from tenants at Fasach to the Glendale estate's trustees is indicative of general crofting attitudes:

> Our poverty is not our fault. We have worked . . . to pay you for what should be our houses. But we are now so poor that we must first obey the law of nature to feed and clothe ourselves, and we cannot therefore pay you the rent which you wish to exact from us.

In the context of the crofting community's long history of non-resistance to a particularly exploitative landlordism, such proclamations, together with the rent strikes and land seizures they announced, smacked of little less than insurrection. And though north-west Scotland quietened down as usual in the summer when its menfolk left for the herring fishings, the climate of crofting opinion was such as to make it obvious – despite the government taking advantage of the summer lull to withdraw its armed forces from Skye in June 1885 – that the Highland land war was far from over. Unsurprisingly, then, the winter of 1885–86 brought renewed manifestations of discontent. In districts as far apart as Ardnamurchan and Lewis, peatstacks and haystacks were burned and other acts of intimidation committed. In Skye, it remained 'impossible to get officers to serve writs', with the result, as ministers were informed by in October 1885 by Lord Lovat – then emerging as something of a spokesman for the landed class – that 'the queen's writ . . . does not now run in the island. The lands seized are still mostly in the hands of the law breakers, rents and taxes are unpaid, and many defaulters are still at large'.

To Lovat and his fellow landowners, the most worrying aspect of the general lawlessness among their tenantries was the rapid proliferation of rent strikes. In September 1885, Lord MacDonald's estate managers – desperate to see at least some cash come in – appealed to crofters to pay such rents as they could afford. But as Lord MacDonald's factor observed ruefully, 'not a single farthing was paid, and not a tenant appeared'. Much the same was true of the rest of Skye. In 1880, Kilmuir crofters had owed their landlord only £63. In 1883, some three years after the first rent strike on the estate, they had owed him £990. By the end of 1885, however, their arrears totalled £5,718. On the MacDonald estate the pattern was identical – crofters' arrears rising from £464 in 1883 to £4,816 in 1885. And in the Outer Isles the overall situation, from the landlords' viewpoint, was no better.

Applied locally, as in Braes and Glendale in 1882, rent strikes were mere irritants – significant in terms of the protest they registered but quite incapable of inflicting serious damage to landowners' finances. But applied on a massive scale, as it was in all of north-west Scotland in 1885–86, the rent strike was a potentially deadly weapon – especially in the context of the serious slump produced in estate revenues by the then accelerating collapse of the market for wool. When, in September 1885, a Skye factor declared that 'unless the law is enforced a good many west coast proprietors must succumb', his warning, though perhaps a little premature, was not without foundation in fact. As a result of the crofting community's rent strikes on the one hand, and the impact of agricultural depression on the other, Highland and Hebridean landlords were undoubtedly facing the most serious crisis they had known since the early nineteenth century.

Their mounting financial difficulties had the effect of inducing in Highland landowners that 'general desire . . . to come to terms with their crofting tenants' which was noted by Cameron of Locheil in December 1884 – and which assumed a concrete shape the following month when some 50 Highland lairds or their representatives met in Inverness to discuss crofting issues. The outcome of this proprietorial summit was an offer to provide crofters with leases, revise croft rents downward and guarantee the payment of compensation for any improvements made by crofters to their homes or holdings. Had they been made two or three years earlier, these proposals would almost certainly have evoked a favourable response – for even in 1883, as the minister of Glenelg had remarked to the Napier Commission, many crofters would have been satisfied with 'some little concession' from their landlords. By 1885, however, that time had passed. The landed class's offer was universally, and correctly, interpreted as a indication of weakness rather than generosity. 'The Highland lairds are on their knees,' the *Oban Times* editorialised. And crofters everywhere agreed. 'No concessions of the landlords can settle matters,' a Kilmuir crofter declared at an HLLRA meeting in January 1885. 'We want no concessions. We want our just rights.'

Opinions of that sort were given dramatic political expression in the results of the general election held towards the end of 1885. With no fewer than four of the five crofting constituencies falling to its candidates, rather than to the Liberal or Tory lairds who were their traditional incumbents, the election was an HLLRA triumph – the crofting community celebrating the occasion by staging torchlit processions and lighting bonfires on several Highlands and Islands hilltops. 'The enemy have left the spoils and fled before the conquering hosts of land law reform,' proclaimed the *Oban Times*. 'From the Mull of Kintyre to the Butt of Lewis the land is before us.'

What were the reasons for this remarkable success? Liberal and Tory discomfiture in the Highlands, *The Scotsman* informed its readers, whom it had previously assured of the certain defeat of HLLRA 'carpet-baggers', was attributable to the fact that crofters, knowing 'nothing of politics', had been 'deluded with promises of nearly everything they desire'. An alternative explanation – one that is at once more convincing and less insulting to the collective intelligence of the crofting community – is to be found in the strength and effectiveness of the HLLRA's organisation on the ground. As was discovered in the course of a secret investigation carried out on behalf of the government in the summer of 1886, a majority of the mainland crofting population were members of the HLLRA. And in the islands, the association's strength was even more impressive. In Skye, for example, it was 'probable that every man of the crofter and cottar classes, with many merchants and artisans besides, [was] an enrolled member'. It was this almost unanimous adherence of the crofting population to its aims and objectives which made possible the HLLRA's spectacular triumph at the polls.

———————

As a political organisation, and it has some claim to the title of Britain's first mass-membership political party, the HLLRA was clearly organised from outside the crofting community. From a crofting perspective, however, this – in the conditions of the time – was a source of some strength. But for their having had access to leadership of the HLLRA variety, crofters would not have achieved either the all-embracing unity or the well developed sense of political purpose which became key facts of Highlands and Islands life during the 1880s. At a more localised level, moreover, the fact that they possessed allies more able than they in the arts of politics and publicity greatly boosted crofting morale – something of which both sides in the Highland land war were well aware. In 1886 John MacPherson, Glendale crofters' leader, 'could say in all truth and sincerity that, if it had not been for the . . . HLLRA, he would have lost heart long ago'. Two years previously, one of the Glendale estate's trustees had made essentially the same point in a letter to William Ivory. 'The people could easily be dealt with,' this man wrote. 'But the London agitators cannot.'

The HLLRA, however, was more than a political party. It was a social movement – and, as such, its inspiration came from within the crofting community itself. Of the many thousands of people who took part in the HLLRA's campaign of protest in the rural Highlands and Islands only a handful were not crofters or cottars. A few teachers – of whom the best known was Donald MacRae, a highly effective organiser of direct action in Lewis in the later 1880s – played some part in the association's proceedings. And in Catholic areas like Barra, South Uist and Arisaig, local priests gave occasionally outspoken support to the movement. The vast majority of the Protestant clergy were, however, opposed to the HLLRA and all it stood for. An occasional Free Church minister, of whom the Revd Finlay Graham of Sleat was the outstanding example, urged his congregation to join the HLLRA. But most of his colleagues – while refraining from following the example of the Revd Hector Cameron of Barvas, Lewis, a man who denounced rent strikes as sinful – did not hesitate to join the Church of Scotland's parish ministers in what the *Oban Times* called an 'unholy alliance' against the association.

That the HLLRA was able to overcome clerical opposition to its policies is a further tribute to its own strength – a truth grasped by Donald H. MacFarlane when he remarked that he won the 1885 election in Argyll, where he was the HLLRA's candidate, 'with the powers of heaven and earth against him'. 'The landlords,' MacFarlane explained, 'were the earth, and the ministers were the heavens.'*

In view of what was said in an earlier chapter about the Free Church's part in promoting a sense of community among crofters, its role in the land war – in which the church's general stance, on any objective reading, was hostile to the crofting interest – might seem a strange one. By the 1880s, however, the Free Church had generally lost its initial identification with the forces of anti-landlordism. Most of its ministers had embraced a political quietism which precluded any challenge to the social order. Some Free Church clerics, in fact, felt themselves indebted to those landlords – of whom, by the 1880s, there were several – who had rendered their denomination a number of valuable services. Thus the Free Church minister of Kilmuir, in his evidence to the Napier Commission, went out of his way to express his gratitude to William Fraser, the parish's owner and arguably the worst landlord in the northern half of Scotland, for all that he had done for the Free Church. As such statements suggest, the 1880s, then, witnessed a partial reversal in the earlier roles of the Free and Established Churches. It was ministers drawn from the latter church – many of them with little in the way of a congregation – who had least to lose by joining the HLLRA. The clergymen who took the most active part in the association's activities, therefore, were Church of Scotland ministers – led by the young and fervently radical Donald MacCallum who was minister at Waternish at

---

*Macfarlane's victory was all the more notable because he was a Catholic standing in an overwhelmingly Protestant constituency. He was the first Catholic to become an MP in Scotland.

the height of the troubles in Skye. This grouping's members greatly distinguished themselves – Donald MacCallum, for instance, enjoying the distinction both of having been tried before the presbytery of Skye on a charge of having 'incited crofters to class hatred' and of having been arrested and imprisoned during an 1886 round up of HLLRA 'agitators' in Skye. But for all the huge affection felt for MacCallum by crofters, his part in the land reform movement was, in the last analysis, quite minimal when compared to the part played by crofters themselves.

Most committed to the HLLRA and to the cause it represented were those men who had grown up in the relatively prosperous and secure 1860s and 1870s and who were not prepared, as some older crofters undoubtedly were, fatalistically to accept a relapse into social and economic uncertainty. As a Lochcarron crofter told an HLLRA conference in 1886:

> The old men had not had the same advantages of education that the young men had. They must put the fear of the landlord and his satellites, the factors, out of the old men. They must try and make them realise that the powers that be are nothing to the powers that the generality of the people possess.

As such comments indicate, the younger generation of crofters tended to be a lot more receptive than their elders to politically radical notions of the sort introduced into the Highlands by John Murdoch and his associates. Despite its being influenced by such ideas, however, the crofters' movement of the 1880s by no means represented a clean break with the past. This movement's local organisation, though standardised in accordance with HLLRA instructions, was broadly developed by crofters themselves and in it the influences of the crofting community's earlier and formative experiences were clearly visible. HLLRA meetings, it was observed during the 1880s, were 'always held in the open air in defiance of rain and tempest' and at them, 'the person selected to preside opens and closes the proceedings with prayer'. The consequent resemblance between such HLLRA gatherings and the assemblages convened by *na daoine* of earlier times was not coincidental. Nor was the fact that the HLLRA's local leaders – men cast in the mould of John MacPherson whose meetings were punctuated by passionately delivered Gaelic prayers and whose eloquence in his native tongue was said to be such as to move an audience to tears or to fury – occupied positions in the townships that were in all respects analogous to those held by *na daoine* of a preceding generation. By the 1880s, when the Highland land war was at its height, *na daoine* had largely faded from the scene and their populist religion – drained of most of its subversive content in the process – had been institutionalised within the framework of the Free Church. But while the Free Church inherited Highland evangelicalism, it was John MacPherson and a host of other HLLRA activists who inherited *na daoine*'s leadership of, and influence over, the crofting community.

Being thus rooted deeply in the crofting population, the HLLRA – in ways that extended far beyond such debt as it owed to the religious revivalism of some decades previously – drew heavily on the many longstanding beliefs carried forward into the nineteenth century from the era of clans and clanship.

As an earlier chapter suggested, such beliefs, notably those concerning the bond between chiefs and their clansfolk, could be, and indeed were, a retarding influence on the development of a radical challenge to Highland landlordism. Not every aspect of the crofting community's cultural heritage fell within this category, however. On the contrary, there survived in the nineteenth-century Highlands a number of concepts – most of them deriving from the more or less remote past of the Celtic peoples – that were quite capable of being transformed into important components of a distinctive critique of landlordism. Crofters, for example, never became reconciled to the right of private ownership of game – a fact which caused Highland lairds no little trouble. 'It is not easy to convince a Highlander that a landlord has a better right to a deer, a moor fowl, or a salmon than he has himself,' it had been noted despairingly in 1802, 'because he considers them the unconfined bounty of heaven.' And in the face of all that landed proprietors could subsequently provide in the way of game laws and gamekeepers, those notions – enshrined in the common Gaelic saying that everyone has a right to a deer from the hill, a tree from the wood and a fish from the river – exhibited such remarkable staying power as to make it possible for them to be deployed against landlords by the HLLRA. A speech delivered by a crofter at an HLLRA meeting in Skye in 1884 makes the point perfectly:

> The fish that was yesterday miles away from the land was claimed by the landlord the moment it reached the shore. And so also were the birds of the air as soon as they flew over his land. The law made it so, because landlords were themselves the lawmakers, and it was a wonder that the poor man was allowed to breathe the air of heaven and drink from the mountain stream without having the factors and the whole of the county police pursuing him as a thief.

Of similar derivation, but of even greater significance, was the longstanding belief that all the members of a tribe, a clan or a community were entitled, simply by virtue of their belonging to such entities, permanently to occupy the land on which they lived.

This conviction, as far as landlords were concerned, had no historical or legal validity. Throughout recorded history, they thought, their ancestors – as chiefs and feudatories – had been the outright and recognised possessors of the land. Thus the Duke of Argyll, writing at the height of the land war, saw in the earliest feudal charters of the Highland nobility 'all the well known powers and obligations of ownership in land' – a view shared by MacLeod of Dunvegan who could see no historical basis for the 'extraordinary assumption' that the Highland people possessed ancient and widely recognised rights in the land. Of the duke's theories, however, crofters held a very low opinion – a Lochaline crofter remarking to the Napier Commission that he was 'not to be bamboozled by his grace's scientific conundrums.' And with an equally sweeping disregard for the claims both of their landlords and of the many historians who – in this regard at least – have taken landlords' part, virtually every other crofter descendant of the commons of the clans has similarly clung steadfastly to the notion of the indissolubility of his ties with the land from which he has scraped a part of his livelihood.

In the medieval and early modern Highlands this notion usually took the form of a profound conviction that prolonged occupation of land gave a right to what amounted to a permanent tenancy of it. Referred to in Gaelic as *duthchas*, such a right was felt to have been established when a family had maintained the effective occupancy of a township or farm for three generations or more. Being recognised by the whole community, *duthchas* was, in principal, inviolable. Thus the tacksmen holders of Highland farms commonly followed each other in patrilineal succession – any attempt by the feudal superior of the farms in question to establish other families on them being resisted by the entire clan, even to the point of bloodshed. Especially strongly expressed among clans like the MacGregors or the MacDonalds of Islay, whose feudal rights were inadequate or uncertain, this age-old concept of the inalienability of the land of the kindred persisted into the eighteenth and nineteenth centuries. In 1750, for example, it was noted:

> Throughout Lochaber, and the adjacent wild countries, the farms have always been given to the cadets of the lesser families . . . which they possess for ages, without any lease, and look upon them as their right of inheritance. And when they are not able to pay their rent and are turned out, they look upon the person who takes these farms after them, as usurping their right. These people have often refused to take a written lease, thinking that by so doing they give up their right of possession.

From this perspective, to accept a lease was also to accept that one's occupancy of a piece of territory could be curtailed by the man who proclaimed himself that same piece of territory's landlord. It is of some significance, in this connection, that the crofters of the 1880s were to reject landlords' offers of leases for exactly the same reason as the tacksmen of the 1750s had rejected them, the Portree branch of the HLLRA resolving, in March 1886:

> That the land of the Highlands, belonging as it does to the people of the Highlands, the acceptance of leases by crofters is not necessary, and is besides a tacit admission of rights which they repudiate as inconsistent with the security of tenure to which they are entitled.

This persistent belief that Highland tenants had, and have, 'a kind of hereditary right' to their holdings survived the state-supported enforcement of private property in land for the simple reason that, as far as crofters were concerned, the claims of their landlords – whatever courts and parliaments might contend – had no foundation in a moral code far older than any Act or charter. Highland tenants, the Earl of Selkirk observed in 1805, well knew 'of how little avail was a piece of parchment and a lump of wax under the old system of the Highlands':

> They reproach their landlord with ingratitude and remind him that, but for their fathers, he would now have no estate. The permanent possession which they had always retained of their paternal farms they consider only as their just right from the share they had borne in the general defence, and can see no difference between the title of the chief and their own.

Another early nineteenth-century writer, John MacCulloch, went so far as to attribute all crofting discontents to this one – utterly outmoded, as he thought – belief:

> But all these complaints, against servitudes as against rent, are the remains of those ancient feelings, from which the Highland people were used to consider the lands as their own – a feeling which was in full force in many places not many years ago . . . [Then] the people considered themselves the proprietors of their farms, as not liable to be ejected at the will of their chief, and scarcely [liable] even to compulsory rent.

Transmuted from one generation of crofters to the next, those views were as strongly held in the 1880s as they had been when tenants in the Strath of Kildonan told Patrick Sellar and his associates 'that they were entitled to keep *their* grounds'. Thus the delegates who came forward from crofting townships to give evidence to the Napier Commission 'often expressed' the opinion 'that the small tenantry of the Highlands have an inalienable title to security of tenure in their possessions'. This opinion, the commission noted, was 'indigenous to the country though it has never been sanctioned by legal recognition and has long been repudiated by the actions of the proprietors'. And as was widely recognised by land reformers both in Scotland and in Ireland, whose peasant farmers had inherited the same Celtic traditions as their Highland counterparts, all such sentiment – however backward-looking it might appear – could readily be accommodated into the radical anti-landlordism of the later nineteenth century.

When parliament recognised the validity of the customary landholding system of Ulster – a region where tenants were also held to have some sort of permanent stake in the land – and incorporated this system's guiding principals into Irish land legislation, John Murdoch drew the appropriate conclusion. Developments in Ireland, Murdoch wrote, 'show very forcibly the importance of cherishing at least some of the traditions which have been handed down from father to son'. 'It would never do,' he commented in the course of an article dating from 1876 'for Highlanders to lose sight of their ancient rights . . . in the land.' And nine years later, when the land war which Murdoch had done so much to foment was well under way, he was still hammering home the same message. 'Highlanders had never forgotten,' Murdoch declared in a speech at Portree in September 1885, 'that the land was theirs and that landlordism was a violent encroachment upon the divine rights of the people.'

All such doctrine, of course, integrated very neatly with the commonly held view – examined in a previous chapter – that clan society had been distinguished by equity, harmony and plenty. Until 1745, according to Charles Cameron, the Liberal MP who was one of the crofting community's earliest parliamentary advocates, 'the cultivators of the soil had a proprietary right in it'. Like other features of the Highlands' golden age, Cameron argued, that right had been destroyed at Culloden:

> It was only after the Highland rising in 1745, when the tribal jurisdiction was swept away, that the Highland chief was transformed into a position analogous to that of the English landlord.

To some of Cameron's land reforming allies, most of all to Alexander MacKenzie who was also a historian, such a sweeping claim appeared 'crude and inaccurate'. And as a piece of historical analysis it did, indeed, leave a lot to be desired. But Cameron's summary of Highland history, for all its over-simplification of complex realities, had the merit of corresponding closely with the beliefs of crofters themselves – beliefs which, as the leading English politician, Joseph Chamberlain, discovered during a tour of north-west Scotland in the spring of 1887, existed 'deep down in the minds of the people'. 'You find it universal,' Chamberlain observed of Highlanders' continuing tendency to base their land reform aspirations on what their ancestors had called *duthchas*. 'They are all of the opinion that they have claims which no lapse of time can possibly extinguish'.

To such claims, statesmen like William Gladstone and – more surprisingly – Lord Salisbury, a Conservative prime minister, paid lip service. If confirmation of their validity was needed it could be found, reformers maintained, in the writings of liberal economists like John Stuart Mill – whose opinion that 'the land of every country belongs to the people of that country' was naturally regarded with some favour by John Murdoch. For much the same reason as they appealed to Murdoch, Mill's theories also appealed to the Irish Land League. Thus Charles Stewart Parnell said of the speech with which he had helped to launch the league:

> We went down to Mayo and we preached the eternal truth that the land of a country, the water of a country, the air of a country, belong to no man. They were not made by any man and they belong to all the human race.

Parnell's language, in this instance, was much the same as that employed by the Revd Donald MacCallum when he proclaimed: 'The land is our birthright, even as the air, the light of the sun, and the water belong to us as our birthright.' And while such declarations could be substantiated from the writings of eighteenth-century philosophers like Rousseau as well as from the works of Victorian commentators like Mill, a more obvious source of enlightenment on such matters, as far as most crofters were concerned, was the bible. Its vital place in crofting life has already been mentioned. And in the bible, more especially in the Old Testament, crofters found lots of instructive parallels between their own plight and that of the Jews more than two millennia before. The point is well made in an 1884 pamphlet dealing with the Highland land question:

> By the Mosaic legislation, the land was to be held under a tribal tenure, the soil being apportioned among the families by whom it was cultivated or used for pasturing their flocks and herds; and this also appears for ages to have been the custom among the Celtic population of the British Isles . . . These ancient Hebrew land laws . . . were set aside by the greedy selfishness of nobles and princes . . . And if the land secured to the tribes of Israel could be filched from the people in such a manner, it is not to be wondered at that the Scottish Highlander, whose Bible is his *vade mecum*, should come to view his present condition, in respect to the land, as somewhat analogous to that of the poorer Jews in the later days of the Jewish monarchy.

Again, the history may be suspect. But there can be no question as to the sincerity of crofters' belief that the bible both sanctioned the notion that landlords had usurped the land and confirmed the validity of their own claim to that land. The statement made by a Tiree crofter imprisoned for his part in a land raid on the Duke of Argyll's Tiree estate speaks for itself:

> He held that he was standing on the side of justice and he had the bible as his authority. The earth belonged to the people and not to the Duke of Argyll or any landlord.

The texts on which those views were based were the common currency of HLLRA politics and were to be seen emblazoned on banners and placards at any one of scores of crofters' meetings:

> The earth is mine . . . The earth is the Lord's and the fullness thereof . . . Woe unto them that join house to house, that lay field to field, till there be no place . . . The earth He hath given to the children of men.

'Unless landlords can prove that we are not of Adam's race at all,' John MacPherson observed in the course of an 1884 letter to MacLeod of Dunvegan, there were to be found in the bible 'letters of agreement from God pronouncing our claim and right in the land.' Much the same point was made by Norman Stewart, a crofter at Valtos on the Kilmuir estate and an HLLRA branch chairman:

> If the landlords consulted Moses or Joshua, they would find there substantial evidences as to who are the rightful owners of the soil. The lord advocate and Sheriff Ivory can quote Acts Georges and John, but we can quote the Act of God – the bible.

The 1880s were a time of widespread agrarian unrest. Within the confines of the British Isles alone, existing tenurial arrangements were effectively challenged, during that decade, in Ireland and Wales as well as in the Highlands. Land reform and land reformers were consequently much in vogue, the latter ranging from Joseph Chamberlain, who saw in land reform a means of capturing rural votes for the Liberal party, to Henry George, the American propagandist to whom a tax on land values seemed the obvious panacea for all social and economic ills. Both Chamberlain and Henry George took an active interest in crofting affairs. But Georgite ideals – rather like those of the socialists with whom John Murdoch became increasingly involved – made no great impact on the crofters' movement which, as preceding paragraphs make clear, was, in its philosophy as well as in its organisation, a distinctively Highland creation. While it would be unwise as well as unjust to minimise the contribution made to that movement by men who were not crofters – John Murdoch, Donald H. MacFarlane, G. B. Clark and their colleagues to mention only a few – it remains the case that crofting protest was fuelled primarily by an ideology stemming ultimately from within the crofting population itself.

By the mid-1880s, then, the crofting community had emerged as a coherent political – as well as social – entity, and crofters had at last begun to take control of their own destinies. It is this fact that made the 1880s – on the face of it, a period of increasing poverty and misery – a time of hope for crofters. The commercial landlordism introduced into the Highlands in the eighteenth century was at last on the retreat. Change was in the air. And for the first time in the nineteenth century, Gaelic poetry took on an optimistic tone – best exemplified in the work of *Mairi Mhor nan Oran*, Mary MacPherson, that committed and outspoken land reformer whose songs, it is said, contributed significantly to the HLLRA's success. As a newspaper correspondent reported from Skye on polling day in 1885, one immediately apparent result of the land war, therefore, was that the crofters involved in it acquired a new and striking self-confidence:

> The crofters were most enthusiastic and each approached the polling station with an air of independence which would have seemed singularly strange to any visitor who had not seen a Skye crofter during the last five years.

The political consequence of that 'air of independence' was the arrival of a Crofters' Party at Westminster in January 1886. Although lacking in numbers, the four members of that party represented a mass movement which had thrown down the gauntlet to Highland landlordism and had plunged north-west Scotland into its greatest political, administrative and social crisis since the demise of Jacobitism. It was the extent of their support among crofters that gave Donald H. MacFarlane (Argyll), Charles Fraser-MacIntosh (Inverness-shire), Roderick MacDonald (Ross and Cromarty), and G. B. Clark (Caithness) their political significance. And it is a measure of what the crofting community had accomplished over the preceding three or four years that the four crofter MPs took their seats in a parliament preparing to devote more time to Highlands and Islands affairs than any of its predecessors since the 1740s.

By 1885, it had become apparent to William Gladstone's government and indeed to every thinking observer – with the exception of Highland landlords who should not, perhaps, be included in the latter category – that the only possible solution to the crofting question lay in a legislative reform of the Highland land system. The requisite legislation should logically have been based on the recommendations contained in the Napier Commission's report. But those recommendations, as was remarked on more than one occasion by the home secretary, Sir William Harcourt, had not met with acceptance in any quarter. One landlord thought Napier's report 'hardly worth discussing'. Another dismissed it as 'full of inconsistencies and anomalies'. And crofters, as already mentioned, had indicated a very strong preference for a measure more akin to the Irish Land Act of 1881 than to the proposals of Lord Napier and his colleagues. To this, Liberal cabinet members were not averse. Gladstone, together with Harcourt and Joseph Chamberlain, felt a great deal of sympathy for crofters and wanted to do something for them. Besides, the Irish Act by which crofters set so much store was the prime minister's own creation and one of which he was inordinately proud. It was consequently resolved, in Gladstone's words, to endorse 'the substantial application of the Irish Land Act to the Highland parishes'. And a Bill to that effect was introduced in the Commons in May 1885.

That particular Bill fell with the government a month later. By New Year, however, a new Liberal administration was in power, there were four crofter MPs in the Commons, and so effective had the HLLRA campaign in the north become that even *The Scotsman* – the paper most committed to the landlords' cause – felt obliged to admit that 'the condition of some parts of the Highlands has become so serious that the urgency of the crofter question can scarcely be exaggerated'. Conservatives and Liberals alike having concluded – by this point – that some sort of remedial legislation was urgently required, the refurbished version of the previous year's Bill which was hastily introduced by the government met with little opposition. Even the Duke of Argyll – who had resigned from Gladstone's cabinet in protest against its Irish land legislation and who had subsequently become Highland landlordism's principal parliamentary spokesman – agreed not to oppose the new measure, 'not because he thought it was a good Bill', but because 'he could not deny that they were in a position that compelled them to agree to something being done'. Arthur Balfour, soon to be secretary of state for Scotland and already the Conservative party's principal spokesman on Highland affairs, took a similar line. On 25 June, therefore, the Bill passed into law.

The Crofters Act of 1886, the only substantial piece of legislation to be enacted by William Gladstone's short-lived third administration, applied to parishes in Argyll, Inverness-shire, Ross and Cromarty, Sutherland, Caithness and the Northern Isles where there were in 1886, or had been during the preceding 80 years, holdings tenanted on a year-to-year basis, rented at under £30 annually and consisting of arable land held in conjunction with rights of common pasturage. The Act, therefore, affected almost every crofter in north-west Scotland – the exceptions consisting of the tiny minority who held leases. And the Act, more to the point, gave the force of law to much of what the HLLRA had been demanding. Subject only to certain easily fulfilled conditions, the June 1886 measure guaranteed security of tenure to crofters – however small their holdings – and gave each crofter the right, on his relinquishing a holding, to claim compensation from the landlord for improvements made to it by himself or by a family predecessor. The Act also enabled a tenant to bequeath his croft to a member of his family and, in a further important provision, set up a land court, the Crofters Commission, which was empowered to fix fair rents, subject these rents to regular revision, cancel all or part of any accumulated arrears, and generally administer both the Act of 1886 and any subsequent crofting legislation.

By the standards of an age accustomed to regarding landed property as inviolable, even sacrosanct, the Crofters Act was a measure so radical as to be little short of revolutionary. Thus *The Scotsman* condemned it as 'a great infringement of the rights of property' – while Fraser of Kilmuir, owner of one of the most disturbed districts in the Highlands, discerned in it an indication of 'communism looming in the future'. Such shrieks of alarm from the propertied classes were inevitable and not very important. Of more significance was the reaction of the crofting community and of its parliamentary representatives. Should the Crofters Act meet with their approval, peace would return to the Highlands and Islands. Should they reject it, unrest would continue. And from the first it was clear that crofters thought the Act far from satisfactory.

Because it was explicitly modelled on the Irish Land Act of 1881, the Crofters Act met, as already noted, many of the demands embodied in the HLLRA's Dingwall Programme for the simple reason that the programme had been drawn up with the Irish precedent in mind. In one crucial respect, however, the 1886 Act fell seriously short of meeting crofters' wishes: it contained little provision for making more land available to them. In part, perhaps, this was the fault of the HLLRA leadership. By harping constantly on the similarities between the Irish tenantry's case – a case whose justice had already been conceded – and that of the crofting community, they had obscured a key distinction between the Irish and Highland situations. Irish agriculture was essentially arable, and Irish smallholders' greatest need was for freedom from rack-renting and capricious eviction. These things, it is true, were not unknown in the Highlands. But Highland agriculture was essentially pastoral and crofters' greatest requirement was for more land – something that was not always appreciated by some of the HLLRA's urban adherents.

Government ministers, on the other hand, were far from unaware of the peculiarities of the Highland situation. At the start of 1885, for instance, J. B. Balfour, the lord advocate, noted that crofters' calls for land redistribution were 'by far the most important' of their demands. He was 'sensible', Balfour added, 'that the expectations, or at all events the hopes, which the crofting class . . . cherish, will not be satisfied unless legislative provision is made for giving them more land'. The Liberal administration of which Balfour was part, however, felt unable to make any such provision. Crofters were too poor to buy land on their own account. The only conceivable way of giving them what they wanted, therefore, was that the government should itself purchase the necessary land and lease it to crofters. Exactly this procedure, in fact, was eventually and successfully adopted. But to the Liberal Party of the mid-1880s it seemed to involve too damaging a departure from the cherished principle of non-intervention in economic affairs. That, at least, was J. B. Balfour's opinion. He did 'not suppose', he informed the Commons, that such a proposal 'would be entertained'.

The 1886 Act consequently made only one very minor concession to crofters' demands for more land. Where land was available for the enlargement of crofts and where its owner refused to let it to crofting tenants on reasonable terms, any five or more tenants whose holdings were near or adjacent to the land in question could apply to the Crofters Commission for the compulsory enlargement of their crofts. The amount of land that could be regarded as available for such a purpose was very restricted. Land subject to existing leases was, for example, excluded – a provision which had the effect of placing most sheep farms and deer forests outwith the measure's already limited scope. Thus, although even this weak gesture in the direction of redistribution, made the Crofters Act more daring than the Irish measure on which it was modelled, the enlargement clause proved quite ineffective in practice and, from the outset, did absolutely nothing to mollify the land-hungry crofters it was intended to appease.

In the House of Commons, then, the four crofters' MPs declared that, as conceived by the government, the Crofters Bill of 1886 was 'of no advantage to the Highland people' and was likely to prove 'a sham and a delusion'. Supported by Irish nationalists who recognised the crofting community's struggle against landlordism to be analogous to that in which their own rural constituents were engaged, Donald H. MacFarlane and his colleagues accordingly opposed the Bill through all its parliamentary stages. But since both front benches were determined to accept no amendments to it, the Bill passed into law without the far-reaching land settlement clauses which the four HLLRA members attempted to attach to it. It did so, however, in the midst of an angry chorus of rejection from the crofting community. Thus Kilmuir crofters resolved 'utterly [to] condemn the so-called Crofters Bill . . . and to continue the agitation till the full measure of their just rights to the soil of their ancestors [be] recognised and secured to them by the legislature'. Glendale crofters similarly pledged themselves 'not to rest satisfied without getting all the land of the Highlands for the people of the Highlands'. And though these declarations were made in districts of above-average crofting militancy, virtually identical resolutions were carried unopposed at scores of HLLRA meetings from Mull to Cape Wrath, and from Helmsdale to the western seaboard of Lewis.

Crofters, of course, had actually gained a great deal from the 1886 Act. But there was one group which had gained nothing. A spokesman for this group had made its aspirations clear at an HLLRA meeting in Skye in December 1884:

> There was considerable talk about the crofters, but there was another class more needful of relief, the cottars . . . It would not benefit the cottars a bit though others got a reduction in rent and more land unless they got land for themselves . . . and he strongly urged that in any . . . settlement of the land question provision should be made for giving land to cottars.

The 1886 Act made no such provision, cottars, in fact, falling almost completely outwith its scope. Their anger was consequently intense and soon manifested itself in a new wave of land seizures. In the spring of 1886, while the Crofters Bill was passing through parliament, 20 cottars living at Morvich in Kintail met and declared that they were 'in such a low condition that we must take the land which is lying waste into our own hands to provide food for ourselves and our families'. In April, the cottars in question began ploughing fields near their landlord's residence, Morvich House, at the head of Loch Duich. There were similar developments in Benbecula. And an HLLRA meeting in the Tiree township of Baugh on 16 April resolved:

> That as the Government has rejected all or any amendments proposed on behalf of cottars, some of the lands unjustly taken from themselves and their fathers and now lying waste be taken possession of and planted with potatoes.

The land raid thus agreed took place within weeks. Other seizures followed and were given fresh impetus when, in September, the 300 delegates attending the HLLRA's annual conference at Bonar Bridge decided to reconstitute the association as the Highland Land League – the league's principal task being 'to restore to the Highland people their inherent rights in their native soil'.

By the autumn of 1886, however, the political context had altered fundamentally. Gladstone's government had fallen on the Irish home rule issue, the Liberal Party had split on the same question, and a Conservative administration headed by Lord Salisbury had been returned to power. Arthur Balfour, Salisbury's nephew, had taken over the recently created Scottish Office – while the Highland Land League, itself in some disarray on the question of home rule for Ireland, was already showing signs of the dissensions that were, within a very few years, to bring about its fragmentation and collapse. The political disagreements of their leaders did not, it is true, affect crofters' and cottars' determination to regain lands lost during the clearances. But the new government, it rapidly emerged, was determined to put down disorder and to make no more concessions to crofting opinion. The passing of the Crofters Act, Arthur Balfour believed, had simultaneously deprived Highland unrest of any justification it might once have possessed and given him the moral authority to suppress it. He was, he told the House of Commons in August 1886, 'no fanatical admirer' of the previous administration's crofting legislation:

> But one advantage of that Bill I foresaw . . . It makes it quite certain that we can exercise the forces of the law and yet be guilty of no hardship to the tenants of the Highlands and Islands.

The explicitly coercive policy thus announced was one that Balfour sought to implement immediately. The 1886 Act was followed, therefore, not by a return to tranquillity but by a series of encounters between the crofting community and the forces of law and order that were more bitter and more violent than any which had hitherto occurred.

10

THE HIGHLAND LAND WAR:
COERCION AND CONCILIATION

1886–1896

First to feel the effects of Conservative coercion were the crofters of Tiree who, as already mentioned, had resolved, in April 1886, to reoccupy lands of which the island's tenantry had been deprived some 30 or 40 years before. Adopted with the then tenantless farm of Greenhill very much in its proposers' minds, this April resolution was soon nullified by an unexpected turn of events: in early May it became known that the island's proprietor, the Duke of Argyll, had let Greenhill to an unusually prosperous crofter, Lachlan MacNeill. The duke – a man, it is worth repeating, who was land reform's bitterest opponent in the world of politics – may, by this action, have been seeking to cause trouble for the HLLRA. If so, he succeeded. By taking over Greenhill, the farm's new tenant was widely considered to have betrayed his fellow crofters. The ensuing ill-feeling – aggravated by the offending crofter being both an HLLRA member and a brother of the chairman of the association's Tiree branch – played no little part in precipitating the confrontation which followed. On 22 May, Greenhill's tenant and his brother, Neil MacNeill, were expelled from the HLLRA. Days later, Greenhill was occupied by over 300 men who at once proceeded to divide the farm among crofters and cottars from nearby townships.

Because Gladstone's government – still in power when these events occurred – refused to sanction renewed military intervention in the Hebrides, the 40 policemen who landed on the island, on 21 July, to serve the writs which the Duke of Argyll had taken out against Greenhill's illegal occupants were unescorted by troops. They were thus no match for the island's crofters. Confronted at Greenhill by a force of men and youths armed with sticks and clubs, the police – outnumbered by about six to one – were obliged to withdraw to the relative security of the inn at Scarinish, their mission unaccomplished. The problem of what they should do next was solved for them by Tiree's crofting population. On the morning of 22 July, Scarinish Inn was surrounded by the men responsible for the seizure of Greenhill. The police contingent, it was demanded, should immediately withdraw from Tiree. They left that afternoon.

With the police in full retreat and the Duke of Argyll complaining that Tiree was 'under the rule of savagery', military involvement became inevitable. On 31 July 1886, the day after Arthur Balfour took over at the Scottish Office, a detachment of 50 police escorted by five times that number of marines was landed on the island. Eight crofters, including the new chairman of Tiree's HLLRA branch, were promptly arrested and conveyed to the mainland where they were subsequently found guilty of mobbing and rioting as well as of deforcement – five being sentenced to six months' imprisonment, the others to four months. Since crofters found guilty of similar offences in the past had been fined a few shillings or jailed for two or three weeks, the Scottish Secretary became the recipient of a spate of protests and representations about the severity of the sentences imposed on the Tiree men. By way of demonstrating how he meant henceforth to conduct policy in the Highlands, Balfour ignored them. It was a fitting beginning to his Highland policy.

The Tiree difficulty behind him, Balfour turned his attention to Skye where, in the summer of 1886, the crofters' rent strike was as solid as ever – the total of outstanding arrears having passed the £20,000 mark. And because estate factors invariably doubled as local authority rates collectors, receiving rents and taxes at the same place on the same day, the non-payment of rents entailed an effective embargo on rates payment also. The outcome – seriously aggravated by Skye landlords' refusal to pay *their* rates until they had received their rents – was that, from 1884 onwards, local government finances plunged into deficit. Deprived of funds, poor law and school boards were forced to borrow heavily until, in the spring of 1886, their credit was exhausted and local government in Skye threatened with complete collapse.

As this crisis developed, cries of woe went up on all sides. Reginald MacLeod, son of MacLeod of Dunvegan, declared Skye to be 'in a state of anarchy'. *The Scotsman* – inevitably – agreed, and added that the chaos in Skye was entirely the fault of the Liberal government which had, the paper alleged, conspicuously failed to restore some degree of order to the island's affairs. Gladstone's ministers, however, had had their fill of Skye and its seemingly endless troubles, and appeals to them to use troops to enforce the collection of rates elicited only an uncompromising refusal. This policy Balfour at once cast aside. The law enforcement agencies in Skye, the newly installed secretary of state noted in September 1886, had been 'demoralised by the ill-usage they [had] received from the population of the island' – ill-usage, Balfour added, which had 'usually [gone] altogether unpunished and [had] never [been] punished adequately'. To restore respect for the law in Skye accordingly became Arthur Balfour's number one priority. A delighted Sheriff William Ivory was duly informed that the Conservative government considered it 'imperatively necessary' to take 'exceptional measures . . . to restore order' to the island – measures involving the despatch of a force of marines whose task it would be to ensure that outstanding rates were paid in full.

On being informed of his intentions, estate owners and their agents hailed Balfour as the saviour of Highland landlordism from the embattled position into which it had been thrust by the success of the crofters' movement – the landed class's new-found optimism being reflected in the reception accorded to the Scottish Secretary's proposals by Alexander MacDonald, Skye's 'uncrowned king' and a man whose many roles included that of solicitor to the island's school and poor law boards. At MacDonald's instigation, summonses for arrears of rates were quickly taken out against crofters. But landed proprietors, most of whom owed more money to the local authorities than all the crofters of Skye put together, MacDonald left severely alone. 'Defaulting landlords,' he thought, 'should be proceeded against, if proceeded against at all, by some different and less summary process.' In so acting, Alexander MacDonald was simply assuming that there continued to be in the Highlands and Islands, as there had always been in the past, one law for the rich and another – altogether harsher and more oppressive – law for the poor. By the 1880s, however, the political influence of the landowning class was on the wane even in the Tory Party. And to MacDonald's chagrin it soon became clear that Balfour, who was subsequently to describe Irish landlords in terms that were little short of contemptuous, had an equally low opinion of the pretensions of their Highland counterparts. Unless landlords and tenants were 'placed on exactly the same footing', the Scottish Secretary declared, he would forbid the deployment of troops in Skye and leave the island's lairds to sort out their own problems.

Even with a Conservative administration in power, then, there was evidently to be no return to the days when a Highland landlord was automatically assured of government support in dealing with an unruly tenantry. To that extent, the Crofters Act – itself the product of political pressures generated by the crofting community – marked a decisive decline in Highland proprietors' power to influence Highland affairs. That power was by no means eliminated. After 1886, however, the pattern of events in the Highlands was increasingly controlled – or at least dominated by – central government and by public agencies which government had established. Those agencies (the first of which was, of course, the Crofters Commission), though seldom subject to democratic control in any real sense of the term, have always been to some extent responsive to crofters' demands – especially when these demands have been vociferously expressed. Thus while British governments – after 1886 as before – have had an interest in maintaining order in the Highlands and Islands, their policies, despite the continuing political influence of landlordism, have not always been the ones that landowners would have chosen. The great achievement of the crofters of the 1880s, in other words, was that they made impossible a continuation of the situation in which north-west Scotland was ruled in flat defiance of the interests of the crofting community. In the autumn of 1886, in tacit recognition of this novel state of affairs, Skye landlords were forced to give way and to pay their outstanding rates.

At once, however, a new difficulty arose – one that showed that, although the balance of power had shifted against them, Highland landlords were still able to act vindictively against their tenants. The military, it had originally been agreed on all sides, were not to be used to collect rents, as opposed to rates, until the Crofters Commission had fixed fair rents for crofters – a task that would obviously take several years to complete. As soon as Skye landowners' rates had been paid, however, Alexander MacDonald informed the authorities that it was landlords' opinion that the payment of rates 'on rents not recovered' entitled them to enforce the collection of overdue rents and to expect military support in so doing. MacDonald, Arthur Balfour observed angrily, 'thinks he can presume on our known desire to restore law and order, and that, once having got the troops, he can use them in his way and for his purposes'. Equally suspicious of MacDonald's intentions were Skye's crofting tenants who saw in their landlords' manoeuvrings an attempt to circumvent the provisions of the 1886 Act by forcibly collecting arrears of rent before the Crofters Commission had had time to decide what proportion of such arrears should be paid. Sharing these concerns, Balfour's officials appealed to Skye's proprietors to desist from the collection of outstanding rents. This appeal having failed to produce the desired result, landlords found themselves the targets of fresh legislation introduced, in Balfour's words, with the aim of mitigating the 'considerable local disturbance and political difficulty' the collection of arrears had caused. This aim was achieved, in effect, by making the collection of arrears illegal. In the end, as a result, only 58 crofters were proceeded against for arrears of rent. But the tenants singled out for attention were, as Sheriff Ivory put it, 'those who had taken a prominent part in refusing to pay any rent whatever for the last three or four years'. They were, in other words, the local leaders of the Highland Land League – as the HLLRA had now become. And while landlord-instigated harassment and persecution of this sort was not at all uncongenial to Sheriff William Ivory, it undoubtedly contributed to the troubles which followed the arrival of Balfour's expeditionary force on Skye.

Under Ivory's personal command and consisting of 40 policemen and 75 marines, this force reached Skye at the beginning of October 1886, the sheriff commencing operations at dawn on 7 October by landing a contingent of police and marines at Loch Pooltiel – their objective being the serving of summonses for arrears of rates on the crofters of Glendale. Although both Ivory and his men were subjected to volleys of 'coarse epithets in Gaelic', their mission was accomplished without violence. The same was true of a series of ensuing forays to other parts of Skye – 358 summonses being served in the course of two weeks that were remarkably free from clashes of any kind. There remained, however, the delicate – and to most people offensive – task of poinding (in other words, seizing) and selling in lieu of rates the effects of the 243 crofters who, despite all William Ivory's endeavours, refused to settle their tax accounts. A week before the poinding process was due to begin, the authorities experienced something of the type of difficulty they were soon to encounter more widely: a number of crofters whose rates were still outstanding drove their cattle into the hills in an attempt to prevent their confiscation.

The Skye rate-recovery force's second phase, like the first, opened in Glendale. But on this occasion peace did not prevail, verbal abuse being supplemented with clods and stones. And on the Kilmuir estate, a few days later, the 'uncompromising attitude of hostility' observed among the Glendale tenantry erupted into open violence. At Bornaskitaig on 25 October, sheriff-officers were forcibly prevented from entering crofters' houses – they and their police escorts being pelted with rocks, mud and 'handfuls of filth from the manure heaps'. An accompanying detachment of marines were ordered to intervene, and – while the troops held back an angry crowd at bayonet point – six crofters were arrested. At the nearby township of Heribusta, also on 25 October, a sheriff-officer and two policemen – who did not have the benefit of military protection – were similarly assaulted. And on the following day, a crowd of about 30 men and women – armed with sticks, graips and other weapons – successfully prevented a sheriff-officer from serving writs for arrears of rent on some of Lord MacDonald's tenants at Woodend, a township near Portree.

To Ivory, who was clearly looking for a chance to get revenge for all the reverses he had suffered in Skye since the Battle of the Braes, these events were a godsend. Suspending his poinding operations, he launched a purge against the crofters responsible for them. During the next few days, Heribusta was raided repeatedly by troops and police: on one occasion, every house in the township was searched at one a.m; on another, the local Free Church was surrounded by weapon-carrying marines while a Sunday service was in progress. At first, those endeavours proved vain. The Heribusta men Sheriff Ivory wanted, in connection with the 25 October troubles in the township, had fled to the hills in a manner reminiscent of the aftermath of Culloden, and only one woman was arrested. The fugitives no doubt hoped that on this, as on former occasions, the authorities would eventually abandon their quest. But Ivory persisted. And in the end the November weather forced his elusive quarries to surrender.

At Woodend, meanwhile, Ivory was getting more rapid results. Before daybreak on 29 October, a strong force of police took up positions on high ground above the settlement while another police contingent, commanded by the sheriff himself, approached it along the road from Portree. Ten men and a woman, all of whom had participated in the events of three days before, were apprehended while trying to escape.

Those arrests were the first of a whole series. At the beginning of November, a youth and two boys were taken into custody for placing boulders on the road to Elgol, and when crofters at Broadford demonstrated against this development, two more men found themselves jailed on charges of mobbing and rioting. On 9 November, a speaker at a Land League meeting in Portree referred to Ivory as a liar. He was promptly imprisoned on a charge of slandering a judge and magistrate. Next day, two more Land League members were arrested on similar charges. And on 13 November, John MacPherson and the Revd Donald MacCallum – the most prominent Land Leaguers in Skye – were arrested on charges of 'promoting an unlawful agitation'. Since 13 November was a Saturday, the following morning was a Sunday. It found the incumbent of Waternish parish church languishing in a cell in Portree Jail.

Horrified by what was occurring in Skye, the Highland Land League leadership launched verbal attack after verbal attack on William Ivory. Inverness-shire's sheriff, Alexander MacKenzie declared, was instigating a 'veritable reign of terror' – while G. B. Clark, for his part, compared Ivory's 'high handed proceedings' to those of 'a Turkish pasha in Macedonia'. But to criticism from such sources, the sheriff was quite immune. His conduct of affairs in Skye had the backing of the island's landlords – MacLeod of Dunvegan, for example, remarking that Ivory had shown Skye crofters that the 'slumbering' forces of 'law and order . . . [had at last been] restored to life and vigour'. Still more critically, the sheriff had the Scottish Secretary's unquestioning public support. On the latter being moved to Dublin in 1887, he was to be dubbed 'Bloody Balfour' in consequence of his wholehearted endorsement of the Royal Irish Constabulary's brutal suppression of unrest in the Irish countryside. This stance was one which had its origins in Balfour's treatment of Skye crofters in the autumn of 1886. It is not surprising, therefore, that the man to whom John MacPherson referred as 'that most heartily hated member Mr Balfour', was, in William Ivory's opinion, a heroic figure: 'the first to show the true way of restoring law and order in a disaffected district'.

That Skye had been pacified was certain. In December, with most of his numerous prisoners being despatched to jail for periods of one, two or three months, and with the greater part of the crofting population's rates arrears at last collected, Ivory was able to inform a suitably gratified Balfour that the island was 'in a much more tranquil and law-respecting state than it has been since the land agitation first commenced' – a diagnosis confirmed by police reports reaching the Scottish Office from 'disturbed districts'. The winter of 1886–87, those reports show, was the most uneventful that Skye had experienced for several years. In part, this was clearly due to the effects of Ivory's campaign of repression. In part, however, it had other causes.

Of those, much the most important was a marked change in crofters' attitudes to the 1886 Act – a change produced by the Crofters Commission's announcement, in January 1887, of its first decisions on the level of croft rents.

The crofters affected by those decisions were the tenants of a number of Sutherland lairds. Their rents were reduced, on average, by about a quarter – while no less than half their arrears were cancelled. The commission's legally-binding rent reductions were no larger, as it happened, than those then being put into effect on Highland sheep farms. But crofters and their allies had expected next to nothing from the commission and were, it followed, pleasantly amazed. 'It must be admitted,' remarked the *Oban Times* on reappraising the Crofters Act in the light of these decisions, 'that it inaugurated a new era for Highlanders'. That judgement was reinforced in May 1887 by the commission's publication of the results of its initial investigations in Skye. There 262 of Lord MacDonald's crofting tenants were awarded an average rent reduction of 22 per cent – half their arrears being cancelled. But even those concessions were overshadowed by the commission granting Kilmuir crofters an average rent reduction in the order of 40 per cent – together with the cancellation of some 65 per cent of their accumulated arrears.

Rent reductions of between 20 and 40 per cent were important victories for crofters – psychologically as well as financially. But even more significant, given the fact that few of Skye's crofting tenants had paid any rent at all since 1883, was the extraordinarily high proportion of arrears cancelled by the Crofters Commission. In a typically aggressive editorial of early 1886, the *Oban Times* had asserted: 'The landlords' game all along was to starve the people, and now the people can starve the landlords by adhering in a body to the No Rent Policy'. A year later, although landowners might not have been at much risk of dying from hunger, it was certainly the case that they were, as one of their representatives put it in January 1887, 'reduced to great straits for want of money'. To Skye's proprietors, therefore, the prospect of losing a substantial part of three or four years' crofting rental was far from welcome. They duly made a new attempt to 'insist', in Alexander MacDonald's words, 'upon the payment of their rents'. The outcome was renewed violence – most marked in Elishader, the township on the Kilmuir estate where the first rent strike of the Highland land war had occurred, and where, in January 1887, a sheriff-officer serving summonses for arrears of rent was assaulted by crofters. The Scottish Office was not prepared, however, to jeopardise the recently established and still fragile peace in Skye for the sake of landlords who were clearly acting contrary to the spirit, if not the letter, of the Crofters Act. No attempt of any kind was made to apprehend the offending Elishader tenants. And in the spring, the government having concluded 'that some restraint should be placed upon action [of the Elishader sort] by landlords', the 1886 Act was amended in such a way as to give the Crofters Commission powers to halt all legal proceedings involving crofters' rents until the rents in question had been reviewed by the Commission.

While helping to placate crofters, the Crofters Act, even when amended, did absolutely nothing – as the Highland Land League had predicted – to alleviate the predicament of the landless. By 1887, in fact, the latter's situation and prospects were deteriorating rapidly. In the Outer Isles, where landlessness was most common, the spring of 1887 was an exceptionally bleak and cheerless one. Stock prices were low. Supplies of food and seed were scanty. 'There can be no doubt,' the sheriff-substitute at Lochmaddy commented in the course of one of his regular reports to his superiors in Inverness, 'that the mass of the people are very poor, and I am unable to understand how a large portion of the cottar class manage to keep life and soul together'. One cause of hardship – as mentioned previously – was the steep, and continuing, fall in cattle prices. But much more serious, as far as cottars, in particular, were concerned, was the slump which had begun to affect the herring fishing industry.

Between 1884 and 1886, as a result of record catches and the imposition of higher import duties in the industry's continental markets, herring prices fell catastrophically. Boats, as a result, were laid up and fewer additional hands hired for the summer fishings – a state of affairs which had dire consequences for the many crofters and cottars accustomed to obtaining seasonal employment on herring drifters. At the same time, and also because of the depression gripping the industry, herring curers abandoned the traditional practice of buying catches at prices fixed before the season opened – a practice which had involved them in heavy losses when prices collapsed. Instead curers insisted that herring be sold, as they have ever since been sold, at pierhead auctions. Losses were thus passed on to boat-owners. They, in their turn, ended the old system of fixed wages and adopted a method of payment which turned on each hired hand receiving a small proportion of the proceeds resulting from the sale of his employer's catch. Intended to give owners some protection from price falls, this new wage structure took little account of the needs of the men who had long met the herring fleet's labour requirements. With scarcely any warning, crofters and cottars who had come to rely on the herring industry for a regular seasonal income found their earnings reduced, as an official report noted, 'from an assured maintenance . . . to a mere precarious subsistence'. Many such cottars and crofters, the same report added, now thought themselves 'fortunate . . . to obtain an engagement at all'.

Although those developments affected almost all of north-west Scotland, the island of Lewis was hardest hit. Its crofts were smaller and its crofters consequently more dependent on the fishing industry than was the case elsewhere in the region. And, to make matters worse, Lewis's population contained a much higher than average proportion of landless families – families whose incomes had come to consist almost entirely of wages earned on herring drifters. In 1887, it was estimated, about £40,000 was lost to the crofting population of Lewis because of the slump in the herring industry – the average wage brought back from the east coast fishings falling from the £20 or £30 of the early 1880s to a mere £1 or £2. The social consequences of that wage collapse are illustrated by the plight of Mary MacLeod, a widow and cottar living at Crossbost in the south-eastern corner of the island. Until 1884, her two sons had earned good wages on the herring fleets and the family had, by the standards of their time and place, lived fairly well. By 1887, the MacLeod household had been reduced to poverty. And what was true of Mary MacLeod's family was true of cottar families everywhere in Lewis. As the winter of 1887–88 set in, it became apparent that there was, as one official put it, 'a most lamentable state of destitution' among the island's landless population.

The loss of the greater part of their non-agricultural income gave a new edge to the land hunger that had always been felt so acutely by those who, unlike their crofter neighbours, had no holdings they could call their own. Hence the feeling given expression at a Highland Land League meeting in the Lewis township of Garrabost in April 1887:

> Such are the straits of the people of this island owing to the want of land, that the time has come for decisive action; and if relief is not obtained during the current year, it will be necessary to go at the large farms without waiting for the passing of a new law on the subject.

Far from bringing relief, ensuing months brought a further worsening of the overall position in Lewis. With the onset, towards the close of 1887, of a winter of hunger and deprivation, a new round of land raids thus became a virtual certainty.

The raiders' target, in the first instance, was Park, the hilly peninsula in the south-eastern part of Lewis which MacKenzie of Seaforth's estate managers had converted into a sheep farm, as detailed in an earlier chapter, by means of an especially comprehensive series of clearances. In 1882, the farm's latest lease had expired and no new tenant could be found for it – a common experience at that time of steeply falling wool prices. A number of crofters and cottars had asked Lady Matheson, widow of the late Sir James and owner of Lewis, to divide the farm among them. But their request was rejected and the more remunerative expedient of transforming Park into a deer forest adopted instead. The 80,000-acre deer forest thus established was let to an English industrialist by the name of Platt. And nowhere, according to a Victorian gazetteer which listed lots of such properties, was there 'a more attractive sporting place'.

Deer forests and grouse moors – which, both in the 1880s and in the decades that followed, became more and more common in the Highlands and Islands – were decidedly unpopular among the crofting community and its political allies. Such moors and forests, it was felt, were swallowing up vacated sheep farms which could otherwise have been made available for settlement by crofting tenants. The proliferation of sporting preserves was consequently condemned repeatedly by the Highland Land League – while individual crofters vented their feelings on the subject by smashing grouse eggs and, at Sconser in Skye, slaughtering a number of Lord MacDonald's deer by the simple expedient of driving them into the sea. The action which Lewis crofters and cottars planned to take against Park was to be – or so it was hoped at any rate – on an altogether grander and more decisive scale. The forest, it was resolved at a meeting convened on 12 November 1887 at Balallan, a township on Park's northern fringe, 'must be cleared and given to the people'.

At further meetings during the next few days – most of them chaired by Donald MacRae, Balallan's schoolmaster and an enthusiastic Land Leaguer – strategy was discussed, duties assigned and firearms collected. Rumours of these activities spread inexorably across Lewis. But, it seems, they were not believed by the authorities. Nothing, at all events, was done to forestall the raid which began, as intended, on the morning of 22 November. Fortunately for the raiders, the day dawned bright and clear, and before sunrise bands of young men – consisting, for the most part, of the 'cottars and squatters' who had been 'represented in force' at the meetings at which the raid was planned – set out from Balallan, Leurbost and other townships within striking distance of the forest. Between them they carried about 50 serviceable rifles, a number of red flags and a considerable quantity of baggage – the intention being to camp out for more than one night. The old men, women and children of the various townships they passed through turned out to cheer the raiders on their way. And the only opposition they encountered came from an understandably alarmed Mrs Platt whose husband, Park's shooting tenant, was in England on business. Accosting several of the raiders on their way to the forest, she pleaded with them to turn back. Their reply was crushingly unanswerable. 'My lady,' one raider said as he marched past, 'we have no English.'

Having got together, as arranged, near the head of Loch Seaforth, the raiders, of whom there were about 700 in all, at once set about the task of killing as many deer as possible. The riflemen among them were stationed on strategic ridges and passes – while their companions, acting as beaters, drove the deer south-eastwards into the forest, into the wind, and under the muzzles of the guns. All that day, the slaughter continued and, as night fell, the raiders made camp on the shores of Loch Seaforth. Makeshift tents consisting of the sails of fishing boats were pitched. Bonfires were lit, and over them were roasted haunches of venison – part of the day's kill. The obtaining of such venison was, in itself, an important reason for participating in the raid – indeed the sheriff of Ross-shire, who arrived in Lewis within 24 hours of the raid's commencement and who personally interviewed a number of the raiders, thought that 'many who took part in it did so mainly from a desire to get food for their starving families'. In that, they succeeded. At least 100 deer were killed, and several boats laden with carcasses destined for the townships from which the various groups of raiders had come were seen slipping away from Park.

But if Park's invaders were hungry for food, they were still more hungry for land. And as was made perfectly clear in the interview which one of them afterwards gave to a newspaperman, the raiders' desire to have land in Park stemmed largely from the fact that many of them were the sons and grandsons of men who had occupied holdings there some 40 or 50 years before:

> He stated that his father's family were among those evicted . . . and it is impossible to imagine with what intense bitterness he gave expression to the feelings with which he said he gazed upon the ruins of his grandfather's cottage.

That man, and others like him, thought it possible that, as a result of the deer cull they conducted, the sporting value of Park forest would be so drastically reduced that its tenant would give it up – thereby forcing Lady Matheson to reverse her decision of 1882 and hand the forest over to such crofters and cottars as wanted it. The chance of this actually happening, as all the numerous intruders on Park were well aware, was, of course, minimal. But at worst, the raiders believed, their craving for land, together with the tragic state of affairs existing in Lewis that winter, would – thanks to their actions – receive extensive coverage in the press. 'Their object,' several raiders commented, 'was to draw the attention of the whole country to their case.'

As it happened, more than 30 years were to pass before any part of Park was resettled with official blessing, and the raiders' primary objective thus remained out of their reach. Publicity for their grievances, however, they received at once and in full measure. And with this, they decided, for the moment, to be content. On the raid's third day, and before any of the police or troops who had been despatched to Lewis could be deployed against them, the Park raiders moved out of the now devastated deer forest – Donald MacRae and the 13 others for whose arrests warrants had been issued voluntarily surrendering themselves to the authorities in Stornoway.

That the Park raid had not been in vain became clear in December when the government agreed to look into the social condition of Lewis. The enquiry which followed, as was remarked at the time by a journalist accompanying the officials charged with the task of conducting it, at once laid bare the causes of the island's discontent:

> In one township after another the same state of matters was met with: half-clad and half-starved people living in squalor within wretched and over-crowded houses.

Lewis's landless population, the enquiry team's findings made clear, were suffering acutely from the effects of the downturn in the herring industry. And though some poor law administrators – a singularly hard-faced breed – continued to believe that there was no more to the crisis on the island than 'a spurious cry of destitution bolstered up . . . by agitators', the nature of the reports reaching him from Lewis were such as to convince Lord Lothian, Arthur Balfour's successor at the Scottish Office, that something would have to be done to tackle the underlying causes of crofting difficulties. The consequent shift towards a notably more conciliatory policy in crofting areas, however, did not materialise in time to prevent the winter of 1887–88 turning into the most violent phase of the entire land war in the Highlands.

In December 1887, the following despatch was submitted by the Lewis correspondent of the *Oban Times*:

> The crofters' agitation has come to an end. It is the cottars' turn now . . . The cottars not only demand the restoration of Park . . . but all the other lands under sheep and deer, with compensation for the loss suffered by themselves and their fathers through the conduct of the evictors who ruined them and left them landless in pauperism.

Because of the prevalence of such sentiments, the withdrawal of the raiders from Park produced no diminution of tension in Lewis. Some 80 soldiers of the Royal Scots, sent to the island while the deer raid was in progress, were retained in Stornoway where they were joined, in December, by a gunboat and by a force of marines. Goaded by their growing poverty, cottars throughout Lewis were meanwhile preparing to follow the example set at Park. A few days before Christmas, about 200 men from Shader, Borve and other townships on the island's north-west coast marched on to the sheep farm of Galson and informed its tenant that his lands would soon be taken from him. Two or three days later, another sheep farm, at Aignish near Stornoway, was visited by almost 1,000 crofters and cottars who told its tenant 'that they required [his] farm . . . to provide holdings for the starving landless cottars and their families in the district, whose ancestors had it under cultivation'. On 29 December, at a mass meeting, it was resolved that, on 9 January, Aignish, together with the neighbouring farm of Melbost, would be forcibly expropriated. The stock on the two farms, it was decided, would be driven to new pastures: the grounds of Stornoway Castle, residence of Lady Matheson. And with a view to facilitating the forthcoming raid, Aignish's boundary fence was torn down under cover of darkness.

During the first week of 1888, Stornoway's sheriff-substitute circulated printed notices which warned, in Gaelic as well as English, that participants in the proposed occupation of Aignish and Melbost farms would be liable to heavy penalties. His proclamations were without effect, however.

On the appointed day, a crowd of several hundred people – 'a large, excited, and determined . . . mob', the sheriff-substitute called them in a hastily despatched telegram to the Scottish Office – marched on Aignish. There they were confronted by a strong force of police, Royal Scots and marines. The Riot Act was read, as the law demanded. But it did nothing to prevent what quickly turned into one of the Highland land war's bitterest and bloodiest confrontations.

The strong military presence meant the abandonment of the original plan to drive the Aignish sheepstock to Stornoway. Instead, a number of animals were deliberately driven into the sea, while others had their backs and legs broken by the stout sticks and clubs wielded by the raiders. On troops and police attempting to clear the farm, they were pelted with stones and other missiles. Several constables and the Royal Scots' commanding officer were more or less badly hurt, while Stornoway's procurator fiscal – who, revolver in hand, was observing the scene from a nearby knoll – found himself assaulted. In the midst of all the confusion, 13 men, picked at random from the crowd, were somehow or other arrested. A rescue attempt was then organised by their comrades, but this was eventually defeated by a group of marines who – forming a cordon round the prisoners and holding off an angry, yelling and jeering crowd at bayonet point – marched them off to jail in Stornoway.

These arrests did absolutely nothing to restore tranquillity to the island. Four days after the Aignish fracas, cottars' delegates from every part of Lewis met in Stornoway. There they resolved to urge government ministers 'to restore to the descendants of the clansmen . . . the whole of the lands formerly tilled by their ancestors for centuries, the restoration to the people of the said lands being the only solution to the land question'. The implementation of such a solution was still a long way off, however, and Lewis cottars, their resolution of 13 January notwithstanding, were in no mood to put their trust in politicians. In the face of threats to burn down its farmhouse and steading, Aignish was placed under permanent military protection. Elsewhere in Lewis, meanwhile, there were new manifestations of unrest.

On 5 January, some 300 men from Barvas, on Lewis's Atlantic coast, made the long trek to Stornoway in order to present Lady Matheson with a petition asking that Galson farm be divided among them. 'These lands are mine,' Lady Matheson told a wet and weary deputation, 'and you have nothing to do with them.' Events soon proved her wrong. By the middle of January, Lewis's increasingly overstretched police authorities had found it necessary to station eight constables at Galson in an attempt to prevent the nightly demolition of dykes and fences. The men responsible for this destruction were not easily deterred, however; and, while patrolling the farm on the night of 16 January, the police detachment encountered several of them busily engaged in tearing down a fence. A hand-to-hand fight ensued. Several constables were seriously cut about the face – prior to the raiders making their escape into the darkness.

As those events were occurring in the neighbourhood of Galson, a part of the farm of Coll near Stornoway was occupied by cottars – while, on the other side of the island, fences around Dalbeg and Linshader were destroyed. And when, on 18 January, an Edinburgh jury acquitted the 14 Park raiders – a development which Ross-shire's sheriff found 'most disheartening', but one which was greeted with predictable delight in Lewis – a fresh impetus was given to Lewis's mounting campaign of land seizures. 'Lawlessness,' the Scottish Office was informed at the end of January, 'is prevalent in almost every district in Lewis.' The overnight destruction of farm dykes and fences had become so frequent as to be hardly worthy of comment. And at the Land League meetings being held regularly in almost every township on the island, the 'wildest resolutions' were commonly adopted – 'the avowed object,' it was noted, 'being to obtain possession, if necessary by violence, of land presently occupied by sheep farms or deer forests'.

Landlessness lay at the root of all such unrest. 'A portion of the land which belonged to their forefathers,' a Lewis cottars' spokesman had argued as far back as 1883, 'should be given to them.' Now, having gained nothing from the Crofters Act and faced with a catastrophic decline in their living standards, Lewis's cottar population were making plain their desperate need for land in the only effective way open to them: they were taking it by force. And since the younger men among Lewis's cottars were almost invariably in the Naval Reserve, which had a large membership on the island, the protest movement which those same men led showed clear signs of having been organised on military lines. The thousand cottars and crofters who marched on Aignish did so in line abreast, with pipes playing and flags flying. At Galson, too, it was observed by the police, raiders responded to military-style commands given by one of their number. And since Lewis branches of the Highland Land League are known to have made clear to each of their members 'that, if he will offend against the rules of the league, he'll pay for it', neither the police or the military, for all their efforts to gain some insight into protesters' intentions, were able to get any real grip of a situation that more than once threatened to slip totally beyond their control.

Throughout the winter of 1887–88, it looked as if the troubles in Lewis might spread to other parts of north-west Scotland. At Clashmore in Sutherland's Assynt district, for instance, farmland of which crofters had been deprived as recently as the 1870s was raided by its former occupants. Dykes were demolished and a farm steading burned to the ground. Military intervention followed. At Lochcarron and in Glenelg, too, there was talk of land seizures. And in Skye – where the poverty caused by the fishing crisis and low cattle prices, though somewhat less acute than in Lewis, was nevertheless 'very widespread' – there were indications that the island's year-old

peace was more precarious than had been thought. At the beginning of
January 1888, for example, Glendale crofters resolved to take possession of
lands in Bracadale from which, as one local man put it, their fathers and
grandfathers had been evicted 'in the days when sheep were more thought
of than men'. On the Kilmuir estate, too, there was renewed unrest. The
crofters and cottars of Bornaskitaig, Hunglader and Kilvaxter petitioned
their landlord for the restoration of their former grazings on Duntulm and
Monkstadt farms which, it was claimed, 'were in the hands of strangers
while . . . the rightful owners were huddled together on rocks and moss not
fit for cultivation'. On 17 January, by way of giving effect to their demands,
a party of about 50 individuals carried out a detailed survey of Duntulm
and Monkstadt in order to allow old men to point out pre-clearance township boundaries to their sons and grandsons.

Across the Minch in Harris, meanwhile, factors and landlords were
presented with petitions requesting that more land be made available
to crofters and cottars – one particularly unpopular sheep farmer being
informed by an anonymous letter that 'some of the poor landless people . . .
are bent on making an example of you first'. The letter's recipient, in the
event, escaped unscathed. But in Harris, every bit as much as in Lewis,
there was acute poverty and suffering among the landless population. It is
not surprising, therefore, that the agitation in the island should be described
as 'more of a cottar than a crofter one', or that representatives of the former
group should openly threaten 'to imitate the Lewismen'. In this intention,
it appeared, Harris folk were not alone. Throughout the Uists and Barra,
the sheriff-substitute at Lochmaddy reported:

> The disturbances in Lewis have had a very serious effect; they are, of course,
> much talked of, and the conduct of the people applauded, and opinions held
> and expressed that it would be well to follow suit.

At meetings held in South Uist in the opening weeks of 1888, the island's
cottars resolved that they would not 'let ourselves or our families starve as
long as there is cultivable land growing under sheep in Uist, or as long as
there is anything in Uist that we can lay our hands upon to prevent such
starvation'. They would, South Uist's cottars accordingly agreed, continue
'to agitate against policemen, and soldiers, and landlords, till big farms are
demolished and granted to such crofters and cottars that are in need of
them'. In Barra – and indeed at cottars' meetings throughout the Hebrides –
similarly aggressive sentiments were very freely expressed. The Clashmore
episode excepted, however, there were – outside Lewis – no actual seizures
of land.

In part, this may have been due to what Alexander MacKenzie called
the 'cruel sentences' – of between nine and 15 months' imprisonment –
imposed on the 14 Lewismen who, at the High Court in Edinburgh on 30
January 1888, were found guilty on mobbing and rioting charges arising

from events at Aignish. The pacifying effect of this unarguably repressive development – which, in the authorities' opinion, reversed the damage done by the Park raiders' acquittal – was strongly enforced, however, by a quite unexpected upturn in the crofting community's economic prospects. The Hebridean white fishings having proved exceptionally good, the spring and early summer of 1888 brought crofter and cottar households more money than they had seen for several years. For the moment at least, therefore, the edge of cottars' land hunger was decisively blunted. Only in Lewis – which had taken on Skye's earlier role of unchallenged storm centre of crofting unrest – did trouble of any kind continue. In May, crofters and cottars from Balallan held a meeting inside the boundaries of Park forest, and some crofters' cattle were driven on to Aignish farm. That month, too, the island's owner, Lady Matheson – under police protection since February when anonymous threats had been made on her life – left Stornoway to take up residence in the south of France. But when the summer – thanks to improved herring prices – proved as prosperous as the spring had been, tranquillity returned even to Lewis. In September, the troops who had been stationed on the island since the previous November's raid on Park were finally withdrawn.

The military withdrawal from Lewis in the early autumn of 1888 marked the end of the land war which had begun in Skye more than six years before. In comparison with the winters that had preceded it, that of 1888–89 was virtually uneventful. By the end of 1890, the Inverness-shire constabulary had been reduced to normal strength. During that year, in the case of Skye, and during 1891, in the case of the Outer Isles, the police were told to cease submitting regular reports to Edinburgh on crofters' activities. The gradual winding down of violent protest, moreover, was accompanied by a steep decline in political activity of the sort which had commenced with the founding of the HLLRA in 1883. Some part of that decline can undoubtedly be attributed to the crofting community's disenchantment with the manoeuvrings* of its erstwhile leaders – manoeuvrings which, in the expressive phrase of a Barra crofters' leader, reduced the HLLRA's successor, the Highland Land League, to the status of, 'a mere political association'. But of equal importance in explaining the Land League's demise – and of considerably more importance in accounting for the tapering away of the land seizures, rent-strikes and other activities which had given rise to it – were the enhanced financial circumstances of the crofting population.

By the end of the 1880s, the worst of the crisis in the herring industry having been successfully surmounted, hired hands' wages were rising once

---

*These manoeuvrings are explored in J. Hunter, 'The Politics of Highland Land Reform', *Scottish Historical Review*, LIII, 1974.

again – as were the prices obtained by crofters for their cattle. In the course of the next 20 years, the crofting community's fishing earnings returned to, indeed exceeded, the levels they had reached before 1884. And though cattle prices did not show the same improvement, any ensuing loss in income was more than offset by the plummeting price of the meal which, as mentioned earlier, most crofters and all cottars had to buy to supplement such food as they grew themselves. Resulting from the growth of grain imports from America as well as from improved transport facilities in the Highlands themselves, this latter development was of great benefit to everyone involved in crofting. In Scourie on Sutherland's west coast, to give a particular instance of a general process, the price of a boll of imported meal fell from around 50s. in 1880 to 12s. 6d. in the early years of the twentieth century.

Of even greater benefit was a significant shift in the government's Highland policy: away from the unrelieved repression of the years immediately following the Crofters Act and towards the officially sponsored development of the Highland economy in general, and of its crofting sector in particular. From this shift, modern Highlands and Islands policy largely stems. But because of the magnitude of the reappraisal involved, it was not something that could be accomplished overnight. Initially, in fact, it seemed that government intervention in the Highlands and Islands would be confined to the promotion of an age-old nostrum – with Lord Lothian declaring, in May 1887, that 'the first step towards an immediate solution' of crofting problems lay in 'an attractive and well financed scheme of state-aided emigration'. Support for such a view could be found in the Napier Commission's report and – predictably – among north-west Scotland's landlords, to whom the removal of the region's 'surplus population' seemed as needful and beneficial as it had done to their predecessors of half a century before. To such a proceeding, however, the crofting community was unalterably opposed. In 1883, a Lewis crofter had remarked of his compatriots' feelings on the subject:

> There is no doubt they are strongly against emigrating and, is it not rather a hard thing that they should be made to emigrate while sheep are being fed at home?

Five years later, when an officially sponsored emigration scheme was put into operation, such opinions were, if anything, more strongly held than ever – crofters resolving at meetings held in all the crofting areas 'to oppose with their might and main . . . any scheme of emigration . . . until all the land available for cultivation in the Highlands and Islands be used . . . to form new crofts for the landless'. Emigration was not ruled out completely – Glendale crofters, for example, announcing that they would not stand in the way of anyone proposing to transport landlords and sheep farmers to Manitoba. But if a government-financed exodus of population was to win the backing of the crofting community, it would clearly have to be preceded by redistribution of land.

Among the Conservative government's supporters there were, it is true, one or two men, the most notable of whom was Joseph Chamberlain, who favoured the granting of more land to crofters. But as a recent defector from the Liberal Party, which he had left because of his opposition to Gladstone's policy of granting home rule to Ireland, Chamberlain's influence on Salisbury's administration was not, in the 1880s at least, decisive. For the moment, then, a Highland land settlement programme remained off the political agenda. But in the face of unyielding crofting opposition to the pro-emigration strategy with which the government had briefly flirted, there was an obvious need for an alternative policy. It was his awareness of this need that induced the secretary of state for Scotland to undertake, in the early summer of 1889, a personal tour of the north-west – his objective, in his own words, being to discover what could be done 'to ameliorate the conditions of the inhabitants of these parts'. The outcome was Lothian's personal conversion to a programme of economic development for the Highlands and Islands. In August 1889, he recommended to the Treasury that no less than £150,000 should be spent on developing the fisheries and on the construction of roads, railways and piers. A royal commission set up to conduct a more detailed enquiry into prospects for the Highlands and Islands economy recommended further such expenditure. By 1892, when the Conservatives fell from office, £237,291 had been assigned, as a result, to development schemes in crofting areas. The first of a continuing series of attempts to stimulate the Highland economy by means of judicious applications of financial assistance, this spending both attracted support in the Highlands and produced lasting improvements to the region's communications system. At the time, however, its undoubtedly beneficial effects on crofting life were completely eclipsed by the still more beneficial consequences of the Crofters Act – consequences which did not become generally and fully apparent until the 1890s.

Responsible for rent reductions of up to 50 per cent and the cancellation of the bulk of the arrears which had accumulated during the rent strikes and economic difficulties of the 1880s, the Crofters Commission was, by the mid-1890s, held almost in reverence – Donald MacRae, the man who had led the 1887 raid on Park, remarking of it that there was 'not an institution, except . . . perhaps the Sabbath, that the Highland people cling to with more determination'. And of even greater importance than the work of the commission, it was generally agreed, were the good effects produced by the decision to grant security of tenure to crofters. The enduring significance of that decision had been summed up thus by a Glendale crofter within a few months of the Crofters Act of 1886 having passed into law:

> If a crofter formerly built a house, it belonged to the laird, as well as other improvements effected by the crofter. Now the crofter could call the house

and croft his own, along with any improvements which he made. Fifty years ago, could their fathers have believed that such a change could be effected?

The great achievement of the Crofters Act, then, was to bring crofters' tenurial position into a close alignment with their traditional beliefs about the nature of their stake in the land – and it is for this reason that, even today, the surest way to arouse the crofting community to anger is to suggest an alteration to the 1886 Act's basic principles. Crofting tenants had always thought they had a right to permanent occupancy of their holdings. To this notion, the Crofters Act gave the force of statute law. The results, as was pointed out by a royal commission in 1895, were dramatic:

> Our opinion is that, speaking generally, the Act has had a beneficial effect, and particularly in the following directions. In the first place, the fixing of a fair rent has to a large extent removed from the minds of crofters the sense of hardship arising from the belief that they were made to pay rent on their own improvements, or otherwise made to pay at an excessive rate for soil of a poor quality. In the second place, the combination of a fair rent with statutory security of tenure has not only taken away or allayed causes of discontent, but has imparted a new spirit to crofters and imbued them with fresh energy. The abiding sense produced that the permanent improvements which a crofter makes upon his holding will, if he complies with certain reasonable statutory conditions, accrue either to himself or to his family successor, will not be taxable by the landlord in the form of increased rent, and moreover will have a money value under a claim for compensation on renunciation of tenancy . . . has led to vigorous efforts towards improvement by crofters in many quarters. For instance, we found that more attention is being paid to cultivation, to rotation of crops, to reclamation of outruns, to fencing, and to the formation or repair of township roads; but most conspicuous of all the effects perceptible, is that upon buildings, including both dwelling-houses and steadings. In a considerable number of localities we found new and improved houses and steadings erected by the crofters themselves since the passing of the Act.

By way of substantiating that last point, it is worth recording that, in the 20 years after 1886, nearly 1,600 of the 4,000 crofters in Skye, Harris and the Uists built new homes on their holdings. And it was appropriate that, in the final report which its members published on their powers being transferred in 1912 to the Scottish Land Court, the Crofters Commission took some pride in the fact that 'the black hovels in which too many of the people lived are now passing away, and have been largely replaced by smart, tidy cottages that would do credit to any part of the country'.

Although recognised by crofters as the foundation of a new and more equitable social order in the region, the Crofters Act was not, of itself, an answer to crofing problems. The crofting community's original criticism of the Act – that it did nothing to restore cleared lands – remained as valid in the 1890s as it had been in the previous decade. Within the confines of the very limited land settlement powers bestowed upon them by the Act the Crofters Commission, admittedly, did their by no means negligible best. They succeeded, for instance, in enlarging 2,051 holdings and making available to crofters, as a result, an additional 72,341 acres – mostly in the form of hill grazings. In relation to the millions of acres occupied as sheep farms and deer forests, however, the Crofters Commission's endeavours were pitifully inadequate – the more so since, having no power to create new holdings, commission members could do absolutely nothing for north-west Scotland's large landless population. The Crofters Act, the *Oban Times* commented in 1901, had 'left the cottars out in the cold':

> The cottar lives in a circumscribed and discouraging sphere well calculated to create discontent and one that holds out no prospect of future betterment by the exercise of self-exertion and enterprise. The claim of the crofter to an inherited title to the soil has been recognised, but that of the cottar has never been acknowledged.

But despite – or maybe because of – their privations, landless families continued to hope that 'some day they [would] come into possession of holdings of their own'. This situation – as had been obvious in the troubled winter of 1887–88 and was to become so again in the opening years of the twentieth century – was a perfect recipe for renewed agrarian unrest. And for all that discontent was generally muted, as already indicated, during the comparatively prosperous 1890s, it was not, significantly enough, entirely absent.

In Lewis, north-west Scotland's undisputed stronghold of landlessness, the destruction of sheep farm boundary fences continued to be a recurring event – while, in the spring of 1891, there took place a second, if less ostentatiously conducted, raid on Park. The raiders, about 40 in all, settled for some weeks at Ornsay, one of the townships cleared half a century before. Among them there was at least one man who had witnessed his father's eviction from an Ornsay holding, and it was with considerable justice, therefore, that the raiders claimed they had come 'to retake the homes of their ancestors'. Reroofing one or two ruined houses, they set about planting potatoes in long-abandoned fields from which they were eventually removed by the police – 32 of the raiders being subsequently sentenced to one or two weeks' imprisonment on trespass charges.

Also in the early 1890s, there were a number of raids by cottars on the farm of Borve on the island of Berneray in the Sound of Harris where, in 1890, a stable was demolished and a stackyard burned and where, some three years later, the illegal occupation of a part of the disputed farm – from which people had been removed during the clearances – led to four cottars being jailed for 60 days on charges of mobbing and rioting. Elsewhere in the north-west – in the Uists and in the neighbourhood of the hotly disputed Assynt farm of Clashmore, for example – fences and dykes were destroyed. And in Skye in 1893, a part of the Kilmuir farm of Duntulm, as well as a small island off Staffin, were subjected to illegal incursions of one kind or another.

Such incidents, the sheriff of Ross-shire pointed out in 1891, were the inevitable consequence of the existence in north-west Scotland, especially in the Hebrides, of a large and dissatisfied cottar population. Unless some provision was made to give land to the landless, the sheriff went on, he could discern 'little hope of entire immunity from disturbance . . . for many years to come'. By the 1890s, as it happened, the notion of redistributing land in the direction of the crofting community, despite its having attracted nothing but condemnation from government when canvassed by the HLLRA, was starting to attract more and more support – some of it from surprising quarters. Like the preceding decade, the 1890s were a time of serious difficulties for the Highlands' sheep farming economy.* With sheep farmers pulling out of the region, and with estate rentals tumbling in consequence, the entire *raison d'être* of the agrarian system established during the clearances seemed on the point of vanishing. This, from the crofting community's standpoint, was excellent news. As the *Oban Times* remarked in 1889, there was no longer 'keen competition on the part of capitalists for lands that may be claimed by the people', and there seemed, therefore, to be no compelling reason for landlords to oppose the return of these lands to the crofting community. In fact, there was one such reason: the immense profits to be made from converting vacated grazings into deer forests. These profits had led, for example, to the Park peninsula being denied to its cottar claimants – and Park was but one instance of a very general phenomenon. Not every unprofitable sheep farm could be devoted to deer, however. By the later 1880s, some landlords were accordingly reaching the *Oban Times'* conclusion – though from an opposite direction. Thus in 1887, in a petition which, as an astonished civil servant commented, 'practically asks for a Land Purchase Bill for Skye', a number of that island's owners asked the government to 'relieve them' of several bankrupt sheep farms as a prelude to handing those farms over to crofters for settlement purposes.

The purchase of privately owned land by government, together with the subsequent resale of such land to its former tenants who were thus converted into owner-occupiers or – in the jargon of the time – peasant proprietors, was an important element in the Conservative administration's attempts to solve the Irish land question. On their being granted a permanent stake in the land, Irish peasants, it was hoped, would be rendered more prosperous, more contented and, therefore, less prone to involvement in political unrest and agitation. Irish landlords, for their part, were compensated with a generosity sufficient to ensure their general support for

---

*For developments in the sheep farming sector at this time, see J. Hunter, 'Sheep and Deer: Highland Sheep Farming, 1850–1900', *Northern Scotland*, I, 1974.

the scheme. And it was, no doubt, the latter aspect of it which attracted the financially hard-pressed proprietors of Skye to the concept of land purchase. They were, they told the government, quite willing to see the crofting system expanded – as long as they received 'just and equitable' compensation for such farmland as might be needed to make such expansion happen.

The determination on Highland landlords' part to do well financially out of any land settlement scheme – a determination evident even in 1887 when no such scheme was being seriously considered – was to prove a major obstacle in the way of achieving a quick and radical redistribution of land in north-west Scotland. Thus the first and extremely tentative step taken in the direction of the creation of new holdings – the Conservative government's 1892 decision to bestow on Scotland's then newly created county councils the power to provide allotments in areas where there was demand for them – came to nothing in the Highlands because of proprietorial opposition. Later in 1892, however, there was another, and apparently more hopeful, development: the setting up by the Liberal government which came to power that year – and did so in the Highlands with strong crofting support – of a royal commission whose task it was to report on the availability, in the crofting counties, of land which, though still under sheep or deer, could conceivably be utilised for land settlement purposes.

In its report, published in April 1895, this latest royal commission not unsurprisingly concluded that there was, especially among north-west Scotland's landless population, an unabated demand for more land:

> Very many [cottars] are deserving and intelligent, and owe their unfortunate position to adverse circumstances. Their ambition almost invariably [is] to get a croft such as their crofter neighbours possess. While the position of the crofter is one of difficulty . . . the position of the cottar is still more difficult, and any scheme that would result in affording cottars the opportunity of obtaining crofts . . . would operate a substantial relief both to the cottars themselves and to the neighbouring crofters.

The land needed to create the necessary crofts, the royal commission's painstaking enquiries had shown, was, in principle anyway, readily to be had. There were in the Highlands and Islands, the commission concluded, no less than 439,188 acres that could be used to extend existing holdings, and a further 794,730 acres that were suitable for the creation of new crofts.

By the spring of 1897, however, Lord Rosebery's Liberal government was tottering towards its imminent collapse. Instead of the sweeping land settlement measure expected by crofters, Rosebery and his colleagues reacted to the report of their own commission by introducing a lukewarm Bill which did not even mention the formation of new holdings. That measure, which fell with its promoters in the early summer, destroyed the credibility in the Highlands and Islands – for the moment at least – both of the Liberal

Party and the Land League which, by this point, had effectively merged with that party. In the ensuing election, therefore, Liberal and Land League fortunes suffered a decisive reverse – the latter organisation, now a tattered remnant of its former self, being swept completely from the scene. The field was thus left open to Conservative candidates who based their Highland campaign on their advocacy of land reforms similar to those carried out by the Conservatives in Ireland between 1886 and 1892. Thus one Tory election address declared:

> The real solution of the question lies in the intervention of the government with financial assistance on the principle of the Irish Land Purchase Acts: first, to take up suitable tracts of land and utilise them for crofters' holdings; and, secondly, to enable these crofters who are capable and desire to do so, to become owners of their land.

More imaginative and much more far-reaching than anything offered by the Liberal–Land League alliance, these proposals were welcomed as such by – among others – the crofters of Glendale, one of the places where the land war had begun some 13 years before. And in 1897, the Conservatives – having easily won power – did indeed implement the policy their Highland candidates had advocated by equipping the Highlands and Islands with an organisation entitled the Congested Districts Board. The board's tasks included that of making more land available to the crofting community, and among its achievements was the conversion of Glendale's crofting tenants into the owners of their holdings.

11

LAND RAIDS AND
LAND SETTLEMENT

1897–1930

The phrase 'congested districts' was originally coined to describe those parts of the West of Ireland where, as Lord Salisbury explained to Queen Victoria, 'a dense population of half starving multitudes' lived on constricted holdings and where hunger, even famine, were seldom absent for long. There, as in Scotland's crofting areas, the cheek-by-jowl existence of peasants (clinging determinedly to their miserable patches of unproductive soil) and well-to-do graziers (occupying enormous tracts of pasture) produced a desperate land hunger which, it seemed, could be assuaged only by a far-reaching redistribution of land. As one of Ireland's nationalist politicians wrote in a passage that could have referred to any one of a hundred townships in north-west Scotland:

> To look over the fence of [a] famine-stricken village and see the rich, green solitudes which might yield full and plenty spread out at the very doorsteps of the ragged peasants was to fill a stranger with a sacred rage and make it an unshirkable duty to strive towards undoing the unnatural divorce between the people and the land.

It was in an attempt to eliminate, or at least reduce, the discontent thus engendered that the Conservative government included in its Irish Land Purchase Act of 1891 the clauses which set up the Congested Districts Board (CDB) – the board's function being to promote the economic development of the West of Ireland by financially assisting indigenous industries, by supplying instruction in farming techniques and, most significantly, by providing new holdings on land which the board was empowered to purchase for that purpose. The CDB, it was rapidly concluded by nationalists as well by unionists, was a resounding success. Hence the decision by Conservative politicians to establish an analogous body to deal with the problems posed by Scotland's 'congested districts' – districts defined in terms of their own under-development and reckoned to comprise parts of Mull, all of Tiree, Barra, the Uists, Harris, Lewis and Skye, together with the bulk of the mainland coastal periphery from Ardnamurchan to Caithness.

Greeted by the HLLRA veteran G.B. Clark as 'a fair and honest attempt' to come to grips with the crofting problem, the new Congested Districts Board, constituted in 1897, possessed powers and was assigned duties similar to those of its Irish predecessor. Under its auspices, roads, paths, bridges, piers and slipways were constructed, the inshore fisheries developed and the then nascent Harris tweed industry aided by grants for looms as well as by the provision of technical instruction. Agricultural shows were sponsored, fencing and draining encouraged, improved varieties of seed provided, the spraying of crofters' potatoes to protect them from blight made possible, the cultivation of turnips, kale and other crops promoted. And because north-west Scotland, as the CDB noted, was 'more suited to pastoral than to agricultural farming', board staff 'endeavoured', in particular, 'to encourage the improvement of stock by all means in their power' – attempting, with considerable success, to educate crofters as to the importance of keeping rather than selling good breeding animals and providing townships, or groups of townships, with bulls, tups and stallions for breeding purposes. The 15 years of the CDB's existence thus constitute an undeservedly forgotten chapter in the history of Highland development. Its endeavours – the more so as a result of the board's bull and tup schemes being kept going by its successor agencies – laid the basis of much of the comparative prosperity of modern crofting life and proved that, with appropriate assistance, the crofting community was quite capable of effecting improvements which Highland landlords had long believed – or had certainly said – were beyond their tenantries' competence.

As its title indicates, however, the board's principal function was to relieve congestion. And that could be done only by providing land for the landless – whose applications for holdings began to pour into the CDB's Edinburgh headquarters within weeks of its being set up. Unfortunately for applicants and for the board's eventual reputation, its efforts to provide the required crofts, either by buying land for resale as smallholdings or by grant-aiding those proprietors prepared to subdivide one or more of the farms on their estates, were gravely handicapped from the outset: partly by financial restrictions imposed by the government; partly by the fact that, in its human aspect at least, north-west Scotland's land problem was not, after all, the same as Ireland's.

Although able to help a settler to equip his new holding with buildings, fences and other permanent fixtures, the CDB was not permitted to assist him to stock his land. And since few cottars could raise the funds needed to purchase the sheep they were expected to take over from the owner or tenant of the former sheep farm on which they were usually settled, this was a serious drawback – as was the CDB's inability to buy more than a tiny proportion of the land needed for settlement purposes. That the board was not empowered to borrow and had, therefore, to buy estates out of its very inadequate budget of £35,000 a year was limiting enough. But equally restrictive in its impact was the CDB's discovery that crofters had no strong desire to become the owners of their holdings – a state of affairs which rather paralysed the board's activities because it could not, like its Irish counterpart, spend money on land purchase in the sure knowledge that such money would eventually be recouped from the purchasing occupiers, whether established or newly settled, of the land in question.

Unlike Irish peasant farmers, whose fervent desire to own their plots the Irish CDB met by means of 49-year purchase schemes, most crofters were content with the recognition – enshrined in the Crofters Act – of their longstanding claim to secure tenures. As early as 1887, and in reply to a suggestion from Joseph Chamberlain that peasant ownership on the Irish model should be introduced into the crofting counties, the Lewis branches of the Land League had observed:

> A fair rent is preferred to purchasing their holdings at 49-years purchase, when most of the existing tenants and claimants would be in their graves . . . Moreover they consider themselves most solemnly now to be part-owners, according to English [sic] law which granted them fixity of tenure.

Crofting reluctance to move towards individual ownership of crofts was reinforced by the fact that such ownership, in Highland circumstances, was attended by marked financial disadvantages. The capital value of a croft rented at £5 a year – a typical holding, in other words – was considered, for purchase purposes, to be about £100. And the annuity by which this sum, principal and interest, was to be repaid to the CDB, over a 50-year period, was £3.14s. – an apparent annual saving of about 25 per cent. But the purchasing owner was held responsible for the payment of owner's, as opposed to tenant's, rates. And these, in almost every part of north-west Scotland, were so high as to practically extinguish the original saving. As owners, moreover, crofters lost the various protections and privileges (such as the right of appeal to the Crofters Commission for settlement of grazing and other disputes) bestowed on them by the 1886 Act – which applied, by definition, to crofting tenants only. The upshot was that of all the crofting tenants on the estates bought by the CDB – Syre in Strathnaver, Northbay in Barra, the island of Vatersay, and the extensive Skye properties of Glendale and Kilmuir – only those of Glendale adhered, in the long-term, to their original agreement to buy their holdings, the remainder opting for the status of tenants of the board or its successor body, the Board (afterwards the Department) of Agriculture for Scotland.

These difficulties, coupled with the CDB's lack of compulsory purchase powers, made land settlement an unavoidably slow and expensive process. Between the few new holdings actually provided by the board and what a Highland newspaper described as 'the glowing promises held out . . . by the Tory Party' there was, as a result, a very obvious contrast. One outcome was a resurgence of crofting support for the Liberals whose 1906 election pledges included a commitment to sweeping land reform in the Highlands. Another outcome of the CDB's creation having aroused expectations which the board, in the event, could not fulfil was the commencement, in 1900, of another round of land seizures.

Like earlier such occurrences, these raids on north-west Scotland's sheep farms were a manifestation of the deep and enduring discontent produced by an agrarian system characterised by a gross imbalance between the amounts of land allotted to farmers on the one hand, and to the crofting community on the other. But between the unrest of the twentieth century's opening decades and that of the 1880s there was a vital difference. During the land war there had been – outside the ranks of the Highland Land League – little acceptance of the principle of land settlement. Some 20 years later, however, the redistribution and resettlement of a good deal of the land that had been cleared 100 or so years before was almost universally admitted to be the only real solution to Highland problems. Since the 1890s, when Liberals set up a royal commission to investigate the region's land settlement potential and when Conservatives established the CDB, the resettlement of landless families on lands to be acquired for that purpose by the state had become an important component of the Highland policies propounded by both Britain's major political parties. Indeed the only – if occasionally profound – disagreement between them concerned the methods by which resettlement was to be achieved: the Liberals being prepared to envisage a degree of compulsion that would have been anathema to their predecessors of the 1880s and was, until about 1917 at least, unacceptable to their Conservative opponents.

The political context of the latest round of the crofting population's long battle to regain the land lost during the clearances, therefore, was one dictated primarily by Liberal and Tory rivalries. The crofting community's southern supporters, to be sure, attempted on more than one occasion to revive the Highland Land League and to re-establish it as the accepted vehicle for the crofting community's political aspirations. But this new league, having failed completely to gain a mass membership in the crofting counties, tended to be dominated, for the most part, by an exotic amalgam of socialists, Gaelic revivalists and Scottish nationalists whose careers – though not uninteresting in themselves – can safely be left out of a history of crofting.* This is not to say, of course, that the struggle for more land had become altogether easier and more respectable than had been the case in the HLLRA's heyday. There was, admittedly, less violence than during the troubles of the 1880s: partly because the state's coercive apparatus was much less freely employed; partly because cottars and squatters, the group who naturally dominated the new land seizure campaign, could not make

---

*The careers in question are outlined in J. Hunter, 'The Gaelic Connection: The Highlands, Ireland and Nationalism, 1873-1922', *Scottish Historical Review*, 54, 1975.

use, because they had no holdings to start with, of landlord-provoking tactics like the rent strike. But land raids and the grievances which gave rise to them were quite capable, for all that, of producing, as events were amply to demonstrate, their own peculiar brand of bitterness.

As if to demonstrate that nineteenth-century issues still demanded resolution, the year 1900 was marked in Skye by the MacDonald estate management's decision to take legal proceedings against crofters at Sconser whose sheep, it was alleged, were being deliberately pastured on Lord MacDonald's extensive – and by now very valuable – deer forest. Sconser's inhabitants claimed, accurately enough, that the land in question had belonged to the townships of Moll and Torramhichaig – from which their forefathers had been evicted in the 1850s. And when a sheriff-officer arrived at Sconser to serve writs which instructed the offending tenants to remove their sheep from the forest, he was duly surrounded by an angry crowd who pelted him with mud and stones before chasing him back the way he had come. The Sconser dispute having thus achieved newsworthy status, the estate management then attempted to solve it by offering to remove Sconser's occupants to vacant lands in Sleat where, with the help of the CDB, they were to be settled on holdings which, it was suggested, were in all respects superior to those they were being asked to abandon. This gesture Sconser residents interpreted as an attempt further to extend Lord MacDonald's hated deer forest at their expense. They accordingly rejected it – making the telling point that the CDB could as easily spend its money on a fence between their common grazings and their landlord's sporting preserves. Sconser's crofting tenants remained, therefore, where they were, the CDB eventually acceding to their demands for a march fence. And as a demonstration of the limits placed on Highland landlords' powers by the developments of the nineteenth century's last 20 years – limits that would have seemed inconceivable in the 1850s when townships could, quite literally, be cleared to order – their victory was not without significance. More typical of the times, however, and certainly more indicative of the troubles to come, were occurrences in Barra.

The small beginning of resettlement legislation represented by the Conservative government's Allotments (Scotland) Act of 1892 was warmly welcomed in Barra where a large landless population lived in appallingly overcrowded, often squalid, conditions. And a considerable number of Barra's cottars – along with landless families in the Uists – had at once put the measure to the test by applying to Inverness-shire County Council, the responsible authority in the matter, for the plots to which they now thought themselves entitled. There followed a protracted wrangle: the council's allotments committee being of the opinion that the Barra cottars' claims should be met; the council's landlord members being determined that no allotments should be conceded. Eventually, in 1899, the question was shelved – an outcome which, as the *Oban Times* remarked, provoked 'a widespread feeling of disappointment and irritation'. Their subsequent appeals to the CDB – which had appeared on the scene in the interim – having elicited no positive response, Barra's cottars decided to take the law into their own hands. On 8 September 1900, the farm of Northbay, one of the largest on the island, was occupied, the cottars responsible for its seizure 'holding that it is better to go to prison than suffer longer as they are doing'. To Lady Gordon Cathcart, owner of Barra and South Uist, the raiders commented:

> All their efforts during the last five years to induce the County Council of Inverness-shire to help them to obtain some small portion of land . . . have signally failed . . . They feel that they are becoming an intolerable burden on their crofter friends upon whose lands, already much too small for their own needs, their cattle and horses drag out a half-starving existence.

One farm having thus been occupied illegally, others quickly suffered the same fate, the most spectacular raid occurring on 26 September when a group of cottars from townships in the southern part of Barra landed on the adjacent island of Vatersay – then let as pasture to a sheep farmer – where they proceeded to peg out a number of 'crofts' for themselves. By the beginning of October, Barra was so unsettled that its owner's lawyers were demanding that some sort of action be taken to stop 'organised bands of cottars . . . marching hither and thither, marking out for their own occupation ground in the lawful occupation of other people'. The crisis at Northbay, in the event, was brought to an end in March 1901 when the CDB bought the entire farm as well as a part of the neighbouring farm of Eoligarry – and, on the land thus acquired, proceeded to provide almost 60 new crofts. This did nothing, however, to alleviate the plight of the many landless families living, at the other end of Barra, in and around Castlebay – some of whom again invaded Vatersay in the spring of 1901.

The moral to be drawn from the decision to hand Northbay over to its illegal occupants was obvious – and its impact was not confined to Barra. Openly expressing their belief that 'they never had a better chance of having their congestion relieved seeing the Barra people got more land', more than 100 cottars from the South Uist townships of Stoneybridge, Howbeg, Howmore and Snishival met in May 1901 and resolved to petition the CDB for holdings on Ormaclett and Bornish farms. 'Why be cottars or landless squatters any longer,' proclaimed a placard tied to a fence at the cottars' meeting place, 'while land in abundance is quite ready for instant habitation?' At that and many similar gatherings, the restoration of the farms 'from which our forefathers were so illegally evicted' was accordingly demanded – and the threat made that, if land was not promptly made available, South Uist's cottars would be 'reluctantly compelled' to take 'forcible possession' of it.

A subsequent – if largely token – occupation of Bornish and Ormaclett had its counterpart in North Uist where cottars had been urging the CDB to buy lands at Valley, Griminish and Scolpaig in the north-western corner of the island – a district which North Uist's owner, Sir Arthur Orde, was then offering for sale. The board having intimated that the area in question was quite unsuitable for settlement, the cottars concerned met at Bayhead, stated bluntly that 'over half a century ago their forefathers were ruthlessly evicted from their homes at Griminish to make way for sheep' and – encouraged by an old man who had witnessed these and other clearances and who was of the understandable opinion that 'it was all very good to talk of justice and agitating on constitutional lines, but he had seen nothing come of that for 65 years' – proceeded to occupy Griminish farm in order 'to show the board' that it was 'well fitted' for crofts.

While attempting to deal with these and other difficulties in the southern part of the Outer Isles, the CDB's harassed officials received, from landless families living in the township of Tobson on the island of Bernera, off Lewis' west coast, a request that the farm of Croir, adjacent to their township, be purchased and allotted among them:

> It is ridiculous to have a farm on our small island when there are so many cottar fishermen on the land of others . . . There are 43 souls of us and surely our lives are of more account than one man and his sheep.

This appeal, both the CDB and Lewis's owner, Major Duncan Matheson, categorically refused to consider. In April 1901, the board consequently received this letter from eight of Tobson's cottars:

> Gentlemen, We have been seeking this farm [of Croir] from the factor and landlord and parliament for the last seven years and so far we have made no progress . . . We are on the land of others and are not allowed to build a proper house and are in constant dread of eviction . . . We now give you due notice that we shall take Croir Farm on the 17th of April. If we break the law, we are compelled to do so; so look out.

On the appointed day, the eight petitioners, as they had promised, appropriated a part of Croir Farm and began to plant potatoes on it. Having defied a court order to relinquish the land thus occupied, they were eventually removed by the police and bound over to keep the peace for six months.

Elsewhere in the Hebrides, there were similar manifestations of unrest. In Tiree, where the Duke of Argyll's response to landless families' appeals for a measure of land redistribution elicited only an offer of assisted passages to the colonies, land raids were threatened in the early months of 1902 and again in the spring of 1903. Among cottars on the island of Taransay – in West Loch Tarbert on the Atlantic coast of Harris – there was talk of land raids at about the same time. And in the spring of 1903, a number of South Uist cottars translated identical mutterings into action by once again occupying farmland.

Throughout this period, however, unrest remained centred on Barra where a CDB attempt to placate the island's landless population by buying and settling Vatersay came to nothing – the selling price being quite beyond the board's resources. The ensuing discontent was aggravated by a series of bad seasons for Barra's numerous cottar-fishermen. All he wanted, one of the latter declared, was 'a piece of land to plant a barrel or two of potatoes and grazing for a cow, to fall back upon when the fishing failed'. In an attempt to obtain exactly such plots, Vatersay was reoccupied in the spring of 1902. In the following spring – with a view to forestalling renewed incursions of a similar nature – the CDB bought some 60 acres of distinctly inferior land on Vatersay from Lady Gordon Cathcart for the grossly inflated price of £600, divided this land into 50 or so potato plots, and let those plots to landless families in Barra's more southerly townships. The peace thus achieved proved transient, however. In February 1906, around 50 cottars landed on the disputed island. There they declared themselves 'determined to get possession of the whole farm of Vatersay and to remove their dwelling houses to Vatersay as soon as possible' – which intention they began to put into effect in June by ferrying their sheep and cattle across the Sound of Vatersay and by commencing to build houses on what they defiantly referred to as their crofts.

As had happened in 1901, the Barra cottars' example proved contagious. Tiree's landless families renewed their appeals for holdings – while the tenants of Skye's Kilmuir estate, bought by the CDB in 1904, met to request the more rapid division of sheep farms and to threaten to 'take possession of the land'. Demands for the resettlement of sheep farms were made at Glenshiel in Wester Ross. And towards the end of February 1906, cottars from the Stoneybridge district of South Uist marched in procession – with flags flying and with pipers at their head – on to Ormaclett and Bornish sheep farms in order, as a cottar spokesman remarked, 'to let the authorities see that they were badly off and that more land was required'. This at least was achieved. A sheep farm at Geirinish in the northern part of South Uist having been similarly invaded, the sheriff of Inverness-shire – a man of a markedly more humane disposition than his predecessor, William Ivory – visited the island and had 'a friendly interview' with the raiders. He formed, the sheriff reported to the Scottish Office, 'a favourable impression of the people, but . . . was struck by the indications of their poverty'. That the South Uist raiders' need for land was genuine and urgent, the sheriff had no doubt whatsoever. The newly installed Liberal government, he believed, should quickly honour its pre-election pledges on Highland land settlement and, to this end, 'should introduce the [requisite] Bill . . . as early as possible'.

That the Liberal party had come to power committed to ambitious and radical land reforms was undoubted. So was the determination of the new administration's Scottish secretary, John Sinclair (later Lord Pentland), to transmute into effective legislation his party's good intentions towards the Highlands – where it had secured a clean sweep of the crofting constituencies. Sinclair's proposals – which envisaged a wider and more comprehensive land settlement programme presided over by a new body to be called the Board of Agriculture for Scotland – had the backing of the prime minister, Henry Campbell-Bannerman. Those proposals, however, were opposed utterly by the Conservatives – reverting, at this point, to their traditional pro-landlord stance. To the region's misfortune, Highland land reform thus became one of the victims of the rapidly developing conflict between a Liberal-dominated House of Commons and a Tory-dominated House of Lords. Although the relevant legislation passed through the Commons in 1907 and again in 1908, it did so only to be rejected out of hand by Conservative peers – many of them, of course, Highland landlords themselves.

To the landless people of the Hebrides, whose hopes of land reform were thus frustrated, the Lords became an object of the most bitter detestation and John Sinclair something of a hero – Lewis cottars, for instance, thanking him 'for his faithful services' to their cause and declaring that the legislative veto exercised by 'selfish, cruel Lords' should be terminated at the earliest opportunity. Sinclair and his cabinet colleagues were eventually to come to the same conclusion. But until the constitutional crisis of 1910 and the subsequent curtailment of the peerage's legislative powers, northwest Scotland's landless population, seeing little prospect of John Sinclair's endeavours having a successful outcome, continued to assert their claims in the only way open to them – the prevalent attitude being reflected in resolutions adopted at a mass meeting in Skye in April 1908. Since the Lords were evidently determined to frustrate Highlanders' democratically expressed aspirations, the proposers of those resolutions stated, 'the only weapon left for us is to take forcible possession of the land'.

That was certainly the course adopted by Vatersay's occupiers. By the autumn of 1907, they had built more than 20 houses on the island where, it was clear, they were determined to remain. By the Vatersay raiders, the secretary of state was informed:

> Up to 50 years ago, their grand-parents and remoter ancestors had crofts on Vatersay at the very place where the raiders' huts were now set up – and though their grand-parents had been evicted their descendants had never given up their claim. Throughout all the years, their descendants, down to this day, have continued to bury their dead on Vatersay.

Claims so securely rooted in history were not likely to be abandoned without a struggle – especially in view of the fact that the people making them had established a firm foothold on the land in question. And to John Sinclair, whose sympathies lay with the cottars and who had absolutely no desire to provoke a confrontation with them, the obvious solution to the problem was to regularise the raiders' position by giving them legal as well as moral rights to Vatersay. Towards the end of 1907, therefore, he informed Lady Gordon Cathcart that, if she agreed to establish a crofting township on Vatersay, the CDB would be instructed to provide the financial and other assistance needed to make the project a success. This plan the island's owner at once rejected. Instead Lady Gordon Cathcart offered to sell Vatersay to the board – at a considerable profit to herself and at a price, as soon became apparent, that was beyond the CDB's resources.

Their negotiations with John Sinclair having thus collapsed, the Barra estate management proceeded to take legal action against the raiders. In June 1908, as a result, ten of the latter were imprisoned for two months. A storm of protest followed. The government was forced to reopen its talks with Vatersay's owner. And in October it was agreed that the CDB should buy Vatersay for £6,250. The raiders, all of whom were granted holdings on the island, thought the price extortionate – which, by 1908 standards, it was. But they were, as they informed the Scottish secretary, 'genuinely grateful' to him for 'bringing about this settlement'. Others were less delighted. Conservative spokesmen and newspapers alleged that in 'giving in' to the raiders the newly ennobled Lord Pentland was condoning, even encouraging, lawlessness. This contention, of course, took no account of the extent to which such lawlessness was a consequence of Conservative obstruction of the Liberal land settlement programme. But it was, for all that, an accurate enough representation of the overall Highlands and Islands situation – the Vatersay settlement having the inevitable effect of precipitating still more land raids.

In Barra itself, for example, a number of landless families living in the undeniably congested east-coast townships of Bruernish, Balnabodach and Ersary pointed out that they were 'exactly in the same circumstances as the Vatersay people before they obtained the land' and announced that, if their wants were not attended to, they would 'by dire necessity . . . be forced' to embark on their own equivalent of the Vatersay raiders' campaign. In March 1909, despite Pentland's warning that illegal action would only 'prejudice their case', the Bruernish, Balnabodach and Ersary people proceeded to occupy the part of Eoligarry farm which had been unaffected by the CDB purchase of eight years before. In South Uist, where the farms of Milton and Glendale were raided, there were identical occurrences. And declaring themselves 'compelled . . . to take forcible possession of a farm as in the case of the Barra men', six cottars from the Lewis township of South Shawbost occupied a field on Dalbeg farm in order to provide themselves with land on which to grow potatoes. On their defying a court order to quit Dalbeg, the members of this particular raiding party were jailed for a week. When released, however, they returned to the farm because, as they said, they 'had nowhere else to go and could not live in the air or on the sea' – an attitude that led to their being imprisoned for another 21 days.

Raids and threats of raids on Hebridean sheep farms having become a part of the accepted order of things, and the land settlement powers of the CDB being demonstrably inadequate, there was, by the end of the twentieth century's first decade, an obvious and urgent need for new legislation on the Highland land question – legislation which at length materialised in the shape of the Small Landholders (Scotland) Act of 1911. Made possible by the curbing of the Lords' prerogatives, the Act – though a private member's measure – had the Liberal government's support and was, in essence, a refurbished, if somewhat watered down, version of Sinclair's ill-fated Bills of 1907 and 1908. A new departure in agricultural policy, the 1911 Act extended many of the original Crofters Act's provisions to smallholders outside the crofting counties, abolishing, in the process, both the Crofters Commission and the Congested Districts Board – the functions of the former being taken over by the Scottish Land Court and those of the latter by the Board of Agriculture for Scotland. On this second organisation there was bestowed a wide range of land settlement powers and an annual budget of £200,000. The greater part of that budget was to be expended on settlement schemes in the north-west, especially in the Hebrides. The owners and farming tenants of lands utilised for settlement purposes were entitled, the Act laid down, to compensation which, failing agreement, was to be determined by the Land Court or – if the compensation claimed was in excess of £300 – by an arbitrator appointed by the Court of Session. Compulsory purchase of land by the state was still ruled out. But should a proprietor or tenant refuse to enlarge existing, or to constitute new, smallholdings on his land, the Board of Agriculture was entitled to lay its case before the Land Court and, if the court was satisfied that the board's proposals were reasonable and would meet genuine needs, it was empowered to issue an order instructing objectors to comply with the Board of Agriculture's wishes.

At last, it seemed, the crofting community's demands for a redistribution of land in their favour – demands which had their origins in the clearances and which had been incessantly and vociferously expressed since the 1880s – were about to be met. The establishment of the Board of Agriculture in the spring of 1912 was accordingly welcomed at scores of meetings in the crofting areas. And by the end of that year the board had received 3,370 applications for holdings – almost half of them from cottars living in the Outer Isles.

Before the Board of Agriculture's first 12 months had elapsed, however, it was clear that it was little better equipped than the CDB had been to tackle the problem of transferring land from one class of occupant to another. The board's funds were inadequate and – what was worse – its procedures, especially those regarding compensation claims, were woefully complex and slow as well as being notably generous to landowning and sheep farming objectors to its plans. Without the eager and enthusiastic co-operation of the latter, therefore, the Act was clearly liable to prove a dead letter. And from the first it was evident that such co-operation was not to be forthcoming.

In part, Highland landlords' opposition to the 1911 Act derived from their Conservative politics. But political calculation was enforced, as is usually the case, by financial self-interest. Sheep farming, the traditional prop of Highland landlordism, had long ceased, it was true, to be a profitable enterprise in much of northern Scotland. But the region's landowners, while amenable to the idea of selling land to the state at prices that were – to put the matter mildly – conspicuously inflated, had no wish to see crofting tenants settled, with state assistance, on land that remained their property. Such settlement would result, landlords feared, in their being unable, in the future, to cash in on any improvement that might eventually occur in the agricultural situation. Crofters, once established, enjoyed security of tenure and could not easily be shifted. Nor could croft rents easily be raised. As was pointed out by a member of one landowning family:

> [The crofting landlord] is at the mercy of a commission [or land court] whose sympathies are entirely with the tenants, and who, if they allow any increase of rent at all, will give the very smallest increase possible, while, if prices fall, they will give the most generous concessions in rent.

Sheep farmers, though for different reasons, were as likely as proprietors to obstruct settlement schemes. Writing from South Uist in 1909, one of the CDB's officials had observed:

> It seems to me that farmers in this district just now, even although they wish to leave, pretend they don't, in the expectation of the government asking for the farm for smallholdings when compensation will be paid for break of lease.

Like their landlords and like the latter's Edinburgh lawyers who, as a civil servant at the Board of Agriculture ruefully remarked, became 'very expert in the preparation of claims for every conceivable item connected with a farm', sheep farmers tended, therefore, to react to the new board's land settlement proposals by initiating legal proceedings as to the amount of compensation due to them. The consequent thicket of writs, processes, claims and arbitrations in which the board became entangled served quickly to nullify all optimistic expectations of a final and speedy solution to agrarian problems in north-west Scotland – only 502 new holdings being created in the first seven years of the Board's existence.

In the spring of 1914, to give an example of the difficulties that ensued, the Board of Agriculture requested the Scottish Land Court to authorise the establishment of 32 new crofts and 14 enlargements to existing crofts on the North Uist farm of Cheese Bay. Having inspected the farm and heard representations from the various parties involved, the board issued the requisite orders in November 1915 – at which point North Uist's owner, Sir Arthur Campbell Orde, intimating that his claim for compensation would exceed £300, asked the Court of Session to appoint the arbitrator to which the law entitled him. In April 1918, an arbitrator having at last been nominated, Sir Arthur lodged a claim for £16,852. And although he was eventually awarded only £4,770 the Board, as the 1911 Act had stipulated, was found liable for all the expenses of the case. The inordinate amount of time taken to appoint an arbitrator was, in this particular instance, attributable to wartime circumstances. In other respects, however, the case was not untypical of those in which the Board of Agriculture became embroiled from its inception. The ensuing and seemingly interminable delays – in the course of which neither the board nor its prospective settlers knew whether or not a particular scheme might eventually have to be abandoned – caused a great deal of bitterness and frustration among the many Hebridean cottars whose hopes of obtaining land had yet again been raised only to be dashed.

It is not surprising, therefore, that, by 1913, there was, as a Highland newspaper remarked, 'ample evidence of a coming revolt'. In Lewis that year, the island's proprietor, Duncan Matheson, opposed Board of Agriculture plans to create 131 new holdings on the farms of Galson, Gress, Carnish, Ardroil, Orinsay and Stimervay – on the grounds both that the farmland in question was not suitable for crofts and that he would lose more by way of rent than he would gain by way of compensation. Lady Gordon Cathcart adopted a similar stance with regard to the proposed subdivision of a number of farms in South Uist where, it was pointed out in the course of the summer, 'some of the applicants in anticipation of getting land had kept stock for almost two years, and . . . [were having] to struggle hard to maintain that stock'. Resolutions to the effect that 'if the Board of Agriculture would not hurry up there would be nothing for it but to seize the land' began to be adopted at meetings in these and other areas. One result, in December 1913, was the occupation of the Lewis farm of Reef by cottars from adjacent townships.

A letter from the Reef raiders to the Scottish Office made their position and predicament crystal clear:

> We were applying for land since the year 1908: applying to the proprietor at first . . . then to the CDB and latterly to the Land Court . . . We were getting replies giving neither encouragement nor discouragement, as if the whole proceedings were in mockery. The only reply we get now is 'that our applications are under consideration'. Anyhow, we were believing we would get land and that caused us to remain at home in anticipation of getting to work on the land – and that was not in our favour as we did not go elsewhere for work. If we won't have immediate possession, we shall be compelled to dispose of our stock which we were diligently gathering and keeping together in order to have some for the new land . . . As is well known, an Act of Parliament [the Act of 1911] was passed to give land to the landless and, as is equally well known, no land was received by anyone under the Act. Surely no one can blame us for the steps we have decided to take. But whether we get blamed or not is of no moment. We have suffered long enough as we are,

and though we were to suffer in another way we would hardly be worse off than we were.

Reef, its occupiers declared, 'was for ages cultivated by smallholders before the clearances'. But whatever their moral and historical rights to it, their legal claims to the farm were non-existent and Duncan Matheson thus had no difficulty in obtaining court orders forbidding the offending cottars from trespassing on his property. The court's instructions, as was usual in such cases, were ignored and the raiders sentenced to six weeks' imprisonment. But their actions, as the under-secretary of state for Scotland wrote at the time, were both 'a symptom and a warning' – a timely indication of the 'widespread dissatisfaction at the slow progress in acquiring holdings'. The accuracy of this statement was underlined by the troubles at Reef having been accompanied by raids on farms in Barra and South Uist and followed, in the spring and early summer, by illegal occupations of land elsewhere in the Hebrides.

Like the incipient civil war in Ireland, the suffragette campaign and the endemic labour unrest which together belie the common notion that Edwardian Britain was as socially tranquil as it was prosperous, the growing discontent among north-west Scotland's landless population was submerged in the wider and more awful violence of the European war which broke out in August 1914. And when that war was finally over, attitudes to Highland land, like attitudes to much else, were found to have undergone a number of significant changes. The exigencies of the war itself, it was true, had caused land settlement to be practically suspended. But its suspension had been accompanied by repeated assurances that, once victory had been secured, 'the land question in the Highlands' would, as T. B. Morrison, lord advocate in Lloyd-George's wartime coalition government declared at Inverness in 1917, 'be settled once and for all . . . Everyone is agreed that the people of the Highlands must be placed in possession of the soil'.

Such pledges, like all the other promises featuring in the 'homes fit for heroes' rhetoric of the time, were more freely made than kept. They did, however, represent a genuine realignment of opinion – a realignment typified both by newfound Liberal–Conservative unity on the need for a comprehensive land settlement policy in the Highlands and by the waning of proprietorial opposition to such a policy. Interestingly, if a trifle paradoxically, the British establishment's sudden interest in undoing the consequences of the Highland Clearances stemmed, in part anyway, from a dawning realisation that redistribution of land – though an apparently radical, even socialist, policy and one, moreover, embraced enthusiastically by the Communists who, in 1917, seized power in Russia – might help to preserve a British social order which, in the years immediately following the First World War, more than once seemed in danger of collapse. The debt the country owed to Highland servicemen was one element in the growing support for a Highland land settlement programme, it was noted in a document drafted in the post-war Scottish Office. But 'the dread of Marxism' was another such element: 'a landholder [has] no time for revolution . . . the holder feels he has a stake in his country and his face is turned towards stability and security'.

Political commitment, even when inspired by fear of Bolshevism, was one thing; legislation another. The tentative additions made to the Board of Agriculture's land settlement powers in 1916 did nothing to mollify irate feelings in the Highlands, where land raids, temporarily stilled by the war, showed every sign of commencing once again. In the spring of 1917, for example, land was seized at Sconser in Skye and at Eoligarry in Barra. And as was remarked in a police report on events at Eoligarry, where women had taken the lead in planning and organising Barra's latest land raid, the war had evidently done nothing to weaken cottars' resolve to possess what had been so long denied to them:

> There has grown up with the war a new feeling, a determination to cast aside legal methods and, by force of seizure, obtain what they deem their rights. They openly state their position thus: 'Why is it that our husbands and sons who are serving their country – some killed and some wounded – cannot obtain . . . a place to build a decent house upon? Why is it that the government asks us to cultivate the land, yet will not give us the land to cultivate? Why is it that two old bachelors [the tenants of the farm which had been raided] . . . are allowed to have all Eoligarry lands for themselves, while we, who are risking our sons' lives to defend that land, can by no means obtain an inch of it?'

Soon similar questions were to be posed elsewhere. In January 1918, for instance, a number of cottars from the Tiree township of Cornaigbeg took possession of a 13-acre field on Belephetrish farm and at once proceeded to prepare it for a spring planting of potatoes. Their actions, they said, were dictated by the wartime government's injunctions to increase agricultural production as well as by their own poverty. The prime minister, the Balephetrish raiders pointed out, 'had asked the people to get food and that was what they were doing'. And they were doing it, moreover, on land which would have been settled by the Board of Agriculture before the war, had not the amount of compensation demanded by its landlord and tenant been so high. The Balephetrish raiders were all old men – two at least being in their seventies – and all had sons on active service. But none of that prevented them from being sentenced to ten days' imprisonment as a result of legal proceedings initiated by the Duke of Argyll, Tiree's owner. Nor were the Duke of Argyll's actions in any way unique. That summer, a group of cottars from the Sutherland township of Portgower, a little to the south of Helmsdale, took over a corner of one of the very many sheep farms on the Duke of Sutherland's estate. One of the Portgower raiders was a widow whose two sons were then at the front line in France. With her companions, she was jailed for ten days. As far as the Highland nobility were concerned, it appeared, not a great deal had changed since the clearances.

Between parliamentarians' pledges and the all too harsh realities of the cottar population's existence, there was thus a yawning gap of mutual mistrust. Events in Tiree and Sutherland were paralleled in the Uists. And with the demobilisation in 1919 of the many young and landless Highlanders and Hebrideans who had seen service in the war, the demand for holdings became, as the Board of Agriculture reported, more insistent than ever. 'When we were in the trenches down to our knees in mud and blood,' a Harris cottar remarked, 'we were promised all good things when we should return home victorious.' 'We returned home,' another ex-serviceman observed, 'firmly believing that the promised land would be given us.' The reverse, however, proved to be the case. Excessive costs, lack of powers, limited funds, unduly high expectations: these are the phrases that characterised official thinking on Highland land settlement during the 12 months following Britain's armistice with Germany in November 1918. And nowhere, during this period, were the problems and frustrations of landlessness more acute than in Lewis.

That there was not enough land in Lewis to provide holdings for all its people was common knowledge – among the island's cottars as well as among the seemingly endless procession of commissions of enquiry into Lewis's uniquely insoluble agrarian problem. But to Lewis cottars at least, this was a situation which made the existence of the island's larger farms more, not less, intolerable than it would otherwise have been. And in 1917, when four island seamen wrote to the editor of the newly established *Stornoway Gazette* to express the hope that his paper would 'help us to get the land of our forefathers . . . that they were deprived of cruelly', Lewis's farms – under pressure since the 1880s – were clearly due for division into crofts. That was certainly the wartime government's opinion. In June 1917, the Board of Agriculture began preparing a Lewis land settlement scheme which was to be enacted at the end of the war and which was to involve practically every scrap of the island's potentially arable land. Lewis then being up for sale, the government actually considered buying it in its entirety. If the island had then passed into public ownership, its post-war history would undoubtedly have been more peaceful, if considerably less eventful, than proved to be the case. In the event, however, Lewis was purchased for £143,000 by Lord Leverhulme, a man who had made a fortune from the manufacture and promotion of mass-produced soaps and who planned to invest a part of this fortune in his huge but by no means prosperous Hebridean estate – to the benefit, Leverhulme hoped, of Lewis's inhabitants as well as to the eventual profit of himself.

Unable to understand an attachment to land that transcended the calculations of profit and loss which had ruled his own life, Leverhulme had little time for crofters and still less for crofting – which Lewis's new proprietor considered a decidedly uncommercial mode of living. And that anyone should wish to *extend* the crofting system was, quite literally, beyond Leverhulme's comprehension. Land settlement, he informed the Board of Agriculture, was 'a gross waste of public money' and, in his opinion, 'the only solution of the land question in Lewis' was to be found in his own planned development of the island's fishing industry. That Lewis was in need of economic aid of some description was certainly all too plain. Even before the war, Lewismen's traditional source of work and income, the herring industry, was beginning to fail them – largely because of the lower manpower needs of a fleet that was being increasingly remodelled around steam drifters. And after the war, when the industry's long-established markets in central and eastern Europe were denied to it by revolutionary turmoil and politically motivated trade embargoes, there began, as the latest official report on Lewis was to acknowledge, a prolonged and disastrous slump:

> Fomerly, Lewismen went in considerable numbers as hired men on the east coast fishing boats, but the general depression of the herring fishing industry now leaves fewer openings of this kind . . . and taking . . . the summer and autumn herring fishery as a whole, it may be said that only a few hundred Lewismen now get employment in this fashion.

So bleak were employment prospects on Scotland's east coast that, in the summer of 1920, not a few of the Lewismen who made their way there in search of work had to borrow the money they needed to get home again. Emigration, in consequence, began to rise and the population of Lewis to fall for the first time in 200 years. With the island's inshore white fisheries also in trouble, its crofters and cottars were consequently in no way opposed in principle to Leverhulme's employment-providing schemes.

They were, however, sceptical – and with justice – of their new landlord's claims that Lewis's economic salvation lay in the development of Stornoway as a herring port equipped with canneries, processing factories and all the other paraphernalia of industrialised fishing. Long used to the vagaries of the fishing business, and more aware than Leverhulme of the dimensions of the crisis then gripping the herring industry, Lewis's cottars were not prepared to trust their island's owner to the extent of abandoning their claims to the land. It was on this point that Leverhulme's ambitions and those of Lewis's large landless population came into – as it proved – irreconcilable conflict. Something of the nature of that conflict is beautifully encapsulated in this account – penned by one of the Board of Agriculture's representatives, Colin MacDonald – of a meeting between Lord Leverhulme and a group of island residents. Leverhulme is addressing the crowd:

> And then there appeared in the next few minutes the most graphic word picture it is possible to imagine – a great fleet of fishing boats – a large

fish-canning factory (already started) – railways – an electric power station; then one could see the garden city grow – steady work, steady pay, beautiful houses for all – every modern convenience and comfort. The insecurity of their present income was referred to; the squalor of their present houses deftly compared with the conditions in the new earthly paradise. Altogether it was a masterpiece; and it produced its effect; little cheers came involuntarily from a few here and there – more cheers! – general cheers!! . . .

And just then, while the artist was still adding skilful detail, there was a dramatic interruption.

One of the ringleaders managed to rouse himself from the spell, and in an impassioned voice addressed the crowd in Gaelic, and this is what he said:

'So so, fhiribh! Cha dean so gnotach! Bheireadh am bodach mil-bheulach sin chreidsinn oirnn gu'm bheil dubh geal 's geal dubh! Ciod e dhuinn na bruadairean briagha aige, a thig no nach tig? 'Se am fearann tha sinn ag iarraidh. Agus 'se tha mise a faighneachd (turning to face Lord Leverhulme and pointing dramatically towards him): *an toir thu dhuinn am fearann?'*
The effect was electrical. The crowd roared their approbation.

Lord Leverhulme looked bewildered at this, to him, torrent of unintelligible sounds, but when the frenzied cheering with which it was greeted died down he spoke.

'I am sorry! It is my great misfortune that I do not understand the Gaelic language. But perhaps my interpreter will translate for me what has been said?'

Said the interpreter: 'I am afraid, Lord Leverhulme, that it will be impossible for me to convey to you in English what has been so forcefully said in the older tongue; but I will do my best' – and his best was a masterpiece, not only in words but in tone and gesture and general effect:

'Come, come, men! This will not do! This honeymouthed man would have us believe that black is white and white is black. We are not concerned with his fancy dreams that may or may not come true! What we want is the *land* – and the question I put to him now is: *will you give us the land?'*

The translation evoked a further round of cheering. A voice was heard to say:

'Not so bad for a poor language like the English!'

Lord Leverhulme's picture, so skilfully painted was shattered in the artist's hand!

In that exhange are echoes of everything this book is about. And though Leverhulme's ultimate failure in the Hebrides was more a product of wider economic circumstances – particularly the difficulties then threatening to overwhelm the herring industry – than it was of Leverhulme's inability to win the backing of Lewis people, that same exchange highlights exactly why, as far as the landless families among those people were concerned, no such backing was forthcoming.

Believing that 'the agitation for land was old fashioned and irrelevant', declaring that 'the retention of the whole of the existing farms in Lewis is an essential foundation of the schemes I have for development', and threatening that 'if the farms are taken I shall be forced . . . to stop the development work', Leverhulme was implacably opposed both to land redistribution in general and to the subdivision of the farms of Coll and

Gress in particular. Situated within a few miles of Stornoway, those two farms were needed, Leverhulme said repeatedly, to supply the town with milk – a contention which, like his dislike of crofting agriculture *per se,* became something of an obsession with him. To Lewis's many hundreds of applicants for holdings, however, Leverhulme's anti-settlement stance was ultimately unacceptable. It was unfortunate, therefore, that Robert Munro, secretary of state for Scotland in the post-war coalition government, allowed himself to be persuaded – in much the same way that the meeting described by Colin MacDonald allowed itself, at least temporarily, to be persuaded – that Lord Leverhulme might singlehandedly provide Lewis with a brighter future than would otherwise be available to the island. The upshot was a government decision that the Lewis land settlement programme should be suspended 'until Lord Leverhulme,' as a Scottish Office memorandum noted, 'should have an opportunity of showing whether by the development of his schemes he would convince the Lewismen that it was in their best interests to fall in with his proposals and cease their demands for smallholdings'. Lewismen, however, were in no mood to be so convinced. In the spring of 1919, by way of making this point clear to Robert Munro as well as to Lord Leverhulme, a number of cottars, most of them ex-servicemen, occupied Coll and Gress farms.

The raiders' motives and justifications were summed up by one of their number, a man who had first applied for a holding as far back as 1906:

> While we were engaged in our country's battles, promises without number were made that . . . the land from which our forefathers were evicted would be placed in our possession . . . While we were fighting nothing seemed too good for us, but now that the enemy has been overcome, through our help, these promises seem to take time in being fulfilled.

Besides, the conditions in which they and their families lived, the Coll and Gress raiders pointed out in a letter to Robert Munro, had become intolerable:

> We were squatting under revolting conditions in hovels situated on other men's crofts. Into one of these hovels, containing two apartments, no fewer than 25 people were crowded. Our families were suffering unspeakably not only from insufficient accommodation but also from want of milk and other food, while hundreds of acres of good land were lying untilled at our doors.

The raiders thus considered themselves 'reluctantly compelled to take matters into [their] own hands'. And having once installed themselves on Coll and Gress, they were not to be easily moved by all Leverhulme's appeals and blandishments. He was not at all opposed to the proprietor's plans, one raider remarked. But he 'wanted to have land whatever happened'. 'We fought for this land in France,' another raider commented, 'and we're prepared to die for it in Lewis.'

In April, Gress's new occupants planted potatoes on their hastily pegged-out 'crofts'. And as if to show that Leverhulme's troubles were not to be confined to that particular locality, Galson, the farm on the other side of the island which had featured so frequently in the events of the 1880s, was also subjected to a number of illegal incursions. Elsewhere in north-west Scotland, meanwhile, there were similar manifestations of discontent. Before 1919 was over, land had been seized in Harris and in North and South Uist – developments that were accompanied by threats to occupy farms in areas as far apart as Tiree, Sutherland and Wester Ross. It was against this background of virtual guerilla warfare between north-west Scotland's cottar population and the authorities that the coalition government's Land Settlement (Scotland) Act passed into law on 23 December 1919.

The 1919 Act – which a Highland newspaper described as the first measure to have any 'real chance' of establishing 'a contented people on the soil of their native land', and which even the Duke of Sutherland hoped would finally lay 'that ghost of unrest which has haunted the Highland glens for so long' – greatly expanded the powers and responsibilities of the Board of Agriculture to which it granted some £2,750,000 for settlement purposes. Enabled now to advance substantial loans to landholders in order to allow them to take over the stocks of newly settled sheep farms as well as to buy seeds, fertilisers and implements of every kind, the board was also authorised to compulsorily purchase land for settlement. And since the new Act's purchase procedures, though by no means rapid, were somewhat less complex than those involved in enforcing – under the provisions of the 1911 Act – land settlement schemes on privately owned land, the majority of the crofts established after 1919 were constituted on land bought for that purpose, and owned ever since, by the state.

Despite the fact that – as was afterwards noted officially – 'instructions were given that land was to be secured as quickly as possible' and that the question of cost was 'to be a secondary consideration', the 1919 Act provided no instant or automatic solution to the problem of landlessness in the Highlands and Hebrides. The difficulties of the purchase negotiations in which the Board was then involved meant that, in 1920, only 227 applicants were actually settled on new holdings. Among the many landless families whose ambitions seemed as far from realisation as they had ever been, 'suspicion and resentment' continued to be prevalent, therefore. And from the time and money which the Board of Agriculture and its staff spent satisfying the claims of the landlords from whom land was beginning to be acquired, the crofting community drew an inevitable conclusion. 'From the conduct of the board,' a group of Skye crofters declared, 'it can easily be seen that they are prejudiced against the landless people, doing their utmost to protect and please the landowners.' This was an opinion that events in Lewis did little to refute.

In January 1920, the farms of Coll and Gress, from which raiders had withdrawn the previous autumn, were once more invaded and, by way of confirming their intention of staying, the farms' occupiers began to build houses on them. Leverhulme promptly retaliated by dismissing from his employment every man from the district of Back in which the disputed farms were situated – conduct that was as indiscriminate as it was dictatorial. Far from intimidating the island's cottar population, however, Leverhulme's action merely generated more hostility – the happenings at Coll and Gress being quickly emulated on other farms in the south and west of Lewis. Soon raiding had broken out, as a Scottish Office civil servant put it, 'on a larger scale' than at any time since the 1880s. Taken somewhat aback by the 'determined nature' of the unrest he had helped unleash, Leverhulme reverted to more conciliatory tactics – offering to provide the Coll and Gress raiders with quarter-acre allotments of arable land or ten-acre crofts to be constituted on the common grazings of existing townships. On those offers being rejected, Leverhulme next attempted to split the Lewis crofting community and to arouse public opinion against the raiders by halting all his building programmes – an action which meant the loss to Lewis of a weekly wage bill calculated to exceed £3,000. One effect of this action was to persuade the secretary of state that something would have to be done to 'mitigate the situation' in Lewis. Since the passing of the Land Settlement Act, Robert Munro pointed out in a letter he sent to Leverhulme in June 1920, settlement schemes had been initiated in lots of places. Only in Lewis, where requests for holdings had been most strongly voiced 'and where expectations had been held out before the war of substantial concessions to the popular demand', had absolutely nothing been done. In such circumstances, Munro opined, 'the action of the raiders, while legally wrong and punishable, was at least intelligible'.

That summer, however, Leverhulme won a series of notable victories in what he was increasingly prone to think of as his war with Robert Munro, with the Board of Agriculture and with the Coll and Gress raiders. Having conceded the need for land settlement schemes on Lewis's Atlantic coast, he intimated his intention of keeping the east coast farms intact, announced that his development projects would not be resumed until Coll and Gress were vacated, and, on that basis, conducted a series of meetings in every part of Lewis at which he unsurprisingly – considering the amount of employment at stake – succeeded in winning majority support for his stance. The Board of Agriculture, however, remained unpersuaded:

> The situation appears to the board to be that Lord Leverhulme is now endeavouring to prevent them from carrying out the duties of land settlement imposed upon them by parliament by threatening to withdraw his schemes for developing the island unless the board further suspend their operations in

regard to Lewis. The board feels that the time has now come when it is their clear duty to proceed with (at any rate) a partial scheme of land settlement in Lewis.

With that view, the occupiers of Coll and Gress would – had they been informed of it – have cordially concurred. Recalling how promptly the British government of 1887 had despatched its troops to put down unrest in Lewis, they pointed out that 'the government was always ready to enforce the law when unfavourable to the landless' – adding, with understandable bitterness, that it had perhaps been too much to expect 'that when it [the law] is favourable to them [the landless] it will be enforced without delay'.

Uneasily aware of their growing isolation in Lewis, the Coll and Gress raiders eventually allowed the lord advocate – who visited the island, in October 1920, for that purpose – to persuade them to withdraw from the disputed farms. By leaving, they made clear, they were not abandoning their claims – merely giving the Board of Agriculture time to put a settlement scheme into operation and allowing Leverhulme to recommence his various activities on the island. Rightly or wrongly, the raiders left in the belief that they had been given 'an undertaking that if we would withdraw . . . the Board of Agriculture would deal with our demand for holdings'. The lord advocate, for his part, was convinced he had given no such undertaking. In such misunderstandings were the seeds of future trouble. But the truce thus achieved in Lewis did at least allow more attention to be paid to events elsewhere in north-west Scotland – events which showed that the Lewis cottars' discontents were widely shared.

The spring of 1920 was marked by raids on lands in North Uist, on the MacLeod estate in Skye, and on a farm in Raasay. In the summer, the focus of activity shifted to the north coast of Sutherland where cottars from the townships of Melvich and Portskerra took possession of a sheep farm promised them by the Duke of Sutherland in 1915 but sold by him four years later. In conjunction with contemporary happenings in Lewis and with the fact that almost 50 other farms were then being threatened with illegal occupations or incursions of one kind or another, these developments went some way to justify the Duke of Sutherland's August declaration that there was a 'danger of the Highlands becoming something like Ireland' – embroiled, at this point, in its people's violent struggle for independence – and certainly seemed to bear out his contention that the Board of Agriculture was 'displaying an attitude of helplessness in meeting the situation'.

The winter of 1920–21 brought a rapid increase in tension and a still more widespread tendency on the part of the Hebrides' landless population to resort to direct action against the farms they had coveted for so long. In December, in what was said to be 'one of the largest raids that has [ever] taken place in the Western Isles', several thousand acres of farmland in North Uist were occupied by a large number of cottars. Hundreds of sheep and cattle having been driven off, an immediate start was made on building huts and houses and on preparing the land for cultivation. By March, over 30 acres had been ploughed while an area twice that size had been thoroughly manured and otherwise made ready for turning over. Handed sheriff court orders which instructed them to quit the farms they had seized, the raiders – most of whom had seen service in France – refused to budge, one of them remarking, 'We don't care a damn for the sheriff. We are soldiers.'

Having been eventually arrested, six of the more defiant of these North Uist raiders were sentenced to two months' imprisonment. But as a Skye ex-serviceman remarked in an exasperated letter to the Board of Agriculture, 'It will not frighten us although people are imprisoned for land raiding – better that than four years under German fire.' And in South Uist, where other ex-servicemen publicly declared their intention to 'fight this time for ourselves and not for others' and where the sheep farms of Drimore and Dremisdale were occupied by cottars in the opening weeks of 1921, the same very general sentiments obviously prevailed.

'From past experience,' the Drimore and Dremisdale raiders announced, they were 'convinced that the only way to get the Board of Agriculture to move' was to 'take the law into their own hands'. The board disagreed:

> Though the board have in some cases promoted schemes on raided lands, it is not the case that scheme has followed on raid as effect on cause, but rather that the raiders disturbed a situation which was tending towards solution.

Such exercises in semantics, however, did little to convince the many southern critics of the Board of Agriculture that its own dilatoriness was more than anything else responsible for the unrest in the Highlands. Nor were such statements, however well intentioned, at all helpful in dispelling the aura of mistrust and confusion surrounding the board's intentions in the Hebrides.

In 1921, admittedly, some progress was made in the Uists where settlement schemes were officially inaugurated on several farms. In Harris, however, there were a number of raids on farmland in the vicinity of Rodel – while in Raasay the ex-servicemen who had appropriated a field near Raasay House in March 1920 were joined, in the spring of 1921, by a party of raiders from the nearby island of Rona to which a number of families from Raasay had been removed during the clearances of the 1850s. Conditions on Rona, the Scottish Land Court reported, were 'miserable in the extreme', the land being of 'the poorest quality' and the houses of 'the most primitive description'. 'It is difficult to know,' court members went on, 'how anyone can carry on under such conditions, and still more so to understand how a living can be obtained.' With that view, Rona's applicants for holdings in Raasay were in full agreement:

The circumstances under which we live here are most deplorable, the place being hardly fit for goats, far less human beings, while the good land on the south end of Raasay from which we could have a decent living and for which the best of our manhood has bled and died in Flanders and elsewhere is as a sporting ground for an . . . English gentleman.

The gentleman in question, acting in conjunction with Raasay's owners, a Glasgow firm which had worked the island's iron ore deposits during the war, at once initiated legal proceedings against the raiders who had begun to rebuild some of the ruined houses at Fearns – one of the several Raasay townships cleared 70 years before – and to prepare their 'holdings' for cultivation. Instructed to relinquish the land they had seized, the raiders refused to do so. Five of them, as a result, were sentenced to 40 days' imprisonment – an outcome which provoked outrage on Raasay and Rona. A mass meeting was summoned. And to Lloyd-George and Robert Munro, to whom copies of the unanimously adopted resolutions were despatched, it was pointed out:

The offence of these men was that . . . they reclaimed, at their own expense, for food production small patches of extensive arable land on the island of Raasay now devoted to the rearing of sheep and deer . . . [The] sentences [imposed on the raiders] constitute an outrage upon, and an insult to, the memory of the gallant deeds performed by . . . islemen in this war and past wars.

As far as government ministers were concerned, however, such sentiments counted for little. Although Raasay was purchased by the Board of Agriculture in 1922, the government reacted to the disquiet produced by the jailing of the Raasay raiders, not by issuing a conciliatory statement, but by proclaiming 'that in future land raiding is to operate as an absolute bar to land settlement, and that persons taking part in such raiding shall be removed from the Board [of Agriculture's] lists of approved applicants for smallholdings'. In the circumstances of the early 1920s, however, threats of this sort were not taken very seriously. Raiding duly continued – especially in Lewis where, in the course of 1921, the concordat established between Leverhulme, the government and the island's landless population broke down completely and irrevocably.

In December 1920, Lord Leverhulme had organised meetings in almost every township in Lewis with a view to asking the island's population to give him a guarantee that there would be no interference with his remaining farms for at least ten years – the time needed, he believed, to ensure the success of his plans. Except in Back, the district which contained the farms of Coll and Gress and where there were nine dissensions from the pro-Leverhulme resolution, he won unanimous approbation. In response to the pressure thus engendered, Robert Munro had little option but to accede to Leverhulme's demands. And in January 1921, he assured Lewis's owner that no part of his estate would be compulsorily acquired for settlement purposes until the stipulated ten years had elapsed.

Because Robert Munro had no authority thus to set aside the provisions of the Land Settlement Act, this agreement was of dubious legality. As far as the cottar families of the Highlands and Islands were concerned, moreover, it served mainly to confirm their growing belief that there was one law for landlords, another for the landless. The 1919 Act had clearly stated that – on the Board of Agriculture being 'satisfied' of the existence, in a particular area, both of a 'demand for small holdings' and of the availablity, in the same area, of 'suitable land' – the board had a 'duty' to proceed with appropriate settlement schemes. That the Back district of Lewis met all these requirements was certain. Hence the question addressed to Robert Munro by a disillusioned applicant for a holding on Coll farm:

> If one Act of Parliament can be overruled, why not another? Why should some men be sent to prison for failing to comply with the law and others be paid huge salaries for the same thing? The board cannot deny that we have satisfied them that there is a demand for small holdings and that there is suitable land available here to meet our demands.

Convinced in the previous autumn that their claims to Coll and Gress were about to be sympathetically considered, the cottars of Back felt betrayed. Nor were their feelings in any way mollified by Leverhulme's decision to make the farms of Reef, Carnish, Ardroil, Mealista, Timsgarry, Croir, Dalmore and Dalbeg available for settlement. All were situated in the southwestern corner of Lewis, the nearest being 30 miles from Back and the most distant some 60 miles away. Although 67 new holdings and 166 enlargements to existing holdings were constituted on these farms at Whitsun 1921, they were awarded, naturally and fairly enough, to local applicants rather than to men from Back.

That Gress and Coll were again raided in the spring of 1921 was no great surprise, therefore, to anyone. More unexpected, however, was the slowing down and eventual suspension of work on Leverhulme's development projects on Lewis: ostensibly in response to events at Coll and Gress; in actuality, because of the steadily increasing financial difficulties of Lewis's proprietor. Matters came to a head at the end of August when Leverhulme announced his intention to leave Lewis to its own devices and to concentrate instead on Harris, which he had bought in 1919 and where he hoped to construct a large and profitable fishing port at Obbe – afterwards renamed Leverburgh in his honour. Among Leverhulme's supporters in Lewis, this announcement caused consternation. At Coll and Gress, however, the raiders were convinced that Leverhulme had abrogated his understanding with the government and with the people of Lewis and consequently believed themselves entitled to expect the Board of Agriculture to recommence its operations in the island. With this view, Robert Munro could see no reason to disagree. 'In the circumstances as they now are,' he informed Lord Leverhulme on 6 September 1921, 'I feel that I would not be justified in refraining any longer from putting into operation a generous measure of land settlement.' Within the next few months, land settlement schemes were accordingly drawn up for most of Lewis's remaining farms.

By the end of 1921, therefore, the worst of the troubles in Lewis were at an end. And with the Board of Agriculture's settlement programme at last moving into high gear, it began to appear as if the process initiated by the establishment of the Congested Districts Board almost a quarter of a century earlier was at last approaching a satisfactory conclusion. Delays still occurred, however, and those affected by them felt – not unnaturally – that their claims were not receiving the attention they deserved. A group of Hebridean cottars gave forceful expression to those feelings in a letter despatched to the Board of Agriculture in October 1922:

> The Great European War was finished in about four years, and the British government through their Board of Agriculture has failed in about the same time to acquire small plots of land for those to whom they were promised . . . We may be candid enough to tell you that our patience is now at breaking point, and that any untoward action on our part will be exonerated by every honest man in the kingdom, unless by your board and its officials.

The men who signed that letter occupied a farm in North Uist in the early part of 1923. And their action was merely one of a long series of land raids which affected Sutherland, Lewis, Harris, Benbecula and Skye in the months that followed.

By previous standards, however, these were mostly minor affairs. And by 1924, the post-war crisis in the Hebrides was clearly over – if only for the reason that, as was pointed out in the Board of Agriculture's annual report for that year, practically all the potentially arable land in the areas where land hunger was, or had been, most acute had been restored to crofting tenants. In Skye, for instance, the board had added 51,000 acres to the area previously purchased by the CDB and, by creating more than 200 new holdings, had practically eliminated landlessness on the island. On the mainland, where cottars had always been fewer than in the islands, the Board of Agriculture's activities had generally been confined to extending the pastures of coastal townships at the expense of neighbouring deer forests. In Sutherland, however, the congestion which had characterised the county's crofting townships since the clearances of a hundred years before was considerably eased by the breaking up of several sheep farms – a process carried to its ultimate conclusion in Tiree, Barra and South Uist where practically all the farms created between the 1820s and 1850s were returned to crofting occupation. More than a third of Tiree and Barra residents gained holdings as a result – and though landlessness had been considerably more prevalent in these islands than in Skye, the problems caused by it were well on the way to being solved. In North Uist and Harris, too, many long-deserted townships were repeopled – while in Lewis practically every one of the island's large farms was divided into crofts. In Lewis, of course, congestion and landlessness were so acute that resettlement failed 'to make such an appreciable difference to the welfare of the community . . . as [was] noted in the case of some of the other islands'. But the more glaring injustices inherent in the post-clearance agrarian order had at least been removed.

Land settlement did not, in itself, provide an automatic answer to all the crofting community's problems. That more land had been placed under crofting tenure did nothing to mitigate the serious effects of the post-war collapse of stock prices and the continuing decline of the fishing industry. The consequently precarious state of the crofting economy in general, and the economy of the island of Lewis in particular, was dramatically under-lined by the calamity produced by the extraordinarily wet summer and autumn of 1923. Crops having failed, cattle prices being low and employ-ment practically unobtainable, the following winter was distinguished in the Outer Isles by conditions which were more than faintly reminiscent of those that had prevailed in the region in the 1840s. An emergency road construction programme was instituted to provide work and wages – while a government grant of £100,000, supplemented by various charitable contributions, was made available for the purchase of seed oats and seed potatoes.

As a means of tackling grievances stemming ultimately from the High-land Clearances, however, the land settlement programme was an imme-diate and conspicuous success. Between 1886 and the early 1950s some 52,000 acres of arable land and 732,000 acres of pasture were added to the area occupied by crofters – a process which involved the creation of 2,742 new holdings and the enlargement of 5,160 previously existing crofts. The Crofters Commission and the Congested Districts Board had contributed to this total. But the greater part of it must be attributed to the endeavours of the Board of Agriculture in the years immediately following the First World War. And not only had more land been made available to crofters: sheep stocks had been taken over from outgoing farmers and managed with considerable success; financial and agricultural aid to crofters every-where had been increased; the improvement in agricultural techniques and in housing conditions – first apparent in the immediate aftermath of the Crofters Act of 1886 – had been maintained, indeed accelerated.

Some insight into the benefits of what was thus accomplished can be gained from statistics relating to the Kilmuir estate in Skye: the scene of some of the last clearances in the Highlands and Islands; the scene, too, of many of the more violent events of the 1880s. Kilmuir, as already mentioned, was bought by the CDB in 1904. After 25 years of public ownership, the acreage under tillage had risen from 2,450 to 3,325, and the acreage occupied by crofters from 24,332 to 44,600 – ten large sheep farms being swept away, 85 new crofts created and 268 existing holdings enlarged in the process. Landlessness had been done away with, the number of thatched houses had fallen from 336 to 137, and the number of houses with slated roofs had increased from 20 to 304.

By the end of the 1920s, therefore, the crofting community's long struggle for the land – a struggle which constitutes the theme of the second half of this book – had produced enormous dividends. The agrarian and social inequalities perpetrated by the creators of the land system that had taken shape during the clearances had been permanently removed – from the crofting community's Hebridean heartland at any rate. In the Outer Isles, in Tiree and in Skye, the majority of the farms so brutally established in the nineteenth century's first 60 years were occupied once more by crofting tenants – many of them former cottars whose ancestors had been evicted from the localities to which their descendants now returned. And if islands like Mull and the straths of Sutherland, Ross-shire and Inverness-shire are still deserted, that is not the crofting community's fault; rather it is an enduring testimonial to evictors more thorough, more ruthless and – by their own criteria – more successful than those most of the Hebrides had known.

CONCLUSION

To end this history of the crofting community by reporting that all is well with contemporary crofting society would be pleasant. But it would not be true. Despite almost 90 years of officially inspired efforts to solve them, crofting problems are with us still: changed in some respects, but all too recognisable in others. Thus, although the extreme poverty of the past has been eliminated, crofters' living standards remain, in many respects, below those prevailing elsewhere in Britain. In 1972, for instance, a survey of houses in North and South Uist and in Barra showed that 68 per cent, 58 per cent and 74 per cent respectively of such houses were below the officially tolerable standard – many being quite unfit for habitation. In those depressing statistics is to be found one cause of the most alarming symptom of crofting decline, the departure of young people – a development which, in the last 40 or so years, has everywhere made depopulation rather than congestion and land hunger symptomatic of crofting difficulties.* The drift from the land, however, is not solely the consequence of crofters' comparatively low standards of living. It is also the result of twentieth-century circumstances – especially of changes which have occurred in the crofting community's relationships with the industrial, and nowadays increasingly affluent, society to the south of the Highlands. Immeasurably better educational facilities and increased communications with the south – in the social and intellectual as well as in the physical senses – have combined to bring the crofter more and more completely into the mainstream of British life. In the process, his expectations and aspirations have changed fundamentally.

Throughout the nineteenth century, crofters – as kelpers, migrant

---

*Readers should be aware that many of those comments, dating from the mid-1970s, have been overtaken by events. Some crofting areas – notably in the Western Isles – have continued to lose population. Others – such as Skye and many parts of the West Highland mainland – have experienced rapid population growth. These and other developments are explored in J. Hunter, *The Claim of Crofting: The Scottish Highlands and Islands, 1930–1990*, Edinburgh, 1991. See also, J. Hunter, *Last of the Free: A Millennial History of the Highlands and Islands of Scotland*, Edinburgh, 1999.

labourers and fishermen – participated actively in the capitalist economy. They did so, however, not in order to escape from their lives on the land, but with a view to obtaining the funds needed to sustain that life. As long as he retained his hold on the land, in other words, the nineteenth-century crofter, in spite of his poverty, was essentially at ease with himself. Until the 1920s, therefore, the crofting community's efforts were accordingly directed not so much towards improving living standards as towards confirming and extending traditional rights in, and claims to, the land on which crofters lived – or of which they had been deprived. This intense emotional attachment to territory – an attachment stemming ultimately from the place of land in the kin-based society of the old Highlands and one that has often been commented on in this book – is still fairly prevalent among crofters. In the 1950s, a royal commission described it thus:

> Above all they [crofters] have the feeling that the croft, its land, its houses, are their own. They have gathered its stones and reared its buildings and occupied it as their own all their days. They have received it from their ancestors who won it from the wilderness and they cherish the hope that they will transmit it to the generations to come. Whatever be the legal theory, they feel it to be their own – and in this respect the provisions of the Crofters Acts do no more than set the seal of parliamentary approval on their own deepest convictions.

Such feelings keep many crofters on their holdings in defiance of the dictates of financial self-interest – their attitude typified by the testimony of a crofting witness to the royal commission mentioned above. 'If I was not born there and the very dust of the place dear to me,' this witness concluded his account of the many disadvantages of his holding, 'I would quit tomorrow.' Lots of other crofters have been of like mind. But it is nevertheless the paradoxical crux of the contemporary crofting problem that, at the very time when the crofter's rights to his land were guaranteed, his increasing absorption into the wider society around him ensured that land, in itself, could no longer be considered enough.

Unaccompanied by living standards and amenities of the sort taken for granted in the south, crofting life has, during the past 30 or 40 years, become increasingly unattractive to a large proportion of the younger population of north-west Scotland. The steadily widening educational opportunities of the same period have provided these same young people with an alternative to crofting. And they have gained immeasurably thereby. But because of the absence of local job opportunities, 'getting on' – whether in a profession or a skilled trade – has almost invariably meant 'getting out'. Individuals have benefited. But the crofting community as a whole has been impoverished as talent, enthusiasm, energy and leadership have been drained from it into distant urban centres. The effects of outward migration of this sort are evident in the way that the age structure of the crofting population has been grossly distorted. In Scotland as a whole, the proportion of people over the age of 65 to those under that age is 1:8. In parts of Lewis and Harris, however, it is as high as 1:4 or even 1:2; in some townships it is as high as 1:1. The consequences of such a situation are as inevitable as they are disastrous. Enterprise and initiative are often lacking. The quality of social life has declined. And because of these developments, still more people are tempted to give up the crofting life.

Given the difficulties currently confronting the crofting community, of which depopulation is easily the most serious, it is clear that the various measures taken between 1886 and the 1920s in order to give security of tenure and more land to crofters were not, in themselves, sufficient to ensure the survival of a healthy crofting society. The contemporary crisis in crofting has duly led both to a widespread questioning of the validity of the crofting policies which have prevailed since the 1880s and to attempts to evolve new solutions to crofters' problems. The essential weakness of the 1886 Crofters Act and of the land settlement programme of the early twentieth century, according to their recent critics, was that, instead of reforming crofting agriculture, they perpetuated, even extended, the traditional crofting system. And being dependent on the fragmentation of arable land into a mass of tiny holdings, that system, it has been argued, is quite unsuited to modern conditions. Hence the conclusion of the last royal commission of enquiry into crofting affairs that crofting, 'as now organised, is fighting a losing battle against the social and economic forces of the day'. And hence that commission's recommendation that everything possible should be done to amalgamate existing crofts into economically viable units.

Expressing its regret that governments of the 1880s had not seen fit to implement the Napier Commission's virtually identical proposals, that commission – which was chaired by Aberdeen University principal, Thomas Taylor, and which reported in 1954 – was highly critical of the Crofters Act of 1886:

> The legislature [in 1886] . . . was concerned in the main with the individual crofter's position, and the form which this protection took has, in the long run, created a rigidity in the crofting structure which is the cause of many of its difficulties today.

Subsequent commentators, particularly Farquhar Gillanders, a Glasgow-based academic, have expressed the same verdict in even more forceful language – with Gillanders declaring for example, that the 1886 Crofters Act 'heralded the doom of crofting life, insulating it from normal economic trends and legally ensuring that crofting land could not now be developed into viable economic units'. The import of that contention is, to all intents and purposes, the same as that of the Napier Commission's somewhat patronising suggestion that 'the most humble and helpless class' of crofting tenants – in other words, the large majority who, in 1883, were paying annual rents of £6 or under – should be denied immunity from eviction in order that they might be 'resolutely though gently withdrawn' from the land with a view to their emigrating 'or [taking] their position . . . as labourers, mechanics, or fishermen'. That suggestion, of course, the crofting community of the 1880s rejected. Instead, crofters held out for, and won in 1886, security of tenure for each and every crofting tenant. This resulted, as observed earlier, in the Crofters Act being bitterly condemned, at the time of its passing, by landowning interests. And to the historian, it follows, much the most striking feature of the criticisms made of the Crofters Act by Farquhar Gillanders and others of like mind is the resemblance those criticisms bear to the attacks made on the Act, at the time of its passing, by the then Duke of Argyll and other representatives of the late nineteenth-century landowning class.

The principal weakness of the Gillanders critique of the 1886 Act – depending, as it does, on the argument that the legislation in question tended to promote agricultural inefficiency and backwardness – is that, whatever may be said for it economically, it leaves social and political considerations out of account. The Crofters Act was the Gladstone government's response to pressures generated by the crofting community. As such, it laid aside the Napier Commission's recommendations regarding the need for the consolidation of existing holdings and granted crofters' forcibly expressed wish that every tenant, no matter how small his croft, be granted security of tenure. The subsequent land settlement programme was shaped by similar forces. The sheep farms created during the clearances were taken over and used, not to provide a few large holdings, but to ensure – in response to the crofting community's insistently expressed demands – that as many cottars and squatters as possible were provided with crofts. The people responsible for implementing land settlement never denied that financial returns from the land they subdivided into smallholdings might have been higher had the land in question been left as large farms:

> But the comparison is between two entirely different things. A sheep farm is a commercial undertaking and has to be judged as such; a crofting community is a way of living and cannot be judged in terms of a profit and loss account. The people were there and insisted upon staying there. Their conditions were a reproach to the nation of which they form part, and the only way to remove that reproach was to give them the available land.

Nor was such a policy as divorced from economic realities as it may seem in retrospect. The essential fallacy in the continuing quest for an economically and agriculturally viable crofting system is that crofting, as was demonstrated in this book's opening chapters, was not created as an agriculturally efficient method of landholding – but, rather, as a means of simultaneously disposing of a displaced population (the population removed from inland parts of the Highlands and Islands to make way for sheep farmers) and satisfying an urgent demand for labour (in the landlord-controlled kelp industry). For better or worse, therefore, crofting, as the Crofters Commission observed in 1963, 'has always meant the sum total of activities which yield the crofter some return – whether it is agriculture, fishing, public works, knitting, etc.' The common factor, to be sure, has been agriculture. But over the last 100 years, as living standards have risen and the need to assiduously cultivate every scrap of potentially arable land has disappeared, its contribution to the crofting economy has declined rather than increased – a tendency that seems likely to continue.

Unfortunately, the present pattern of government aid to crofting, though praiseworthy and helpful in many respects, betrays a lack of insight into this central reality of crofting life – the generous cropping and agricultural improvement grants for which provision was made in the Crofters Acts of 1955 and 1961 being unmatched by measures intended to boost returns from crofters' non-agricultural activities. As far as recent legislators are concerned, then, the model croft is one which aspires to the status of a small farm. The pattern of grant aid consequently favours the crofters of areas like Caithness and Orkney – where the land is more fertile and holdings larger than is the case in the north-west. In the early 1960s, for instance, the annual average total of cropping grant to the 245 crofters of the Sutherland parish of Assynt was £146 as compared with an average total payment of £12,585 to the 227 crofters of the Caithness parish of Watten and Wick. The 535 crofters of Harris, to give another example, were then receiving an annual average total of £3,772 from the same source – a sum which, when contrasted with the £29,848 paid to the 532 crofters of Orkney, seems little better than derisory.

At a superficial level, those figures appear to add weight to the argument that crofting, as conducted on the north-western seaboard and in the Western Isles at any rate, is economically moribund. What these and similar statistics really indicate, however, is that the crofting community of the region in question is still, as it has been since the heyday of the kelp industry, highly dependent for its livelihood on occupations that are essentially ancillary to the purely agricultural side of crofting. Indeed in a situation in which 85 per cent of existing holdings provide their occupants with less than the equivalent of two days' work a week, the crofter's non-agricultural employment – in fishing, weaving, tourism, forestry, construction, service industry and so on – is usually of much greater financial importance to him than his work on the land. A policy which involved the wholesale consolidation of smallholdings – apart from being of dubious agricultural value in that the amalgamation of two, three or even more crofts might well fail to produce financially viable farms in a part of the country where costs are high, markets distant and soil and climate unfavourable – would, therefore, be socially disastrous in that its main effect would be to break the crofting community's historic ties with the land and thus accelerate the already alarming movement of people from the crofting areas to places where employment prospects are better and living standards higher. The probable outcome can be seen in Mull, an island where clearances were ruthlessly carried through to their logical conclusion, where large agricultural units consequently prevail and where depopulation has, as a result, become critical – a state of affairs which may be contrasted with that prevailing in Lewis where a system of undersized holdings maintains a very large number of people.

Had all previous attempts to 'modernise', 'rationalise' and 'improve' Highland agriculture been successful, in other words, the entire north of Scotland would have suffered the fate of the interior of Sutherland. And had not the crofting community successfully fought for its right to retain its grip on the land, Skye, Tiree and the Outer Isles would now be as empty as Mull. That is why the Highlands and Islands Development Board (HIDB) has commented:

> [Crofting] helps to maintain communities and their essential services in remote areas which might now otherwise be deserted. [Indeed] . . . if one had to look . . . for a way of life that would keep that number of people in such relatively untractable territory, it would be difficult to contrive a better system.

To have a good chance of achieving economic success without at the same time causing social dislocation and cultural collapse, therefore, a development policy for the crofting areas ought ideally to be founded on a commitment, first, to maintaining people on the land and an equal commitment, second, to providing employment of a type that can be combined with the management of a small croft.

It is to the credit of members of the present Crofters Commission, then, that – despite the commission having been constituted by an Act of Parliament which, as already noted, set considerable store by the need for an agriculturally viable crofting system – they have placed less stress on amalgamation and consolidation than on the need to promote and facilitate the crofting community's involvement in commercial and industrial enterprises of one kind or another:

> The willingness of crofters to work in industry combined with a desire to own their own homes and cultivate or stock a piece of land which they regard as their own, and which, for practical purposes is their own, gives us an opportunity in the Highlands of working towards a new form of industrial society which will be healthier and more stable than any community which is completely urbanised. This is the true value of the small croft, and as new opportunities for employment are provided, it will increase rather than diminish.

About such a vision of the Highland future there is nothing that is intrinsically utopian. It is merely an extension into present circumstances of the historic role of crofting as examined in this book. And when, on its being set up by the then Labour government in 1966, the HIDB adopted a similar policy with regard to crofting, longstanding hopes for the regeneration of the crofting community seemed on the point of realisation. But despite its first chairman having remarked that 'no matter what success is achieved in the Eastern or Central Highlands . . . the board will be judged by its ability to hold population in the true crofting areas', the HIDB has rather lost interest, of late, in crofting affairs. With the notable exception of its fishery development schemes, its attempts to provide crofters with non-agricultural employment opportunities have not been notable successes.

Symptomatic of the HIDB's failure to make any real impression on crofting problems has been its attitude to land. For – though the land cannot, of itself, provide crofters with more than a fraction of their economic requirements – it is, to quote from the HIDB's first annual report, the 'basic natural resource' of the Highlands and Islands. And it is by virtue of its unique relationship with the land that the crofting community, of course, exists. But in spite of its professed eagerness to learn from the experience of other countries and in spite of the fact that such experience has tended to show that the vesting of an underdeveloped region's land in a few large landowners is inimical to its effective development, the HIDB's policy on land reform has been practically non-existent and its policy on land use timorous and contradictory. In 1968, to give but one example of the latter characteristic, the HIDB announced its intention to promote 'schemes for land reclamation and regeneration where the estimated return justifies the expense involved, or where *the social advantage in any comprehensive scheme is sufficiently strong to offset any doubt that the project is economically viable*'. Two years later, when reporting on the development potential of the Strath of Kildonan, the HIDB, observing that its planning was 'primarily *economic rather than social* in its orientation', and concluded that land settlement in the strath could not be *economically* justified.

That the HIDB can thus employ arguments which the Congested Districts Board of 1900 or the Board of Agriculture of 1920 would not have dared to use is indicative of the extent to which politicians – and those of the left in particular – have recently refused to grapple with the still contentious issue of landholding and land tenure in the Highlands. That Conservative administrations should have no desire to dismantle the apparatus of landlordism in the region is understandable. But that successive Labour governments have not advanced the good work begun by the Highland Land League and the Liberal Party is a lot less comprehensible. It is a failure which, in view of the recent enhancement of Highlands and Islands economic prospects – as a result, in particular, of the expansion of tourism and the commencement of oil-related industrialisation – could prove disastrous for the crofting community. For the existing tennurial system gives crofters little opportunity to exercise control over, and reap benefits from, changes which are imminent.

The crofting community's victories of the 1880s and subsequent decades –

victories enshrined in the 1886 Act and ensuing legislation – were won at a time of acute difficulty for Highland landlordism. Sheep farming was in decline. Farming tenants were difficult to find. It made financial sense, in these circumstances, to leave crofters in possession of the lands they already occupied; it even made financial sense, for a time, to make more land available for crofting settlement. Within the last few years, however, that situation has altered radically. Throughout the Highlands and Islands, land values are soaring – while changes in land use from agricultural to commercial or industrial purposes, once thought unlikely, are now inevitable. The crofter, whose hard-won security of tenure applies only as long as his land is used agriculturally, can neither stop development nor benefit from it financially – since increased land values resulting from a change in land use accrue to landlord rather than tenant. Thus in a recent and notorious case in Skye, a number of crofters were deprived of a part of their common grazings on which their landlord wished to build several houses. As in all such cases, compensation for the crofters was assessed by the Scottish Land Court with reference to the land's agricultural value only, and – although their landlord's profits from the deal were expected to amount to many thousands of pounds – the affected crofters received exactly £1.25 apiece. It was in an attempt to enable crofters to cope with this sort of situation that the Crofters Commission proposed, in October 1968, that crofters be given full rights of ownership to their crofts.

This revival of the concept of crofting owner-occupation, or peasant proprietorship as it used to be called, some 60 years after the Congested Districts Board's failure to persuade significant numbers of crofters to buy their holdings, has resulted, then, from the changed economic circumstances mentioned above. The Crofters Commission's 1968 proposals – which the commission rightly claimed to constitute 'the most important reform in crofting since the first Crofters Act of 1886' – were designed to overhaul the entire crofting system in such a way as to give crofters a positive, and hopefully profitable, role in developments which they cannot, in any case, prevent. Ownership, the Crofters Commission contended, would make crofters – as opposed to crofting landlords – the beneficiaries of such development as occurs on croft land. As owners of their holdings, moreover, crofters would be better placed to participate in development on their own account. They could, for example, raise capital on the security of their house and buildings – something they cannot do as crofting tenants.

The way in which the Crofters Commission originally intended its proposals to be implemented was as simple as it was sweeping. On an appointed day, all holdings held under crofting tenure were to be compulsorily converted to owner occupation. Crofters' purchase prices were to take the form of an annuity no greater than their current rents. And landlords were to be compensated from public funds – the latter expenditure to be partly offset by savings resulting from the abolition of the legal and administrative apparatus necessitated by crofters' unique tenurial status. To the immediately expressed fear that a free market in crofting land would lead to crofters selling out to holiday home seekers and property developers, the Crofters Commission responded both by dismissing such fears as stemming from a misplaced paternalism and by proposing some degree of control over the resale of croft land.

Since the Crofters Commission's ownership recommendations were, in essence, an elaboration of views first advanced by the Federation of Crofters Unions, a grouping established in the early 1960s, those recommendations received, when first made, a general, if understandably cautious, welcome from crofters. Since 1968, however, the crofting community's enthusiasm for reform has measurably diminished. This development is due principally to the fact that the crofting reforms actually advanced by Edward Heath's Conservative government – reforms embodied in a Bill presented to parliament in 1973 – bore little relation to the Crofters Commission's original proposals and were, in fact, quite different from them in scope and intention. The eventual rights and status of the crofter remained substantially as envisaged by the commission. But the means by which the change was to be effected had been drastically revised. Along with several subsidiary reforms – including land resale controls – the concept of compulsory conversion to ownership was abandoned. The crofter had now to elect to buy his holding. And his purchase price, failing agreement with the landlord, was to be determined by the Scottish Land Court in such a way as to include at least some part of the holding's 'market' as opposed to 'crofting' value. Since purchase prices thus calculated would include at least a proportion of a holding's development value as well as a sum related to the cash likely to be realised by the sale of its house and buildings, it seemed likely that crofters who opted for ownership would be asked to pay high, perhaps exorbitant, prices rather than the virtually nominal annuities originally proposed.

The Conservative Bill fell with Edward Heath's government in February 1974. Four months later, William Ross, secretary of state for Scotland in the succeeding Labour administration, stated that the new government would proceed to enact the Crofters Commission's proposals regarding owner occupancy and added that the purchase price of holdings would relate to their crofting value only – a considerable advance on the Conservative measure. At the time of writing, the promised Bill is about to become law. Its provisions will make it possible for holdings (along with their houses and buildings) to be purchased by their tenants for not more than one or two hundred pounds. By its opponents, Mr Ross's Crofting Reform Bill has been castigated as a measure which will destroy the crofting community by exposing crofters to the full force of commercial development. Its supporters have portrayed it as a constructive and liberating influence. In fact, the Bill's ultimate effects are difficult, if not impossible, to predict. But it certainly marks a turning point. And as such it constitutes an appropriate stopping place.*

With regard to the present crofting situation, the past may be thought of little significance. But the past, in the Highlands and Islands at any rate, casts a long shadow. Hence a comment made in the course of the Taylor Commission's 1954 report:

> In order to make an appreciation of current crofting conditions, it is necessary to have regard to the historical background. This is important not only to enable the trend of events to be established but because the events of the past have a powerful influence on the minds of the crofting population. It was clear from the evidence put before us during our visits to the crofting areas that the history of the past remains vivid in the minds of the people and, in some measure, conditions their attitudes to current problems.

To study the Highlands and Islands past, then, is to gain valuable insights into the Highlands and Islands present. Indeed some knowledge of crofting history – as immediately preceding paragraphs have suggested – may well be essential if contemporary crofting problems are to be tackled effectively. The explanation of the present in historical terms is not, however, the historian's prime function. Historical investigation undertaken for such an entirely utilitarian end is apt to degenerate into propaganda – the task of uncovering and analysing the past being subsumed in that of reinforcing a preconceived view of the world. Absolute objectivity, in the sense of being quite uninfluenced by the circumstances of one's own time and place is, on the other hand, as unattainable a goal for the historian as for anyone else. The Highlander or Hebridean who can approach the history of the crofting community in a spirit of utter detachment has yet to be born. And I have no doubt that my own sympathy with crofters, whether past or present, could be deduced from a casual reading of practically any page of this book. That sympathy, however, has not taken the form of uncritically reproducing crofters' understandably prejudiced view of their own history. Rather, as indicated at the outset, it has taken the form of explaining that view. Myths have been treated as myths, not as facts. Little or no space has been devoted to unprofitable speculation about what might have been – about ways, for example, in which the catastrophe of the clearances might have been avoided. But in taking events as they happened, I have tried to understand how crofters saw them, how they influenced crofters and what crofters did about them. The result, whatever its imperfections, is the first full-length history of the crofting community. And its fundamental conten-

---

*These and subsequent developments are analysed in J. Hunter, *The Claim of Crofting*, Edinburgh, 1991.

tion and conclusion is simply that the modern history of the Highlands and Islands, certainly of crofters' part in it, can properly be understood only if that history is considered in its entirety.

For example: while it became clear in the course of the research on which this book is based that the origins of the Highland land war of the 1880s are partly to be found in the economic and other circumstances of that decade, it became equally clear that crofters were then fighting to secure legal recognition of traditional rights in the land – rights of which they had been deprived, they believed, in the late eighteenth and early nineteenth centuries. The troubles of the 1880s, it was obvious, too, were about lost lands as well as about lost rights. And even the men who returned from the Great War and set about seizing scores of Hebridean sheep farms knew, and said, that they were merely reoccupying townships from which their grandfathers or great-grandfathers had been evicted.

All this implied that the clearances at least would have to be taken into account – and described in starker terms than those employed by most recent historians. By landlords and by many historians, the Highland Clearances, however regrettable, were, and are, considered explicable in the jargon of historic necessity and economic inevitability. To crofters, past and present, they are explicable only as a brutal betrayal of traditional custom and belief, a reckless assertion of the interests of the few at the expense of those of the many. If that fact is not grasped, the passions of the 1880s, indeed the entire legacy of bitterness bestowed by clearing landlords on succeeding generations of crofters, are unintelligible. And without an understanding of these things, a study of the crofting community's history would be meaningless and futile.

The clearances are not, however, the beginning of modern Highland history. The evictions of the nineteenth century had their origin in the events of the eighteenth century; in the transformation and modernisation of the traditional society of the Highlands; above all, in the conversion of clan chieftains into commercial landowners. From that extraordinarily successful absorption of the Gaelic aristocracy into the capitalist order all else stemmed. The rise of kelp and the coming of crofting; the clearance of inland glens and the settling of evicted tenantries on the coast; the initial proprietorial opposition to emigration as well as the subsequent conversion of estate managements to a pro-emigration stance when the kelp industry collapsed and crofters were seen to be of no more use to their landlords; the further extension and consolidation of the sheep farming system at crofters' expense: all these twists and turns of landlord policy can be seen to originate in the philosophy of commercial land management which was firmly implanted in the Highlands during the eighteenth century. That philosophy gave pride of place to the pursuit of profit and was, as far as crofters were concerned, brutal, alien and wrong. But it was legitimised by a moral and economic code which sanctified self-interest, which derided the communal traditions of the past, and which was supported by British governments in their role of guardians and representatives of the capitalist class whose creed it was.

That their chieftains mostly survived the turmoils of the eighteenth century – albeit in new roles – made it immeasurably more difficult for the people of the Highlands to grasp the extent of the transformation which had occurred and to cope with the social and moral complexities of a situation in which the wellbeing of the kindred was subordinated to landlords' need to make more and more money from the land. In the summer of 1973, to give a modern example of the sort of thinking engendered by the manner in which commercial capitalism came to the Highlands, I talked to a Skye crofter who, while bitterly condemning lawyers, factors and other agents and representatives of the MacDonald estate management, told me that neither he nor his predecessors had ever had any quarrel with the MacDonalds of Sleat who, he assured me, had always been 'good landlords'. The MacLeods of Dunvegan, however, he damned to eternity as the proprietors responsible for some of the most brutal clearances in the Highlands. Had that old man been born in the north-west instead of in the east of Skye, he would have reversed, I have no doubt, the roles he attributed to the island's principal families – between whom, incidentally, there is little to choose as far as numbers of evictions are concerned. Such was, and still is, the strength of a kin-based society allegedly destroyed more than 200 years ago.

The persistence of such attitudes into the 1970s goes far to explain why effective resistance to Highland landlordism took so long to materialise. What was required was not just the courage to stand up to evictors who had the majesty of the law and the power of the state on their side, but a whole new way of looking at the world – a way of coming to terms with the reality of landlordism. The task of overthrowing the immense corpus of practice and belief inherited from a society with a continuous history of at least a thousand years was begun by the religious revivals of the first half of the nineteenth century – which gave a demoralised people a new confidence in themselves – and continued by the movement which eventually became known as the Highland Land League. But while the crofters of the 1880s owed a considerable debt to their predecessors of the Disruption era, their actions also mark the commencement of a new epoch in crofting history. The incipient conflict between the crofting community and the Highlands' landowning class broke into open warfare for the first time. An effective alliance was established between crofters and their sympathisers in the south. Landlordism was effectively challenged in the political arena – while the social and economic foundations of landlords' power and authority were menaced by rent strikes and land raids. Highland landowners' consequent difficulties were compounded by the collapse of the sheep-farming economy established at the time of the clearances. And the outcome was that successive governments, prodded after 1900 by a new campaign of land seizures, conceded practically every one of the crofting community's demands. In 1886, 1911 and 1919 crofters gained security of tenure, judicially determined rents, compensation for improvements, more land and a steadily increasing amount of economic and financial assistance.

These were tremendous victories. Between the early 1880s, when the land war began in Skye, and the later 1920s, when a massive land settlement programme had been virtually completed, the whole trend of early nineteenth-century crofting history was reversed. Insecurity of tenure was eliminated and a great deal of land given back to crofters – developments which laid the basis for, and were accompanied, by a new prosperity symbolised by the gradual demise of the black house. In more recent times, especially in the years since 1945, the prosperity of crofters has generally continued to increase. New and larger grants are available for housing. Public funds have been invested in agricultural support structures. Electricity, roads, and other services have been provided in all but the most remote localities. The welfare state has made its presence felt in the provision of old age pensions and other benefits. But for all that, crofters and their families remain, as already stressed, worse off – sometimes much worse off – than people in the south. All the attractions of crofting life – and there are not a few – cannot compensate, in twentieth-century circumstances, for lack of employment opportunities, relatively low standards of living, high costs, remoteness and all the other disadvantages of life in crofting areas.

Thus it has come about that a crofting problem still remains – a problem now of how to halt depopulation and thus keep the crofting community on the land. Hence the importance of ensuring that crofters are given the chance to capitalise on the opportunities becoming available in the Highlands and Islands as a result of the arrival and growth of industries associated with the exploitation of North Sea oil. Oil-related industrialisation, it needs emphasising in this context, is not without its hazards from a crofting point of view. The Crofters Commission has made the point thus:

> It would be ironic in the extreme if crofting townships, having lost a high proportion of their indigenous population over the past century through lack of employment opportunities, should be finally destroyed because of overwhelming and over-rapid development now.

Unrestricted and uncontrolled industrialisation, then, could prove to be an unmitigated disaster – especially in areas affected by essentially transient activities like the construction of the production platforms needed to extract oil from the bed of the North Sea. It is in this sense that oil-related industrial development can be seen as a continuation of the pattern of Highland exploitation established more than two centuries ago. For the majority of the multinational corporations now involved in oil-related industry in the Highlands are interested, like sheep farmers and owners of kelping estates before them, only in the short-term exploitation of the region's natural resources. In the past, the Highland resources targeted for such exploitation were the seaweeds of the Atlantic seaboard and the pastures of the region's inland glens and straths. Now the resource at issue is the deep and sheltered water needed by platform builders – or, if the Highlands' boundaries are extended seawards, oil itself. The combines and conglomerates of the 1970s, it might be said in this context, bring prosperity to the localities in which they operate – thus demonstrating their superiority over the clearing landlords of the nineteenth century. But they will do so for a comparatively short period only. And the wages they pay are high only because they result from a 12–14-hour working day, a 6–7-day working week. Like nineteenth-century landlords, moreover, twentieth-century oil majors and platform construction companies will not invest the profits of their Highland activities in the Highlands. And even the bulk of the tax revenues derived from such activities seem likely, given Britain's ailing economy and existing constitutional arrangements, to be appropriated by the British exchequer and set against the deficit on Britain's balance of payments account. The proportion of North Sea oil revenues which will find its way back to the Highlands will consequently be small. And though it may be asserted that oil-related industry – on its eventual and inevitable withdrawal from the Highlands – will be replaced by other industries, the extent to which such replacement will actually occur is problematical. It is especially problematical in the area with which this book is concerned. There is a real danger, therefore, that oil-related industrialisation will prove, in the long run, to be the prelude to yet another downward spiral in the Highlands' long history of decline.

But if certain types of industry are likely to bring little benefit to the crofting community, this is not true of industry as such. It is consequently arguable that the crofting community's survival is currently imperilled less by industrialisation than by those who are determined to preserve the existing social and economic situation in the Highlands. That there is much in the Highlands that ought to be conserved is undoubted. But to promote a policy of absolute and unwavering opposition to change, often in the name of preserving the Highland or crofting way of life, is implicitly or explicitly to condemn the indigenous population of the Highlands, repository of the way of life which is held to be at stake, to depressed, even falling, living standards. And from such a situation there would almost certainly ensue more migration, more depopulation.

For – as has already been remarked – the modern crofter, particularly the younger crofter, knows all about the material benefits of urban civilisation and feels himself entitled to a share in these benefits. The Crofters Commission has made the point well:

> The crofter is utterly bored with the romantic conception of his life and what the city dweller thinks good for him. He has long since rejected the role of the noble son of Nature who rejoices in homely fare and draws strength from stern privation. He now wants above all to be a citizen of this country as others are, not a curiosity or a 'character' or a being apart . . . He prizes his Gaelic culture, but not to the extent of being treated as a museum piece on account of it; he will assuredly prize it still more highly when it is no longer the bedfellow of poverty and underprivilege.

The key to the solution of today's crofting problems is to be found, therefore, in giving crofters living standards and job opportunities equal to those elsewhere in Britain. And since sufficient income can never be won from the land, higher living standards can be achieved – to reiterate the most vital single fact about crofting life, past and present – only by providing adequate and remunerative employment opportunities which are entirely outside, though ancillary to, crofting agriculture.

Massive and temporary oil-related industrialisation will not provide such opportunities. More permanent and more slowly developing oil-related industrialisation may do so. Only time will tell. But throughout the crofting areas there is a need for more and better jobs – whether in new or traditional industries. There is also a need for a more imaginative Highland development policy – one that is concerned not merely with the provision of employment but with the regeneration of the social and cultural, as well as the economic, life of north-west Scotland. In this respect, there is now some cause for optimism.* For instance, in the newly created Western Isles Island Council or, to give its more manageable Gaelic designation, Comhairle nan Eilean, there exists, for the first time, an official body committed to the pursuit of economic development in conjunction with a vigorous policy of bilingual education and the fostering of Gaelic culture. To be successful, of course, such policies require money. And money can come only from central government which, as earlier chapters of this book have amply demonstrated, has customarily taken a constructive interest in Highland affairs only when forced to do so.

The necessary funds could be made available from the tax revenues which will accrue from the exploitation of North Sea oil – exploitation which the deep, sheltered waters of the Highlands have made possible. And it is in this context that it is worth recalling an argument frequently heard at Highland Land League meetings in the 1880s: that the crofting problem

---

*This optimism proved well-founded. Since those words were written, policy with regard to Gaelic, in particular, has undergone something of a revolution – with a huge expansion of Gaelic broadcasting and with the emergence, still more significantly, of Gaelic-medium education. It would have seemed virtually inconceivable in 1976 that the Sleat area of Skye would have, by the twentieth century's close, a college, Sabhal Mòr Ostaig, delivering university degrees through Gaelic. But that has happened.

will not be solved until self-government is restored to Scotland. For it may be that only the creation of a fairly autonomous Scottish government will lead to North Sea oil wealth being made available in sufficient quantities to make possible the meaningful development of the Highlands or, for that matter, other parts of Scotland. It should be stressed, however, that Scottish autonomy, even Scottish independence, would not, in itself, do anything for the crofting community. There would still be a need for an imaginative, and no doubt costly, Highland development policy. And there would certainly still be a need for further reform of the Highlands' land-holding structure. A recent and highly successful play (John McGrath's *The Cheviot, the Stag and the Black, Black Oil*) which dealt with the same subject matter as this book concluded by declaring: 'The people do not own the land. The people do not control the land.' Not until that situation is finally remedied will the crofting community be master of its own destiny.

Index